Generation X

Americans Born
1965 to 1976

8th EDITION

Generation X

Americans Born 1965 to 1976

8th EDITION

The American
Generations Series

BY THE NEW STRATEGIST EDITORS

New Strategist Press, LLC
Amityville, New York

New Strategist Press, LLC
P.O. Box 635, Amityville, New York 11701
800/848-0842; 631/608-8795
www.newstrategist.com

ISBN 978-1-940308-84-5 (hardcover)
ISBN 978-1-940308-85-2 (paper)
ISBN 978-1-940308-86-9 (pdf)

Printed in the United States of America

Table of Contents

Chapter 4. Housing

Chapter 5. Income

Chapter 6. Labor Force

Chapter 7. Living Arrangements

List of Tables

Chapter 3. Health

Chapter 4. Housing

Chapter 5. Income

Chapter 6. Labor Force

List of Illustrations

Chapter 5. Income

Chapter 6. Labor Force

Chapter 7. Living Arrangements

Chapter 8. Population

Chapter 9. Spending

Chapter 10. Time Use

Chapter 11. Wealth

Introduction

Generation X gained fame simply by following the Baby-Boom generation onto the stage of youth decades ago, a stage Boomers created and made the center of the nation's attention. Generation X was everything Boomers were not—small in number, cynical rather than idealistic, they were expected to make their way easily through life because of the swath Boomers had carved. But it did not turn out that way. Gen Xers have struggled to compete with the masses of Boomers ahead of them and the large Millennial generation at their heels. Perhaps no generation has been hit as hard by the Great Recession and collapse of the housing market as Generation X. Now they face a tough job market as millions of Boomers postpone retirement. The eighth edition of *Generation X: Americans Born 1965 to 1976* tells the sometimes grim story of the small generation spanning the ages of 38 to 49 in 2014.

Although their numbers are small, Generation X is a vital part of the nation's commerce and culture because of their lifestage. People in their forties are in their peak earning and spending years. They are supposed to be at the height of their career, their incomes should be rising, and their spending should be climbing. *Generation X: Americans Born 1965 to 1976* shows how Gen Xers are coping with midlife and what to expect in the future.

Gen Xers are a diverse segment of the population, with minorities accounting for a large share of the whole. One issue binds together this diversity: the struggle to reach and remain in the middle class. While other generations face the same issue, getting ahead and staying there is proving more difficult for Generation X because of their position between two larger generations. Only 16 percent of Americans are Gen Xers, while 24 percent are Boomers and 25 percent are Millennials (see the Population chapter). In part because they are overshadowed by others, Gen Xers are suffering economically. The percentage of men in their late thirties and forties who have worked for their current employer for 10 or more years has fallen (see the Labor Force chapter). The median household income of people ranging in age from 35 to 54 is 11 to 13 percent lower today than it was in 2000, after adjusting for inflation. The median incomes of men aged 35 to 54 have declined by more than 10 percent (see the Income chapter). Even women in the age group have lost ground since 2007.

It is not easy to study Generation X. Few surveys focus on the generation, and the ages spanned by the members of the generation make it difficult to tease them out of the government's traditional five- or 10-year age brackets. Many of the data in this edition of *Generation X* are for 2013, when the generation was aged 37 to 48. When possible, New Strategist's editors produced estimates to create a precise profile of the Gen X age group for the year in which data are shown. Consequently, *Generation X: Americans Born 1965 to 1976* provides real insight into the status of this struggling generation.

How to Use This Book

Generation X: Americans Born 1965 to 1976 is designed for easy use. It is divided into 11 chapters, organized alphabetically: Attitudes, Education, Health, Housing, Income, Labor Force, Living Arrangements, Population, Spending, Time Use, and Wealth.

The eighth edition of *Generation X* includes the latest data on the changing demographics of homeownership, based on the Census Bureau's 2013 Housing Vacancies and Homeownership Survey. The Income chapter, with 2013 income statistics, reveals the struggle of so many Americans to stay afloat. The Spending chapter reveals trends in Gen X spending through 2013, and examines how their spending changed after the Great Recession. *Generation X* includes the latest labor force numbers and the government's labor force projections that show rising participation among the Baby-Boom generation—not good news for Gen Xers anxious to advance in their career. The Wealth chapter presents data from the Survey of Consumer Finances revealing the impact of the Great Recession on household wealth, with a look at the trends from 2007 to 2013. The Health chapter includes 2013 statistics on health insurance coverage. The Attitudes chapter, based on New Strategist's analysis of the 2012 General Social Survey, compares and contrasts the perspectives of the generations.

Most of the tables in *Generation X* are based on data collected by the federal government, in particular the Census Bureau, the Bureau of Labor Statistics, the National Center for Education Statistics, the National Center for Health Statistics, and the Federal Reserve Board. The federal government is the best source of up-to-date, reliable information on the changing characteristics of Americans. By having *Generation X* on your bookshelf you can get the answers to your questions faster than online. Even better, visit www.newstrategist.com and download the PDF version of *Generation X* with links to each table in Excel.

The chapters of *Generation X* present the demographic and lifestyle data most important to researchers. Within each chapter, most of the tables are based on data collected by the federal government, but they are not simple reproductions of government spreadsheets—as is the case in many reference books. Instead, each table is individually compiled and created by New Strategist's editors, with calculations designed to reveal the trends. The task of extracting and processing data from the government's web sites to create a single table can require hours of effort. New Strategist has done the work for you, each table telling a story about Gen Xers—a story explained by the accompanying text and chart, which analyze the data and highlight future trends. If you need more information than the tables and text provide, you can plumb the original source listed at the bottom of each table.

The book contains a comprehensive list of tables to help you locate the information you need. For a more detailed search, see the index at the back of the book. Also at the back of the book is the glossary, which defines the terms and describes the many surveys referenced in the tables and text.

With *Generation X: Americans Born 1965 to 1976* on your bookshelf, an in-depth understanding of this influential and struggling generation is at hand.

1

Attitudes

■ Only 25 percent of Gen Xers (aged 36 to 47 in 2012) are satisfied with their financial situation, well below the 40 percent of Older Americans who are satisfied.

■ Older Americans are the only generation in which the majority identifies itself as middle class, with 60 percent saying so. Only 42 percent of Gen Xers consider themselves middle class.

■ Most Gen Xers think they are better off than their parents were at the same age, and most also think their children will be better off than they themselves are today.

■ Only 43 percent of Gen Xers identify themselves as Protestant compared with 51 percent of Boomers and 63 percent of Older Americans.

■ In 2012, the 51 percent majority of Gen Xers thought gays and lesbians should have the right to marry. A larger 62 percent of Millennials support gay and lesbian marriage.

■ Among Gen Xers, 35 percent identify themselves as politically moderate, 34 percent as conservative, and 30 percent as liberal.

■ Only 42 percent of Gen Xers favored legalizing marijuana in 2012, less than the 49 percent among Boomers and 55 percent among Millennials.

Television Remains the Most Important Source of News

The Internet is more important for Millennials and Gen Xers, however.

When asked where they get most of their information about current news events, 46 percent of Millennials say the Internet and 40 percent say television, according to the 2012 General Social Survey. Among Gen Xers, 40 percent name the Internet and 39 percent television.

Most Boomers and Older Americans say television is their most important source of news about current events. The Internet is the number-two choice for Boomers, and newspapers is number two for Older Americans.

Among Millennials, only 15 percent say they read a newspaper every day. Among Older Americans, the figure is 55 percent. One in four Americans never reads a newspaper.

■ The media preferences of younger generations are revolutionizing the news industry.

Media use varies sharply by generation

(percent of people aged 18 or older who name selected medium as their most important source of information about current events, by generation, 2012)

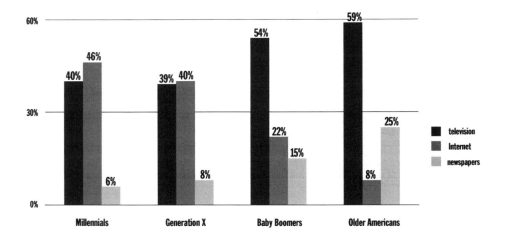

Table 1.1 Main Source of News, 2012

"Where do you get most of your information about current news events?"

(percent of people aged 18 or older responding by generation, 2012)

	television	Internet	newspapers	radio	other
Total people	**47.9%**	**30.0%**	**12.4%**	**4.7%**	**5.0%**
Millennial (18 to 35)	40.5	45.8	5.9	1.2	6.6
Generation X (36 to 47)	38.5	39.8	8.1	9.2	4.4
Baby Boom (48 to 66)	54.1	22.1	14.7	4.3	4.8
Older Americans (67 or older)	58.5	7.7	24.8	5.9	3.1

Source: Survey Documentation and Analysis, Computer-assisted Survey Methods Program, University of California, Berkeley, General Social Survey, 1972–2012 Cumulative Data Files, Internet site http://sda.berkeley.edu/cgi-bin/hsda?harcsda+gss12; calculations by New Strategist

Table 1.2 Daily Newspaper Readership, 2012

"How often do you read the newspaper?"

(percent of people aged 18 or older responding by generation, 2012)

	every day	few times a week	once a week	less than once a week	never
Total people	**26.7%**	**16.3%**	**15.7%**	**16.5%**	**24.8%**
Millennial (18 to 35)	14.8	18.0	19.3	20.3	27.6
Generation X (36 to 47)	22.8	12.7	17.0	18.8	28.8
Baby Boom (48 to 66)	31.0	17.7	13.2	16.4	21.7
Older Americans (67 or older)	54.9	14.9	9.2	3.1	17.9

Source: Survey Documentation and Analysis, Computer-assisted Survey Methods Program, University of California, Berkeley, General Social Survey, 1972–2012 Cumulative Data Files, Internet site http://sda.berkeley.edu/cgi-bin/hsda?harcsda+gss12; calculations by New Strategist

Internet Is Most Important Source of Science News

Television is number one for Boomers and Older Americans, however.

When asked where they get most of their information about science and technology, the largest share of the public now says the Internet (41 percent), followed by television (36 percent). Most Millennials and Gen Xers say the Internet is their most important source of science news, according to the 2012 General Social Survey. In contrast, a larger share of Boomers and Older Americans turn to television rather than the Internet for science news.

Most Americans, regardless of generation, disagree with the notion that "science makes our way of life change too fast." Fully 52 percent of the public disagrees with the statement, with little variation by age.

Sixty-one percent of Millennials believe in evolution. Among Gen Xers and Boomers, the figures are 59 and 56 percent, respectively. Among Older Americans, only 38 percent believe in evolution.

■ Older Americans are almost as likely to depend on magazines (13 percent) as the Internet (15 percent) for their science news.

Millennials are most likely to believe in evolution

(percent of people aged 18 or older who think the statement "human beings developed from earlier species of animals" is true, by generation, 2012)

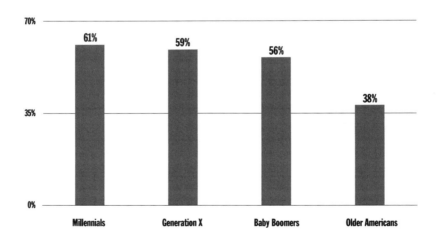

Table 1.3 Main Source of Information about Science and Technology, 2012

"Where do you get most of your information about science and technology?"

(percent of people aged 18 or older responding by generation, 2012)

	Internet	television	magazines	newspapers	radio	books	other
Total people	**41.5%**	**35.9%**	**7.0%**	**5.5%**	**2.8%**	**2.7%**	**4.6%**
Millennial (18 to 35)	59.8	25.8	1.5	3.2	1.0	2.7	6.0
Generation X (36 to 47)	51.6	25.4	8.7	4.5	2.9	2.5	4.4
Baby Boom (48 to 66)	33.4	41.9	7.7	5.8	4.1	2.4	4.7
Older Americans (67 or older)	14.7	54.8	12.7	9.9	2.9	3.9	1.1

Source: Survey Documentation and Analysis, Computer-assisted Survey Methods Program, University of California, Berkeley, General Social Survey, 1972–2012 Cumulative Data Files, Internet site http://sda.berkeley.edu/cgi-bin/hsda?harcsda+gss12; calculations by New Strategist

Table 1.4 Science Makes Our Way of Life Change Too Fast, 2012

"Science makes our way of life change too fast.
Do you agree or disagree?"

(percent of people aged 18 or older responding by generation, 2012)

	strongly agree	agree	disagree	strongly disagree
Total people	**9.8%**	**33.7%**	**52.5%**	**4.0%**
Millennial (18 to 35)	5.0	34.9	54.2	5.9
Generation X (36 to 47)	13.1	29.5	54.0	3.4
Baby Boom (48 to 66)	12.1	33.2	50.7	4.0
Older Americans (67 or older)	8.1	39.1	51.4	1.4

Source: Survey Documentation and Analysis, Computer-assisted Survey Methods Program, University of California, Berkeley, General Social Survey, 1972–2012 Cumulative Data Files, Internet site http://sda.berkeley.edu/cgi-bin/hsda?harcsda+gss12; calculations by New Strategist

Table 1.5 Human Evolution, 2012

"Human beings, as we know them today, developed from
earlier species of animals. Is this true or false?"

(percent of people aged 18 or older responding by generation, 2012)

	true	false
Total people	**55.8%**	**44.2%**
Millennial (18 to 35)	61.0	39.0
Generation X (36 to 47)	58.7	41.3
Baby Boom (48 to 66)	55.7	44.3
Older Americans (67 or older)	38.0	62.0

Source: Survey Documentation and Analysis, Computer-assisted Survey Methods Program, University of California, Berkeley, General Social Survey, 1972–2012 Cumulative Data Files, Internet site http://sda.berkeley.edu/cgi-bin/hsda?harcsda+gss12; calculations by New Strategist

Religious Beliefs Shape the Perspectives of Older Americans

Younger generations are more secular in their outlook.

Technology is not the only thing that separates young from old. On religious issues, Millennials and Older Americans are often far apart. Only 32 percent of Millennials identify themselves as Protestant, for example, compared with 63 percent of Older Americans. Thirty percent of Millennials say they have no religious affiliation compared with just 10 percent of the older generation.

Fewer than half of Millennials believe in God without a doubt (48 percent). This is well below the figures for Gen Xers and Boomers (63 percent) and Older Americans (69 percent). Only 46 percent of Millenials say they are very or moderately religious compared with 59 percent of Gen Xers, 66 percent of Boomers, and 70 percent of Older Americans.

■ Millennials are ushering in a more secular society, but it will take many more decades for that to unfold.

Older Americans are the most religious

(percent of people aged 18 or older who say they are moderately or very religious, by generation, 2012)

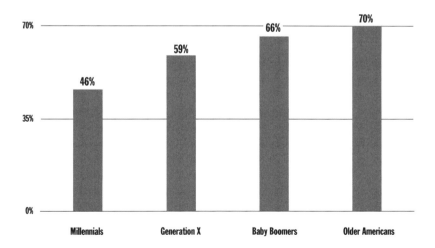

Table 1.6 Religious Preference, 2012

"What is your religious preference? "

(percent of people aged 18 or older responding by generation, 2012)

	Protestant	Catholic	none	Christian	Jewish	Moslem/ Islam	other
Total people	**44.3%**	**24.2%**	**19.7%**	**6.0%**	**1.5%**	**1.1%**	**3.2%**
Millennial (18 to 35)	31.9	24.4	29.5	7.4	0.8	0.7	5.3
Generation X (36 to 47)	42.5	24.7	18.4	7.4	2.7	2.2	2.1
Baby Boom (48 to 66)	50.5	24.7	15.1	5.1	0.9	1.0	2.7
Older Americans (67 or older)	62.9	21.5	9.7	2.5	2.6	0.3	0.5

Source: Survey Documentation and Analysis, Computer-assisted Survey Methods Program, University of California, Berkeley, General Social Survey, 1972–2012 Cumulative Data Files, Internet site http://sda.berkeley.edu/cgi-bin/hsda?harcsda+gss12; calculations by New Strategist

Table 1.7 Attendance at Religious Services, 2012

"How often do you attend religious services?"

(percent of people aged 18 or older responding by generation, 2012)

	more than once a week	every week	nearly every week	two or three times a month	once a month	several times a year	once a year	less than once a year	never
Total people	**6.5%**	**19.7%**	**4.0%**	**8.9%**	**6.8%**	**10.8%**	**13.0%**	**5.0%**	**25.3%**
Millennial (18 to 35)	4.4	13.7	2.2	8.2	8.9	10.4	16.4	5.7	30.1
Generation X (36 to 47)	6.5	21.3	5.0	8.5	6.7	12.1	13.0	3.8	23.2
Baby Boom (48 to 66)	6.5	22.1	4.3	10.8	5.9	10.1	12.2	5.0	23.3
Older Americans (67 or older)	11.6	26.1	5.9	6.7	4.2	11.6	7.2	4.7	22.0

Source: Survey Documentation and Analysis, Computer-assisted Survey Methods Program, University of California, Berkeley, General Social Survey, 1972–2012 Cumulative Data Files, Internet site http://sda.berkeley.edu/cgi-bin/hsda?harcsda+gss12; calculations by New Strategist

Table 1.8 Confidence in the Existence of God, 2012

"Which statement comes closest to expressing what you believe about God? 1) I don't believe in God. 2) I don't know whether there is a God and I don't believe there is any way to find out. 3) I don't believe in a personal God, but I do believe in a Higher Power of some kind. 4) I find myself believing in God some of the time, but not at others. 5) While I have doubts, I feel that I do believe in God. 6) I know God really exists and I have no doubts about it."

(percent of people aged 18 or older responding by generation, 2012)

	1 don't believe	2 no way to find out	3 higher power	4 believe sometimes	5 believe but doubts	6 know God exists
Total people	**3.1%**	**5.6%**	**11.6%**	**4.2%**	**16.5%**	**59.1%**
Millennial (18 to 35)	3.1	7.2	17.7	4.7	19.4	47.9
Generation X (36 to 47)	4.1	5.7	9.5	4.1	13.4	63.2
Baby Boom (48 to 66)	2.7	4.4	9.0	3.6	17.1	63.3
Older Americans (67 or older)	2.2	4.5	6.5	4.4	13.3	69.1

Source: Survey Documentation and Analysis, Computer-assisted Survey Methods Program, University of California, Berkeley, General Social Survey, 1972–2012 Cumulative Data Files, Internet site http://sda.berkeley.edu/cgi-bin/hsda?harcsda+gss12; calculations by New Strategist

Table 1.9 Degree of Religiosity, 2012

"To what extent do you consider yourself a religious person?"

(percent of people aged 18 or older responding by generation, 2012)

	very	moderately	slightly	not
Total people	**18.8%**	**39.5%**	**21.6%**	**20.1%**
Millennial (18 to 35)	11.2	34.5	26.2	28.1
Generation X (36 to 47)	20.3	38.3	20.1	21.3
Baby Boom (48 to 66)	25.0	40.7	18.6	15.7
Older Americans (67 or older)	20.0	50.1	20.5	9.4

Source: Survey Documentation and Analysis, Computer-assisted Survey Methods Program, University of California, Berkeley, General Social Survey, 1972–2012 Cumulative Data Files, Internet site http://sda.berkeley.edu/cgi-bin/hsda?harcsda+gss12; calculations by New Strategist

Table 1.10 Feelings about the Bible, 2012

"Which of these statements comes closes to describing your feelings about the
Bible? 1) The Bible is the actual word of God and is to be taken literally.
2) The Bible is the inspired word of God but not everything in it should
be taken literally, word for word. 3) The Bible is an ancient book of fables,
legends, history, and moral precepts recorded by men."

(percent of people aged 18 or older responding by generation, 2012)

	word of God	inspired word	book of fables	other
Total people	**32.1%**	**44.6%**	**21.8%**	**1.5%**
Millennial (18 to 35)	25.9	45.1	27.8	1.3
Generation X (36 to 47)	33.5	44.7	21.4	0.4
Baby Boom (48 to 66)	33.8	45.1	18.3	2.8
Older Americans (67 or older)	41.2	41.4	16.6	0.8

*Source: Survey Documentation and Analysis, Computer-assisted Survey Methods Program, University of California, Berkeley,
General Social Survey, 1972–2012 Cumulative Data Files, Internet site http://sda.berkeley.edu/cgi-bin/hsda?harcsda+gss12;
calculations by New Strategist*

Younger Generations Support Gay Marriage

The majority of Millennials and Gen Xers think gays and lesbians should have the right to marry.

There is no longer any controversy about working women in our society. That's because most Americans were raised by a working mother. Regardless of age, the majority of the public now disagrees that "traditional" sex roles—where men go to work and women stay home—are best. The oldest generation is the only one in which the majority thinks there is something wrong with premarital sex.

Americans are still ambivalent about homosexuality, but less so with each passing year as more tolerant younger generations replace older people. The 55 percent majority of Millennials say there is nothing wrong with sexual relations between adults of the same sex. Sixty-two percent of Millennials believe gays and lesbians should have the right to marry, as do 51 percent of Gen Xers. Only 43 percent of Boomers and 30 percent of Older Americans support gay marriage.

■ Among Millennials, 6 percent identify as gay, lesbian, or bisexual—nearly four times the share among Older Americans.

Millennials and Gen Xers support gay marriage

(percent of people aged 18 or older who agree that gays and lesbians should have the right to marry, by generation, 2012)

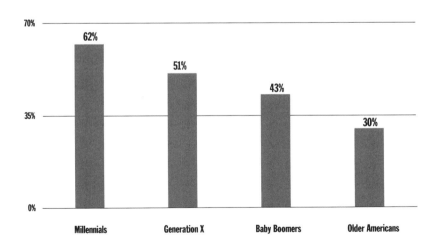

Table 1.11 Sex Roles, 2012

"It is much better for everyone involved if the man is the achiever outside
the home and the woman takes care of the home and family.
Do you agree or disagree?"

(percent of people aged 18 or older responding by generation, 2012)

	strongly agree	agree	disagree	strongly disagree
Total people	**6.5%**	**25.2%**	**48.3%**	**20.0%**
Millennial (18 to 35)	6.0	18.9	51.9	23.2
Generation X (36 to 47)	7.5	19.1	51.9	21.5
Baby Boom (48 to 66)	6.0	30.9	43.6	19.4
Older Americans (67 or older)	7.0	40.0	41.9	11.1

Source: Survey Documentation and Analysis, Computer-assisted Survey Methods Program, University of California, Berkeley, General Social Survey, 1972–2012 Cumulative Data Files, Internet site http://sda.berkeley.edu/cgi-bin/hsda?harcsda+gss12; calculations by New Strategist

Table 1.12 Mother Worked While You Were Growing Up, 2012

"Did your mother ever work for pay for as long as a year
while you were growing up?"

(percent of people aged 18 or older responding by generation, 2012)

	yes	no
Total people	**72.5%**	**27.5%**
Millennial (18 to 35)	82.6	17.4
Generation X (36 to 47)	80.1	19.9
Baby Boom (48 to 66)	67.9	32.1
Older Americans (67 or older)	47.7	52.3

Source: Survey Documentation and Analysis, Computer-assisted Survey Methods Program, University of California, Berkeley, General Social Survey, 1972–2012 Cumulative Data Files, Internet site http://sda.berkeley.edu/cgi-bin/hsda?harcsda+gss12; calculations by New Strategist

Table 1.13 Premarital Sex, 2012

"If a man and a woman have sexual relations before marriage,
do you think it is always wrong, almost always wrong,
sometimes wrong, or not wrong at all?"

(percent of people aged 18 or older responding by generation, 2012)

	always wrong	almost always wrong	sometimes wrong	not wrong at all
Total people	**21.9%**	**5.1%**	**15.5%**	**57.5%**
Millennial (18 to 35)	13.7	4.0	16.6	65.7
Generation X (36 to 47)	24.2	4.5	13.1	58.2
Baby Boom (48 to 66)	23.0	5.7	13.8	57.5
Older Americans (67 or older)	37.0	8.0	20.2	34.8

Source: Survey Documentation and Analysis, Computer-assisted Survey Methods Program, University of California, Berkeley, General Social Survey, 1972–2012 Cumulative Data Files, Internet site http://sda.berkeley.edu/cgi-bin/hsda?harcsda+gss12; calculations by New Strategist

Table 1.14 Homosexuality, 2012

"What about sexual relations between two adults of the same sex—is it always
wrong, almost always wrong, sometimes wrong, or not wrong at all?"

(percent of people aged 18 or older responding by generation, 2012)

	always wrong	almost always wrong	sometimes wrong	not wrong at all
Total people	**45.7%**	**2.9%**	**7.7%**	**43.8%**
Millennial (18 to 35)	32.3	2.7	10.2	54.8
Generation X (36 to 47)	46.8	3.4	5.7	44.0
Baby Boom (48 to 66)	48.7	2.8	8.2	40.3
Older Americans (67 or older)	69.9	2.6	3.7	23.8

Source: Survey Documentation and Analysis, Computer-assisted Survey Methods Program, University of California, Berkeley, General Social Survey, 1972–2012 Cumulative Data Files, Internet site http://sda.berkeley.edu/cgi-bin/hsda?harcsda+gss12; calculations by New Strategist

Table 1.15 Gay Marriage, 2012

"Homosexual couples should have the right to marry one another.
Do you agree or disagree?"

(percent of people aged 18 or older responding by generation, 2012)

	agree	neither agree nor disagree	disagree
Total people	**48.9%**	**12.0%**	**39.1%**
Millennial (18 to 35)	62.3	13.0	24.7
Generation X (36 to 47)	50.7	9.9	39.4
Baby Boom (48 to 66)	42.6	13.8	43.6
Older Americans (67 or older)	29.8	9.1	61.2

Source: Survey Documentation and Analysis, Computer-assisted Survey Methods Program, University of California, Berkeley, General Social Survey, 1972–2012 Cumulative Data Files, Internet site http://sda.berkeley.edu/cgi-bin/hsda?harcsda+gss12; calculations by New Strategist

Table 1.16 Sexual Orientation, 2012

"Which of the following best describes you?"

(percent of people aged 18 or older responding by generation, 2012)

	gay, lesbian or homosexual	bisexual	heterosexual or straight
Total people	**1.5%**	**2.2%**	**96.3%**
Millennial (18 to 35)	1.8	4.0	94.2
Generation X (36 to 47)	2.1	2.4	95.4
Baby Boom (48 to 66)	1.0	0.7	98.3
Older Americans (67 or older)	0.6	0.9	98.5

Source: Survey Documentation and Analysis, Computer-assisted Survey Methods Program, University of California, Berkeley, General Social Survey, 1972–2012 Cumulative Data Files, Internet site http://sda.berkeley.edu/cgi-bin/hsda?harcsda+gss12; calculations by New Strategist

Most Americans Do Not Trust Others

Younger generations are less trusting than older ones.

When Americans are asked whether most people can be trusted, 64 percent say no. The percentage of people who say others cannot be trusted is as high as 75 percent among Millennials and as low as 56 to 57 percent among Boomers and Older Americans.

The 53 percent majority of the public says life is exciting, while 43 percent describe life as pretty routine. There are almost no differences in response to this question among Millennials, Gen Xers, or Boomers. Older Americans, however, are more likely to say life is pretty routine (54 percent) than exciting (43 percent).

■ Regardless of generation, about one-third of the population claims to be "very happy."

Younger generations are most likely to find life exciting

(percent of people aged 18 or older who say life is exciting, by generation, 2012)

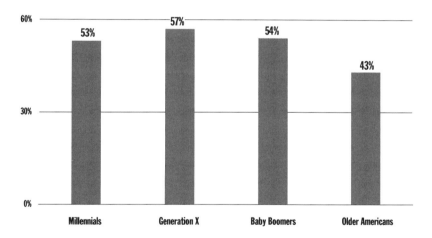

Table 1.17 Trust in Others, 2012

"Generally speaking, would you say that most people can be trusted
or that you can't be too careful in life?"

(percent of people aged 18 or older responding by generation, 2012)

	can trust	cannot trust	depends
Total people	**32.2%**	**64.2%**	**3.7%**
Millennial (18 to 35)	21.2	75.2	3.6
Generation X (36 to 47)	32.5	64.6	2.9
Baby Boom (48 to 66)	39.9	56.5	3.6
Older Americans (67 or older)	38.0	56.8	5.2

Source: Survey Documentation and Analysis, Computer-assisted Survey Methods Program, University of California, Berkeley, General Social Survey, 1972–2012 Cumulative Data Files, Internet site http://sda.berkeley.edu/cgi-bin/hsda?harcsda+gss12; calculations by New Strategist

Table 1.18 Life Exciting or Dull, 2012

"In general, do you find life exciting, pretty routine, or dull?"

(percent of people aged 18 or older responding by generation, 2012)

	exciting	pretty routine	dull
Total people	**52.7%**	**42.6%**	**4.7%**
Millennial (18 to 35)	52.6	41.9	5.5
Generation X (36 to 47)	56.9	40.2	3.0
Baby Boom (48 to 66)	53.6	40.7	5.7
Older Americans (67 or older)	42.9	53.7	3.4

Source: Survey Documentation and Analysis, Computer-assisted Survey Methods Program, University of California, Berkeley, General Social Survey, 1972–2012 Cumulative Data Files, Internet site http://sda.berkeley.edu/cgi-bin/hsda?harcsda+gss12; calculations by New Strategist

Table 1.19 General Happiness, 2012

"Taken all together, how would you say things are these days—would you say that you are very happy, pretty happy, or not too happy?"

(percent of people aged 18 or older responding by generation, 2012)

	very happy	pretty happy	not too happy
Total people	**32.9%**	**54.2%**	**12.9%**
Millennial (18 to 35)	33.4	55.1	11.5
Generation X (36 to 47)	31.6	57.0	11.5
Baby Boom (48 to 66)	33.1	52.1	14.7
Older Americans (67 or older)	33.8	52.9	13.2

Source: Survey Documentation and Analysis, Computer-assisted Survey Methods Program, University of California, Berkeley, General Social Survey, 1972–2012 Cumulative Data Files, Internet site http://sda.berkeley.edu/cgi-bin/hsda?harcsda+gss12; calculations by New Strategist

Millennials Are Least Likely to Be Conservative

Older Americans are the most conservative.

There is a common misconception that people become increasingly conservative with age. In fact, political outlook develops in early adulthood and tends to remain stable throughout life. This stability in political leanings over the life course makes the current findings from the General Social Survey especially interesting. The 2012 results show Millennials to be the least conservative generation and the only one in which liberals are as numerous as conservatives. In 2012, 29 percent of Millennials identified themselves as liberal and 28 percent identified themselves as conservative. Among the oldest Americans, 42 percent are conservative and only 21 percent are liberal.

Millennials also are less likely than the older generations to identify themselves as Republican, with only 29 percent placing themselves on the Republican end of the scale. Among older generations, from 35 to 41 percent identify themselves as Republican at least somewhat.

■ Older Americans, who are protected by the government's Medicare health insurance program, are least likely to think the government should help people pay for medical care.

Millennials are most likely to think the government should help pay for medical care

(percent of people aged 18 or older who believe the federal government should help people pay for their medical care (a 1 or 2 on the scale), by generation, 2012)

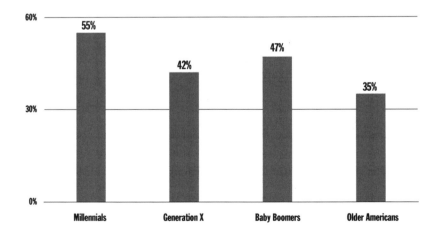

Table 1.20 Political Leanings, 2012

"We hear a lot of talk these days about liberals and conservatives. Where would you place yourself on a seven-point scale from extremely liberal (1) to extremely conservative (7)?"

(percent of people aged 18 or older responding by generation, 2012)

	liberal (1 to 3)	moderate (4)	conservative (5 to 7)
Total people	**27.0%**	**38.5%**	**34.6%**
Millennial (18 to 35)	29.0	42.7	28.2
Generation X (36 to 47)	30.4	35.4	34.3
Baby Boom (48 to 66)	24.9	37.6	37.7
Older Americans (67 or older)	21.4	36.1	42.4

Source: Survey Documentation and Analysis, Computer-assisted Survey Methods Program, University of California, Berkeley, General Social Survey, 1972–2012 Cumulative Data Files, Internet site http://sda.berkeley.edu/cgi-bin/hsda?harcsda+gss12; calculations by New Strategist

Table 1.21 Political Party Affiliation, 2012

"Generally speaking, do you usually think of yourself as a Republican, Democrat, Independent, or what?"

(percent of people aged 18 or older responding by generation, 2012)

	strong Democrat	not strong Democrat	independent, near Democrat	independent	independent, near Republican	not strong Republican	strong Republican	other party
Total people	**16.7%**	**17.0%**	**12.4%**	**19.8%**	**8.2%**	**13.7%**	**9.8%**	**2.3%**
Millennial (18 to 35)	13.5	17.9	13.6	26.2	6.9	14.7	5.2	2.1
Generation X (36 to 47)	13.5	17.3	14.1	20.4	10.3	15.3	7.0	2.1
Baby Boom (48 to 66)	20.1	14.9	12.0	16.7	7.8	11.6	13.9	3.0
Older Americans (67 or older)	21.2	18.9	8.2	10.5	9.4	13.8	16.0	2.0

Source: Survey Documentation and Analysis, Computer-assisted Survey Methods Program, University of California, Berkeley, General Social Survey, 1972–2012 Cumulative Data Files, Internet site http://sda.berkeley.edu/cgi-bin/hsda?harcsda+gss12; calculations by New Strategist

Table 1.22 Government Should Help Pay for Medical Care, 2012

"In general, some people think that it is the responsibility of the government in Washington to see to it that people have help in paying for doctors and hospital bills; they are at point 1. Others think that these matters are not the responsibility of the federal government and that people should take care of these things themselves; they are at point 5. Where would you place yourself on the scale?"

(percent of people aged 18 or older responding by generation, 2012)

	1 government should help	2	3 agree with both	4	5 people should help themselves
Total people	**28.4%**	**18.1%**	**31.4%**	**12.4%**	**9.7%**
Millennial (18 to 35)	29.4	25.2	26.9	13.8	4.6
Generation X (36 to 47)	24.3	17.7	36.3	12.6	9.2
Baby Boom (48 to 66)	31.3	15.3	29.3	11.8	12.3
Older Americans (67 or older)	25.4	9.7	38.7	10.4	15.7

Source: Survey Documentation and Analysis, Computer-assisted Survey Methods Program, University of California, Berkeley, General Social Survey, 1972–2012 Cumulative Data Files, Internet site http://sda.berkeley.edu/cgi-bin/hsda?harcsda+gss12; calculations by New Strategist

Many Think Their Income Is below Average

Fewer than half of Americans identify themselves as middle class.

Forty-six percent of Americans say their family income is average relative to others, while one-third says their income is below average. Only 44 percent identify themselves as middle class, while an equal proportion say they are working class. Among Older Americans, however, 60 percent say they are middle class.

Not surprisingly, as Millennials graduate from college and go to work, they are most likely to say their financial situation is improving. Thirty-nine percent of Millennials report that their finances have gotten better. Boomers are most likely to report worsening finances (38 percent).

When it comes to the American Dream, younger generations typically have the most optimistic outlook. Sixty-four percent of Millennials agree with the statement, "The way things are in America, people like me and my family have a good chance of improving our standard of living," a higher share than in any other generation. The figure is 56 percent among Gen Xers. In contrast, only 43 percent of Older Americans agree.

■ Older Americans are most likely to be satisfied with their financial situation.

Older Americans are most likely to identify themselves as middle class

(percent of people aged 18 or older who say they are middle class, by generation, 2012)

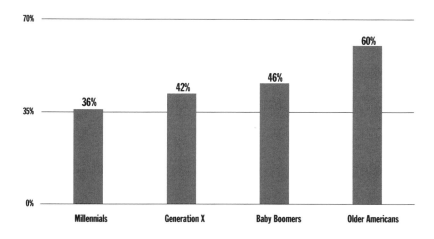

Table 1.23 Family Income Relative to Others, 2012

"Compared with American families in general, would you say
your family income is far below average, below average,
average, above average, or far above average?"

(percent of people aged 18 or older responding by generation, 2012)

	far below average	below average	average	above average	far above average
Total people	**6.8%**	**25.9%**	**45.5%**	**19.0%**	**2.7%**
Millennial (18 to 35)	5.7	27.7	49.9	15.3	1.4
Generation X (36 to 47)	7.7	22.3	40.5	25.3	4.3
Baby Boom (48 to 66)	8.3	24.9	43.6	19.9	3.2
Older Americans (67 or older)	4.6	29.8	48.1	15.0	2.4

Source: Survey Documentation and Analysis, Computer-assisted Survey Methods Program, University of California, Berkeley, General Social Survey, 1972–2012 Cumulative Data Files, Internet site http://sda.berkeley.edu/cgi-bin/hsda?harcsda+gss12; calculations by New Strategist

Table 1.24 Social Class Membership, 2012

"If you were asked to use one of four names for your social class,
which would you say you belong in: the lower class,
the working class, the middle class, or the upper class?"

(percent of people aged 18 or older responding by generation, 2012)

	lower	working	middle	upper
Total people	**8.4%**	**44.3%**	**43.7%**	**3.6%**
Millennial (18 to 35)	9.3	52.3	35.7	2.7
Generation X (36 to 47)	5.6	48.4	42.0	4.1
Baby Boom (48 to 66)	9.0	40.6	46.2	4.2
Older Americans (67 or older)	9.7	27.6	59.6	3.1

Source: Survey Documentation and Analysis, Computer-assisted Survey Methods Program, University of California, Berkeley, General Social Survey, 1972–2012 Cumulative Data Files, Internet site http://sda.berkeley.edu/cgi-bin/hsda?harcsda+gss12; calculations by New Strategist

Table 1.25　Change in Financial Situation, 2012

"During the last few years, has your financial situation been getting better, worse, or has it stayed the same?"

(percent of people aged 18 or older responding by generation, 2012)

	better	worse	stayed same
Total people	**28.2%**	**30.2%**	**41.6%**
Millennial (18 to 35)	39.1	22.7	38.1
Generation X (36 to 47)	29.3	28.9	41.8
Baby Boom (48 to 66)	23.2	38.0	38.8
Older Americans (67 or older)	12.5	32.0	55.5

Source: Survey Documentation and Analysis, Computer-assisted Survey Methods Program, University of California, Berkeley, General Social Survey, 1972–2012 Cumulative Data Files, Internet site http://sda.berkeley.edu/cgi-bin/hsda?harcsda+gss12; calculations by New Strategist

Table 1.26　Satisfaction with Financial Situation, 2012

"We are interested in how people are getting along financially these days. So far as you and your family are concerned, would you say that you are pretty well satisfied with your present financial situation, more or less satisfied, or not satisfied at all?"

(percent of people aged 18 or older responding by generation, 2012)

	satisfied	more or less satisfied	not at all satisfied
Total people	**27.0%**	**45.0%**	**28.0%**
Millennial (18 to 35)	22.4	48.7	28.9
Generation X (36 to 47)	25.2	46.3	28.5
Baby Boom (48 to 66)	27.2	41.9	30.9
Older Americans (67 or older)	39.9	41.2	18.9

Source: Survey Documentation and Analysis, Computer-assisted Survey Methods Program, University of California, Berkeley, General Social Survey, 1972–2012 Cumulative Data Files, Internet site http://sda.berkeley.edu/cgi-bin/hsda?harcsda+gss12; calculations by New Strategist

Table 1.27 Standard of Living Will Improve, 2012

"The way things are in America, people like me and my family have a good chance of improving our standard of living. Do you agree or disagree?"

(percent of people aged 18 or older responding by generation, 2012)

	agree	neither	disagree
Total people	**54.8%**	**17.9%**	**27.4%**
Millennial (18 to 35)	63.9	17.7	18.5
Generation X (36 to 47)	55.6	18.9	25.5
Baby Boom (48 to 66)	50.8	17.5	31.6
Older Americans (67 or older)	43.2	17.8	38.9

Source: Survey Documentation and Analysis, Computer-assisted Survey Methods Program, University of California, Berkeley, General Social Survey, 1972–2012 Cumulative Data Files, Internet site http://sda.berkeley.edu/cgi-bin/hsda?harcsda+gss12; calculations by New Strategist

Younger Generations See a Better Future

Fewer than half of Boomers and Older Americans think their children will be better off.

The 62 percent majority of Americans believe their standard of living is better than that of their parents' at the same age. The percentage who feel this way ranges from a low of 58 percent among Gen Xers to a high of 70 percent among Older Americans.

The public is not this positive about its children's standard of living, however. Overall, 57 percent of American parents think their children's standard of living will be better than their own. Among Millennials, 70 percent believe their children's standard of living will be better, as do 62 percent of Gen Xers. Among Boomers and Older Americans, however, fewer than half have a positive outlook on their children's future. Thirty percent of Boomers and 34 percent of Older Americans think their children's standard of living will be worse.

■ The percentage of parents who think their children's standard of living will be better than their own has fallen from 69 percent in 2000 to the 57 percent of 2012.

Optimism is greatest among younger adults

(percent of parents aged 18 or older who say their children's standard of living will be better than their own, by generation, 2012)

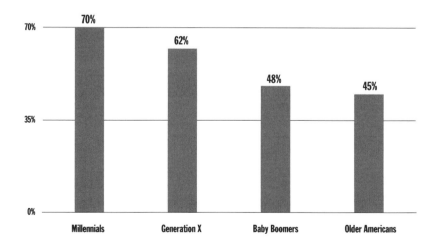

Table 1.28 Parents' Standard of Living, 2012

"Compared to your parents when they were the age you are now, do you think your own standard of living now is much better, somewhat better, about the same, somewhat worse, or much worse than theirs was?"

(percent of people aged 18 or older responding by generation, 2012)

	much better	somewhat better	about the same	somewhat worse	much worse
Total people	**33.5%**	**28.6%**	**21.2%**	**12.0%**	**4.6%**
Millennial (18 to 35)	33.0	30.5	22.2	10.2	4.1
Generation X (36 to 47)	32.1	25.6	21.5	14.6	6.3
Baby Boom (48 to 66)	33.1	27.2	20.5	13.6	5.7
Older Americans (67 or older)	37.7	32.1	20.5	8.6	1.1

Source: Survey Documentation and Analysis, Computer-assisted Survey Methods Program, University of California, Berkeley, General Social Survey, 1972–2012 Cumulative Data Files, Internet site http://sda.berkeley.edu/cgi-bin/hsda?harcsda+gss12; calculations by New Strategist

Table 1.29 Children's Standard of Living, 2012

"When your children are at the age you are now, do you think their standard of living will be much better, somewhat better, about the same, somewhat worse, or much worse than yours is now?"

(percent of people aged 18 or older with children responding by generation, 2012)

	much better	somewhat better	about the same	somewhat worse	much worse
Total people with children	**31.4%**	**25.6%**	**20.5%**	**16.3%**	**6.2%**
Millennial (18 to 35)	42.3	27.4	19.0	8.9	2.5
Generation X (36 to 47)	33.5	28.1	18.8	12.2	7.4
Baby Boom (48 to 66)	24.9	22.7	22.8	22.5	7.2
Older Americans (67 or older)	20.7	24.3	21.3	24.4	9.3

Source: Survey Documentation and Analysis, Computer-assisted Survey Methods Program, University of California, Berkeley, General Social Survey, 1972–2012 Cumulative Data Files, Internet site http://sda.berkeley.edu/cgi-bin/hsda?harcsda+gss12; calculations by New Strategist

Millennials Socialize the Most

Socializing with relatives is more common than socializing with friends.

Thirty-seven percent of Americans socialize with relatives at least weekly. Millennials are most likely to do so, with 46 percent spending a social evening with relatives at least weekly. Millennials are also most likely to socialize on a weekly basis with friends (36 percent). About one-third of Gen Xers and Boomers socialize with relatives on a weekly basis, but only 17 to 20 percent get together with friends that often. Older Americans are almost twice as likely to socialize with family (28 percent) than friends (15 percent) on a weekly basis.

A 34 percent minority of the public owns a gun, and the proportion rises with age. Among Older Americans, 46 percent have a gun in their home. Among Millennials, only 27 percent are gun owners.

■ Support is growing for the legalization of marijuana as Millennials replace older generations.

Millennials are most supportive of legalizing marijuana

(percent of people aged 18 or older who think marijuana should be made legal, by generation, 2012)

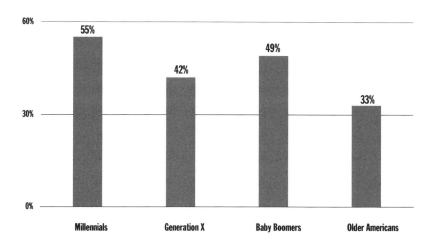

Table 1.30 Spend Evening with Relatives, 2012

"How often do you spend a social evening with relatives?"

(percent of people aged 18 or older responding by generation, 2012)

	almost daily	several times a week	several times a month	once a month	several times a year	once a year	never
Total people	**13.6%**	**23.5%**	**22.4%**	**13.6%**	**15.8%**	**6.7%**	**4.4%**
Millennial (18 to 35)	21.0	25.2	25.3	9.5	11.8	3.6	3.6
Generation X (36 to 47)	12.0	22.1	18.3	18.2	16.2	8.0	5.1
Baby Boom (48 to 66)	9.1	23.4	22.2	14.0	17.9	9.8	3.7
Older Americans (67 or older)	7.0	21.5	21.2	16.0	21.5	5.9	6.9

Source: Survey Documentation and Analysis, Computer-assisted Survey Methods Program, University of California, Berkeley, General Social Survey, 1972–2012 Cumulative Data Files, Internet site http://sda.berkeley.edu/cgi-bin/hsda?harcsda+gss12; calculations by New Strategist

Table 1.31 Spend Evening with Friends, 2012

"How often do you spend a social evening with friends
who live outside the neighborhood?"

(percent of people aged 18 or older responding by generation, 2012)

	almost daily	several times a week	several times a month	once a month	several times a year	once a year	never
Total people	**4.5%**	**19.6%**	**21.0%**	**21.0%**	**16.2%**	**8.3%**	**9.5%**
Millennial (18 to 35)	9.1	26.6	27.7	13.9	12.1	5.7	5.0
Generation X (36 to 47)	2.6	14.7	21.9	27.0	17.2	7.1	9.5
Baby Boom (48 to 66)	2.2	17.3	16.6	25.9	18.4	10.7	8.9
Older Americans (67 or older)	0.7	14.4	11.1	18.4	20.7	12.0	22.8

Source: Survey Documentation and Analysis, Computer-assisted Survey Methods Program, University of California, Berkeley, General Social Survey, 1972–2012 Cumulative Data Files, Internet site http://sda.berkeley.edu/cgi-bin/hsda?harcsda+gss12; calculations by New Strategist

Table 1.32 Have Gun in Home, 2012

"Do you happen to have in your home (or garage) any guns or revolvers?"

(percent of people aged 18 or older responding by generation, 2012)

	yes	no	refused
Total people	**34.4%**	**63.6%**	**2.0%**
Millennial (18 to 35)	26.7	72.5	0.8
Generation X (36 to 47)	33.6	65.3	1.2
Baby Boom (48 to 66)	38.1	58.8	3.1
Older Americans (67 or older)	46.2	50.3	3.5

Source: Survey Documentation and Analysis, Computer-assisted Survey Methods Program, University of California, Berkeley, General Social Survey, 1972–2012 Cumulative Data Files, Internet site http://sda.berkeley.edu/cgi-bin/hsda?harcsda+gss12; calculations by New Strategist

Table 1.33 Should Marijuana Be Made Legal, 2012

"Do you think the use of marijuana should be made legal or not?"

(percent of people aged 18 or older responding by generation, 2012)

	legal	not legal
Total people	**46.9%**	**53.1%**
Millennial (18 to 35)	55.3	44.7
Generation X (36 to 47)	41.7	58.3
Baby Boom (48 to 66)	49.0	51.0
Older Americans (67 or older)	33.0	67.0

Source: Survey Documentation and Analysis, Computer-assisted Survey Methods Program, University of California, Berkeley, General Social Survey, 1972–2012 Cumulative Data Files, Internet site http://sda.berkeley.edu/cgi-bin/hsda?harcsda+gss12; calculations by New Strategist

2

Education

■ The percentage of Americans with a college degree peaks among Generation Xers and Millennials. More than one-third of Gen Xers has a bachelor's degree.

■ The women of Generation X are better educated than the men. Fully 65 percent of women aged 37 to 48 have college experience compared with 59 percent of their male counterparts. Thirty-six percent of the women and 33 percent of the men have a bachelor's degree.

■ Asians are the best-educated Gen Xers, the 60 percent majority having a bachelor's degree. Hispanics are the least-educated Gen Xers, only 16 percent having a bachelor's degree.

■ The Gen X age groups (aged 35 to 49) account for a substantial 11 percent of the nation's college students.

Generation X Is Highly Educated

Only Millennials are better educated than Gen Xers.

Among Generation Xers (aged 37 to 48 in 2013), more than one in three (34.6 percent) has a bachelor's degree. Millennials are barely ahead of them, with 34.9 percent having a bachelor's degree. Boomers were once the best-educated generation, but younger adults have surpassed them as the Great Recession drove them back to school. Thirty-one percent of Boomers have a bachelor's degree. Among Americans aged 68 or older, only 24 percent are college graduates.

Although Generation X is better educated than Boomers overall, some cohorts of Boomer men are better educated than the men of Generation X. Among Boomer men in their sixties, 35 to 36 percent have a bachelor's degree because of draft deferments offered to college students during the Vietnam War. Among the men of Generation X, only 33 percent have a bachelor's degree.

■ The women of Generation X are better educated than Boomer women, boosting the percentage of Gen Xers with a bachelor's degree above that of Boomers.

Generation X is better educated than Boomers

(percent of people aged 25 or older with a bachelor's degree by generation, 2013)

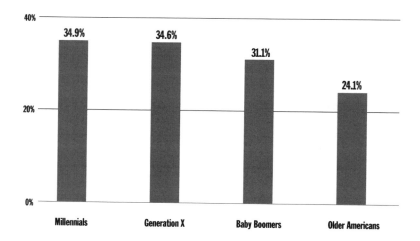

Table 2.1 Educational Attainment by Generation, 2013

(number and percent distribution of people aged 25 or older by highest level of education, by generation, 2013; numbers in thousands)

	total aged 25 or older	Millennials (aged 25 to 36)	Generation X (aged 37 to 48)	Boomers (aged 49 to 67)	Older Americans (aged 68 or older)
Total people	**206,899**	**49,485**	**49,038**	**73,751**	**34,624**
Not a high school graduate	24,517	5,279	5,108	7,680	6,450
High school graduate	61,704	12,902	13,453	22,997	12,350
Some college, no degree	34,805	9,010	8,146	12,516	5,133
Associate's degree	20,367	5,045	5,369	7,603	2,352
Bachelor's degree	41,575	12,084	10,832	13,880	4,778
Master's degree	17,395	3,929	4,558	6,472	2,435
Professional degree	3,066	611	766	1,220	470
Doctoral degree	3,470	627	803	1,384	656
High school graduate or more	182,382	44,208	43,927	66,072	28,173
Some college or more	120,678	31,306	30,474	43,075	15,823
Associate's degree or more	85,873	22,296	22,328	30,559	10,690
Bachelor's degree or more	65,506	17,251	16,959	22,956	8,338
PERCENT DISTRIBUTION					
Total people	**100.0%**	**100.0%**	**100.0%**	**100.0%**	**100.0%**
Not a high school graduate	11.8	10.7	10.4	10.4	18.6
High school graduate	29.8	26.1	27.4	31.2	35.7
Some college, no degree	16.8	18.2	16.6	17.0	14.8
Associate's degree	9.8	10.2	10.9	10.3	6.8
Bachelor's degree	20.1	24.4	22.1	18.8	13.8
Master's degree	8.4	7.9	9.3	8.8	7.0
Professional degree	1.5	1.2	1.6	1.7	1.4
Doctoral degree	1.7	1.3	1.6	1.9	1.9
High school graduate or more	88.2	89.3	89.6	89.6	81.4
Some college or more	58.3	63.3	62.1	58.4	45.7
Associate's degree or more	41.5	45.1	45.5	41.4	30.9
Bachelor's degree or more	31.7	34.9	34.6	31.1	24.1

Source: Bureau of the Census, Educational Attainment in the United States: 2013, detailed tables, Internet site http://www.census .gov/hhes/socdemo/education/data/cps/2013/tables.html; calculations by New Strategist

More than 60 Percent of Gen Xers Have College Experience

More than one-third are college graduates.

Generation X followed the Baby-Boom generation onto the nation's college campuses. Overall, the 62 percent majority of Gen Xers have been to college—17 percent have college experience but no degree, 11 percent have an associate's degree, 22 percent have a bachelor's degree, and 12 percent have a graduate degree.

Although Generation X is better educated than Boomers, the oldest Boomer men are better educated than Generation X men. Among Boomer men in their sixties, 35 to 36 percent have a bachelor's degree—thanks in part to draft deferments offered to college students during the Vietnam War. Among the men of Generation X, a smaller 33 percent have a bachelor's degree. In contrast, Gen X women are better educated than Boomer women. Thirty-six percent of Gen X women have at least a bachelor's degree versus 30 percent of Baby-Boom women.

■ Because most Gen Xers have college experience, they will be eager to see their children go to college as well.

More than 60 percent of Generation X has college experience

(percent distribution of people aged 37 to 48 by educational attainment, 2013)

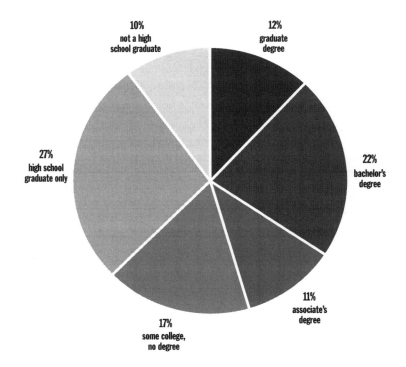

10%
not a high
school graduate

12%
graduate
degree

27%
high school
graduate only

22%
bachelor's
degree

11%
associate's
degree

17%
some college,
no degree

Table 2.2 Educational Attainment of Generation Xers and Age Groups, 2013

(number and percent distribution of people aged 25 or older, aged 37 to 48, and in five-year age groups that include Gen Xers, by educational attainment, 2013; numbers in thousands)

	total aged 25 or older	Gen Xers (aged 37 to 48)	aged 35 to 39	aged 40 to 44	aged 45 to 49
Total people	**206,899**	**49,038**	**19,221**	**20,657**	**21,060**
Not a high school graduate	24,517	5,108	2,168	2,059	2,185
High school graduate	61,704	13,453	4,877	5,576	6,189
Some college, no degree	34,805	8,146	3,228	3,541	3,335
Associate's degree	20,367	5,369	2,022	2,250	2,382
Bachelor's degree	41,575	10,832	4,327	4,525	4,639
Master's degree	17,395	4,558	1,931	2,016	1,729
Professional degree	3,066	766	342	326	294
Doctoral degree	3,470	803	325	363	306
High school graduate or more	182,382	43,927	17,052	18,597	18,874
Some college or more	120,678	30,474	12,175	13,021	12,685
Associate's degree or more	85,873	22,328	8,947	9,480	9,350
Bachelor's degree or more	65,506	16,959	6,925	7,230	6,968

PERCENT DISTRIBUTION

Total people	**100.0%**	**100.0%**	**100.0%**	**100.0%**	**100.0%**
Not a high school graduate	11.8	10.4	11.3	10.0	10.4
High school graduate	29.8	27.4	25.4	27.0	29.4
Some college, no degree	16.8	16.6	16.8	17.1	15.8
Associate's degree	9.8	10.9	10.5	10.9	11.3
Bachelor's degree	20.1	22.1	22.5	21.9	22.0
Master's degree	8.4	9.3	10.0	9.8	8.2
Professional degree	1.5	1.6	1.8	1.6	1.4
Doctoral degree	1.7	1.6	1.7	1.8	1.5
High school graduate or more	88.2	89.6	88.7	90.0	89.6
Some college or more	58.3	62.1	63.3	63.0	60.2
Associate's degree or more	41.5	45.5	46.5	45.9	44.4
Bachelor's degree or more	31.7	34.6	36.0	35.0	33.1

Source: Bureau of the Census, Educational Attainment in the United States: 2013, detailed tables, Internet site http://www.census .gov/hhes/socdemo/education/data/cps/2013/tables.html; calculations by New Strategist

Table 2.3 Educational Attainment of Generation X Men and Age Groups, 2013

(number and percent distribution of men aged 25 or older, aged 37 to 48, and in five-year age groups that include Gen Xers, by educational attainment, 2013; numbers in thousands)

	total aged 25 or older	Gen X men (aged 37 to 48)	aged 35 to 39	aged 40 to 44	aged 45 to 49
Total men	**99,305**	**24,094**	**9,461**	**10,162**	**10,319**
Not a high school graduate	12,277	2,826	1,174	1,141	1,226
High school graduate	30,014	7,101	2,696	2,927	3,196
Some college, no degree	16,508	3,922	1,613	1,733	1,527
Associate's degree	8,775	2,324	836	1,002	1,025
Bachelor's degree	19,860	4,999	1,959	2,082	2,177
Master's degree	7,804	2,015	837	859	817
Professional degree	1,876	425	184	182	166
Doctoral degree	2,192	479	163	236	182
High school graduate or more	87,029	21,266	8,288	9,021	9,090
Some college or more	57,015	14,164	5,592	6,094	5,894
Associate's degree or more	40,507	10,242	3,979	4,361	4,367
Bachelor's degree or more	31,732	7,918	3,143	3,359	3,342

PERCENT DISTRIBUTION

	total aged 25 or older	Gen X men (aged 37 to 48)	aged 35 to 39	aged 40 to 44	aged 45 to 49
Total men	**100.0%**	**100.0%**	**100.0%**	**100.0%**	**100.0%**
Not a high school graduate	12.4	11.7	12.4	11.2	11.9
High school graduate	30.2	29.5	28.5	28.8	31.0
Some college, no degree	16.6	16.3	17.0	17.1	14.8
Associate's degree	8.8	9.6	8.8	9.9	9.9
Bachelor's degree	20.0	20.7	20.7	20.5	21.1
Master's degree	7.9	8.4	8.8	8.5	7.9
Professional degree	1.9	1.8	1.9	1.8	1.6
Doctoral degree	2.2	2.0	1.7	2.3	1.8
High school graduate or more	87.6	88.3	87.6	88.8	88.1
Some college or more	57.4	58.8	59.1	60.0	57.1
Associate's degree or more	40.8	42.5	42.1	42.9	42.3
Bachelor's degree or more	32.0	32.9	33.2	33.1	32.4

Source: Bureau of the Census, Educational Attainment in the United States: 2013, detailed tables, Internet site http://www.census .gov/hhes/socdemo/education/data/cps/2013/tables.html; calculations by New Strategist

Table 2.4 Educational Attainment of Generation X Women and Age Groups, 2013

(number and percent distribution of women aged 25 or older, aged 37 to 48, and in five-year age groups that include Gen Xers, by educational attainment, 2013; numbers in thousands)

	total aged 25 or older	Gen X women (aged 37 to 48)	aged 35 to 39	aged 40 to 44	aged 45 to 49
Total women	**107,594**	**24,944**	**9,759**	**10,495**	**10,742**
Not a high school graduate	12,241	2,282	994	918	960
High school graduate	31,690	6,352	2,181	2,649	2,993
Some college, no degree	18,298	4,223	1,615	1,808	1,808
Associate's degree	11,592	3,043	1,186	1,247	1,355
Bachelor's degree	21,715	5,833	2,368	2,443	2,461
Master's degree	9,591	2,543	1,094	1,157	912
Professional degree	1,191	341	159	144	127
Doctoral degree	1,278	324	162	127	125
High school graduate or more	95,355	22,659	8,765	9,575	9,781
Some college or more	63,665	16,307	6,584	6,926	6,788
Associate's degree or more	45,367	12,083	4,969	5,118	4,980
Bachelor's degree or more	33,775	9,041	3,783	3,871	3,625
PERCENT DISTRIBUTION					
Total women	**100.0%**	**100.0%**	**100.0%**	**100.0%**	**100.0%**
Not a high school graduate	11.4	9.2	10.2	8.7	8.9
High school graduate	29.5	25.5	22.3	25.2	27.9
Some college, no degree	17.0	16.9	16.5	17.2	16.8
Associate's degree	10.8	12.2	12.2	11.9	12.6
Bachelor's degree	20.2	23.4	24.3	23.3	22.9
Master's degree	8.9	10.2	11.2	11.0	8.5
Professional degree	1.1	1.4	1.6	1.4	1.2
Doctoral degree	1.2	1.3	1.7	1.2	1.2
High school graduate or more	88.6	90.8	89.8	91.2	91.1
Some college or more	59.2	65.4	67.5	66.0	63.2
Associate's degree or more	42.2	48.4	50.9	48.8	46.4
Bachelor's degree or more	31.4	36.2	38.8	36.9	33.7

Source: Bureau of the Census, Educational Attainment in the United States: 2013, detailed tables, Internet site http://www.census .gov/hhes/socdemo/education/data/cps/2013/tables.html; calculations by New Strategist

Among Gen Xers, Asians Have the Highest Educational Attainment

Hispanics are least likely to have completed high school or college.

In every generation, including Generation X, Asians are better educated than other race-and-Hispanic-origin groups. Three out of four Asian Gen Xers have college experience and the 60 percent majority has a bachelor's degree. Most Black and non-Hispanic White Gen Xers have college experience as well, but fewer than half have a bachelor's degree—25 percent of Blacks and 39 percent of non-Hispanic Whites are college graduates.

In every generation, Hispanics are the least-educated segment. Only two out of three Hispanic Gen Xers are high school graduates and 16 percent have a bachelor's degree. One reason for the relatively low educational level of Hispanics is that many are immigrants who came to the United States as adults with little schooling.

■ Among Asian Gen Xers, men are more likely than women to have a bachelor's degree. In the other race-and-Hispanic-origin groups, women are more likely than men to be college graduates.

More than half of Asian Gen Xers have a bachelor's degree

(percent of people aged 37 to 48 with a bachelor's degree by race and Hispanic origin, 2013)

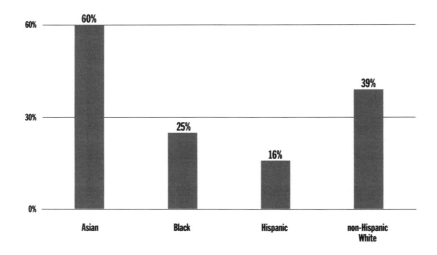

Table 2.5 Educational Attainment of Generation X by Race and Hispanic Origin, 2013

(number and percent distribution of people aged 37 to 48 by educational attainment, race, and Hispanic origin, 2013; numbers in thousands)

	total	Asian	Black	Hispanic	non-Hispanic White
Generation Xers (37 to 48)	**49,038**	**3,241**	**6,611**	**8,599**	**30,473**
Not a high school graduate	5,108	211	697	2,798	1,464
High school graduate	13,453	517	2,090	2,625	8,135
Some college, no degree	8,146	331	1,428	1,122	5,214
Associate's degree	5,369	250	725	645	3,718
Bachelor's degree	10,832	1,018	1,091	969	7,756
Master's degree	4,558	613	495	332	3,122
Professional degree	766	121	45	59	541
Doctoral degree	803	182	44	47	525
High school graduate or more	43,927	3,031	5,917	5,800	29,010
Some college or more	30,474	2,515	3,828	3,174	20,875
Associate's degree or more	22,328	2,183	2,400	2,052	15,661
Bachelor's degree or more	16,959	1,933	1,675	1,407	11,943
PERCENT DISTRIBUTION					
Generation Xers (37 to 48)	**100.0%**	**100.0%**	**100.0%**	**100.0%**	**100.0%**
Not a high school graduate	10.4	6.5	10.5	32.5	4.8
High school graduate	27.4	15.9	31.6	30.5	26.7
Some college, no degree	16.6	10.2	21.6	13.0	17.1
Associate's degree	10.9	7.7	11.0	7.5	12.2
Bachelor's degree	22.1	31.4	16.5	11.3	25.5
Master's degree	9.3	18.9	7.5	3.9	10.2
Professional degree	1.6	3.7	0.7	0.7	1.8
Doctoral degree	1.6	5.6	0.7	0.6	1.7
High school graduate or more	89.6	93.5	89.5	67.5	95.2
Some college or more	62.1	77.6	57.9	36.9	68.5
Associate's degree or more	45.5	67.4	36.3	23.9	51.4
Bachelor's degree or more	34.6	59.6	25.3	16.4	39.2

Note: Asians and Blacks are those who identify themselves as being of the race alone and those who identify themselves as being of the race in combination with other races. Non-Hispanic Whites are those who identify themselves as being White alone and not Hispanic. Numbers do not add to total because not all races are shown and Hispanics may be of any race.
Source: Bureau of the Census, Educational Attainment in the United States: 2013, detailed tables, Internet site http://www.census .gov/hhes/socdemo/education/data/cps/2013/tables.html; calculations by New Strategist

Table 2.6 Educational Attainment of Generation X Men by Race and Hispanic Origin, 2013

(number and percent distribution of men aged 37 to 48 by educational attainment, race, and Hispanic origin, 2013; numbers in thousands)

	total	Asian	Black	Hispanic	non-Hispanic White
Generation X men (37 to 48)	**24,094**	**1,512**	**2,981**	**4,335**	**15,181**
Not a high school graduate	2,826	99	349	1,535	866
High school graduate only	7,101	219	1,055	1,389	4,396
Some college, no degree	3,922	152	601	526	2,618
Associate's degree	2,324	106	315	262	1,619
Bachelor's degree	4,999	447	432	415	3,692
Master's degree	2,015	323	182	149	1,361
Professional degree	425	54	22	25	320
Doctoral degree	479	113	26	34	310
High school graduate or more	21,266	1,415	2,633	2,799	14,316
Some college or more	14,164	1,195	1,578	1,411	9,920
Associate's degree or more	10,242	1,044	977	885	7,302
Bachelor's degree or more	7,918	937	661	623	5,683
PERCENT DISTRIBUTION					
Generation X men (37 to 48)	**100.0%**	**100.0%**	**100.0%**	**100.0%**	**100.0%**
Not a high school graduate	11.7	6.6	11.7	35.4	5.7
High school graduate only	29.5	14.5	35.4	32.0	29.0
Some college, no degree	16.3	10.0	20.2	12.1	17.2
Associate's degree	9.6	7.0	10.6	6.0	10.7
Bachelor's degree	20.7	29.6	14.5	9.6	24.3
Master's degree	8.4	21.4	6.1	3.4	9.0
Professional degree	1.8	3.5	0.7	0.6	2.1
Doctoral degree	2.0	7.5	0.9	0.8	2.0
High school graduate or more	88.3	93.5	88.3	64.6	94.3
Some college or more	58.8	79.0	52.9	32.5	65.3
Associate's degree or more	42.5	69.0	32.8	20.4	48.1
Bachelor's degree or more	32.9	62.0	22.2	14.4	37.4

Note: Asians and Blacks are those who identify themselves as being of the race alone and those who identify themselves as being of the race in combination with other races. Non-Hispanic Whites are those who identify themselves as being White alone and not Hispanic. Numbers do not add to total because not all races are shown and Hispanics may be of any race.
Source: Bureau of the Census, Educational Attainment in the United States: 2013, detailed tables, Internet site http://www.census .gov/hhes/socdemo/education/data/cps/2013/tables.html; calculations by New Strategist

Table 2.7 Educational Attainment of Generation X Women by Race and Hispanic Origin, 2013

(number and percent distribution of women aged 37 to 48 by educational attainment, race, and Hispanic origin, 2013; numbers in thousands)

	total	Asian	Black	Hispanic	non-Hispanic White
Generation X women (37 to 48)	**24,944**	**1,729**	**3,630**	**4,265**	**15,291**
Not a high school graduate	2,282	113	345	1,264	598
High school graduate only	6,352	297	1,035	1,236	3,738
Some college, no degree	4,223	179	826	598	2,595
Associate's degree	3,043	144	410	385	2,100
Bachelor's degree	5,833	569	660	552	4,062
Master's degree	2,543	290	314	182	1,762
Professional degree	341	67	23	33	220
Doctoral degree	324	69	18	15	215
High school graduate or more	22,659	1,615	3,286	3,001	14,693
Some college or more	16,307	1,318	2,251	1,765	10,954
Associate's degree or more	12,083	1,139	1,425	1,167	8,359
Bachelor's degree or more	9,041	995	1,015	782	6,259

PERCENT DISTRIBUTION

	total	Asian	Black	Hispanic	non-Hispanic White
Generation X women (37 to 48)	**100.0%**	**100.0%**	**100.0%**	**100.0%**	**100.0%**
Not a high school graduate	9.2	6.5	9.5	29.6	3.9
High school graduate only	25.5	17.2	28.5	29.0	24.4
Some college, no degree	16.9	10.4	22.8	14.0	17.0
Associate's degree	12.2	8.3	11.3	9.0	13.7
Bachelor's degree	23.4	32.9	18.2	12.9	26.6
Master's degree	10.2	16.8	8.6	4.3	11.5
Professional degree	1.4	3.9	0.6	0.8	1.4
Doctoral degree	1.3	4.0	0.5	0.3	1.4
High school graduate or more	90.8	93.4	90.5	70.4	96.1
Some college or more	65.4	76.2	62.0	41.4	71.6
Associate's degree or more	48.4	65.9	39.3	27.4	54.7
Bachelor's degree or more	36.2	57.5	28.0	18.3	40.9

Note: Asians and Blacks are those who identify themselves as being of the race alone and those who identify themselves as being of the race in combination with other races. Non-Hispanic Whites are those who identify themselves as being White alone and not Hispanic. Numbers do not add to total because not all races are shown and Hispanics may be of any race.
Source: Bureau of the Census, Educational Attainment in the United States: 2013, detailed tables, Internet site http://www.census .gov/hhes/socdemo/education/data/cps/2013/tables.html; calculations by New Strategist

Few Gen Xers Are Still in School

Among those enrolled in school, women far outnumber men.

Not surprisingly, school enrollment is not common in the Generation X age groups. In 2012, only 3.7 percent of people aged 35 to 49 (Gen Xers were aged 36 to 47 in 2012) were in school.

Among those in the Gen X age groups who are enrolled in school, most are in college. In 2012, 2.1 million people aged 35 to 49 were college students, with women accounting for two-thirds of those enrolled. The Gen X age groups account for a substantial 11 percent of college enrollment.

■ The economic downturn boosted the percentage of people in school, including Gen Xers.

More than 1 million Gen X women are in college

(number of people aged 35 to 49 enrolled in college, by sex, 2012)

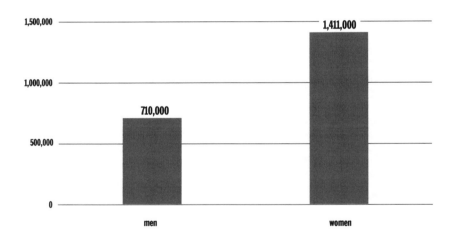

Table 2.8 School Enrollment by Sex and Age, 2012

(number and percent of people aged 3 or older enrolled in school by sex and age, 2012; numbers in thousands)

	total		females		males	
	number	percent	number	percent	number	percent
Total enrolled	**78,426**	**26.4%**	**39,921**	**26.2%**	**38,505**	**26.6%**
Aged 3	1,614	40.5	774	39.6	840	41.5
Aged 4	2,675	66.4	1,362	69.1	1,314	63.7
Aged 5	3,812	89.8	1,902	90.2	1,910	89.4
Aged 6	3,916	96.8	1,900	96.5	2,016	97.1
Aged 7	3,966	98.1	1,923	98.5	2,043	97.8
Aged 8	4,023	98.2	1,976	98.2	2,047	98.1
Aged 9	3,962	97.9	1,945	98.4	2,017	97.4
Aged 10	3,959	97.9	1,980	97.4	1,979	98.4
Aged 11	4,051	97.8	1,927	97.6	2,124	98.0
Aged 12	4,155	98.3	2,053	98.2	2,102	98.5
Aged 13	4,031	98.1	1,945	98.2	2,086	98.0
Aged 14	4,021	98.0	1,967	97.6	2,053	98.5
Aged 15	4,065	98.4	1,987	98.7	2,077	98.1
Aged 16	3,962	97.1	1,958	97.9	2,004	96.4
Aged 17	4,108	94.6	1,991	94.0	2,117	95.1
Aged 18	3,277	77.0	1,627	77.7	1,650	76.3
Aged 19	2,578	61.0	1,392	66.9	1,186	55.3
Aged 20	2,446	56.2	1,375	61.7	1,071	50.3
Aged 21	2,343	51.9	1,261	55.0	1,083	48.7
Aged 22	1,662	38.7	892	41.2	769	36.1
Aged 23	1,243	28.3	591	27.7	652	28.9
Aged 24	1,100	25.4	582	27.3	518	23.5
Aged 25 to 29	2,888	14.0	1,666	16.0	1,222	11.9
Aged 30 to 34	1,532	7.5	951	9.2	581	5.8
Aged 35 to 49	2,233	3.7	1,469	4.7	764	1.6
Aged 35 to 39	936	4.9	610	6.3	326	3.5
Aged 40 to 44	706	3.4	452	4.3	254	2.5
Aged 45 to 49	591	2.8	407	3.8	184	1.8
Aged 50 to 54	416	1.9	261	2.3	156	1.4
Aged 55 to 59	235	1.1	164	1.5	71	0.7
Aged 60 to 64	74	0.4	50	0.5	24	0.3
Aged 65 or older	79	0.2	51	0.2	28	0.2

Source: Bureau of the Census, School Enrollment—CPS October 2012 Detailed Tables, Internet site http://www.census.gov/hhes/school/data/cps/2012/tables.html; calculations by New Strategist

Table 2.9 College Students by Age and Sex, 2012

(number of people aged 15 or older enrolled in institutions of higher education by age and sex and female share of total, 2012; numbers in thousands)

	total	men	women number	women share of total
Total enrolled	**19,930**	**8,602**	**11,327**	**56.8%**
Aged 15 to 19	4,286	1,933	2,353	54.9
Aged 20	2,306	1,004	1,301	56.4
Aged 21	2,257	1,046	1,211	53.7
Aged 22	1,630	756	875	53.7
Aged 23	1,203	626	576	47.9
Aged 24	1,047	499	549	52.4
Aged 25 to 29	2,816	1,196	1,622	57.6
Aged 30 to 34	1,516	576	942	62.1
Aged 35 to 49	2,122	710	1,411	66.5
Aged 35 to 39	893	310	584	65.4
Aged 40 to 44	661	228	432	65.4
Aged 45 to 49	568	172	395	69.5
Aged 50 to 54	389	142	247	63.5
Aged 55 to 59	221	70	150	67.9
Aged 60 to 64	72	24	48	66.7
Aged 65 or older	70	25	43	61.4

Source: Bureau of the Census, School Enrollment—CPS October 2012 Detailed Tables, Internet site http://www.census.gov/hhes/ school/data/cps/2012/tables.html; calculations by New Strategist

3

Health

■ The 52 percent majority of Americans aged 18 or older say their health is very good or excellent. Among 35-to-44-year-olds the figure is 55.5 percent.

■ Americans have a weight problem, and Gen Xers are no exception. The average Gen X man weighs nearly 200 pounds. The average Gen X woman weighs more than 160 pounds.

■ Gen X men have had a median of six opposite-sex partners in their lifetime. Women in the generation have had more than three.

■ The women of Generation X accounted for only 10 percent of the nation's births in 2013.

■ Many Gen Xers do not have health insurance. In 2013, fully 19 percent of people aged 35 to 44 had no health insurance coverage at any time during the year.

■ Twenty-four percent of Americans aged 18 to 44 have experienced lower back pain for at least one full day in the past three months, making it the most common health condition in the age group.

■ Most Gen Xers had a prescription drug expense in the past year, spending a median of $192 on drugs— 20 percent of which they paid out-of-pocket.

Most 35-to-54-Year-Olds Say Their Health Is Very Good or Excellent

The percentage who report very good or excellent health declines with age.

Overall, the 52 percent majority of Americans aged 18 or older say their health is "very good" or "excellent." The figure peaks at 63 percent among adults aged 18 to 24. Among people aged 35 to 54 in 2013 (Gen Xers were aged 37 to 48 in that year), more than half say they are in very good or excellent health. The figure falls with increasing age as chronic conditions become common.

Fewer than half of people aged 55 or older report that their health is very good or excellent. Nevertheless, the proportion in poor health remains below 7 percent, regardless of age. Among people aged 65 or older, the proportion who say their health is very good or excellent (41 percent) surpasses the proportion saying their health is only "fair" or "poor" (24 percent).

■ Medical advances that allow people to manage chronic conditions may boost the proportions of older Americans who report very good or excellent health in the years ahead.

Fewer than half of people aged 55 or older say their health is very good or excellent

(percentage of people aged 18 or older who say their health is "very good" or "excellent," by age, 2013)

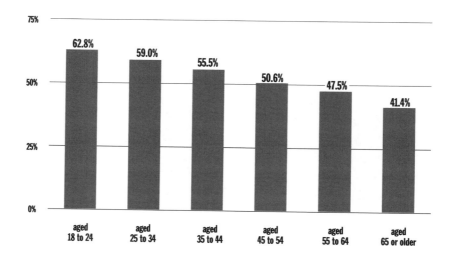

Table 3.1 Health Status by Age, 2013

(percent distribution of people aged 18 or older by self-reported health status, by age, 2013)

	total	excellent or very good			good	fair or poor		
		total	excellent	very good		total	fair	poor
Total people	**100.0%**	**52.2%**	**18.6%**	**33.6%**	**30.9%**	**16.7%**	**12.3%**	**4.4%**
Aged 18 to 24	100.0	62.8	24.9	37.9	28.9	8.6	7.5	1.1
Aged 25 to 34	100.0	59.0	23.0	36.0	30.1	10.5	8.5	2.0
Aged 35 to 44	100.0	55.5	20.6	34.9	30.8	13.6	10.5	3.1
Aged 45 to 54	100.0	50.6	18.0	32.6	30.1	18.3	12.6	5.7
Aged 55 to 64	100.0	47.5	15.3	32.2	31.0	21.1	14.4	6.7
Aged 65 or older	100.0	41.4	12.3	29.1	33.4	23.8	16.9	6.9

Source: Centers for Disease Control and Prevention, Behavioral Risk Factor Surveillance System, Prevalence Data, Internet site http://apps.nccd.cdc.gov/brfss/; calculations by New Strategist

Weight Problems Are the Norm for Gen Xers

Most men and women are overweight.

Americans have a weight problem, and Gen Xers are no exception. The average Gen X man weighs nearly 200 pounds. The average Gen X woman weighs more than 160 pounds. Nearly 80 percent of Gen X men and more than 60 percent of Gen X women are overweight, and more than one-third is obese.

Although many people say they exercise, only 20 percent of adults meet federal physical activity guidelines. The percentage who meet the guidelines falls with age to just 12 percent of people aged 65 or older. The guidelines are fairly complex and demanding, however, which might explain why so few can meet them.

■ Most Gen Xers lack the willpower to eat less or exercise more—fueling a diet and weight loss industry that never lacks for customers.

Most Gen Xers weigh more than they should

(percent of people aged 35 to 54 who are overweight, by sex, 2009–12)

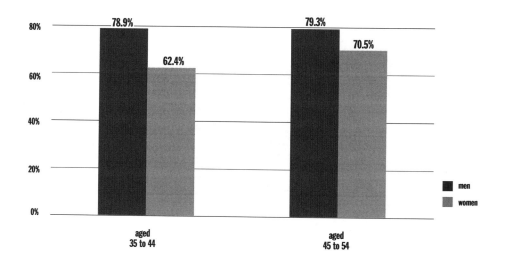

Table 3.2 Average Measured Weight by Age and Sex, 2007–10

(average weight in pounds of people aged 20 or older by age and sex, 2007–10)

	men	women
Total aged 20 or older	**195.5 lbs.**	**166.2 lbs.**
Aged 20 to 29	183.9	161.9
Aged 30 to 39	199.5	169.1
Aged 40 to 49	200.6	168.0
Aged 50 to 59	201.3	170.0
Aged 60 to 69	199.4	170.5
Aged 70 to 79	190.6	164.9
Aged 80 or older	174.9	143.1

Note: Data are based on measured weight of a sample of the civilian noninstitutionalized population.
Source: National Center for Health Statistics, Anthropometric Reference Data for Children and Adults: United States, 2007–2010, Vital Health Statistics, Series 11, No. 252, 2012, Internet site http://www.cdc.gov/nchs/products/series/series11.htm; calculations by New Strategist

Table 3.3 Weight Status by Sex and Age, 2009–12

(percent distribution of people aged 20 or older by weight status, sex, and age, 2009–12)

	total	healthy weight	overweight total	overweight obese
Total people	**100.0%**	**29.2%**	**69.1%**	**35.5%**
Total men	**100.0**	**26.2**	**72.9**	**34.6**
Aged 20 to 34	100.0	37.5	60.9	28.9
Aged 35 to 44	100.0	21.0	78.9	38.1
Aged 45 to 54	100.0	20.0	79.3	38.1
Aged 55 to 64	100.0	21.9	77.4	38.1
Aged 65 to 74	100.0	22.4	76.9	36.4
Aged 75 or older	100.0	28.2	70.4	27.4
Total women	**100.0**	**31.9**	**65.5**	**36.4**
Aged 20 to 34	100.0	40.8	55.2	30.0
Aged 35 to 44	100.0	35.2	62.4	36.0
Aged 45 to 54	100.0	27.3	70.5	38.3
Aged 55 to 64	100.0	23.8	75.1	42.9
Aged 65 to 74	100.0	23.5	73.8	44.2
Aged 75 or older	100.0	35.3	62.4	29.8

Note: Data are based on measured height and weight of a sample of the civilian noninstitutionalized population. "Overweight" is defined as a body mass index of 25 or higher. "Obese" is defined as a body mass index of 30 or higher. Body mass index is calculated by dividing weight in kilograms by height in meters squared. Percentages do not add to 100 because "underweight" is not shown.
Source: National Center for Health Statistics, Health, United States, 2013, Internet site http://www.cdc.gov/nchs/hus.htm

Table 3.4 Physical Activity Status of People Aged 18 or Older, 2012

(percent of people aged 18 or older by leisure-time aerobic and muscle-strengthening guideline activity status, by sex and age, 2012)

	met muscle-strengthening guideline	met aerobic activity guideline	met both guidelines	met neither guideline
Total people	**23.6%**	**49.6%**	**20.3%**	**47.1%**
Aged 18 to 24	32.1	59.6	29.7	37.9
Aged 25 to 44	27.2	54.9	24.2	42.2
Aged 45 to 54	21.4	48.5	18.2	48.3
Aged 55 to 64	19.8	45.0	16.0	51.2
Aged 65 or older	16.1	37.5	11.9	58.4
Total men	**28.4**	**54.0**	**24.6**	**42.2**
Aged 18 to 44	35.4	60.5	31.8	35.9
Aged 45 to 54	22.3	50.3	18.7	45.9
Aged 55 to 64	20.9	46.9	16.8	49.1
Aged 65 to 74	20.6	50.8	17.1	45.9
Aged 75 or older	15.4	33.8	10.5	61.3
Total women	**20.0**	**46.6**	**17.1**	**50.7**
Aged 18 to 44	21.9	51.9	19.8	46.0
Aged 45 to 54	20.5	46.7	17.7	50.5
Aged 55 to 64	18.8	43.3	15.3	53.2
Aged 65 to 74	17.1	39.1	12.8	56.7
Aged 75 or older	10.8	24.3	6.2	71.2

Note: Federal aerobic guideline recommends that adults perform at least 150 minutes per week of moderate-intensity or 75 minutes per week of vigorous-intensity aerobic physical activity or equivalent combination. Federal muscle-strengthening guideline recommends muscle-strengthening activities of moderate or high intensity involving all major muscle groups on two or more days per week.
Source: National Center for Health Statistics, Health, United States, 2013, Internet site http://www.cdc.gov/nchs/hus.htm

Americans Report on Their Sexual Behavior

Men aged 35 to 44 have had a median of six opposite-sex partners in their lifetime.

The federal government's National Survey of Family Growth examines the sexual behavior of Americans aged 15 to 44. Most people in the age group have had at least one opposite-sex partner in their lifetime. Even among 15-to-19-year-olds, 57 percent of men and 52 percent of women are sexually experienced. Overall, men aged 15 to 44 have had a median of 5.1 opposite-sex partners in their lifetime, and women have had a median of 3.2 partners.

Among 15-to-44-year-olds, 93.5 percent of men and 83.3 percent of women identify themselves as attracted only to the opposite sex. Just 2.8 percent of men and 4.6 percent of women identify themselves as homosexual or bisexual—a figure likely to be underreported.

■ The percentage of men who report any sexual activity with a same-sex partner rises from 2.5 percent among teenagers to 8.1 percent in the 40-to-44 age group.

Women are more likely than men to report some same-sex attraction

(percent distribution of men and women aged 15 to 44 by sexual attraction, 2006–08)

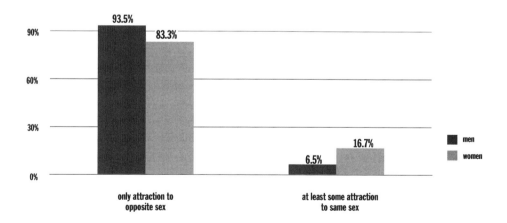

Table 3.5 Lifetime Sexual Activity of 15-to-44-Year-Olds by Sex, 2006–08

(number of people aged 15 to 44 and percent distribution by sexual experience with opposite-sex partners during lifetime, by sex and age, 2006–08; numbers in thousands)

	total		number of opposite-sex partners in lifetime							
	number	percent	0	1 or more	1	2	3 to 6	7 to 14	15 or more	median
Total men aged 15 to 44	**62,199**	**100.0%**	**11.4%**	**88.6%**	**15.0%**	**7.6%**	**26.5%**	**18.1%**	**21.4%**	**5.1**
Aged 15 to 19	10,777	100.0	43.3	56.7	21.2	9.4	17.6	5.4	3.1	1.8
Aged 20 to 24	10,404	100.0	14.4	85.5	19.1	8.0	26.1	18.1	14.2	4.1
Aged 25 to 29	10,431	100.0	3.8	96.2	11.8	8.9	29.5	22.9	23.1	5.7
Aged 30 to 34	9,575	100.0	3.1	96.9	14.2	6.1	26.6	21.7	28.3	6.4
Aged 35 to 39	10,318	100.0	1.4	98.8	13.3	5.6	29.7	19.6	30.6	6.2
Aged 40 to 44	10,695	100.0	1.3	98.8	10.3	7.2	29.7	21.6	30.0	6.4
Total women aged 15 to 44	**61,865**	**100.0**	**11.3**	**88.8**	**22.2**	**10.7**	**31.6**	**16.0**	**8.3**	**3.2**
Aged 15 to 19	10,431	100.0	48.1	51.8	22.7	8.2	15.7	4.1	1.1	1.4
Aged 20 to 24	10,140	100.0	12.6	87.5	24.5	12.5	31.6	11.7	7.2	2.6
Aged 25 to 29	10,250	100.0	3.4	96.6	20.0	12.4	31.0	20.4	12.8	3.6
Aged 30 to 34	9,587	100.0	1.9	98.1	20.9	10.6	31.9	21.3	13.4	4.2
Aged 35 to 39	10,475	100.0	0.9	99.1	22.2	9.9	38.3	20.8	7.9	3.5
Aged 40 to 44	10,982	100.0	0.4	99.7	22.4	10.8	40.5	18.0	8.0	3.4

Source: National Center for Health Statistics, Sexual Behavior, Sexual Attraction, and Sexual Identity in the United States: Data from the 2006–2008 National Survey of Family Growth, National Health Statistics Reports, No. 36, 2011, Internet site http://www .cdc.gov/nchs/nsfg/new_nsfg.htm; calculations by New Strategist

Table 3.6 Sexual Attraction among 18-to-44-Year-Olds, 2006—08

(number of people aged 18 to 44 and percent distribution by sexual attraction, by sex and age, 2006–08; numbers in thousands)

	total		only opposite sex	mostly opposite sex	equally to both	mostly same sex	only same sex	not sure
	number	percent						
Total men aged 18 to 44	**55,399**	**100.0%**	**93.5%**	**3.7%**	**0.5%**	**0.7%**	**1.2%**	**0.4%**
Aged 18 to 19	4,460	100.0	91.7	5.7	–	0.7	1.1	0.6
Aged 20 to 24	9,883	100.0	91.3	5.8	1.1	0.5	0.7	0.7
Aged 25 to 29	9,226	100.0	94.3	3.1	0.3	0.7	1.3	0.4
Aged 30 to 34	10,138	100.0	95.3	2.7	–	0.5	0.8	0.4
Aged 35 to 44	21,692	100.0	93.6	3.1	0.4	0.9	1.7	0.2
Total women aged 18 to 44	**56,032**	**100.0**	**83.3**	**11.9**	**2.8**	**0.6**	**0.8**	**0.7**
Aged 18 to 19	4,598	100.0	82.4	9.4	4.8	0.9	1.3	1.2
Aged 20 to 24	10,140	100.0	77.6	16.7	3.7	0.8	0.8	0.4
Aged 25 to 29	10,250	100.0	81.4	12.9	3.8	0.5	1.1	0.4
Aged 30 to 34	9,587	100.0	81.4	13.0	2.8	0.7	0.9	1.2
Aged 35 to 44	21,457	100.0	87.9	9.1	1.4	0.4	0.5	0.6

Note: "–" means sample is too small to make a reliable estimate.
Source: National Center for Health Statistics, Sexual Behavior, Sexual Attraction, and Sexual Identity in the United States: Data from the 2006–2008 National Survey of Family Growth, National Health Statistics Reports, No. 36, 2011, Internet site http://www .cdc.gov/nchs/nsfg/new_nsfg.htm; calculations by New Strategist

Table 3.7 Sexual Orientation of 18-to-44-Year-Olds, 2006–08

(number of people aged 18 to 44 and percent distribution by sexual orientation, by sex and age, 2006–08; numbers in thousands)

	total		heterosexual or straight	homosexual or gay	bisexual
	number	percent			
Total men aged 18 to 44	**55,399**	**100.0%**	**95.7%**	**1.7%**	**1.1%**
Aged 18 to 19	4,460	100.0	96.6	1.6	1.1
Aged 20 to 24	9,883	100.0	95.1	1.2	2.0
Aged 25 to 29	9,226	100.0	96.3	1.7	0.8
Aged 30 to 34	10,138	100.0	96.2	1.5	0.6
Aged 35 to 44	21,692	100.0	95.2	2.1	1.0
Total women aged 18 to 44	**56,032**	**100.0**	**93.7**	**1.1**	**3.5**
Aged 18 to 19	4,598	100.0	90.1	1.9	5.8
Aged 20 to 24	10,140	100.0	90.4	1.3	6.3
Aged 25 to 29	10,250	100.0	91.9	1.2	5.4
Aged 30 to 34	9,587	100.0	94.4	1.1	2.9
Aged 35 to 44	21,457	100.0	96.6	0.7	1.1

Note: Numbers do not add to 100 percent because "something else" and "not reported" are not shown.
Source: National Center for Health Statistics, Sexual Behavior, Sexual Attraction, and Sexual Identity in the United States: Data from the 2006–2008 National Survey of Family Growth, National Health Statistics Reports, No. 36, 2011, Internet site http://www .cdc.gov/nchs/nsfg/new_nsfg.htm; calculations by New Strategist

Table 3.8 Lifetime Same-Sex Sexual Activity of 15-to-44-Year-Olds, 2006–08

(percent of people aged 15 to 44 reporting any sexual activity with same-sex partners in their lifetime, by age and sex, 2006–08)

	men	women
Total aged 15 to 44	**5.2%**	**12.5%**
Aged 15 to 19	2.5	11.0
Aged 20 to 24	5.6	15.8
Aged 25 to 29	5.2	15.0
Aged 30 to 34	4.0	14.2
Aged 35 to 39	5.7	11.5
Aged 40 to 44	8.1	7.9

Source: National Center for Health Statistics, Sexual Behavior, Sexual Attraction, and Sexual Identity in the United States: Data from the 2006–2008 National Survey of Family Growth, National Health Statistics Reports, No. 36, 2011, Internet site http://www .cdc.gov/nchs/nsfg/new_nsfg.htm; calculations by New Strategist

Most Women of Childbearing Age Use Contraceptives

The pill and female sterilization are the most popular contraceptives.

Among the nation's women of childbearing age—defined as ages 15 to 44—the 62 percent majority uses contraceptives. The pill is most popular, with 17.1 percent of women using it, according to the federal government's National Survey of Family Growth. Female sterilization is the contraceptive choice of 16.5 percent of women, while condoms rank third at 10.2 percent. Use of the pill peaks at 27 percent among women aged 20 to 24, while women aged 30 or older are more likely to have been sterilized than to be on the pill.

Among women not using contraception, most are sexually inactive, pregnant, or postpartum. Only 8 percent of women aged 15 to 44 are not using contraceptives, able to become pregnant, and sexually active.

■ Contraception is a vital element of health care for American women.

The pill is popular among young women

(percent of women aged 15 to 44 who are using the contraceptive pill, 2006–10)

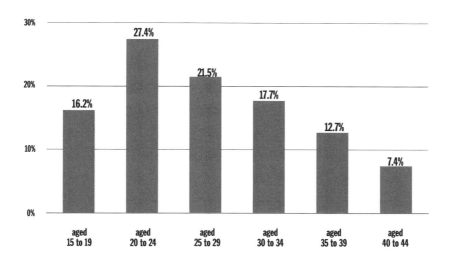

Table 3.9 Contraceptive Use by Age, 2006–10

(total number of women aged 15 to 44 and percent distribution by contraceptive status and age, 2006–10; numbers in thousands)

	total	15 to 19	20 to 24	25 to 29	30 to 34	35 to 39	40 to 44
Total women aged 15 to 44 (number)	61,755	10,478	10,365	10,535	9,188	10,538	10,652
Total women aged 15 to 44 (percent)	100.0%	100.0%	100.0%	100.0%	100.0%	100.0%	100.0%
USING CONTRACEPTION	**62.2**	**30.5**	**58.3**	**65.3**	**69.7**	**74.6**	**75.3**
Female sterilization	16.5	–	1.5	10.7	20.9	27.9	38.1
Male sterilization	6.2	–	0.5	2.7	6.6	12.4	15.1
Pill	17.1	16.2	27.4	21.5	17.7	12.7	7.4
Other hormonal methods	4.5	4.9	7.1	7.4	3.9	2.0	1.4
Implant, Lunelle, or Patch	0.9	0.7	1.1	1.5	0.9	0.5	–
Three-month injectable (Depo-Provera)	2.3	3.5	3.3	3.4	1.7	1.0	0.6
Contraceptive ring	1.3	0.7	2.7	2.4	1.4	0.5	0.4
Intrauterine device (IUD)	3.5	0.8	3.3	4.7	4.9	4.8	2.4
Condom	10.2	6.1	14.9	13.6	10.8	9.0	6.8
Periodic abstinence— calendar rhythm method	0.6	–	0.2	0.5	0.8	1.0	1.1
Periodic abstinence— natural family planning	0.1	0.0	0.0	0.0	0.4	–	–
Withdrawal	3.2	2.1	3.3	4.1	3.2	4.1	2.6
Other methods	0.3	0.2	–	0.3	0.5	0.6	0.4
NOT USING CONTRACEPTION	**37.8**	**69.5**	**41.7**	**34.7**	**30.3**	**25.4**	**24.7**
Surgically sterile, female (noncontraceptive)	0.4	–	–	0.2	–	0.4	1.5
Nonsurgically sterile, female or male	1.7	0.5	1.4	1.4	1.8	2.0	3.1
Pregnant or postpartum	5.0	3.2	8.1	8.4	7.2	2.3	1.4
Seeking pregnancy	4.0	0.6	4.0	6.3	6.0	4.8	2.4
Never had intercourse	11.8	51.4	11.6	3.1	1.9	1.1	0.6
No intercourse in past three months	7.3	7.1	7.9	7.0	6.6	6.5	8.6
Had intercourse during past three months	7.7	6.7	8.7	8.4	6.7	8.4	7.1

Note: "Other methods" includes diaphragm, emergency contraceptive, Today sponge, cervical cap, female condom, and other methods. "–" means sample is too small to make a reliable estimate.
Source: National Center for Health Statistics, Current Contraceptive Use in the United States, 2006–2010, and Changes in Patterns of Use Since 1995, National Health Statistics Reports, No. 60, 2012, Internet site http://www.cdc.gov/nchs/nsfg.htm; calculations by New Strategist

Fertility Rate Is at a Record Low

The rate is rising among women aged 35 or older, however.

The women of Generation X (aged 37 to 48 in 2013) are in their late childbearing years. Because many went to college and delayed marrying, their childbearing has been postponed. The lingering effects of the Great Recession also caused many women to delay having children. Consequently, the fertility rate of women aged 30 or older has increased since 2000, while the rate among women under age 30 has declined.

The delayed childbearing of younger women and the catch-up childbearing of Gen Xers have upended an historic pattern. In 2009, for the first time, the fertility rate of women aged 20 to 24 fell below that of women aged 30 to 34.

■ Despite the Great Recession, the fertility rate increased among women aged 35 or older between 2007 and 2013.

Fertility rate peaks in the 25-to-29 age group

(births per 1,000 women in age group, 2013)

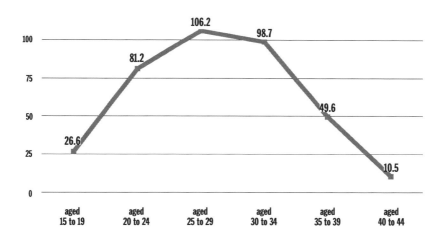

Table 3.10 Fertility Rate by Age, 2000 to 2013

(number of births per 1,000 women aged 15 to 44, and per 1,000 women in specified age group, 2000 to 2013; percent change for selected years)

	total	15 to 19	20 to 24	25 to 29	30 to 34	35 to 39	40 to 44	45 to 49
2013	62.9	26.6	81.2	106.2	98.7	49.6	10.5	0.8
2012	63.0	29.4	83.1	106.5	97.3	48.3	10.4	0.7
2011	63.2	31.3	85.3	107.2	96.5	47.2	10.3	0.7
2010	64.1	34.3	90.0	108.3	96.6	45.9	10.2	0.7
2009	66.2	37.9	96.2	111.5	97.5	46.1	10.0	0.7
2008	68.6	41.5	103.0	115.1	99.3	46.9	9.8	0.7
2007	69.5	42.5	106.3	117.5	99.9	47.5	9.5	0.6
2006	68.5	41.9	105.9	116.7	97.7	47.3	9.4	0.6
2005	66.7	40.4	102.2	115.6	95.9	46.3	9.1	0.6
2004	66.3	41.1	101.7	115.5	95.3	45.4	8.9	0.5
2003	66.1	41.6	102.6	115.6	95.1	43.8	8.7	0.5
2002	64.8	43.0	103.6	113.6	91.5	41.4	8.3	0.5
2001	65.3	45.3	106.2	113.4	91.9	40.6	8.1	0.5
2000	65.9	47.7	109.7	113.5	91.2	39.7	8.0	0.5
PERCENT CHANGE								
2007 to 2013	−9.5%	−37.4%	−23.6%	−9.6%	−1.2%	4.4%	10.5%	33.3%
2000 to 2013	−4.6	−44.2	−26.0	−6.4	8.2	24.9	31.3	60.0

Source: National Center for Health Statistics, Birth Data, Internet site http://www.cdc.gov/nchs/births.htm; calculations by New Strategist

Most Women Are Mothers by Age 30

Among women aged 35 to 50, more than 30 percent have had three or more children.

The proportion of women who have never had a child falls from 95 percent among 15-to-19-year-olds to a much smaller (but still substantial) 17 percent among women aged 45 to 50. Overall, 59 percent of women aged 15 to 50 have had at least one child. The largest share (23 percent) has had two.

Five percent of women aged 15 to 50 had a baby in the past year, according to the 2012 American Community Survey. Women aged 25 to 34 are most likely to have had a baby recently, with 10 percent having given birth in the past year. By race and Hispanic origin, Hispanics are most likely to have given birth in the past 12 months, at nearly 7 percent. By educational attainment, women with graduate degrees are most likely to have had a baby in the past year.

■ The two-child family has been the norm in the United States for several decades.

Most women aged 25 or older have had at least one child

(percent of women aged 15 to 50 who have had one or more children, by age, 2012)

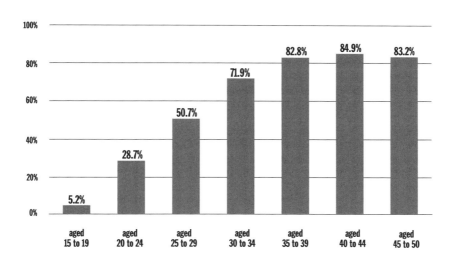

Table 3.11 Number of Children Born to Women Aged 15 to 50, 2012

(total number of women aged 15 to 50, and percent distribution by number of children ever born, by age, 2012; numbers in thousands)

	total			one or more			
	number	percent	none	total	one	two	three or more
Total aged 15 to 50	**75,392**	**100.0%**	**41.3%**	**58.8%**	**17.2%**	**23.1%**	**18.5%**
Aged 15 to 19	10,351	100.0	94.9	5.2	4.0	0.8	0.4
Aged 20 to 24	10,909	100.0	71.4	28.7	18.0	8.5	2.2
Aged 25 to 29	10,437	100.0	49.4	50.7	21.6	18.1	11.0
Aged 30 to 34	10,324	100.0	28.2	71.9	21.6	28.4	21.9
Aged 35 to 39	9,709	100.0	17.2	82.8	17.7	33.8	31.3
Aged 40 to 44	10,516	100.0	15.1	84.9	18.9	34.9	31.1
Aged 45 to 50	13,145	100.0	16.8	83.2	18.1	35.1	30.0

Note: Number of women aged 15 to 50 is based on Current Population Survey estimates.
Source: Bureau of the Census, Fertility of Women in the United States: 2012, Internet site http://www.census.gov/hhes/fertility/

Table 3.12 Women Having Given Birth in the Past Year, 2012

(total number of women aged 15 to 50 and number and percent who gave birth in the past year by selected characteristics, 2012; numbers in thousands)

| | | gave birth in past year | |
	total	number	percent
Total aged 15 to 50	**76,187**	**4,125**	**5.4%**
Age			
Aged 15 to 19	10,504	225	2.1
Aged 20 to 24	10,964	867	7.9
Aged 25 to 29	10,487	1,083	10.3
Aged 30 to 34	10,402	1,073	10.3
Aged 35 to 39	9,813	584	6.0
Aged 40 to 44	10,617	200	1.9
Aged 45 to 50	13,400	93	0.7
Race and Hispanic origin			
Asian	4,544	259	5.7
Black	10,704	613	5.7
Hispanic	14,102	932	6.6
Non-Hispanic White	44,790	2,207	4.9
Nativity status			
Native born	63,537	3,266	5.1
Foreign born	12,651	859	6.8
Educational attainment			
Not a high school graduate	13,559	635	4.7
High school degree	16,492	951	5.8
Some college or associate's degree	25,636	1,322	5.2
Bachelor's degree	13,863	779	5.6
Graduate or professional degree	6,637	438	6.6

Note: Numbers by race and Hispanic origin do not add to total because Hispanics may be of any race and not all races are shown. Asians and Blacks are those who identify themselves as being of the race alone. Non-Hispanic Whites are those who identify themselves as being White alone and not Hispanic. Number of women aged 15 to 50 is based on American Community Survey estimates.
Source: Bureau of the Census, Fertility of Women in the United States: 2012, Internet site http://www.census.gov/hhes/fertility/

Generation X Is at the End of the Childbearing Years

Most babies are born to women under age 30.

Despite an increase in the number of older mothers during the past few decades, the great majority of women who give birth each year is under age 30. Gen X women (aged 37 to 48) accounted for only 10 percent of births in 2013, while Millennial women accounted for fully 85 percent.

The age at which women give birth varies by race and Hispanic origin. Among Asians, women aged 35 or older account for a substantial 25 percent of births. Among Blacks, the figure is just 12 percent. College attendance is one of the reasons many Asian women postpone childbearing until their mid- to late thirties.

Among women aged 35 or older who gave birth in 2013, fewer than one in four were having their first child. Many were having their third, fourth, or subsequent child.

■ The iGeneration is beginning to enter the years of parenthood.

Women of Generation X account for few births

(percent distribution of births by generation of mother, 2013)

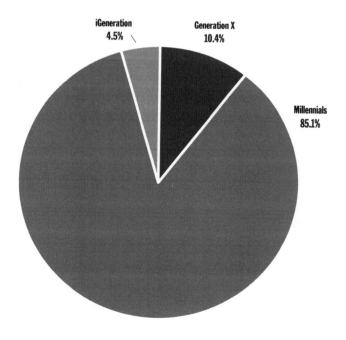

Table 3.13 Births by Age and Generation, 2013

(number and percent distribution of births by age and generation of mother, 2013)

	number	percent distribution
Total births	**3,957,577**	**100.0%**
Under age 15	3,108	0.1
Aged 15 to 17	75,234	1.9
Aged 18 to 19	199,407	5.0
Aged 20 to 24	902,146	22.8
Aged 25 to 29	1,127,561	28.5
Aged 30 to 34	1,044,029	26.4
Aged 35 to 39	487,476	12.3
Aged 40 to 44	110,332	2.8
Aged 45 to 54	8,284	0.2
Total births	**3,957,577**	**100.0**
iGeneration (under age 19)	178,046	4.5
Millennials (aged 19 to 36)	3,368,430	85.1
Gen X (aged 37 or older)	411,102	10.4

Source: National Center for Health Statistics, Births: Preliminary Data for 2013, National Vital Statistics Reports, Vol. 63, No. 2, 2014, Internet site http://www.cdc.gov/nchs/births.htm; calculations by New Strategist

Table 3.14 Births by Age, Race, and Hispanic Origin, 2013

(number and percent distribution of births by age, race, and Hispanic origin of mother, 2013)

	total	American Indian	Asian	Black, non-Hispanic	Hispanic	White, non-Hispanic
Total births	**3,957,577**	**46,167**	**268,559**	**587,612**	**907,859**	**2,140,273**
Under age 15	3,108	70	59	1,045	1,221	717
Aged 15 to 19	274,641	5,729	5,132	62,439	93,585	108,334
Aged 20 to 24	902,146	15,035	27,534	186,863	239,401	433,617
Aged 25 to 29	1,127,561	12,721	71,621	154,864	246,164	640,732
Aged 30 to 34	1,044,029	8,175	96,895	113,416	197,976	624,279
Aged 35 to 39	487,476	3,605	53,482	53,920	103,476	270,872
Aged 40 to 44	110,332	784	12,805	13,953	24,678	57,243
Aged 45 to 54	8,284	49	1,033	1,114	1,358	4,479
PERCENT DISTRIBUTION BY RACE AND HISPANIC ORIGIN						
Total births	**100.0%**	**1.2%**	**6.8%**	**14.8%**	**22.9%**	**54.1%**
Under age 15	100.0	2.3	1.9	33.6	39.3	23.1
Aged 15 to 19	100.0	2.1	1.9	22.7	34.1	39.4
Aged 20 to 24	100.0	1.7	3.1	20.7	26.5	48.1
Aged 25 to 29	100.0	1.1	6.4	13.7	21.8	56.8
Aged 30 to 34	100.0	0.8	9.3	10.9	19.0	59.8
Aged 35 to 39	100.0	0.7	11.0	11.1	21.2	55.6
Aged 40 to 44	100.0	0.7	11.6	12.6	22.4	51.9
Aged 45 to 54	100.0	0.6	12.5	13.4	16.4	54.1
PERCENT DISTRIBUTION BY AGE						
Total births	**100.0**	**100.0**	**100.0**	**100.0**	**100.0**	**100.0**
Under age 15	0.1	0.2	0.0	0.2	0.1	0.0
Aged 15 to 19	6.9	12.4	1.9	10.6	10.3	5.1
Aged 20 to 24	22.8	32.6	10.3	31.8	26.4	20.3
Aged 25 to 29	28.5	27.6	26.7	26.4	27.1	29.9
Aged 30 to 34	26.4	17.7	36.1	19.3	21.8	29.2
Aged 35 to 39	12.3	7.8	19.9	9.2	11.4	12.7
Aged 40 to 44	2.8	1.7	4.8	2.4	2.7	2.7
Aged 45 to 54	0.2	0.1	0.4	0.2	0.1	0.2

Note: Births by race and Hispanic origin do not add to total because Hispanics may be of any race and "not stated" is not shown.
Source: National Center for Health Statistics, Births: Preliminary Data for 2013, National Vital Statistics Reports, Vol. 63, No. 2, 2014, Internet site http://www.cdc.gov/nchs/births.htm; calculations by New Strategist

Table 3.15 Births by Age of Mother and Birth Order, 2013

(number and percent distribution of births by age of mother and birth order, 2013)

	total	first child	second child	third child	fourth or later child
Total births	**3,957,577**	**1,555,614**	**1,251,721**	**657,578**	**472,270**
Under age 15	3,108	3,038	50	3	1
Aged 15 to 19	274,641	226,650	40,478	5,567	753
Aged 20 to 24	902,146	456,161	293,099	108,760	39,641
Aged 25 to 29	1,127,561	421,982	371,466	203,371	125,021
Aged 30 to 34	1,044,029	311,003	356,382	207,433	163,724
Aged 35 to 39	487,476	110,071	157,067	108,664	108,974
Aged 40 to 44	110,332	24,320	31,056	22,503	31,736
Aged 45 to 54	8,284	2,390	2,124	1,277	2,420
PERCENT DISTRIBUTION BY BIRTH ORDER					
Total births	**100.0%**	**39.3%**	**31.6%**	**16.6%**	**11.9%**
Under age 15	100.0	97.7	1.6	0.1	0.0
Aged 15 to 19	100.0	82.5	14.7	2.0	0.3
Aged 20 to 24	100.0	50.6	32.5	12.1	4.4
Aged 25 to 29	100.0	37.4	32.9	18.0	11.1
Aged 30 to 34	100.0	29.8	34.1	19.9	15.7
Aged 35 to 39	100.0	22.6	32.2	22.3	22.4
Aged 40 to 44	100.0	22.0	28.1	20.4	28.8
Aged 45 to 54	100.0	28.9	25.6	15.4	29.2
PERCENT DISTRIBUTION BY AGE					
Total births	**100.0**	**100.0**	**100.0**	**100.0**	**100.0**
Under age 15	0.1	0.2	0.0	0.0	0.0
Aged 15 to 19	6.9	14.6	3.2	0.8	0.2
Aged 20 to 24	22.8	29.3	23.4	16.5	8.4
Aged 25 to 29	28.5	27.1	29.7	30.9	26.5
Aged 30 to 34	26.4	20.0	28.5	31.5	34.7
Aged 35 to 39	12.3	7.1	12.5	16.5	23.1
Aged 40 to 44	2.8	1.6	2.5	3.4	6.7
Aged 45 to 54	0.2	0.2	0.2	0.2	0.5

Note: Numbers do not add to total because "not stated" is not shown.
Source: National Center for Health Statistics, Births: Preliminary Data for 2013, National Vital Statistics Reports, Vol. 63, No. 2, 2014, Internet site http://www.cdc.gov/nchs/births.htm; calculations by New Strategist

Many Generation X Mothers Are Not Married

Out-of-wedlock births fall with age.

Nearly 41 percent of babies born in 2013 had a mother who was not married. There are large differences by age in the percentage of new mothers who are not married, however. The younger the woman, the more likely she is to give birth out of wedlock.

Among babies born to women under age 25 in 2013, most were born to single mothers. The figure falls to 36 percent in the 25-to-29 age group. Among babies born to women aged 30 or older, from 21 to 24 percent had a single mother.

■ Out-of-wedlock childbearing has increased enormously over the past few decades and has become common even among older mothers.

More than one in five babies born to women aged 30 or older are born out of wedlock

(percent of babies born to unmarried women by age, 2013)

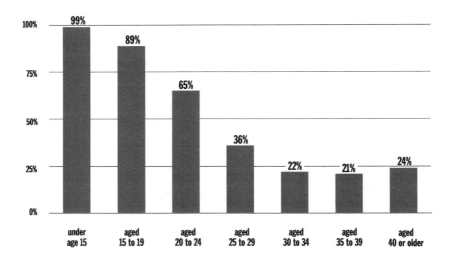

Table 3.16 Births to Unmarried Women by Age, 2013

(total number of births and number and percent to unmarried women, by age, 2013)

	total	unmarried women		
		number	percent distribution	percent of total
Total births	**3,957,577**	**1,605,643**	**100.0%**	**40.6%**
Under age 15	3,108	3,081	0.2	99.1
Aged 15 to 19	274,641	243,480	15.2	88.7
Aged 20 to 24	902,146	590,385	36.8	65.4
Aged 25 to 29	1,127,561	404,443	25.2	35.9
Aged 30 to 34	1,044,029	233,078	14.5	22.3
Aged 35 to 39	487,476	103,101	6.4	21.1
Aged 40 or older	118,616	28,075	1.7	23.7

Source: National Center for Health Statistics, Births: Preliminary Data for 2013, National Vital Statistics Reports, Vol. 63, No. 2, 2014, Internet site http://www.cdc.gov/nchs/births.htm; calculations by New Strategist

More than One in Five 35-to-44-Year-Olds Smoke Cigarettes

Smoking rate peaks among 25-to-34-year-olds.

The percentage of Americans who smoke cigarettes is sharply lower than what it was a few decades ago. Nevertheless, a substantial 19 percent of people aged 18 or older were current smokers in 2012. Among people aged 35 to 44, a larger 22 percent smoke cigarettes. Twenty percent of 35-to-44-year-olds are former smokers.

Drinking is much more popular than smoking. Overall, 55 percent of people aged 18 or older have had an alcoholic beverage in the past month. The proportion peaks at 64 percent in the 25-to-34 age group, then falls to 59 percent in the 35-to-44 age group.

Although many Gen Xers have experience with illicit drugs, particularly marijuana, few continue to use them. Only 7 to 9 percent of people aged 35 to 44 have used illicit drugs in the past month. But most between the ages of 18 and 59 have used illicit drugs at some point in their lives. Nearly half of 35-to-44-year-olds have used marijuana in the past, although only 5 to 7 percent have used it in the past month.

■ As Gen Xers age and health concerns become increasingly important, the proportion who smoke or drink should decline.

Most Gen Xers never smoked

(percent distribution of people aged 35 to 44 by cigarette smoking status, 2012)

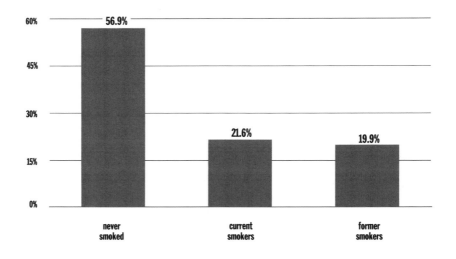

Table 3.17 Cigarette Smoking Status by Age, 2012

(percent distribution of people aged 18 or older by age and cigarette smoking status, 2012)

	total	all current smokers			former smoker	never smoked
		total	smoke every day	smoke some days		
Total people	**100.0 %**	**19.2%**	**13.5%**	**5.7%**	**25.2%**	**54.4%**
Aged 18 to 24	100.0	20.8	13.2	7.6	6.7	71.9
Aged 25 to 34	100.0	26.9	18.8	8.1	17.4	55.0
Aged 35 to 44	100.0	21.6	15.6	6.0	19.9	56.9
Aged 45 to 54	100.0	22.3	16.8	5.5	24.2	53.1
Aged 55 to 64	100.0	18.2	13.3	4.9	32.8	47.9
Aged 65 or older	100.0	8.8	6.4	2.4	43.1	47.0

Source: Centers for Disease Control and Prevention, Behavioral Risk Factor Surveillance System Prevalence Data, 2012, Internet site http://apps.nccd.cdc.gov/brfss/

Table 3.18 Alcohol Use by Age, 2012

(percent distribution of people aged 18 or older by whether they have had at least one drink of alcohol within the past 30 days, by age, 2012)

	total	yes	no
Total people	**100.0%**	**55.3%**	**44.7%**
Aged 18 to 24	100.0	52.6	47.4
Aged 25 to 34	100.0	64.3	35.7
Aged 35 to 44	100.0	59.1	40.9
Aged 45 to 54	100.0	57.3	42.7
Aged 55 to 64	100.0	53.1	46.9
Aged 65 or older	100.0	42.9	57.1

Source: Centers for Disease Control and Prevention, Behavioral Risk Factor Surveillance System Prevalence Data, 2012; Internet site http://apps.nccd.cdc.gov/brfss/v

Table 3.19 Illicit Drug Use by People Aged 12 or Older, 2012

(percent of people aged 12 or older who ever used any illicit drug, who used an illicit drug in the past year, and who used an illicit drug in the past month, by age, 2012)

	ever used	used in past year	used in past month
Total people aged 12 or older	**48.0%**	**16.0%**	**9.2%**
Aged 12 to 17	24.2	17.9	9.5
Aged 18 to 25	57.8	36.3	21.3
Aged 26 to 29	61.7	26.4	14.6
Aged 30 to 34	60.0	21.5	13.2
Aged 35 to 39	55.5	15.7	8.8
Aged 40 to 44	54.5	13.8	7.3
Aged 45 to 49	59.0	13.4	7.7
Aged 50 to 54	60.7	12.1	7.2
Aged 55 to 59	56.8	10.8	6.6
Aged 60 to 64	47.6	6.0	3.6
Aged 65 or older	19.3	2.3	1.3

Note: Illicit drugs include marijuana, hashish, cocaine (including crack), heroin, hallucinogens, inhalants, or any prescription-type psychotherapeutic used nonmedically.
Source: SAMHSA, Office of Applied Studies, 2012 National Survey on Drug Use and Health, Detailed Tables, Internet site http://www.samhsa.gov/data/NSDUH/2012SummNatFindDetTables/Index.aspx

Table 3.20 Marijuana Use by People Aged 12 or Older, 2012

(percent of people aged 12 or older who ever used marijuana, who used marijuana in the past year, and who used marijuana in the past month, by age, 2012)

	ever used	used in past year	used in past month
Total people aged 12 or older	**42.8%**	**12.1%**	**7.3%**
Aged 12 to 17	17.0	13.5	7.2
Aged 18 to 25	52.2	31.5	18.7
Aged 26 to 29	56.2	20.1	11.9
Aged 30 to 34	54.3	16.5	10.8
Aged 35 to 39	49.6	10.8	6.6
Aged 40 to 44	47.8	9.1	5.1
Aged 45 to 49	53.7	9.4	5.2
Aged 50 to 54	56.7	8.0	5.1
Aged 55 to 59	53.0	7.4	4.8
Aged 60 to 64	44.4	4.4	2.4
Aged 65 or older	14.8	1.2	0.9

Source: SAMHSA, Office of Applied Studies, 2012 National Survey on Drug Use and Health, Detailed Tables, Internet site http://www.samhsa.gov/data/NSDUH/2012SummNatFindDetTables/Index.aspx

Many Gen Xers Lack Health Insurance

Among 35-to-44-year-olds, nearly one in five did not have health insurance coverage at any time in the past year.

Nineteen percent of 35-to-44-year-olds did not have health insurance at any time in 2013. While Gen Xers are more likely to have health insurance than younger adults, many are at risk of medical bankruptcy.

Most Americans obtain health insurance coverage through their employer. Among 35-to-44-year-olds with health insurance, 79 percent had employment-based coverage in 2013. But a smaller 57 percent had their own employment-based coverage.

Not surprisingly, health care expenses rise with age. Median health care expenses for Gen Xers exceed $1,000 annually. Most (57 percent) of their health care expenses are paid for by private insurance. Gen Xers account for only 11 percent of total health care spending.

■ The Affordable Care Act is reducing the number of Americans without health insurance.

Many Americans under age 65 are not covered by health insurance

(percent of people aged 18 or older not covered by health insurance at any time during the year, by age, 2013)

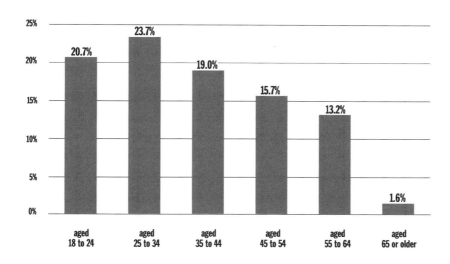

Table 3.21 Health Insurance Coverage by Age, 2013

(number and percent distribution of people by age and health insurance coverage status, 2013; numbers in thousands)

	total	covered by some type of health insurance during the year	not covered at any time during the year
Total people	**313,395**	**271,442**	**41,953**
Under age 65	268,888	227,627	41,260
Under age 18	74,055	68,613	5,441
Aged 18 to 24	30,054	23,846	6,208
Aged 25 to 34	42,466	32,397	10,069
Aged 35 to 44	39,789	32,233	7,556
Aged 45 to 54	42,898	36,159	6,739
Aged 55 to 64	39,626	34,380	5,247
Aged 65 or older	44,508	43,815	693
PERCENT DISTRIBUTION BY COVERAGE STATUS			
Total people	**100.0%**	**86.6%**	**13.4%**
Under age 65	100.0	84.7	15.3
Under age 18	100.0	92.7	7.3
Aged 18 to 24	100.0	79.3	20.7
Aged 25 to 34	100.0	76.3	23.7
Aged 35 to 44	100.0	81.0	19.0
Aged 45 to 54	100.0	84.3	15.7
Aged 55 to 64	100.0	86.8	13.2
Aged 65 or older	100.0	98.4	1.6
PERCENT DISTRIBUTION BY AGE			
Total people	**100.0**	**100.0**	**100.0**
Under age 65	85.8	83.9	98.3
Under age 18	23.6	25.3	13.0
Aged 18 to 24	9.6	8.8	14.8
Aged 25 to 34	13.6	11.9	24.0
Aged 35 to 44	12.7	11.9	18.0
Aged 45 to 54	13.7	13.3	16.1
Aged 55 to 64	12.6	12.7	12.5
Aged 65 or older	14.2	16.1	1.7

Source: Bureau of the Census, Health Insurance, Internet site http://www.census.gov/hhes/www/hlthins/; calculations by New Strategist

Table 3.22 Health Insurance Coverage by Age and Type of Coverage, 2013

(number and percent distribution of people with health insurance by age and type of coverage, 2013; numbers in thousands)

	total with coverage	total with private	employment based total	employment based own	direct purchase	total with government	Medicaid	Medicare	military
Total people	**271,442**	**201,064**	**169,015**	**87,097**	**34,531**	**107,581**	**54,081**	**48,977**	**14,147**
Under age 65	227,627	177,026	156,000	77,685	22,534	65,913	51,241	7,534	10,853
Under age 18	68,613	44,429	40,556	64	4,828	30,410	27,814	264	2,970
Aged 18 to 24	23,846	19,035	13,793	3,562	2,434	6,404	5,193	254	1,174
Aged 25 to 34	32,397	26,647	23,514	17,479	3,326	7,378	5,522	615	1,581
Aged 35 to 44	32,233	27,661	25,447	18,324	2,960	6,214	4,501	948	1,256
Aged 45 to 54	36,159	31,250	28,290	20,313	4,277	6,641	3,943	1,931	1,553
Aged 55 to 64	34,380	28,003	24,400	17,944	4,710	8,866	4,270	3,523	2,318
Aged 65 or older	43,815	24,039	13,015	9,413	11,996	41,668	2,840	41,442	3,294

PERCENT DISTRIBUTION BY TYPE OF COVERAGE

	total with coverage	total with private	employment based total	employment based own	direct purchase	total with government	Medicaid	Medicare	military
Total people	**100.0%**	**74.1%**	**62.3%**	**32.1%**	**12.7%**	**39.6%**	**19.9%**	**18.0%**	**5.2%**
Under age 65	100.0	77.8	68.5	34.1	9.9	29.0	22.5	3.3	4.8
Under age 18	100.0	64.8	59.1	0.1	7.0	44.3	40.5	0.4	4.3
Aged 18 to 24	100.0	79.8	57.8	14.9	10.2	26.9	21.8	1.1	4.9
Aged 25 to 34	100.0	82.3	72.6	54.0	10.3	22.8	17.0	1.9	4.9
Aged 35 to 44	100.0	85.8	78.9	56.8	9.2	19.3	14.0	2.9	3.9
Aged 45 to 54	100.0	86.4	78.2	56.2	11.8	18.4	10.9	5.3	4.3
Aged 55 to 64	100.0	81.5	71.0	52.2	13.7	25.8	12.4	10.2	6.7
Aged 65 or older	100.0	54.9	29.7	21.5	27.4	95.1	6.5	94.6	7.5

PERCENT DISTRIBUTION BY AGE

	total with coverage	total with private	employment based total	employment based own	direct purchase	total with government	Medicaid	Medicare	military
Total people	**100.0**	**100.0**	**100.0**	**100.0**	**100.0**	**100.0**	**100.0**	**100.0**	**100.0**
Under age 65	83.9	88.0	92.3	89.2	65.3	61.3	94.7	15.4	76.7
Under age 18	25.3	22.1	24.0	0.1	14.0	28.3	51.4	0.5	21.0
Aged 18 to 24	8.8	9.5	8.2	4.1	7.0	6.0	9.6	0.5	8.3
Aged 25 to 34	11.9	13.3	13.9	20.1	9.6	6.9	10.2	1.3	11.2
Aged 35 to 44	11.9	13.8	15.1	21.0	8.6	5.8	8.3	1.9	8.9
Aged 45 to 54	13.3	15.5	16.7	23.3	12.4	6.2	7.3	3.9	11.0
Aged 55 to 64	12.7	13.9	14.4	20.6	13.6	8.2	7.9	7.2	16.4
Aged 65 or older	16.1	12.0	7.7	10.8	34.7	38.7	5.3	84.6	23.3

Note: Numbers do not add to total because some people are covered by more than one type of health insurance.
Source: Bureau of the Census, Health Insurance, Internet site http://www.census.gov/hhes/www/hlthins/; calculations by New Strategist

Table 3.23 Spending on Health Care by Age, 2012

(percent of people with health care expense, median expense per person, total expenses, and percent distribution of total expenses by source of payment, by age, 2012)

	total (thousands)	percent with expense	median expense per person	total expenses amount (millions)	total expenses percent distribution
Total people	**313,490**	**84.7%**	**$1,286**	**$1,350,721**	**100.0%**
Under age 18	73,913	86.7	541	133,951	9.9
Aged 18 to 25	35,050	71.0	681	68,081	5.0
Aged 26 to 34	37,139	74.9	947	112,697	8.3
Aged 35 to 44	39,769	80.1	1,098	116,212	8.6
Aged 45 to 54	43,598	85.8	1,539	215,894	16.0
Aged 55 to 64	38,751	92.3	2,509	281,776	20.9
Aged 65 or older	45,271	96.3	4,292	422,109	31.3

	percent distribution by source of payment total	out of pocket	private insurance	Medicare	Medicaid
Total people	**100.0%**	**14.1%**	**42.5%**	**24.5%**	**10.5%**
Under age 18	100.0	15.0	50.6	1.3	27.5
Aged 18 to 25	100.0	15.3	56.3	1.7	18.9
Aged 26 to 34	100.0	14.9	55.9	2.8	15.0
Aged 35 to 44	100.0	16.6	55.9	7.6	11.7
Aged 45 to 54	100.0	14.4	55.7	9.5	11.6
Aged 55 to 64	100.0	13.9	54.7	13.1	6.9
Aged 65 or older	100.0	12.8	15.5	61.3	4.1

Note: Source of payment does not sum to 100 because "other" is not shown.
Source: Agency for Healthcare Research and Quality, Medical Expenditure Panel Survey, 2012, Internet site http://meps.ahrq .gov/mepsweb/survey_comp/household.jsp; calculations by New Strategist

Table 3.24 Spending on Health Care by Generation, 2012

(percent of people with health care expense, median expense per person, total expenses, and percent distribution of total expenses by source of payment, by generation, 2012)

	total (thousands)	percent with expense	median expense per person	total expenses	
				amount (millions)	percent distribution
Total people	**313,490**	**84.7%**	**$1,286**	**$1,350,721**	**100.0%**
iGeneration (under age 18)	73,913	86.7	541	133,951	9.9
Millennials (aged 18 to 35)	76,263	73.4	831	193,924	14.4
Generation X (aged 36 to 47)	47,418	81.1	1,143	149,346	11.1
Baby Boomers (aged 48 to 66)	77,615	90.1	2,202	503,104	37.2
Older Americans (aged 67 or older)	38,281	96.7	4,481	370,397	27.4

	percent distribution by source of payment				
	total	out of pocket	private insurance	Medicare	Medicaid
Total people	**100.0%**	**14.1%**	**42.5%**	**24.5%**	**10.5%**
iGeneration (under age 18)	100.0	15.0	50.6	1.3	27.5
Millennials (aged 18 to 35)	100.0	14.9	56.5	2.9	16.0
Generation X (aged 36 to 47)	100.0	16.5	56.8	7.1	11.4
Baby Boomers (aged 48 to 66)	100.0	13.9	52.0	15.5	8.1
Older Americans (aged 67 or older)	100.0	12.8	13.5	63.5	4.4

Note: Source of payment does not sum to 100 because "other" is not shown.
Source: Agency for Healthcare Research and Quality, Medical Expenditure Panel Survey, 2012, Internet site http://meps.ahrq
.gov/mepsweb/survey_comp/household.jsp; calculations by New Strategist

Health Problems Are Few in the 18-to-44 Age Group

Lower back pain is by far the most common health condition in the age group.

Twenty-four percent of Americans aged 18 to 44 have experienced lower back pain for at least one full day in the past three months, making it the most common health condition in the age group. Migraines or severe headaches are second, with 17 percent experiencing them. Chronic joint symptoms are third, with 15 percent reporting this problem. The 18-to-44 age group accounts for more than half of those who have ever had asthma.

More than 1 million Americans have been diagnosed with AIDS over the decades. The largest share were diagnosed in their thirties and early forties—the age groups now filled with Generation X.

■ As Generation X ages into its late forties and fifties, the percentage with chronic health problems will rise.

Percentage of people with diabetes rises with age

(percent of people with diabetes, by age, 2010)

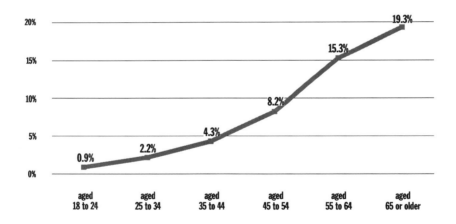

Table 3.25 Number of Adults with Health Conditions by Age, 2012

(number of people aged 18 or older with selected health conditions, by type of condition and age, 2012; numbers in thousands)

				65 or older		
	total	18 to 44	45 to 64	total	65 to 74	75 or older
Total people aged 18 or older	234,921	111,034	82,038	41,849	23,760	18,089
Selected circulatory diseases						
Heart disease, all types	26,561	4,168	9,939	12,453	5,792	6,661
Coronary	15,281	980	5,796	8,505	3,848	4,657
Hypertension	59,830	9,187	27,578	23,065	12,404	10,661
Stroke	6,370	635	2,293	3,441	1,505	1,936
Selected respiratory conditions						
Emphysema	4,108	292	1,853	1,964	1,121	843
Asthma, ever	29,660	14,929	10,380	4,352	2,863	1,489
Asthma, still	18,719	8,943	6,852	2,925	1,837	1,088
Hay fever	17,596	6,774	7,965	2,857	1,882	975
Sinusitis	28,504	10,889	12,542	5,074	3,291	1,783
Chronic bronchitis	8,658	2,721	3,831	2,105	1,165	940
Chronic obstructive pulmonary disease	6,790	512	3,074	3,204	1,646	1,558
Selected types of cancer						
Any cancer	20,073	2,265	7,629	10,179	5,014	5,165
Breast cancer	3,312	171	1,242	1,898	909	989
Cervical cancer	1,330	524	558	247	156	91
Prostate cancer	2,453	–	546	1,902	907	995
Other selected diseases and conditions						
Diabetes	21,319	2,673	10,273	8,372	4,863	3,509
Ulcers	15,435	4,555	6,452	4,428	2,393	2,035
Kidney disease	3,882	633	1,548	1,700	746	954
Liver disease	3,034	688	1,662	684	491	193
Arthritis	51,830	7,582	24,223	20,025	11,111	8,914
Chronic joint symptoms	63,085	16,734	28,984	17,367	10,076	7,291
Migraines or severe headaches	32,453	18,920	11,136	2,396	1,545	851
Pain in neck	33,515	12,528	15,053	5,934	3,452	2,482
Pain in lower back	65,823	26,611	26,495	12,717	7,104	5,613
Pain in face or jaw	11,326	5,457	4,296	1,574	963	611
Selected sensory problems						
Hearing	37,567	6,830	15,731	15,005	6,992	8,013
Vision	20,609	6,014	9,292	5,303	2,607	2,696
Absence of all natural teeth	17,952	2,785	6,345	8,823	4,164	4,659

Note: The conditions shown are those that have ever been diagnosed by a doctor, except as noted. Hay fever, sinusitis, chronic bronchitis, and chronic obstructive pulmonary disease have been diagnosed in the past 12 months. Kidney and liver diseases have been diagnosed in the past 12 months and exclude kidney stones, bladder infections, and incontinence. Chronic joint symptoms are shown if respondent had pain, aching, or stiffness in or around a joint (excluding back and neck) and the condition began more than three months ago. Migraines and pain in neck, lower back, face, or jaw are shown only if pain lasted a whole day or more. "–" means sample is too small to make a reliable estimate.
Source: National Center for Health Statistics, Summary Health Statistics for U.S. Adults: National Health Interview Survey, 2012, Vital and Health Statistics, Series 10, No. 260, 2014, Internet site http://www.cdc.gov/nchs/nhis.htm

Table 3.26 Percent of Adults with Health Conditions by Age, 2012

(percent of people aged 18 or older with selected health conditions, by type of condition and age, 2012)

	total	18 to 44	45 to 64	65 to 74	75 or older
Total people aged 18 or older	100.0%	100.0%	100.0%	100.0%	100.0%
Selected circulatory diseases					
Heart disease, all types	11.3	3.8	12.1	34.4	36.9
Coronary	6.5	0.9	7.1	16.2	25.8
Hypertension	25.5	8.3	33.7	52.3	59.2
Stroke	2.7	0.6	2.8	6.3	10.7
Selected respiratory conditions					
Emphysema	1.7	0.3	2.3	4.7	4.7
Asthma, ever	12.6	13.4	12.7	12.1	8.2
Asthma, still	8.0	8.1	8.4	7.8	6.0
Hay fever	7.5	6.1	9.7	7.9	5.4
Sinusitis	12.1	9.8	15.3	13.9	9.9
Chronic bronchitis	3.7	2.5	4.7	4.9	5.2
Chronic obstructive pulmonary disease	2.9	0.5	3.8	6.9	8.6
Selected types of cancer					
Any cancer	8.5	2.0	9.3	21.1	28.6
Breast cancer	1.4	0.2	1.5	3.8	5.5
Cervical cancer	1.1	0.9	1.3	1.2	0.8
Prostate cancer	2.2	–	1.4	8.2	13.7
Other selected diseases and conditions					
Diabetes	9.2	2.4	12.7	21.1	19.8
Ulcers	6.6	4.1	7.9	10.1	11.3
Kidney disease	1.7	0.6	1.9	3.1	5.3
Liver disease	1.3	0.6	2.0	2.1	1.1
Arthritis	22.1	6.8	29.6	46.8	49.4
Chronic joint symptoms	26.9	15.1	35.3	42.5	40.4
Migraines or severe headaches	13.8	17.1	13.6	6.5	4.7
Pain in neck	14.3	11.3	18.4	14.5	13.7
Pain in lower back	28.0	24.0	32.3	29.9	31.1
Pain in face or jaw	4.8	4.9	5.2	4.1	3.4
Selected sensory problems					
Hearing	16.0	6.2	19.2	29.4	44.4
Vision	8.8	5.4	11.3	11.0	14.9
Absence of all natural teeth	7.6	2.5	7.7	17.5	25.8

Note: The conditions shown are those that have ever been diagnosed by a doctor, except as noted. Hay fever, sinusitis, chronic bronchitis, and chronic obstructive pulmonary disease have been diagnosed in the past 12 months. Kidney and liver diseases have been diagnosed in the past 12 months and exclude kidney stones, bladder infections, and incontinence. Chronic joint symptoms are shown if respondent had pain, aching, or stiffness in or around a joint (excluding back and neck) and the condition began more than three months ago. Migraines and pain in neck, lower back, face, or jaw are shown only if pain lasted a whole day or more. "–" means sample is too small to make a reliable estimate.
Source: National Center for Health Statistics, Summary Health Statistics for U.S. Adults: National Health Interview Survey, 2012, Vital and Health Statistics, Series 10, No. 260, 2014, Internet site http://www.cdc.gov/nchs/nhis.htm

Table 3.27 Distribution of Health Conditions among Adults by Age, 2012

(percent distribution of people aged 18 or older with selected health conditions, by type of condition and age, 2012)

				65 or older		
	total	18 to 44	45 to 64	total	65 to 74	75 or older
Total people aged 18 or older	**100.0%**	**47.3%**	**34.9%**	**17.8%**	**10.1%**	**7.7%**
Selected circulatory diseases						
Heart disease, all types	100.0	15.7	37.4	46.9	21.8	25.1
Coronary	100.0	6.4	37.9	55.7	25.2	30.5
Hypertension	100.0	15.4	46.1	38.6	20.7	17.8
Stroke	100.0	10.0	36.0	54.0	23.6	30.4
Selected respiratory conditions						
Emphysema	100.0	7.1	45.1	47.8	27.3	20.5
Asthma, ever	100.0	50.3	35.0	14.7	9.7	5.0
Asthma, still	100.0	47.8	36.6	15.6	9.8	5.8
Hay fever	100.0	38.5	45.3	16.2	10.7	5.5
Sinusitis	100.0	38.2	44.0	17.8	11.5	6.3
Chronic bronchitis	100.0	31.4	44.2	24.3	13.5	10.9
Chronic obstructive pulmonary disease	100.0	7.5	45.3	47.2	24.2	22.9
Selected types of cancer						
Any cancer	100.0	11.3	38.0	50.7	25.0	25.7
Breast cancer	100.0	5.2	37.5	57.3	27.4	29.9
Cervical cancer	100.0	39.4	42.0	18.6	11.7	6.8
Prostate cancer	100.0	–	22.3	77.5	37.0	40.6
Other selected diseases and conditions						
Diabetes	100.0	12.5	48.2	39.3	22.8	16.5
Ulcers	100.0	29.5	41.8	28.7	15.5	13.2
Kidney disease	100.0	16.3	39.9	43.8	19.2	24.6
Liver disease	100.0	22.7	54.8	22.5	16.2	6.4
Arthritis	100.0	14.6	46.7	38.6	21.4	17.2
Chronic joint symptoms	100.0	26.5	45.9	27.5	16.0	11.6
Migraines or severe headaches	100.0	58.3	34.3	7.4	4.8	2.6
Pain in neck	100.0	37.4	44.9	17.7	10.3	7.4
Pain in lower back	100.0	40.4	40.3	19.3	10.8	8.5
Pain in face or jaw	100.0	48.2	37.9	13.9	8.5	5.4
Selected sensory problems						
Hearing	100.0	18.2	41.9	39.9	18.6	21.3
Vision	100.0	29.2	45.1	25.7	12.6	13.1
Absence of all natural teeth	100.0	15.5	35.3	49.1	23.2	26.0

Note: The conditions shown are those that have ever been diagnosed by a doctor, except as noted. Hay fever, sinusitis, chronic bronchitis, and chronic obstructive pulmonary disease have been diagnosed in the past 12 months. Kidney and liver diseases have been diagnosed in the past 12 months and exclude kidney stones, bladder infections, and incontinence. Chronic joint symptoms are shown if respondent had pain, aching, or stiffness in or around a joint (excluding back and neck) and the condition began more than three months ago. Migraines and pain in neck, lower back, face, or jaw are shown only if pain lasted a whole day or more. "–" means sample is too small to make a reliable estimate.
Source: National Center for Health Statistics, Summary Health Statistics for U.S. Adults: National Health Interview Survey, 2012, Vital and Health Statistics, Series 10, No. 260, 2014, Internet site http://www.cdc.gov/nchs/nhis.htm

Table 3.28 Diabetes Diagnosis by Age, 2010

(percent distribution of people aged 18 or older by age and diabetes diagnosis status, 2010)

	total	diagnosed with diabetes by a doctor	
		yes	no
Total people	**100.0%**	**8.7%**	**91.3%**
Aged 18 to 24	100.0	0.9	99.1
Aged 25 to 34	100.0	2.2	97.8
Aged 35 to 44	100.0	4.3	95.7
Aged 45 to 54	100.0	8.2	91.8
Aged 55 to 64	100.0	15.3	84.7
Aged 65 or older	100.0	19.3	80.7

Source: Centers for Disease Control and Prevention, Behavioral Risk Factor Surveillance System Prevalence Data, 2010, Internet site http://apps.nccd.cdc.gov/brfss/

Table 3.29 AIDS Cases by Age, through 2011

(cumulative number and percent distribution of AIDS cases by age at diagnosis, 2011)

	number	percent distribution
Total cases	**1,155,792**	**100.0%**
Under age 13	9,521	0.8
Aged 13 to 14	1,452	0.1
Aged 15 to 19	8,129	0.7
Aged 20 to 24	46,957	4.1
Aged 25 to 29	135,135	11.7
Aged 30 to 34	219,784	19.0
Aged 35 to 39	239,749	20.7
Aged 40 to 44	199,727	17.3
Aged 45 to 49	133,612	11.6
Aged 50 to 54	77,843	6.7
Aged 55 to 59	42,372	3.7
Aged 60 to 64	22,369	1.9
Aged 65 or older	19,143	1.7

Source: Centers for Disease Control and Prevention, Diagnoses of HIV Infection in the United States and Dependent Areas, 2011, Internet site http://www.cdc.gov/hiv/surveillance/resources/reports/2011report/index.htm; calculations by New Strategist

Gen Xers Are Approaching the Age when Prescription Drug Use Becomes the Norm

Most Americans aged 45 or older have taken at least one prescription drug in the past month.

The use of prescription drugs to treat a variety of illnesses, particularly chronic conditions, has become the norm among middle-aged and older Americans. In the 18-to-44 age group, 39 percent have taken at least one prescription drug in the past month. In the 45-to-64 age group, the figure climbs to 66 percent. Gen Xers (aged 37 to 48 in 2013) are straddling these two age groups.

As prescription drug use becomes common with age, spending on prescription drugs rises. Fully 62 percent of adults incurred a prescription drug expense in 2012, according to the federal government's Medical Expenditure Panel Survey. Expenses for prescription drugs rise with age to a median of $989 per person among people aged 65 or older. The 60.5 percent majority of Gen Xers had a prescription drug expense in 2012, with a median of $192 spent on these medications. Only 20 percent of that cost came out-of-pocket and half was paid by private insurance.

■ Behind the increase in the use of prescriptions is the introduction and marketing of new drugs to treat chronic health problems.

Most Gen Xers have had a prescription drug expense in the past year

(percent of people with prescription drug expenses, by generation, 2012)

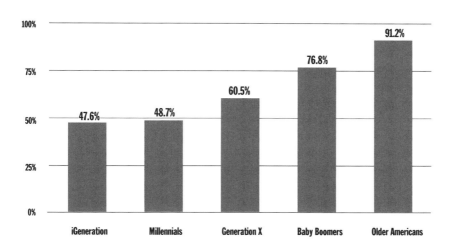

Table 3.30 Prescription Drug Use by Sex and Age, 2007–10

(percent of people aged 18 or older taking at least one or three or more prescription drugs in the past month, by sex and age, 2007–10)

	at least one in past month	three or more in past month
Total people	**48.5%**	**21.7%**
Under age 18	24.0	3.8
Aged 18 to 44	38.7	9.7
Aged 45 to 64	66.2	34.4
Aged 65 or older	89.7	66.6
Total females	**53.8**	**24.2**
Under age 18	23.5	3.1
Aged 18 to 44	47.6	12.2
Aged 45 to 64	70.8	38.1
Aged 65 or older	90.4	66.4
Total males	**43.0**	**19.0**
Under age 18	24.5	4.4
Aged 18 to 44	29.5	7.1
Aged 45 to 64	61.3	30.4
Aged 65 or older	88.8	66.8

Source: National Center for Health Statistics, Health, United States, 2013, Internet site http://www.cdc.gov/nchs/hus.htm; calculations by New Strategist

Table 3.31 Spending on Prescription Medications by Age, 2012

(percent of people with prescription medication expense, median expense per person, total expenses, and percent distribution of total expenses by source of payment, by age, 2012)

	total (thousands)	percent with expense	median expense per person	total expenses	
				amount (millions)	percent distribution
Total people	**313,490**	**62.4%**	**$253**	**$292,957**	**100.0%**
Under age 18	73,913	47.6	52	25,558	8.7
Aged 18 to 25	35,050	44.2	95	9,554	3.3
Aged 26 to 34	37,139	52.0	109	18,611	6.4
Aged 35 to 44	39,769	58.4	179	27,742	9.5
Aged 45 to 54	43,598	68.4	329	53,153	18.1
Aged 55 to 64	38,751	80.9	593	68,316	23.3
Aged 65 or older	45,271	90.8	961	90,023	30.7

	percent distribution by source of payment				
	total	out of pocket	private insurance	Medicare	Medicaid
Total people	**100.0%**	**19.1%**	**38.7%**	**25.5%**	**9.8%**
Under age 18	100.0	10.7	46.5	5.2	35.6
Aged 18 to 25	100.0	22.8	42.5	8.8	19.1
Aged 26 to 34	100.0	19.8	33.5	13.6	12.8
Aged 35 to 44	100.0	18.7	49.6	12.2	13.7
Aged 45 to 54	100.0	19.1	51.3	12.3	10.9
Aged 55 to 64	100.0	20.0	47.6	19.7	7.3
Aged 65 or older	100.0	20.6	19.7	51.8	0.9

Note: Source of payment does not sum to 100 because "other" is not shown.
Source: Agency for Healthcare Research and Quality, Medical Expenditure Panel Survey, 2012, Internet site http://meps.ahrq
.gov/mepsweb/survey_comp/household.jsp; calculations by New Strategist

Table 3.32 Spending on Prescription Medications by Generation, 2012

(percent of people with prescription medication expense, median expense per person, total expenses, and percent distribution of total expenses by source of payment, by generation, 2012)

	total (thousands)	percent with expense	median expense per person	total expenses amount (millions)	total expenses percent distribution
Total people	**313,490**	**62.4%**	**$253**	**$292,957**	**100.0%**
iGeneration (under age 18)	73,913	47.6	52	25,558	8.7
Millennials (aged 18 to 35)	76,263	48.7	106	30,976	10.6
Generation X (aged 36 to 47)	47,418	60.5	192	33,782	11.5
Baby Boomers (aged 48 to 66)	77,615	76.8	502	125,950	43.0
Older Americans (aged 67 or older)	38,281	91.2	989	76,692	26.2

	percent distribution by source of payment total	out of pocket	private insurance	Medicare	Medicaid
Total people	**100.0%**	**19.1%**	**38.7%**	**25.5%**	**9.8%**
iGeneration (under age 18)	100.0	10.7	46.5	5.2	35.6
Millennials (aged 18 to 35)	100.0	20.6	38.0	11.5	15.0
Generation X (aged 36 to 47)	100.0	19.8	50.3	11.3	12.4
Baby Boomers (aged 48 to 66)	100.0	19.2	47.0	19.3	8.0
Older Americans (aged 67 or older)	100.0	20.9	17.8	54.4	0.9

Note: Source of payment does not sum to 100 because "other" is not shown.
Source: Agency for Healthcare Research and Quality, Medical Expenditure Panel Survey, 2012, Internet site http://meps.ahrq
.gov/mepsweb/survey_comp/household.jsp; calculations by New Strategist

Most Gen Xers Have Seen a Health Care Provider in the Past Year

Most also have a usual place of care.

Nearly 80 percent of adults visited a health care provider at least once in 2012. Among 18-to-44-year-olds, the figure is 71 percent (Gen Xers were aged 36 to 47 in 2012). Most of the adult population also has a usual place of care, and for the majority that place is a doctor's office or HMO.

When adults who visited a doctor or health care clinic are asked to rate the care they received, only half give it the highest rating (a 9 or 10 on a scale of 0 to 10). Only 43 percent of Millennials and 44 percent of Gen Xers give the health care they received the highest rating. A much larger 63 percent of Older Americans—almost all on Medicare—give their health care the highest rating.

■ Many Gen Xers struggle to maintain health insurance coverage, a factor that contributes to their jaded view of the quality of care they receive.

Fewer than half of Gen Xers give their health care provider the highest rating

*(percent of people aged 18 or older who visited a health care provider
in the past year who rated the health care they received a 9 or 10
on a scale from 0 (worst) to 10 (best), by generation, 2012)*

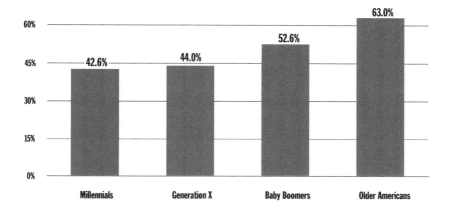

Table 3.33 Health Care Office Visits by Age, 2012

(number of people aged 18 or older and percent distribution by number of office visits to a health care provider in past 12 months, by selected characteristics, 2012; numbers in thousands)

	total	no visits	one or more visits total	one	two to three	four to nine	10 or more
Total people	**234,921**	**45,321**	**184,823**	**41,398**	**59,307**	**53,239**	**30,879**
Aged 18 to 44	111,034	29,657	79,328	22,923	26,482	18,419	11,504
Aged 45 to 64	82,038	12,900	67,495	14,058	22,149	20,126	11,162
Aged 65 to 74	23,760	1,759	21,542	2,925	6,428	7,930	4,259
Aged 75 or older	18,089	1,005	16,458	1,492	4,249	6,764	3,953
PERCENT DISTRIBUTION							
Total people	**100.0%**	**19.3%**	**78.7%**	**17.6%**	**25.2%**	**22.7%**	**13.1%**
Aged 18 to 44	100.0	26.7	71.4	20.6	23.9	16.6	10.4
Aged 45 to 64	100.0	15.7	82.3	17.1	27.0	24.5	13.6
Aged 65 to 74	100.0	7.4	90.7	12.3	27.1	33.4	17.9
Aged 75 or older	100.0	5.6	91.0	8.2	23.5	37.4	21.9

Note: Health care visits exclude overnight hospitalizations, visits to emergency rooms, home visits, dental visits, and telephone calls. Numbers do not add to total because "unknown" is not shown.
Source: National Center for Health Statistics, Summary Health Statistics for U.S. Adults: National Health Interview Survey, 2012, Vital and Health Statistics, Series 10, No. 260, 2014, Internet site http://www.cdc.gov/nchs/products/series/series10.htm; calculations by New Strategist

Table 3.34 Usual Place of Health Care for Adults, 2012

(number and percent distribution of people aged 18 or older by usual place of care status and type of place, by age, 2012; numbers in thousands)

	number	without a usual place of care	with a usual place of care				
			total	doctor's office or HMO	clinic or health center	hospital emergency room or outpatient department	some other place
Total people	**234,921**	**37,458**	**194,933**	**145,366**	**40,518**	**5,463**	**2,049**
Aged 18 to 44	111,034	26,361	83,537	57,795	20,597	2,974	1,108
Aged 45 to 64	82,038	9,733	71,466	54,716	13,821	1,860	694
Aged 65 to 74	23,760	869	22,633	18,386	3,698	369	139
Aged 75 or older	18,089	495	17,298	14,469	2,403	261	108
PERCENT DISTRIBUTION							
Total people	**100.0%**	**15.9%**	**83.0%**	**61.9%**	**17.2%**	**2.3%**	**0.9%**
Aged 18 to 44	100.0	23.7	75.2	52.1	18.6	2.7	1.0
Aged 45 to 64	100.0	11.9	87.1	66.7	16.8	2.3	0.8
Aged 65 to 74	100.0	3.7	95.3	77.4	15.6	1.6	0.6
Aged 75 or older	100.0	2.7	95.6	80.0	13.3	1.4	0.6

Source: National Center for Health Statistics, Summary Health Statistics for U.S. Adults: National Health Interview Survey, 2012, Vital and Health Statistics, Series 10, No. 260, 2014, Internet site http://www.cdc.gov/nchs/products/series/series10.htm; calculations by New Strategist

Table 3.35 Rating of Health Care Received from Doctor's Office or Clinic by Age, 2012

(number of people aged 18 or older visiting a doctor or health care clinic in past 12 months, and percent distribution by rating for health care received on a scale from 0 (worst) to 10 (best), by age, 2012; people in thousands)

	with health care visit		rating		
	number	percent	9 to 10	7 to 8	0 to 6
Total adults	**159,173**	**100.0%**	**50.6%**	**36.1%**	**12.2%**
Aged 18 to 25	17,745	100.0	45.7	39.0	14.7
Aged 26 to 34	20,172	100.0	39.7	45.0	14.5
Aged 35 to 44	24,353	100.0	43.0	41.2	14.7
Aged 45 to 54	28,240	100.0	47.1	38.4	13.6
Aged 55 to 64	30,738	100.0	55.3	32.5	10.9
Aged 65 or older	37,925	100.0	62.2	28.1	8.2

Source: Agency for Healthcare Research and Quality, Medical Expenditure Panel Survey, 2012; Internet site http://meps.ahrq .gov/mepsweb/survey_comp/household.jsp; calculations by New Strategist

Table 3.36 Rating of Health Care Received from Doctor's Office or Clinic by Generation, 2012

(number of people aged 18 or older visiting a doctor or health care clinic in past 12 months, and percent distribution by rating for health care received on a scale from 0 (worst) to 10 (best), by generation, 2012; people in thousands)

	with health care visit		rating		
	number	percent	9 to 10	7 to 8	0 to 6
Total adults	**159,173**	**100.0%**	**50.6%**	**36.1%**	**12.2%**
Millennials (aged 18 to 35)	40,331	100.0	42.6	42.3	14.4
Generation X (aged 36 to 47)	29,748	100.0	44.0	40.4	14.4
Baby Boomers (aged 48 to 66)	57,110	100.0	52.6	34.5	11.8
Older Americans (aged 67 or older)	31,983	100.0	63.0	27.4	8.2

Source: Agency for Healthcare Research and Quality, Medical Expenditure Panel Survey, 2012; Internet site http://meps.ahrq .gov/mepsweb/survey_comp/household.jsp; calculations by New Strategist

Many Deaths of Younger Adults Are Preventable

Accidents are the leading cause of death for 25-to-44-year-olds.

When adults under age 45 die, it is often preventable. Accidents are the leading cause of death among 25-to-44-year-olds, accounting for 26 percent of the total in 2011 (Gen X was aged 35 to 46 in that year). Suicide ranks fourth among 25-to-44-year-olds, and homicide is fifth. Cancer is the second most important cause of death in the age group, followed by heart disease. HIV infection ranks eighth.

Although more could be done to reduce deaths among younger adults, some progress has been made. The life expectancy of Americans continues to rise. At age 35, life expectancy is another 45 years. At age 40, another 41 years of life remain—marking the true midpoint of life.

■ As Gen Xers age, heart disease and cancer will become the two leading causes of death.

Cancer and heart disease are important causes of death among 25-to-44-year-olds

(percent of deaths among 25-to-44-year-olds caused by top four causes of death, 2011)

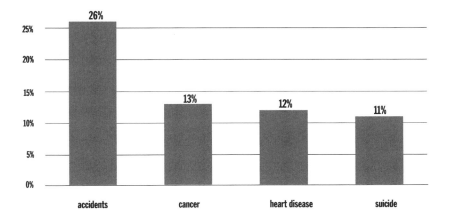

Table 3.37 Leading Causes of Death for People Aged 25 to 44, 2011

(number and percent distribution of deaths accounted for by the 10 leading causes of death for people aged 25 to 44, 2011)

	number	percent
All causes	**113,341**	**100.0%**
1. Accidents (5)	29,424	26.0
2. Malignant neoplasms (cancer) (2)	15,210	13.4
3. Diseases of the heart (1)	13,479	11.9
4. Suicide (10)	12,269	10.8
5. Homicide	6,639	5.9
6. Chronic liver disease and cirrhosis	2,919	2.6
7. Diabetes mellitus (7)	2,474	2.2
8. Human immunodeficiency virus infection	2,262	2.0
9. Cerebrovascular diseases (4)	2,245	2.0
10. Influenza and pneumonia (8)	1,341	1.2
All other causes	25,079	22.1

Note: Number in parentheses shows rank for all Americans if the cause of death is in top 10.
Source: National Center for Health Statistics, Deaths: Preliminary Data for 2011, National Vital Statistics Report, Vol. 61, No. 6, 2012, Internet site http://www.cdc.gov/nchs/deaths.htm; calculations by New Strategist

Table 3.38 Life Expectancy by Age and Sex, 2011

(average years of life remaining at selected ages, by sex, 2011)

	total	females	males
At birth	78.7 yrs.	81.1 yrs.	76.3 yrs.
Aged 1	78.2	80.5	75.8
Aged 5	74.3	76.6	71.9
Aged 10	69.3	71.6	66.9
Aged 15	64.4	66.7	62.0
Aged 20	59.5	61.8	57.2
Aged 25	54.8	56.9	52.5
Aged 30	50.0	52.0	47.9
Aged 35	45.3	47.2	43.2
Aged 40	40.6	42.5	38.6
Aged 45	36.0	37.8	34.0
Aged 50	31.5	33.2	29.6
Aged 55	27.2	28.8	25.5
Aged 60	23.1	24.5	21.5
Aged 65	19.2	20.4	17.8
Aged 70	15.5	16.5	14.3
Aged 75	12.1	12.9	11.0
Aged 80	9.1	9.7	8.2
Aged 85	6.5	6.9	5.9
Aged 90	4.6	4.8	4.1
Aged 95	3.2	3.3	2.9
Aged 100	2.3	2.3	2.1

Source: National Center for Health Statistics, Deaths: Preliminary Data for 2011, National Vital Statistics Report, Vol. 61, No. 6, 2012, Internet site http://www.cdc.gov/nchs/deaths.htm

4

Housing

■ The homeownership rate in the United States reached a peak of 69.0 percent in 2004. By 2013, the rate had fallen 3.9 percentage points to 65.1 percent. During those years, the homeownership rate fell the most among 35-to-39-year-olds—a 10.4 percentage point drop.

■ Two out of three Gen Xers own their home. Generation X accounts for 21 percent of the nation's homeowners and 22 percent of all renters.

■ Most Asian and non-Hispanic White Gen Xers are homeowners. Among Black and Hispanic Gen Xers, the homeownership rate is 41 and 47 percent, respectively.

■ The majority of American households (69 percent) live in a single-family home. Three out of four householders ranging in age from 35 to 64 live in this type of housing unit.

■ Only 11.7 percent of Americans aged 1 or older moved between March 2012 and March 2013. The proportion was a slightly smaller 10.6 percent among Gen Xers.

Homeownership Rate Has Declined

Rate has fallen the most for 35-to-39-year-olds.

The homeownership rate in the United States reached a peak of 69.0 percent in 2004. Then the Great Recession set in and the housing market collapsed. The overall homeownership rate fell 3.9 percentage points between 2004 and 2013, to 65.1 percent. The 2013 rate is 2.4 percentage points below the rate of 2000.

Since the peak of 2004, the homeownership rate has fallen the most among households headed by 35-to-39-year-olds. This drop occurred primarily as younger renters aged into their thirties and found themselves unable or unwilling to buy a home. In 2013, the homeownership rate of householders aged 35 to 39 was more than 10 percentage points below the rate for that age group in 2004. Among householders in their forties, the homeownership rate fell 7 percentage points during those years. Householders aged 75 or older were the only ones more likely to be homeowners in 2013 than in 2004.

■ No generation was hit harder by the Great Recession and the collapse of the housing market than Generation X.

After peaking in 2004, homeownership rate is lower among 35-to-49-year-olds

(percentage point change in homeownership rate for householders aged 35 to 49, by age, 2004 and 2013)

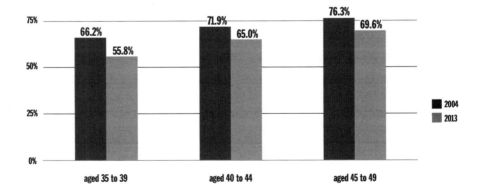

Table 4.1 Homeownership Rate by Age of Householder, 2000 to 2013

(percentage of householders who own their home by age of householder, 2000 to 2013; percentage point change for selected years)

	2013	2010	2004	2000	percentage point change 2004–13	2000–13
Total households	**65.1%**	**66.8%**	**69.0%**	**67.5%**	**–3.9**	**–2.4**
Under age 25	22.2	22.8	25.2	21.8	–3.0	0.4
Aged 25 to 29	34.1	36.8	40.2	37.8	–6.1	–3.7
Aged 30 to 34	48.1	51.6	57.4	54.5	–9.3	–6.4
Aged 35 to 39	55.8	61.9	66.2	65.2	–10.4	–9.4
Aged 40 to 44	65.0	67.8	71.9	70.6	–6.9	–5.6
Aged 45 to 49	69.6	72.0	76.3	75.0	–6.7	–5.4
Aged 50 to 54	72.6	75.0	78.3	78.7	–5.7	–6.1
Aged 55 to 59	75.8	77.7	81.2	79.8	–5.4	–4.0
Aged 60 to 64	77.6	80.4	82.4	80.6	–4.8	–3.0
Aged 65 to 69	80.5	81.6	83.2	83.4	–2.7	–2.9
Aged 70 to 74	82.8	82.4	83.4	81.6	–0.6	1.2
Aged 75 or older	80.0	78.9	78.8	78.2	1.2	1.8
Total households	**65.1**	**66.8**	**69.0**	**67.5**	**–3.9**	**–2.4**
Under age 35	36.8	39.0	43.1	40.7	–6.3	–3.9
Aged 35 to 44	60.6	65.0	69.2	68.0	–8.6	–7.4
Aged 45 to 54	71.2	73.5	77.2	76.8	–6.0	–5.6
Aged 55 to 64	76.6	79.0	81.7	80.2	–5.1	–3.6
Aged 65 or older	80.8	80.5	81.1	80.5	–0.3	0.3

Source: Bureau of the Census, Housing Vacancies and Homeownership, Internet site http://www.census.gov/housing/hvs/; calculations by New Strategist

Homeownership Rises with Age

Nearly two out of three Gen Xers own their home.

Homeownership becomes the norm in the 35-to-39 age group, which is now filled with Gen Xers. In 2013, the 55.8 percent majority of householders aged 35 to 39 owned their home. The homeownership rate rises to 65.0 percent among 40-to-44-year-olds and approaches 70 percent among 45-to-49-year-olds.

Young adults are least likely to own a home because they have not yet accumulated the savings for a down payment and are not yet earning enough to qualify for a mortgage. Only 39 percent of Millennial households own their home. The homeownership rate is 76 percent among Boomers and peaks at 81 percent among older Americans.

■ Although homeownership rates are down from their peak, the pattern of homeownership—with rates rising as people age—is unchanged.

Homeownership varies greatly by generation

(percent of households that own their home by generation, 2013)

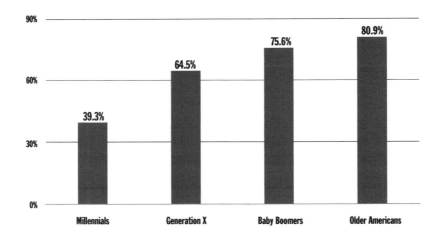

Table 4.2 Owners and Renters by Generation of Householder, 2013

(number and percent distribution of householders by homeownership status, by generation of householder, 2013; numbers in thousands)

	total	owners	renters
Total households	**114,673**	**74,668**	**40,005**
Millennials (under age 37)	28,619	11,251	17,368
Generation Xers (aged 37 to 48)	24,617	15,875	8,742
Baby Boomers (aged 49 to 67)	40,241	30,402	9,839
Older Americans (aged 68 or older)	21,197	17,141	4,056
PERCENT DISTRIBUTION BY HOMEOWNERSHIP STATUS			
Total households	**100.0%**	**65.1%**	**34.9%**
Millennials (under age 37)	100.0	39.3	60.7
Generation Xers (aged 37 to 48)	100.0	64.5	35.5
Baby Boomers (aged 49 to 67)	100.0	75.6	24.4
Older Americans (aged 68 or older)	100.0	80.9	19.1
PERCENT DISTRIBUTION BY AGE OF HOUSEHOLDER			
Total households	**100.0**	**100.0**	**100.0**
Millennials (under age 37)	25.0	15.1	43.4
Generation Xers (aged 37 to 48)	21.5	21.3	21.9
Baby Boomers (aged 49 to 67)	35.1	40.7	24.6
Older Americans (aged 68 or older)	18.5	23.0	10.1

Source: Bureau of the Census, Housing Vacancies and Homeownership, Internet site http://www.census.gov/housing/hvs/; calculations by New Strategist

Table 4.3 Households by Homeownership Status, Generation, and Age Group, 2013

(number and percent distribution of total households, households headed by people aged 37 to 48, and households in age groups that include Gen Xers, by homeownership status, 2013; numbers in thousands)

	total	owners	renters
Total households	**114,673**	**74,668**	**40,005**
Generation Xers (aged 37 to 48)	**24,617**	**15,875**	**8,742**
Aged 35 to 39	9,502	5,302	4,200
Aged 40 to 44	10,351	6,729	3,622
Aged 45 to 49	10,706	7,456	3,250
PERCENT DISTRIBUTION BY HOMEOWNERSHIP STATUS			
Total households	**100.0%**	**65.1%**	**34.9%**
Generation Xers (aged 37 to 48)	**100.0**	**64.5**	**35.5**
Aged 35 to 39	100.0	55.8	44.2
Aged 40 to 44	100.0	65.0	35.0
Aged 45 to 49	100.0	69.6	30.4

Source: Bureau of the Census, Housing Vacancies and Homeownership, Internet site http://www.census.gov/housing/hvs/; calculations by New Strategist

Married Couples Are Most Likely to Be Homeowners

Homeownership rate is highest in the Midwest.

The homeownership rate among married couples was 80.7 percent in 2013, much higher than the 65.1 percent for all households. Among married couples, the homeownership rate surpasses 50 percent in the youthful 25-to-29 age group. For other types of households, the homeownership rate does not surpass 50 percent until older age groups. Male-headed families cross the 50-percent threshold in the 40-to-44 age group, female-headed families and men who live alone in the 45-to-49 age group, and women who live alone in the 50-to-54 age group.

In 2013, the homeownership rate was highest in the Midwest (69.7 percent) and lowest in the West (59.4 percent). Homeownership becomes the norm in the 30-to-34 age group in the Midwest, in the 35-to-39 age group in the Northeast and South, and in the 40-to-44 age group in the West. Homeownership peaks at 86.9 percent among householders aged 70 to 74 in the Midwest.

■ The collapse of the housing market and the decline in homeownership did not eliminate differences in homeownership rates by household type.

Three out of four married couples aged 35 to 44 own their home

(percent of married-couple householders who own their home, by age, 2013)

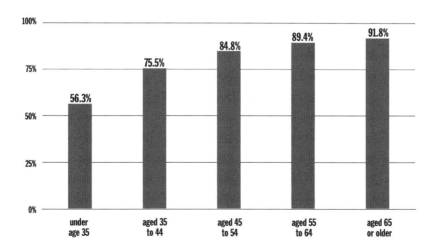

Table 4.4 Homeownership Rate by Age of Householder and Type of Household, 2013

(percent of households owning their home, by age of householder and type of household, 2013)

	total	married couples	female family householder, no spouse present	male family householder, no spouse present	people living alone	
					females	males
Total households	**65.1%**	**80.7%**	**46.7%**	**55.3%**	**57.2%**	**49.8%**
Under age 25	22.2	31.7	25.9	41.9	10.8	13.3
Aged 25 to 29	34.1	51.5	22.0	37.8	20.1	26.4
Aged 30 to 34	48.1	63.9	28.8	42.4	29.3	32.3
Aged 35 to 39	55.8	70.8	33.7	46.6	37.1	39.7
Aged 40 to 44	65.0	79.6	43.6	54.7	43.1	45.1
Aged 45 to 49	69.6	83.4	50.6	62.9	48.8	50.2
Aged 50 to 54	72.6	86.1	58.6	67.9	53.7	51.7
Aged 55 to 59	75.8	88.6	65.0	70.7	59.3	55.6
Aged 60 to 64	77.6	90.4	66.9	69.5	63.3	58.1
Aged 65 to 69	80.5	91.8	72.0	80.1	66.6	62.5
Aged 70 to 74	82.8	92.7	78.5	78.4	71.9	69.4
Aged 75 or older	80.0	91.0	86.1	87.1	71.4	73.0
Total households	**65.1**	**80.7**	**46.7**	**55.3**	**57.2**	**49.8**
Under age 35	36.8	56.3	25.7	40.7	20.3	25.5
Aged 35 to 44	60.6	75.5	38.6	50.8	40.3	42.6
Aged 45 to 54	71.2	84.8	54.5	65.4	51.7	51.0
Aged 55 to 64	76.6	89.4	65.8	70.2	61.4	56.8
Aged 65 or older	80.8	91.8	80.4	83.1	70.4	69.0

Source: Bureau of the Census, Housing Vacancies and Homeownership, Internet site http://www.census.gov/housing/hvs/; calculations by New Strategist

Table 4.5 Homeownership Rate by Age of Householder and Region, 2013

(percent of households owning their home, by age of householder and region, 2013)

	total	Northeast	Midwest	South	West
Total households	**65.1%**	**63.0%**	**69.7%**	**66.7%**	**59.4%**
Under age 25	22.2	22.8	20.1	24.3	20.1
Aged 25 to 29	34.1	30.0	41.5	34.7	28.8
Aged 30 to 34	48.1	42.1	57.9	49.8	40.6
Aged 35 to 39	55.8	53.9	63.4	56.6	48.7
Aged 40 to 44	65.0	64.4	70.7	66.1	58.2
Aged 45 to 49	69.6	67.8	75.4	70.5	63.7
Aged 50 to 54	72.6	71.1	77.6	74.4	66.0
Aged 55 to 59	75.8	72.9	79.2	77.6	71.4
Aged 60 to 64	77.6	74.6	79.6	79.6	74.6
Aged 65 to 69	80.5	75.7	83.6	83.7	75.9
Aged 70 to 74	82.8	75.2	86.9	86.3	78.5
Aged 75 or older	80.0	73.6	79.7	85.4	77.2
Total households	**65.1**	**63.0**	**69.7**	**66.7**	**59.4**
Under age 35	36.8	33.5	42.6	37.9	31.6
Aged 35 to 44	60.6	59.5	67.2	61.6	53.6
Aged 45 to 54	71.2	69.6	76.6	72.5	64.9
Aged 55 to 64	76.6	73.7	79.4	78.5	72.9
Aged 65 or older	80.8	74.6	82.5	85.1	77.1

Source: Bureau of the Census, Housing Vacancies and Homeownership, Internet site http://www.census.gov/housing/hvs/; calculations by New Strategist

Most Black and Hispanic Gen Xers Are Not Yet Homeowners

Among Asian Gen Xers, 60 percent own their home.

Households headed by Asians, Blacks, and Hispanics are less likely than the average household to own a home. The homeownership rate was 65.1 percent for all households in 2010, according to the census. The rate was 58 percent among Asians, 44 percent among Blacks, and 47 percent among Hispanics. Non-Hispanic Whites are the only race-and-Hispanic-origin group with an above-average homeownership rate, at 72 percent in 2010.

Overall, 62 percent of Gen Xers owned a home in 2010. By race and Hispanic origin, the homeownership rate of Gen Xers was 60 percent among Asians, 41 percent among Blacks, 47 percent among Hispanics, and 70 percent among non-Hispanic Whites.

■ Among Gen X homeowners, Hispanics outnumber Blacks.

More than 70 percent of non-Hispanic White Gen Xers own their home

(homeownership rate of householders aged 34 to 45,
by race and Hispanic origin, 2010)

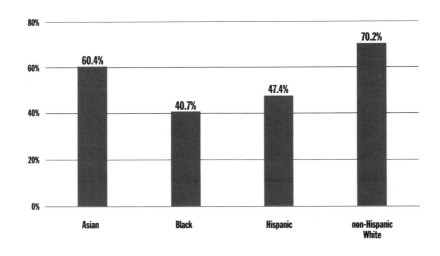

Table 4.6 Homeownership by Generation, Race, and Hispanic Origin, 2010

(number and percent of households that own their home, by generation, race, and Hispanic origin of householder, 2010; numbers in thousands)

	total	Asian	Black	Hispanic	non-Hispanic White
Total households	**116,716**	**4,632**	**14,130**	**13,461**	**82,333**
Millennials (under age 34)	21,562	1,049	3,022	3,695	13,235
Generation Xers (aged 34 to 45)	25,577	1,337	3,456	4,050	16,206
Baby Boomers (aged 46 to 64)	43,757	1,623	5,322	4,220	31,823
Older Americans (aged 65 or older)	25,820	624	2,331	1,496	21,069
HOMEOWNERS					
Total households	**75,986**	**2,689**	**6,261**	**6,368**	**59,484**
Millennials (under age 34)	7,662	313	564	1,012	5,607
Generation Xers (aged 34 to 45)	15,791	808	1,405	1,918	11,375
Baby Boomers (aged 46 to 64)	32,526	1,161	2,832	2,498	25,525
Older Americans (aged 65 or older)	20,007	407	1,460	941	16,977
HOMEOWNERSHIP RATE					
Total households	**65.1%**	**58.0%**	**44.3%**	**47.3%**	**72.2%**
Millennials (under age 34)	35.5	29.9	18.7	27.4	42.4
Generation Xers (aged 34 to 45)	61.7	60.4	40.7	47.4	70.2
Baby Boomers (aged 46 to 64)	74.3	71.5	53.2	59.2	80.2
Older Americans (aged 65 or older)	77.5	65.2	62.6	62.9	80.6

Note: Asians and Blacks are those who identify themselves as being of the race alone. Hispanics may be of any race. Non-Hispanic Whites are those who identify themselves as being White alone and not Hispanic.
Source: Bureau of the Census, 2010 Census, American Factfinder, Internet site http://factfinder2.census.gov/faces/nav/jsf/pages/index.xhtml; calculations by New Strategist

Table 4.7 Homeownership by Age, Race, and Hispanic Origin, 2010

(number and percent of households that own their home, by age, race, and Hispanic origin of householder, 2010; numbers in thousands)

	total	Asian	Black	Hispanic	non-Hispanic White
Total households	**116,716**	**4,632**	**14,130**	**13,461**	**82,333**
Under age 25	5,401	217	802	885	3,333
Aged 25 to 34	17,957	924	2,466	3,122	11,003
Aged 35 to 44	21,291	1,145	2,890	3,457	13,362
Aged 45 to 54	24,907	1,002	3,190	2,808	17,438
Aged 55 to 64	21,340	720	2,450	1,693	16,129
Aged 65 or older	25,820	624	2,331	1,496	21,069
HOMEOWNERS					
Total households	**75,986**	**2,689**	**6,261**	**6,368**	**59,484**
Under age 25	870	26	63	133	622
Aged 25 to 34	7,547	319	557	976	5,538
Aged 35 to 44	13,256	706	1,190	1,659	9,461
Aged 45 to 54	17,804	701	1,594	1,611	13,601
Aged 55 to 64	16,503	530	1,398	1,048	13,285
Aged 65 or older	20,007	407	1,460	941	16,977
HOMEOWNERSHIP RATE					
Total households	**65.1%**	**58.0%**	**44.3%**	**47.3%**	**72.2%**
Under age 25	16.1	12.1	7.8	15.1	18.7
Aged 25 to 34	42.0	34.5	22.6	31.3	50.3
Aged 35 to 44	62.3	61.7	41.2	48.0	70.8
Aged 45 to 54	71.5	69.9	50.0	57.4	78.0
Aged 55 to 64	77.3	73.6	57.0	61.9	82.4
Aged 65 or older	77.5	65.2	62.6	62.9	80.6

Note: Asians and Blacks are those who identify themselves as being of the race alone. Hispanics may be of any race. Non-Hispanic Whites are those who identify themselves as being White alone and not Hispanic.
Source: Bureau of the Census, 2010 Census, American Factfinder, Internet site http://factfinder2.census.gov/faces/nav/jsf/pages/index.xhtml; calculations by New Strategist

Most Gen Xers Live in a Single-Family Home

Only 20 percent of householders aged 35 to 64 live in a multi-unit building.

The majority of American households (69 percent) live in a single-family home. Three out of four householders aged 35 to 64, a broad age group that includes Gen Xers as well as Baby Boomers, live in this type of housing unit. Among householders under age 35, a smaller 49 percent live in a single-family housing unit.

Among homeowners, 88 percent live in a single-family home with little variation by age. Only 5 percent of homeowners are in a multi-unit building. They are outnumbered by the 7 percent who live in a mobile home, boat, or RV.

Among renters, there is more variation in type of structure by age. Thirty-nine percent of renters aged 35 to 64 live in a single-family home or duplex compared with only 26 percent of renters aged 65 or older. Fully 27 percent of older renters live in a building with 50 or more units versus fewer than 10 percent of younger renters.

■ Despite the collapse of the housing market in the wake of the Great Recession, the percentage of Americans who live in a single-family house has barely changed over the years.

Most middle-aged and older householders live in a single-family home

(percent of households living in a single-family house, by age of householder, 2012)

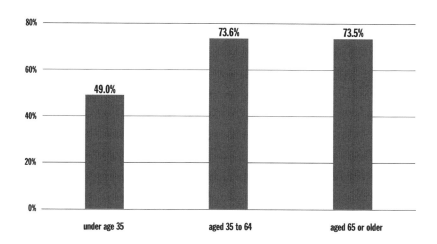

Table 4.8 Number of Units in Structure by Age of Householder, 2012: Total Occupied Units

(number and percent distribution of households by age of householder and number of units in structure, 2012; numbers in thousands)

	total	one detached or attached	multi-unit building total	2 to 4	5 to 19	20 to 49	50 or more	mobile home, boat, RV, etc.
Total households	**115,970**	**79,800**	**29,269**	**9,195**	**10,342**	**4,012**	**5,719**	**6,901**
Under age 35	22,404	10,981	10,219	3,052	4,232	1,412	1,523	1,205
Aged 35 to 64	67,038	49,320	13,735	4,788	4,872	1,765	2,310	3,984
Aged 65 or older	26,527	19,500	5,315	1,356	1,237	835	1,887	1,712
PERCENT DISTRIBUTION OF HOUSEHOLDS BY UNITS IN STRUCTURE								
Total households	**100.0%**	**68.8%**	**25.2%**	**7.9%**	**8.9%**	**3.5%**	**4.9%**	**6.0%**
Under age 35	100.0	49.0	45.6	13.6	18.9	6.3	6.8	5.4
Aged 35 to 64	100.0	73.6	20.5	7.1	7.3	2.6	3.4	5.9
Aged 65 or older	100.0	73.5	20.0	5.1	4.7	3.1	7.1	6.5
PERCENT DISTRIBUTION OF HOUSEHOLDS BY AGE OF HOUSEHOLDER								
Total households	**100.0**	**100.0**	**100.0**	**100.0**	**100.0**	**100.0**	**100.0**	**100.0**
Under age 35	19.3	13.8	34.9	33.2	40.9	35.2	26.6	17.5
Aged 35 to 64	57.8	61.8	46.9	52.1	47.1	44.0	40.4	57.7
Aged 65 or older	22.9	24.4	18.2	14.7	12.0	20.8	33.0	24.8

Source: Bureau of the Census, 2012 American Community Survey, Internet site http://factfinder2.census.gov/faces/nav/jsf/pages/index.xhtml; calculations by New Strategist

Table 4.9 Number of Units in Structure by Age of Householder, 2012: Owner-Occupied Units

(number and percent distribution of homeowners by age of householder and number of units in structure, 2012; numbers in thousands)

	total	one detached or attached	multi-unit building total	2 to 4	5 to 19	20 to 49	50 or more	mobile home, boat, RV, etc.
Total homeowners	**74,119**	**65,249**	**3,914**	**1,537**	**1,009**	**490**	**877**	**4,956**
Under age 35	7,304	6,239	509	161	169	68	112	556
Aged 35 to 64	45,946	40,988	2,058	876	529	232	421	2,899
Aged 65 or older	20,869	18,021	1,347	500	312	190	345	1,501

PERCENT DISTRIBUTION OF HOMEOWNERS BY UNITS IN STRUCTURE

Total homeowners	**100.0%**	**88.0%**	**5.3%**	**2.1%**	**1.4%**	**0.7%**	**1.2%**	**6.7%**
Under age 35	100.0	85.4	7.0	2.2	2.3	0.9	1.5	7.6
Aged 35 to 64	100.0	89.2	4.5	1.9	1.2	0.5	0.9	6.3
Aged 65 or older	100.0	86.4	6.5	2.4	1.5	0.9	1.7	7.2

PERCENT DISTRIBUTION OF HOMEOWNERS BY AGE OF HOUSEHOLDER

Total homeowners	**100.0**	**100.0**	**100.0**	**100.0**	**100.0**	**100.0**	**100.0**	**100.0**
Under age 35	9.9	9.6	13.0	10.5	16.7	13.9	12.7	11.2
Aged 35 to 64	62.0	62.8	52.6	57.0	52.4	47.3	48.0	58.5
Aged 65 or older	28.2	27.6	34.4	32.5	30.9	38.8	39.3	30.3

Source: Bureau of the Census, 2012 American Community Survey, Internet site http://factfinder2.census.gov/faces/nav/jsf/pages/index.xhtml; calculations by New Strategist

Table 4.10 Number of Units in Structure by Age of Householder, 2012: Renter-Occupied Units

(number and percent distribution of renters by age of householder and number of units in structure, 2012; numbers in thousands)

| | total | one detached or attached | multi-unit building | | | | | mobile home, boat, RV, etc. |
			total	2 to 4	5 to 19	20 to 49	50 or more	
Total renters	**41,850**	**14,551**	**25,355**	**7,659**	**9,333**	**3,522**	**4,842**	**1,945**
Under age 35	15,100	4,741	9,710	2,891	4,064	1,344	1,411	649
Aged 35 to 64	21,092	8,331	11,677	3,912	4,344	1,533	1,888	1,084
Aged 65 or older	5,658	1,478	3,969	856	925	645	1,542	211
PERCENT DISTRIBUTION OF RENTERS BY UNITS IN STRUCTURE								
Total renters	**100.0%**	**34.8%**	**60.6%**	**18.3%**	**22.3%**	**8.4%**	**11.6%**	**4.6%**
Under age 35	100.0	31.4	64.3	19.1	26.9	8.9	9.3	4.3
Aged 35 to 64	100.0	39.5	55.4	18.5	20.6	7.3	9.0	5.1
Aged 65 or older	100.0	26.1	70.1	15.1	16.4	11.4	27.3	3.7
PERCENT DISTRIBUTION OF RENTERS BY AGE OF HOUSEHOLDER								
Total renters	**100.0**	**100.0**	**100.0**	**100.0**	**100.0**	**100.0**	**100.0**	**100.0**
Under age 35	36.1	32.6	38.3	37.7	43.5	38.2	29.1	33.4
Aged 35 to 64	50.4	57.3	46.1	51.1	46.5	43.5	39.0	55.8
Aged 65 or older	13.5	10.2	15.7	11.2	9.9	18.3	31.9	10.9

Source: Bureau of the Census, 2012 American Community Survey, Internet site http://factfinder2.census.gov/faces/nav/jsf/pages/index.xhtml; calculations by New Strategist

About One in Ten Gen Xers Moves Annually

Most move for housing-related reasons.

Only 11.7 percent of Americans aged 1 or older moved between March 2012 and March 2013, and the proportion was a slightly smaller 10.6 percent among Gen Xers. Among all movers, the majority stays within the same county. Only 13 percent of people who moved between 2012 and 2013 went to a different state.

Regardless of age, housing is the primary motivation for moving. The 48 percent plurality of movers aged 30 to 44 say housing was the main reason for their move. Family reasons ranked second as a motivation for moving, and employment ranked third.

■ Mobility has been declining in the United States for decades, and the Great Recession lowered mobility rates even further.

Gen Xers are more likely to move than Boomers or older Americans

(percent of people who moved between March 2012 and March 2013, by generation)

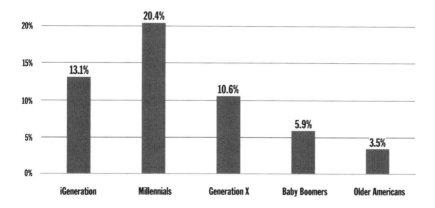

Table 4.11 Geographic Mobility by Generation and Type of Move, 2012–13

(total number of people aged 1 or older, and number and percent who moved between March 2012 and March 2013, by generation and type of move; numbers in thousands)

	total	total movers	same county	different county, same state	different state total	same region	different region	movers from abroad
Total, aged 1 or older	307,243	35,918	23,150	6,961	4,770	2,323	2,447	1,036
iGeneration (under age 19)	74,252	9,735	6,627	1,677	1,167	598	570	263
Millennials (aged 19 to 36)	75,576	15,432	9,839	3,008	2,105	956	1,149	479
Generation Xers (aged 37 to 48)	49,038	5,213	3,355	1,031	660	348	312	167
Baby Boomers (aged 49 to 67)	73,751	4,315	2,634	937	647	336	311	103
Older Americans (aged 68 or older)	34,625	1,222	698	307	193	86	107	24

PERCENT DISTRIBUTION BY MOBILITY STATUS

	total	total movers	same county	different county, same state	different state total	same region	different region	movers from abroad
Total, aged 1 or older	100.0%	11.7%	7.5%	2.3%	1.6%	0.8%	0.8%	0.3%
iGeneration (under age 19)	100.0	13.1	8.9	2.3	1.6	0.8	0.8	0.4
Millennials (aged 19 to 36)	100.0	20.4	13.0	4.0	2.8	1.3	1.5	0.6
Generation Xers (aged 37 to 48)	100.0	10.6	6.8	2.1	1.3	0.7	0.6	0.3
Baby Boomers (aged 49 to 67)	100.0	5.9	3.6	1.3	0.9	0.5	0.4	0.1
Older Americans (aged 68 or older)	100.0	3.5	2.0	0.9	0.6	0.2	0.3	0.1

PERCENT DISTRIBUTION OF MOVERS BY TYPE OF MOVE

	total	total movers	same county	different county, same state	different state total	same region	different region	movers from abroad
Total, aged 1 or older	–	100.0	64.5	19.4	13.3	6.5	6.8	2.9
iGeneration (under age 19)	–	100.0	68.1	17.2	12.0	6.1	5.9	2.7
Millennials (aged 19 to 36)	–	100.0	63.8	19.5	13.6	6.2	7.4	3.1
Generation Xers (aged 37 to 48)	–	100.0	64.4	19.8	12.7	6.7	6.0	3.2
Baby Boomers (aged 49 to 67)	–	100.0	61.0	21.7	15.0	7.8	7.2	2.4
Older Americans (aged 68 or older)	–	100.0	57.1	25.1	15.8	7.0	8.8	2.0

Note: "–" means not applicable.
Source: Bureau of the Census, Geographic Mobility: 2012 to 2013, Internet site http://www.census.gov/hhes/migration/data/cps/cps2013.html; calculations by New Strategist

Table 4.12 Geographic Mobility by Generation, Age, and Type of Move, 2012–13

(number and percent distribution of people aged 1 or older, aged 37 to 48, and in age groups that include Gen Xers, by mobility status between March 2012 and March 2013; numbers in thousands)

	total	total movers	same county	different county, same state	different state total	different state same region	different state different region	movers from abroad
Total, aged 1 or older	307,243	35,918	23,150	6,961	4,770	2,323	2,447	1,036
Generation Xers (aged 37 to 48)	49,038	5,213	3,355	1,031	660	348	312	167
Aged 35 to 39	19,221	2,628	1,600	523	396	194	202	108
Aged 40 to 44	20,657	2,151	1,417	431	238	124	114	66
Aged 45 to 49	21,060	1,857	1,223	358	231	135	96	45
PERCENT DISTRIBUTION BY MOBILITY STATUS								
Total, aged 1 or older	100.0%	11.7%	7.5%	2.3%	1.6%	0.8%	0.8%	0.3%
Generation Xers (aged 37 to 48)	100.0	10.6	6.8	2.1	1.3	0.7	0.6	0.3
Aged 35 to 39	100.0	13.7	8.3	2.7	2.1	1.0	1.1	0.6
Aged 40 to 44	100.0	10.4	6.9	2.1	1.2	0.6	0.6	0.3
Aged 45 to 49	100.0	8.8	5.8	1.7	1.1	0.6	0.5	0.2

Source: Bureau of the Census, Geographic Mobility: 2012 to 2013, Internet site http://www.census.gov/hhes/migration/data/cps/cps2013.html; calculations by New Strategist

Table 4.13 Movers by Generation, Age, and Type of Move, 2012–13

(number and percent distribution of people aged 1 or older, aged 37 to 48, and in age groups that include Gen Xers who moved between March 2012 and March 2013, by type of move; numbers in thousands)

	total movers	same county	different county, same state	different state total	different state same region	different state different region	movers from abroad
Total movers aged 1 or older	35,918	23,150	6,961	4,770	2,323	2,447	1,036
Generation Xers (aged 37 to 48)	5,213	3,355	1,031	660	348	312	167
Aged 35 to 39	2,628	1,600	523	396	194	202	108
Aged 40 to 44	2,151	1,417	431	238	124	114	66
Aged 45 to 49	1,857	1,223	358	231	135	96	45
PERCENT DISTRIBUTION BY MOBILITY STATUS							
Total movers aged 1 or older	100.0%	64.5%	19.4%	13.3%	6.5%	6.8%	2.9%
Generation Xers (aged 37 to 48)	100.0	64.4	19.8	12.7	6.7	6.0	3.2
Aged 35 to 39	100.0	60.9	19.9	15.1	7.4	7.7	4.1
Aged 40 to 44	100.0	65.9	20.0	11.1	5.8	5.3	3.1
Aged 45 to 49	100.0	65.9	19.3	12.4	7.3	5.2	2.4

Source: Bureau of the Census, Geographic Mobility: 2012 to 2013, Internet site http://www.census.gov/hhes/migration/data/cps/ cps2013.html; calculations by New Strategist

Table 4.14 Reason for Moving among People Aged 30 to 44, 2012–13

(number and percent distribution of movers aged 30 to 44 by primary reason for move and share of total movers between March 2012 and March 2013; numbers in thousands)

	total movers	movers aged 30 to 44		
		number	percent distribution	share of total
Total movers	**35,918**	**8,288**	**100.0%**	**23.1%**
Family reasons	10,871	2,289	27.6	21.1
Change in marital status	1,817	561	6.8	30.9
To establish own household	3,753	756	9.1	20.1
Other family reasons	5,301	972	11.7	18.3
Employment reasons	6,979	1,878	22.7	26.9
New job or job transfer	3,242	952	11.5	29.4
To look for work or lost job	750	156	1.9	20.8
To be closer to work/easier commute	1,941	495	6.0	25.5
Retired	237	16	0.2	6.8
Other job-related reason	809	259	3.1	32.0
Housing reasons	17,225	4,006	48.3	23.3
Wanted own home, not rent	2,099	654	7.9	31.2
Wanted better home/apartment	5,332	1,251	15.1	23.5
Wanted better neighborhood/less crime	1,135	306	3.7	27.0
Wanted cheaper housing	2,989	674	8.1	22.5
Foreclosure/eviction	654	117	1.4	17.9
Other housing reasons	5,016	1,004	12.1	20.0
Other reasons	844	115	1.4	13.6
To attend or leave college	215	11	0.1	5.1
Change of climate	20	6	0.1	30.0
Health reasons	136	13	0.2	9.6
Natural disaster	11	0	0.0	0.0
Other reasons	462	85	1.0	18.4

Source: Bureau of the Census, Geographic Mobility: 2012 to 2013, Internet site http://www.census.gov/hhes/migration/data/cps/cps2013.html; calculations by New Strategist

5

Income

■ Between 2000 and 2013, the median income of households headed by people aged 35 to 44 fell by a substantial 11 percent, after adjusting for inflation. (Gen Xers were aged 37 to 48 in 2013.)

■ As Gen Xers fill the 45-to-49 age group, they are in their peak earnings years. The median income of households headed by 45-to-49-year-olds was higher than any other, at $70,879 in 2013.

■ The median income of households headed by Asians aged 35 to 44 stood at $82,676 in 2013, exceeding the median income of non-Hispanic Whites by nearly $7,000.

■ The median income of men aged 35 to 44 fell 9 percent between 2007 and 2013, after adjusting for inflation. The median income of women in the age group fell 2 percent.

■ Generation Xers are less likely to be poor than the average American. Overall, 14.5 percent of Americans were poor in 2013. Among people aged 35 to 44, a smaller 12.2 percent were poor, and the rate bottoms out at 10.6 percent among people aged 45 to 54.

Household Incomes of Gen Xers Have Declined

Incomes are much lower than they were in 2000.

Between 2000 and 2013, the median income of households headed by people aged 35 to 44 fell by a substantial 11 percent, after adjusting for inflation. The median income of households headed by people aged 45 to 54 fell by an even larger 14 percent. (Generation Xers were aged 37 to 48 in 2013.) The decline was well underway before the Great Recession, which started in 2007.

In 2000, householders aged 45 to 54 were indisputably the nation's most affluent, with a median income fully 37 percent above the all-household median. By 2013, their median income was only 29 percent higher than average and barely surpassed that of householders aged 35 to 44.

■ The $67,141 median income of householders aged 45 to 54 in 2013 was only about $2,000 greater than the median of householders aged 35 to 44. The gap was more than $5,000 in 2000.

Since 2000, the median income of households headed by people aged 35 to 54 has declined

*(median income of households headed by people aged 35 to 54,
2000 and 2013; in 2013 dollars)*

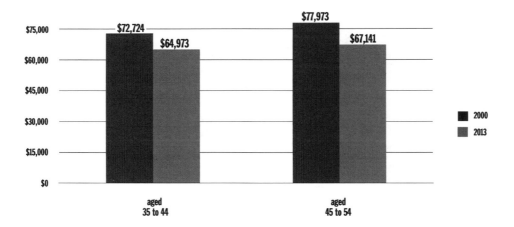

Table 5.1 Median Income of Households Headed by People Aged 35 to 54, 2000 to 2013

(median income of total households and households headed by people aged 35 to 54, and index of age group to total, 2000 to 2013; percent change for selected years; in 2013 dollars)

	total households	35 to 44	45 to 54
2013	$51,939	$64,973	$67,141
2012	51,758	64,554	67,376
2011	51,842	64,128	66,142
2010	52,646	65,619	66,605
2009	54,059	66,338	69,761
2008	54,423	68,111	69,620
2007	56,436	69,795	73,561
2006	55,689	69,789	74,952
2005	55,278	69,308	74,486
2004	54,674	69,902	75,261
2003	54,865	69,717	76,301
2002	54,913	69,302	76,423
2001	55,562	70,157	76,374
2000	56,800	72,724	77,973
PERCENT CHANGE			
2007 to 2013	−8.0%	−6.9%	−8.7%
2000 to 2013	−8.6	−10.7	−13.9
INDEX			
2013	100	125	129
2012	100	125	130
2011	100	124	128
2010	100	125	127
2009	100	123	129
2008	100	125	128
2007	100	124	130
2006	100	125	135
2005	100	125	135
2004	100	128	138
2003	100	127	139
2002	100	126	139
2001	100	126	137
2000	100	128	137

Note: The index is calculated by dividing the median income of the age group by the national median and multiplying by 100.
Source: Bureau of the Census, Historical Income Data, Internet site http://www.census.gov/hhes/www/income/data/historical/index .html; calculations by New Strategist

Household Income Rises with Age

Median household income peaks in the 45-to-49 age group.

The 2013 median income of Gen X households ranges from a low of $61,383 for those headed by 35-to-39-year-olds to a high of $70,879 for those headed by 45-to-49-year-olds. People aged 45 to 49 have a higher median household income than any other age group. (Gen Xers were aged 37 to 48 in 2013.)

In the nation as a whole, 28 million households had an income of $100,000 or more in 2013. More than one-third of those households were headed by people aged 35 to 49. Among all households, 22 percent had an income of $100,000 or more. Among households headed by people aged 35 to 49, the figure is 31 percent.

■ Gen Xers are likely to see little income growth in the years ahead as Boomers postpone retirement and clog up the promotion pipeline.

Households headed by people aged 35 to 49 have above-average incomes

(median income of total households and households headed by people aged 35 to 49, 2013)

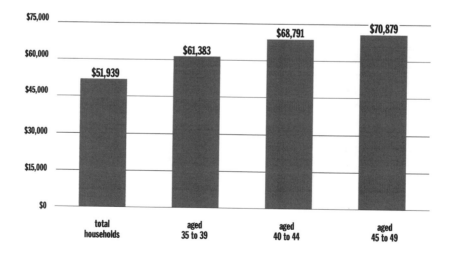

Table 5.2 Income of Households Headed by People Aged 35 to 49, 2013: Total Households

(number and percent distribution of total households and households headed by people aged 35 to 49, by income, 2013; households in thousands as of 2014)

	total	aged 35 to 44 total	35 to 39	40 to 44	45 to 49
Total households	122,952	21,046	10,322	10,724	11,383
Under $10,000	8,939	1,093	525	569	604
$10,000 to $19,999	14,014	1,601	821	781	738
$20,000 to $29,999	12,879	1,718	878	839	827
$30,000 to $39,999	12,281	1,831	922	909	943
$40,000 to $49,999	10,850	1,832	970	862	870
$50,000 to $59,999	9,547	1,624	891	733	850
$60,000 to $69,999	8,240	1,516	778	738	794
$70,000 to $79,999	7,574	1,448	709	738	655
$80,000 to $89,999	6,006	1,121	492	629	767
$90,000 to $99,999	4,980	1,071	477	594	627
$100,000 or more	27,641	6,191	2,859	3,331	3,708
$100,000 to $124,999	9,459	2,163	1,063	1,101	1,143
$125,000 to $149,999	5,806	1,301	565	736	784
$150,000 to $174,999	4,175	957	437	519	578
$175,000 to $199,999	2,288	521	213	308	296
$200,000 or more	5,913	1,249	582	667	905
Median income	**$51,939**	**$64,973**	**$61,383**	**$68,791**	**$70,879**
Total households	**100.0%**	**100.0%**	**100.0%**	**100.0%**	**100.0%**
Under $10,000	7.3	5.2	5.1	5.3	5.3
$10,000 to $19,999	11.4	7.6	8.0	7.3	6.5
$20,000 to $29,999	10.5	8.2	8.5	7.8	7.3
$30,000 to $39,999	10.0	8.7	8.9	8.5	8.3
$40,000 to $49,999	8.8	8.7	9.4	8.0	7.6
$50,000 to $59,999	7.8	7.7	8.6	6.8	7.5
$60,000 to $69,999	6.7	7.2	7.5	6.9	7.0
$70,000 to $79,999	6.2	6.9	6.9	6.9	5.8
$80,000 to $89,999	4.9	5.3	4.8	5.9	6.7
$90,000 to $99,999	4.1	5.1	4.6	5.5	5.5
$100,000 or more	22.5	29.4	27.7	31.1	32.6
$100,000 to $124,999	7.7	10.3	10.3	10.3	10.0
$125,000 to $149,999	4.7	6.2	5.5	6.9	6.9
$150,000 to $174,999	3.4	4.5	4.2	4.8	5.1
$175,000 to $199,999	1.9	2.5	2.1	2.9	2.6
$200,000 or more	4.8	5.9	5.6	6.2	8.0

Source: Bureau of the Census, 2014 Current Population Survey, Internet site http://www.census.gov/hhes/www/income/data/index .html; calculations by New Strategist

Incomes Are Highest for Asian Households

Among Gen Xers, the incomes of Asians are far higher than those of other racial or ethnic groups.

The 2013 median income of households headed by Asians aged 35 to 44 was $82,676. Among Asian householders aged 45 to 49, median income was an even higher $84,315. (Gen Xers were aged 37 to 48 in 2013.) The median household incomes of non-Hispanic Whites in those age groups were almost as high. In contrast, the median incomes of Hispanic and Black householders aged 35 to 49 were much lower. Black households headed by people aged 45 to 49 had a median income of $43,403, and their Hispanic counterparts had a median income of $48,618.

One factor behind income differences by race and Hispanic origin is the number of earners per household. Black households are much less likely to be headed by a married couple, which reduces the number of earners per household and consequently lowers Black household income. Another factor is educational attainment. Hispanics are much less educated than Asians, Blacks, or non-Hispanic Whites, which reduces their earning power and household incomes.

■ The household income gap between Black and non-Hispanic White households will not disappear until dual-earner couples head a larger share of Black households. The gap between Hispanic and non-Hispanic White households will not close until Hispanic educational attainment rises.

The incomes of Gen Xers vary by race and Hispanic origin

*(median income of households headed by people aged 35 to 44,
by race and Hispanic origin, 2013)*

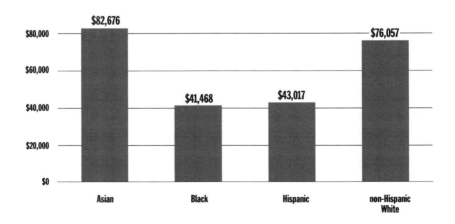

Table 5.3 Income of Households Headed by People Aged 35 to 49, 2013: Asian Households

(number and percent distribution of total Asian households and households headed by Asians aged 35 to 49, by income, 2013; households in thousands as of 2014)

	total	aged 35 to 44			45 to 49
		total	35 to 39	40 to 44	
Total Asian households	**6,111**	**1,400**	**663**	**737**	**609**
Under $10,000	459	44	23	21	16
$10,000 to $19,999	417	48	22	26	18
$20,000 to $29,999	480	81	37	44	41
$30,000 to $39,999	448	62	28	34	50
$40,000 to $49,999	503	126	59	67	33
$50,000 to $59,999	404	102	58	43	38
$60,000 to $69,999	431	110	31	79	46
$70,000 to $79,999	385	96	50	45	39
$80,000 to $89,999	286	69	31	39	36
$90,000 to $99,999	226	46	18	28	35
$100,000 or more	2,072	617	305	312	258
$100,000 to $124,999	647	188	107	82	61
$125,000 to $149,999	365	103	44	59	43
$150,000 to $174,999	339	102	42	59	34
$175,000 to $199,999	198	55	29	26	31
$200,000 or more	522	170	82	87	89
Median income	**$67,366**	**$82,676**	**$86,601**	**$81,443**	**$84,315**
Total Asian households	**100.0%**	**100.0%**	**100.0%**	**100.0%**	**100.0%**
Under $10,000	7.5	3.1	3.5	2.8	2.6
$10,000 to $19,999	6.8	3.5	3.4	3.5	2.9
$20,000 to $29,999	7.8	5.8	5.6	5.9	6.8
$30,000 to $39,999	7.3	4.4	4.1	4.6	8.3
$40,000 to $49,999	8.2	9.0	9.0	9.1	5.4
$50,000 to $59,999	6.6	7.3	8.8	5.8	6.2
$60,000 to $69,999	7.1	7.9	4.7	10.7	7.5
$70,000 to $79,999	6.3	6.8	7.6	6.2	6.3
$80,000 to $89,999	4.7	4.9	4.6	5.2	5.9
$90,000 to $99,999	3.7	3.3	2.7	3.8	5.8
$100,000 or more	33.9	44.1	46.0	42.4	42.4
$100,000 to $124,999	10.6	13.4	16.1	11.1	10.1
$125,000 to $149,999	6.0	7.4	6.7	7.9	7.1
$150,000 to $174,999	5.5	7.3	6.4	8.1	5.6
$175,000 to $199,999	3.2	3.9	4.4	3.5	5.1
$200,000 or more	8.5	12.1	12.4	11.8	14.5

Note: Asians are those who identify themselves as being of the race alone and those who identify themselves as being of the race in combination with other races.
Source: Bureau of the Census, 2014 Current Population Survey, Internet site http://www.census.gov/hhes/www/income/data/index .html; calculations by New Strategist

Table 5.4 Income of Households Headed by People Aged 35 to 49, 2013: Black Households

(number and percent distribution of total Black households and households headed by Blacks aged 35 to 49, by income, 2013; households in thousands as of 2014)

	total	aged 35 to 44 total	35 to 39	40 to 44	45 to 49
Total Black households	**16,855**	**3,246**	**1,606**	**1,640**	**1,731**
Under $10,000	2,385	355	186	169	187
$10,000 to $19,999	2,830	413	189	224	202
$20,000 to $29,999	2,164	383	199	184	175
$30,000 to $39,999	2,006	405	219	186	237
$40,000 to $49,999	1,578	313	151	162	193
$50,000 to $59,999	1,217	272	148	124	126
$60,000 to $69,999	904	161	90	71	110
$70,000 to $79,999	723	179	93	85	70
$80,000 to $89,999	558	131	39	92	82
$90,000 to $99,999	470	127	52	75	51
$100,000 or more	2,018	508	240	268	298
$100,000 to $124,999	870	221	120	101	130
$125,000 to $149,999	443	116	53	63	57
$150,000 to $174,999	278	63	33	29	51
$175,000 to $199,999	136	37	13	24	16
$200,000 or more	291	71	20	51	44
Median income	**$34,775**	**$41,468**	**$40,437**	**$42,701**	**$43,403**
Total Black households	**100.0%**	**100.0%**	**100.0%**	**100.0%**	**100.0%**
Under $10,000	14.2	10.9	11.6	10.3	10.8
$10,000 to $19,999	16.8	12.7	11.7	13.7	11.7
$20,000 to $29,999	12.8	11.8	12.4	11.2	10.1
$30,000 to $39,999	11.9	12.5	13.6	11.3	13.7
$40,000 to $49,999	9.4	9.6	9.4	9.9	11.2
$50,000 to $59,999	7.2	8.4	9.2	7.6	7.3
$60,000 to $69,999	5.4	4.9	5.6	4.3	6.4
$70,000 to $79,999	4.3	5.5	5.8	5.2	4.1
$80,000 to $89,999	3.3	4.1	2.4	5.6	4.8
$90,000 to $99,999	2.8	3.9	3.3	4.6	2.9
$100,000 or more	12.0	15.7	15.0	16.3	17.2
$100,000 to $124,999	5.2	6.8	7.5	6.2	7.5
$125,000 to $149,999	2.6	3.6	3.3	3.8	3.3
$150,000 to $174,999	1.6	1.9	2.1	1.8	3.0
$175,000 to $199,999	0.8	1.1	0.8	1.5	0.9
$200,000 or more	1.7	2.2	1.3	3.1	2.5

Note: Blacks are those who identify themselves as being of the race alone and those who identify themselves as being of the race in combination with other races.
Source: Bureau of the Census, 2014 Current Population Survey, Internet site http://www.census.gov/hhes/www/income/data/index .html; calculations by New Strategist

Table 5.5 Income of Households Headed by People Aged 35 to 49, 2013: Hispanic Households

(number and percent distribution of total Hispanic households and households headed by Hispanics aged 35 to 49, by income, 2013; households in thousands as of 2014)

	total	aged 35 to 44			45 to 49
		total	35 to 39	40 to 44	
Total Hispanic households	**15,811**	**3,744**	**1,906**	**1,838**	**1,639**
Under $10,000	1,467	251	128	123	108
$10,000 to $19,999	2,127	393	201	193	170
$20,000 to $29,999	2,142	508	280	228	216
$30,000 to $39,999	1,968	568	313	255	174
$40,000 to $49,999	1,664	364	170	194	167
$50,000 to $59,999	1,288	321	151	170	116
$60,000 to $69,999	959	218	129	89	126
$70,000 to $79,999	923	217	104	113	101
$80,000 to $89,999	586	151	65	86	84
$90,000 to $99,999	609	175	86	90	97
$100,000 or more	2,077	577	280	297	281
$100,000 to $124,999	895	250	121	129	113
$125,000 to $149,999	461	123	65	57	61
$150,000 to $174,999	298	85	34	51	29
$175,000 to $199,999	136	37	16	21	19
$200,000 or more	287	82	43	39	58
Median income	**$40,963**	**$43,017**	**$41,535**	**$45,176**	**$48,618**
Total Hispanic households	**100.0%**	**100.0%**	**100.0%**	**100.0%**	**100.0%**
Under $10,000	9.3	6.7	6.7	6.7	6.6
$10,000 to $19,999	13.5	10.5	10.5	10.5	10.4
$20,000 to $29,999	13.5	13.6	14.7	12.4	13.2
$30,000 to $39,999	12.4	15.2	16.4	13.9	10.6
$40,000 to $49,999	10.5	9.7	8.9	10.5	10.2
$50,000 to $59,999	8.1	8.6	7.9	9.3	7.1
$60,000 to $69,999	6.1	5.8	6.7	4.9	7.7
$70,000 to $79,999	5.8	5.8	5.4	6.2	6.2
$80,000 to $89,999	3.7	4.0	3.4	4.7	5.2
$90,000 to $99,999	3.9	4.7	4.5	4.9	5.9
$100,000 or more	13.1	15.4	14.7	16.2	17.1
$100,000 to $124,999	5.7	6.7	6.3	7.0	6.9
$125,000 to $149,999	2.9	3.3	3.4	3.1	3.7
$150,000 to $174,999	1.9	2.3	1.8	2.8	1.8
$175,000 to $199,999	0.9	1.0	0.8	1.1	1.2
$200,000 or more	1.8	2.2	2.3	2.1	3.5

Source: Bureau of the Census, 2014 Current Population Survey, Internet site http://www.census.gov/hhes/www/income/data/index .html; calculations by New Strategist

Table 5.6 Income of Households Headed by People Aged 35 to 49, 2013: Non-Hispanic White Households

(number and percent distribution of total non-Hispanic White households and households headed by non-Hispanic Whites aged 35 to 49, by income, 2013; households in thousands as of 2014)

		aged 35 to 44			
	total	total	35 to 39	40 to 44	45 to 49
Total non-Hispanic White households	**83,641**	**12,674**	**6,172**	**6,502**	**7,368**
Under $10,000	4,569	440	191	249	304
$10,000 to $19,999	8,577	758	407	351	355
$20,000 to $29,999	7,996	740	355	385	395
$30,000 to $39,999	7,871	827	393	434	494
$40,000 to $49,999	7,070	1,031	583	448	460
$50,000 to $59,999	6,592	929	531	397	565
$60,000 to $69,999	5,892	1,018	531	487	500
$70,000 to $79,999	5,469	943	461	482	447
$80,000 to $89,999	4,570	774	353	421	563
$90,000 to $99,999	3,660	721	321	400	438
$100,000 or more	21,375	4,493	2,047	2,445	2,847
$100,000 to $124,999	7,032	1,504	728	777	833
$125,000 to $149,999	4,509	953	397	557	624
$150,000 to $174,999	3,242	711	330	381	463
$175,000 to $199,999	1,808	400	155	245	227
$200,000 or more	4,784	924	438	486	701
Median income	**$58,270**	**$76,057**	**$71,599**	**$80,290**	**$82,205**
Total non-Hispanic White households	**100.0%**	**100.0%**	**100.0%**	**100.0%**	**100.0%**
Under $10,000	5.5	3.5	3.1	3.8	4.1
$10,000 to $19,999	10.3	6.0	6.6	5.4	4.8
$20,000 to $29,999	9.6	5.8	5.8	5.9	5.4
$30,000 to $39,999	9.4	6.5	6.4	6.7	6.7
$40,000 to $49,999	8.5	8.1	9.4	6.9	6.2
$50,000 to $59,999	7.9	7.3	8.6	6.1	7.7
$60,000 to $69,999	7.0	8.0	8.6	7.5	6.8
$70,000 to $79,999	6.5	7.4	7.5	7.4	6.1
$80,000 to $89,999	5.5	6.1	5.7	6.5	7.6
$90,000 to $99,999	4.4	5.7	5.2	6.2	5.9
$100,000 or more	25.6	35.4	33.2	37.6	38.6
$100,000 to $124,999	8.4	11.9	11.8	11.9	11.3
$125,000 to $149,999	5.4	7.5	6.4	8.6	8.5
$150,000 to $174,999	3.9	5.6	5.4	5.9	6.3
$175,000 to $199,999	2.2	3.2	2.5	3.8	3.1
$200,000 or more	5.7	7.3	7.1	7.5	9.5

Note: Non-Hispanic Whites are those who identify themselves as being White alone and not Hispanic.
Source: Bureau of the Census, 2014 Current Population Survey, Internet site http://www.census.gov/hhes/www/income/data/index .html; calculations by New Strategist

Married Couples Have the Highest Incomes

Female-headed families have much lower incomes.

The incomes of households headed by people aged 35 to 44 vary greatly by household type. Married couples have the highest incomes by far. Among households headed by people aged 35 to 44, married couples had a median income of $88,536 in 2013. Among married-couple householders aged 45 to 49, median income was an even higher $94,780. (Gen Xers were aged 37 to 49 in 2013.) Behind the high incomes of married couples is the fact that most are dual earners.

Female-headed families in the 35-to-44 age group had a median income of only $35,692 in 2013. Women aged 35 to 44 who live alone had an almost identical median income of $35,736. These incomes are almost identical because in both types of households there is typically only one earner.

■ Married couples have much higher incomes because most are dual earners.

Median income of Gen Xers varies by household type

(median income of households headed by people aged 35 to 44 by household type, 2013)

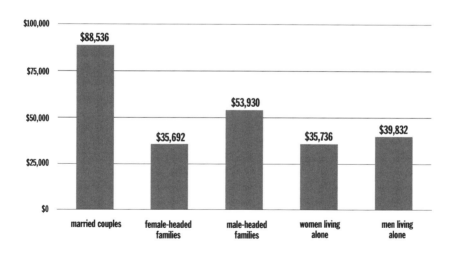

Table 5.7 Income of Households by Household Type, 2013: Aged 35 to 44

(number and percent distribution of households headed by people aged 35 to 44, by income and household type, 2013; households in thousands as of 2014)

| | | family households | | | nonfamily households | | | |
| | | | female householder, no spouse present | male householder, no spouse present | female householder | | male householder | |
	total	married couples			total	living alone	total	living alone
Total households headed by 35-to-44-year-olds	**21,046**	**11,619**	**3,500**	**1,314**	**1,657**	**1,296**	**2,956**	**2,316**
Under $10,000	1,093	139	415	53	216	200	271	254
$10,000 to $19,999	1,601	336	510	128	276	243	352	313
$20,000 to $29,999	1,718	569	523	118	141	125	366	318
$30,000 to $39,999	1,831	642	529	157	167	137	336	276
$40,000 to $49,999	1,832	788	381	140	197	168	325	249
$50,000 to $59,999	1,624	883	269	133	112	92	226	189
$60,000 to $69,999	1,516	858	206	103	96	65	252	191
$70,000 to $79,999	1,448	924	184	66	119	78	154	109
$80,000 to $89,999	1,121	744	99	71	79	60	128	81
$90,000 to $99,999	1,071	793	102	90	38	14	49	28
$100,000 or more	6,191	4,942	282	254	215	114	497	307
$100,000 to $124,999	2,163	1,624	138	116	113	69	172	120
$125,000 to $149,999	1,301	1,079	55	52	42	23	72	38
$150,000 to $174,999	957	791	37	27	16	2	86	59
$175,000 to $199,999	521	411	27	19	10	3	54	30
$200,000 or more	1,249	1,037	25	38	34	17	114	61
Median income	**$64,973**	**$88,536**	**$35,692**	**$53,930**	**$41,095**	**$35,736**	**$43,909**	**$39,832**
Total households headed by 35-to-44-year-olds	**100.0%**	**100.0%**	**100.0%**	**100.0%**	**100.0%**	**100.0%**	**100.0%**	**100.0%**
Under $10,000	5.2	1.2	11.8	4.1	13.0	15.4	9.2	11.0
$10,000 to $19,999	7.6	2.9	14.6	9.7	16.7	18.8	11.9	13.5
$20,000 to $29,999	8.2	4.9	15.0	9.0	8.5	9.6	12.4	13.7
$30,000 to $39,999	8.7	5.5	15.1	12.0	10.1	10.6	11.4	11.9
$40,000 to $49,999	8.7	6.8	10.9	10.7	11.9	13.0	11.0	10.8
$50,000 to $59,999	7.7	7.6	7.7	10.1	6.7	7.1	7.7	8.2
$60,000 to $69,999	7.2	7.4	5.9	7.8	5.8	5.0	8.5	8.2
$70,000 to $79,999	6.9	8.0	5.3	5.0	7.2	6.0	5.2	4.7
$80,000 to $89,999	5.3	6.4	2.8	5.4	4.8	4.6	4.3	3.5
$90,000 to $99,999	5.1	6.8	2.9	6.8	2.3	1.1	1.6	1.2
$100,000 or more	29.4	42.5	8.1	19.3	13.0	8.8	16.8	13.3
$100,000 to $124,999	10.3	14.0	3.9	8.9	6.8	5.3	5.8	5.2
$125,000 to $149,999	6.2	9.3	1.6	4.0	2.5	1.7	2.4	1.7
$150,000 to $174,999	4.5	6.8	1.1	2.1	0.9	0.2	2.9	2.5
$175,000 to $199,999	2.5	3.5	0.8	1.5	0.6	0.2	1.8	1.3
$200,000 or more	5.9	8.9	0.7	2.9	2.1	1.3	3.9	2.6

Source: Bureau of the Census, 2014 Current Population Survey, Internet site http://www.census.gov/hhes/www/income/data/index .html; calculations by New Strategist

Table 5.8 Income of Households by Household Type, 2013: Aged 45 to 54

(number and percent distribution of households headed by people aged 45 to 54, by income and household type, 2013; households in thousands as of 2014)

| | | family households | | | nonfamily households | | | |
| | | | | | female householder | | male householder | |
	total	married couples	female householder, no spouse present	male householder, no spouse present	total	living alone	total	living alone
Total households headed by 45-to-54-year-olds	**23,809**	**13,292**	**3,017**	**1,244**	**2,923**	**2,463**	**3,333**	**2,639**
Under $10,000	1,555	229	268	83	506	490	469	427
$10,000 to $19,999	1,668	396	420	96	371	342	386	340
$20,000 to $29,999	1,753	519	376	130	323	257	405	329
$30,000 to $39,999	1,999	730	372	143	354	318	400	329
$40,000 to $49,999	1,788	778	302	130	274	250	304	270
$50,000 to $59,999	1,879	894	312	93	281	235	300	241
$60,000 to $69,999	1,637	947	237	112	149	112	192	149
$70,000 to $79,999	1,481	869	193	91	174	143	154	114
$80,000 to $89,999	1,413	935	114	57	148	117	158	109
$90,000 to $99,999	1,188	894	100	51	44	29	98	62
$100,000 or more	7,447	6,101	323	259	298	168	466	268
$100,000 to $124,999	2,324	1,780	140	112	129	62	163	101
$125,000 to $149,999	1,445	1,173	78	43	58	32	93	48
$150,000 to $174,999	1,171	971	47	40	66	51	48	28
$175,000 to $199,999	680	573	23	18	15	5	51	33
$200,000 or more	1,827	1,604	35	46	31	18	112	58
Median income	**$67,141**	**$93,180**	**$41,838**	**$52,940**	**$36,755**	**$34,615**	**$40,154**	**$36,772**
Total households headed by 45-to-54-year-olds	**100.0%**	**100.0%**	**100.0%**	**100.0%**	**100.0%**	**100.0%**	**100.0%**	**100.0%**
Under $10,000	6.5	1.7	8.9	6.7	17.3	19.9	14.1	16.2
$10,000 to $19,999	7.0	3.0	13.9	7.7	12.7	13.9	11.6	12.9
$20,000 to $29,999	7.4	3.9	12.5	10.5	11.1	10.4	12.1	12.5
$30,000 to $39,999	8.4	5.5	12.3	11.5	12.1	12.9	12.0	12.5
$40,000 to $49,999	7.5	5.8	10.0	10.4	9.4	10.2	9.1	10.2
$50,000 to $59,999	7.9	6.7	10.3	7.5	9.6	9.6	9.0	9.1
$60,000 to $69,999	6.9	7.1	7.9	9.0	5.1	4.6	5.8	5.6
$70,000 to $79,999	6.2	6.5	6.4	7.3	5.9	5.8	4.6	4.3
$80,000 to $89,999	5.9	7.0	3.8	4.5	5.1	4.8	4.8	4.1
$90,000 to $99,999	5.0	6.7	3.3	4.1	1.5	1.2	3.0	2.4
$100,000 or more	31.3	45.9	10.7	20.8	10.2	6.8	14.0	10.1
$100,000 to $124,999	9.8	13.4	4.6	9.0	4.4	2.5	4.9	3.8
$125,000 to $149,999	6.1	8.8	2.6	3.5	2.0	1.3	2.8	1.8
$150,000 to $174,999	4.9	7.3	1.6	3.2	2.2	2.1	1.4	1.1
$175,000 to $199,999	2.9	4.3	0.8	1.4	0.5	0.2	1.5	1.3
$200,000 or more	7.7	12.1	1.1	3.7	1.1	0.7	3.4	2.2

Source: Bureau of the Census, 2014 Current Population Survey, Internet site http://www.census.gov/hhes/www/income/data/index .html; calculations by New Strategist

Table 5.9 Income of Households by Household Type, 2013: Aged 35 to 39

(number and percent distribution of households headed by people aged 35 to 39, by income and household type, 2013; households in thousands as of 2014)

| | | family households | | | nonfamily households | | | |
| | | | | | female householder | | male householder | |
	total	married couples	female householder, no spouse present	male householder, no spouse present	total	living alone	total	living alone
Total households headed by 35-to-39-year-olds	**10,322**	**5,536**	**1,735**	**694**	**808**	**599**	**1,550**	**1,186**
Under $10,000	525	60	214	28	73	64	150	138
$10,000 to $19,999	821	170	265	71	125	99	191	173
$20,000 to $29,999	878	274	270	75	71	62	187	160
$30,000 to $39,999	922	326	240	81	101	80	174	146
$40,000 to $49,999	970	425	165	69	118	103	192	143
$50,000 to $59,999	891	496	153	71	66	56	105	92
$60,000 to $69,999	778	432	108	53	44	17	141	95
$70,000 to $79,999	709	460	85	34	47	33	83	47
$80,000 to $89,999	492	290	40	54	42	33	65	38
$90,000 to $99,999	477	340	58	27	23	4	30	12
$100,000 or more	2,859	2,263	137	131	98	48	231	143
$100,000 to $124,999	1,063	780	69	76	56	33	82	69
$125,000 to $149,999	565	479	21	16	18	6	32	13
$150,000 to $174,999	437	350	24	14	4	0	45	33
$175,000 to $199,999	213	161	13	13	6	0	19	11
$200,000 or more	582	493	10	12	14	8	52	17
Median income	**$61,383**	**$83,609**	**$35,061**	**$53,164**	**$42,142**	**$38,910**	**$43,115**	**$37,276**
Total households headed by 35-to-39-year-olds	**100.0%**	**100.0%**	**100.0%**	**100.0%**	**100.0%**	**100.0%**	**100.0%**	**100.0%**
Under $10,000	5.1	1.1	12.3	4.1	9.0	10.7	9.7	11.6
$10,000 to $19,999	8.0	3.1	15.3	10.2	15.4	16.6	12.3	14.6
$20,000 to $29,999	8.5	5.0	15.6	10.8	8.8	10.3	12.1	13.5
$30,000 to $39,999	8.9	5.9	13.9	11.7	12.5	13.3	11.3	12.3
$40,000 to $49,999	9.4	7.7	9.5	10.0	14.6	17.2	12.4	12.0
$50,000 to $59,999	8.6	9.0	8.8	10.2	8.2	9.3	6.8	7.8
$60,000 to $69,999	7.5	7.8	6.2	7.6	5.5	2.9	9.1	8.0
$70,000 to $79,999	6.9	8.3	4.9	4.9	5.9	5.5	5.4	4.0
$80,000 to $89,999	4.8	5.2	2.3	7.9	5.2	5.5	4.2	3.2
$90,000 to $99,999	4.6	6.1	3.3	3.8	2.8	0.6	1.9	1.0
$100,000 or more	27.7	40.9	7.9	18.9	12.1	8.1	14.9	12.0
$100,000 to $124,999	10.3	14.1	4.0	11.0	6.9	5.6	5.3	5.8
$125,000 to $149,999	5.5	8.6	1.2	2.2	2.2	1.1	2.0	1.1
$150,000 to $174,999	4.2	6.3	1.4	2.1	0.5	0.1	2.9	2.8
$175,000 to $199,999	2.1	2.9	0.7	1.8	0.8	0.0	1.3	0.9
$200,000 or more	5.6	8.9	0.6	1.7	1.8	1.4	3.3	1.5

Source: Bureau of the Census, 2014 Current Population Survey, Internet site http://www.census.gov/hhes/www/income/data/index .html; calculations by New Strategist

Table 5.10 Income of Households by Household Type, 2013: Aged 40 to 44

(number and percent distribution of households headed by people aged 40 to 44, by income and household type, 2013; households in thousands as of 2014)

| | | family households | | | nonfamily households | | | |
| | | | female householder, no spouse present | male householder, no spouse present | female householder | | male householder | |
	total	married couples			total	living alone	total	living alone
Total households headed by 40-to-44-year-olds	**10,724**	**6,083**	**1,765**	**620**	**850**	**698**	**1,406**	**1,130**
Under $10,000	569	79	201	25	143	136	121	116
$10,000 to $19,999	781	166	245	57	152	144	161	140
$20,000 to $29,999	839	295	253	43	70	63	179	158
$30,000 to $39,999	909	316	288	76	66	57	161	130
$40,000 to $49,999	862	363	216	71	79	66	133	106
$50,000 to $59,999	733	387	117	62	46	36	121	97
$60,000 to $69,999	738	426	99	50	52	48	111	96
$70,000 to $79,999	738	464	99	33	72	45	71	62
$80,000 to $89,999	629	454	59	17	37	27	63	44
$90,000 to $99,999	594	453	43	63	15	11	19	16
$100,000 or more	3,331	2,679	145	123	117	66	266	165
$100,000 to $124,999	1,101	844	69	40	58	36	89	51
$125,000 to $149,999	736	600	34	37	25	16	40	26
$150,000 to $174,999	519	441	13	13	12	2	41	26
$175,000 to $199,999	308	250	14	7	4	3	34	19
$200,000 or more	667	544	15	26	20	9	62	43
Median income	**$68,791**	**$91,742**	**$36,199**	**$55,008**	**$38,118**	**$31,004**	**$44,882**	**$41,187**
Total households headed by 40-to-44-year-olds	**100.0%**	**100.0%**	**100.0%**	**100.0%**	**100.0%**	**100.0%**	**100.0%**	**100.0%**
Under $10,000	5.3	1.3	11.4	4.0	16.8	19.5	8.6	10.3
$10,000 to $19,999	7.3	2.7	13.9	9.2	17.9	20.6	11.5	12.4
$20,000 to $29,999	7.8	4.8	14.3	6.9	8.3	9.0	12.7	14.0
$30,000 to $39,999	8.5	5.2	16.3	12.3	7.8	8.2	11.5	11.5
$40,000 to $49,999	8.0	6.0	12.2	11.5	9.3	9.4	9.5	9.4
$50,000 to $59,999	6.8	6.4	6.6	10.0	5.4	5.2	8.6	8.6
$60,000 to $69,999	6.9	7.0	5.6	8.1	6.1	6.8	7.9	8.5
$70,000 to $79,999	6.9	7.6	5.6	5.3	8.5	6.4	5.0	5.5
$80,000 to $89,999	5.9	7.5	3.3	2.7	4.4	3.9	4.4	3.9
$90,000 to $99,999	5.5	7.4	2.5	10.2	1.8	1.5	1.4	1.4
$100,000 or more	31.1	44.0	8.2	19.8	13.8	9.5	18.9	14.6
$100,000 to $124,999	10.3	13.9	3.9	6.5	6.8	5.1	6.4	4.5
$125,000 to $149,999	6.9	9.9	1.9	5.9	2.9	2.3	2.9	2.3
$150,000 to $174,999	4.8	7.2	0.8	2.1	1.4	0.3	2.9	2.3
$175,000 to $199,999	2.9	4.1	0.8	1.1	0.4	0.5	2.4	1.7
$200,000 or more	6.2	8.9	0.8	4.3	2.3	1.3	4.4	3.8

Source: Bureau of the Census, 2014 Current Population Survey, Internet site http://www.census.gov/hhes/www/income/data/index .html; calculations by New Strategist

Table 5.11 Income of Households by Household Type, 2013: Aged 45 to 49

(number and percent distribution of households headed by people aged 45 to 49, by income and household type, 2013; households in thousands as of 2014)

| | total | family households | | | nonfamily households | | | |
| | | | | | female householder | | male householder | |
		married couples	female householder, no spouse present	male householder, no spouse present	total	living alone	total	living alone
Total households headed by 45-to-49-year-olds	**11,383**	**6,572**	**1,558**	**645**	**1,161**	**937**	**1,447**	**1,107**
Under $10,000	604	85	121	19	169	158	209	190
$10,000 to $19,999	738	197	232	38	128	120	143	118
$20,000 to $29,999	827	233	211	75	130	103	177	126
$30,000 to $39,999	943	357	224	61	136	111	165	136
$40,000 to $49,999	870	364	180	81	109	102	135	122
$50,000 to $59,999	850	395	145	61	124	113	124	96
$60,000 to $69,999	794	459	116	75	54	32	90	68
$70,000 to $79,999	655	419	70	36	58	52	71	53
$80,000 to $89,999	767	518	57	25	83	67	85	63
$90,000 to $99,999	627	490	33	30	23	13	51	28
$100,000 or more	3,708	3,056	167	143	145	67	197	105
$100,000 to $124,999	1,143	890	64	64	66	31	59	41
$125,000 to $149,999	784	652	39	22	29	13	43	14
$150,000 to $174,999	578	489	22	18	25	14	25	18
$175,000 to $199,999	296	245	12	5	9	0	25	17
$200,000 or more	905	780	31	33	16	8	45	16
Median income	**$70,879**	**$94,780**	**$39,526**	**$57,292**	**$41,181**	**$36,936**	**$42,674**	**$37,324**
Total households headed by 45-to-49-year-olds	**100.0%**	**100.0%**	**100.0%**	**100.0%**	**100.0%**	**100.0%**	**100.0%**	**100.0%**
Under $10,000	5.3	1.3	7.8	2.9	14.6	16.9	14.4	17.2
$10,000 to $19,999	6.5	3.0	14.9	5.9	11.1	12.8	9.9	10.7
$20,000 to $29,999	7.3	3.5	13.6	11.7	11.2	11.0	12.2	11.4
$30,000 to $39,999	8.3	5.4	14.4	9.4	11.7	11.9	11.4	12.3
$40,000 to $49,999	7.6	5.5	11.6	12.6	9.4	10.9	9.3	11.1
$50,000 to $59,999	7.5	6.0	9.3	9.5	10.7	12.0	8.6	8.7
$60,000 to $69,999	7.0	7.0	7.5	11.7	4.6	3.4	6.2	6.2
$70,000 to $79,999	5.8	6.4	4.5	5.7	5.0	5.5	4.9	4.8
$80,000 to $89,999	6.7	7.9	3.6	3.8	7.1	7.1	5.9	5.7
$90,000 to $99,999	5.5	7.4	2.1	4.7	2.0	1.4	3.5	2.6
$100,000 or more	32.6	46.5	10.7	22.1	12.5	7.1	13.6	9.5
$100,000 to $124,999	10.0	13.5	4.1	10.0	5.7	3.3	4.1	3.7
$125,000 to $149,999	6.9	9.9	2.5	3.4	2.5	1.4	3.0	1.3
$150,000 to $174,999	5.1	7.4	1.4	2.8	2.2	1.4	1.7	1.6
$175,000 to $199,999	2.6	3.7	0.7	0.8	0.7	0.0	1.8	1.5
$200,000 or more	8.0	11.9	2.0	5.1	1.4	0.9	3.1	1.4

Source: Bureau of the Census, 2014 Current Population Survey, Internet site http://www.census.gov/hhes/www/income/data/index .html; calculations by New Strategist

Median Income of Middle-Aged Men Has Declined

Middle-aged women have lost ground since 2007.

The median income of men aged 35 to 44 fell 10 percent between 2000 and 2013, after adjusting for inflation. Men aged 45 to 54 saw their median fall by an even larger 13 percent during those years. (Gen Xers were aged 37 to 48 in 2013.) In contrast, the median income of women aged 35 to 44 climbed 2 percent between 2000 and 2013, but the median of those aged 45 to 54 fell. Between 2007 and 2013, women in both age groups lost ground.

The Great Recession was not the only factor behind the decline in men's incomes, because the decline began well before 2007. The Great Recession exacerbated the decline, however. The median income of men aged 35 to 44 in 2013 was more than $5,000 below the median income of their counterparts in 2000, after adjusting for inflation. The loss was more than $7,000 for men aged 45 to 54.

■ In 2013, the median income of men aged 45 to 54 was 37 percent higher than the median for all men. The margin was a larger 45 percent in 2000.

Both men and women have lost ground since 2007

(percent change in median income of people aged 35 to 54, by sex, 2007 to 2013; in 2013 dollars)

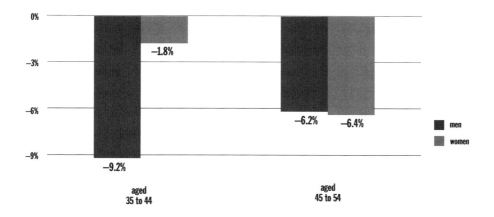

Table 5.12 Median Income of Men Aged 35 to 54, 2000 to 2013

(median income of men aged 15 or older and aged 35 to 54, and index of age group to total, 2000 to 2013; percent change for selected years; in 2013 dollars)

	total men	35 to 44	45 to 54
2013	$35,228	$45,942	$48,300
2012	34,397	45,881	47,141
2011	34,164	45,538	47,592
2010	34,408	45,120	48,556
2009	34,953	45,857	48,579
2008	35,877	47,809	49,270
2007	37,295	50,577	51,510
2006	37,277	49,261	52,792
2005	37,318	48,880	52,057
2004	37,633	49,988	51,629
2003	37,910	49,643	53,296
2002	37,859	49,065	53,049
2001	38,290	50,447	54,083
2000	38,340	51,297	55,514
PERCENT CHANGE			
2007 to 2013	−5.5%	−9.2%	−6.2%
2000 to 2013	−8.1	−10.4	−13.0
INDEX			
2013	100	130	137
2012	100	133	137
2011	100	133	139
2010	100	131	141
2009	100	131	139
2008	100	133	137
2007	100	136	138
2006	100	132	142
2005	100	131	139
2004	100	133	137
2003	100	131	141
2002	100	130	140
2001	100	132	141
2000	100	134	145

Note: The index is calculated by dividing the median income of the age group by the national median and multiplying by 100.
Source: Bureau of the Census, Historical Income Data, Internet site http://www.census.gov/hhes/www/income/data/historical/index
.html; calculations by New Strategist

Table 5.13 Median Income of Women Aged 35 to 54, 2000 to 2013

(median income of women aged 15 or older and aged 35 to 54, and index of age group to total, 2000 to 2013; percent change for selected years; in 2013 dollars)

	total women	35 to 44	45 to 54
2013	$22,063	$30,571	$30,957
2012	21,833	30,498	30,217
2011	21,856	30,134	29,477
2010	22,196	31,274	29,566
2009	22,760	30,294	31,079
2008	22,576	29,613	30,549
2007	23,505	31,123	33,090
2006	23,123	30,464	32,170
2005	22,166	30,350	31,592
2004	21,788	30,093	32,350
2003	21,860	29,729	32,761
2002	21,769	28,904	32,585
2001	21,860	29,567	31,756
2000	21,729	29,864	32,102
PERCENT CHANGE			
2007 to 2013	−6.1%	−1.8%	−6.4%
2000 to 2013	1.5	2.4	−3.6
INDEX			
2013	100	139	140
2012	100	140	138
2011	100	138	135
2010	100	141	133
2009	100	133	137
2008	100	131	135
2007	100	132	141
2006	100	132	139
2005	100	137	143
2004	100	138	148
2003	100	136	150
2002	100	133	150
2001	100	135	145
2000	100	137	148

Note: The index is calculated by dividing the median income of the age group by the national median and multiplying by 100.
Source: Bureau of the Census, Historical Income Data, Internet site http://www.census.gov/hhes/www/income/data/historical/index
.html; calculations by New Strategist

Seventy Percent of Gen X Men Work Full-Time

Asian and non-Hispanic White men have the highest incomes.

Gen X men are in their peak earning years. The incomes of men aged 35 to 49 are well above average (Gen Xers were aged 37 to 48 in 2013). In 2013, men aged 35 to 44 had a median income of $45,942. Among the 73 percent with a full-time job, median income was a higher $53,172. For the 74 percent of men aged 45 to 49 who work full-time, median income was an even larger $57,480.

Among men aged 35 to 44 who work full-time, Asians have the highest median income—$72,102 in 2013, nearly $12,000 more than the median income of their non-Hispanic White counterparts. Black men in the age group who work full-time had a median income of $47,264. Among Hispanics, median income was just $35,949. In the 45-to-49 age group, the median income of non-Hispanic White men who work full-time is slightly greater than the Asian median ($66,306 versus $65,611), while the Hispanic median is the lowest ($37,304).

■ Hispanic men have the lowest incomes because they are the least educated.

Among men aged 35 to 44, Hispanics have the lowest median income

(median income of men aged 35 to 44 who work full-time, by race and Hispanic origin, 2013)

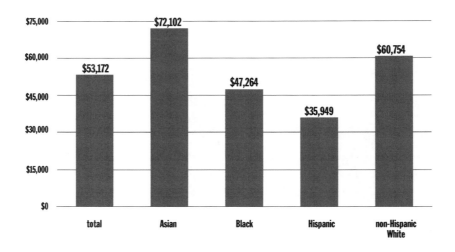

Table 5.14 Income of Men Aged 35 to 49, 2013: Total Men

(number and percent distribution of men aged 15 or older and aged 35 to 49 by income and age, 2013; median income of men with income and of men working full-time, year-round; percent working full-time, year-round; men in thousands as of 2014)

| | | aged 35 to 44 | | | |
	total	total	35 to 39	40 to 44	45 to 49
TOTAL MEN	**122,414**	**19,593**	**9,562**	**10,030**	**10,145**
Without income	**13,707**	**1,116**	**549**	**567**	**489**
With income	**108,706**	**18,477**	**9,014**	**9,463**	**9,656**
Under $5,000	7,073	451	216	235	303
$5,000 to $9,999	7,227	820	398	421	369
$10,000 to $14,999	7,751	856	437	419	362
$15,000 to $19,999	8,834	1,127	576	551	522
$20,000 to $24,999	8,947	1,296	712	584	564
$25,000 to $29,999	7,106	1,110	513	597	583
$30,000 to $34,999	7,054	1,092	546	546	564
$35,000 to $39,999	6,027	1,134	620	514	502
$40,000 to $44,999	6,034	1,120	566	554	610
$45,000 to $49,999	4,608	967	482	485	491
$50,000 to $54,999	5,239	936	500	437	566
$55,000 to $59,999	2,987	652	287	365	280
$60,000 to $64,999	3,837	823	367	455	394
$65,000 to $69,999	2,653	562	294	268	346
$70,000 to $74,999	2,639	603	276	326	319
$75,000 to $79,999	2,339	578	277	300	284
$80,000 to $84,999	2,208	601	281	320	291
$85,000 to $89,999	1,451	298	136	163	237
$90,000 to $94,999	1,605	344	166	179	209
$95,000 to $99,999	1,084	279	124	155	133
$100,000 or more	12,003	2,828	1,239	1,589	1,727
MEDIAN INCOME					
Men with income	$35,228	$45,942	$43,645	$47,617	$49,286
Working full-time	50,943	53,172	51,139	56,807	57,480
Percent full-time	49.7%	73.2%	73.4%	72.9%	74.1%
PERCENT DISTRIBUTION					
TOTAL MEN	**100.0%**	**100.0%**	**100.0%**	**100.0%**	**100.0%**
Without income	**11.2**	**5.7**	**5.7**	**5.7**	**4.8**
With income	**88.8**	**94.3**	**94.3**	**94.3**	**95.2**
Under $15,000	18.0	10.8	11.0	10.7	10.2
$15,000 to $24,999	14.5	12.4	13.5	11.3	10.7
$25,000 to $34,999	11.6	11.2	11.1	11.4	11.3
$35,000 to $49,999	13.6	16.4	17.4	15.5	15.8
$50,000 to $74,999	14.2	18.2	18.0	18.5	18.8
$75,000 to $99,999	7.1	10.7	10.3	11.1	11.4
$100,000 or more	9.8	14.4	13.0	15.8	17.0

Source: Bureau of the Census, 2014 Current Population Survey, Internet site http://www.census.gov/hhes/www/income/data/index .html; calculations by New Strategist

Table 5.15 Income of Men Aged 35 to 49, 2013: Asian Men

(number and percent distribution of Asian men aged 15 or older and aged 35 to 49 by income and age, 2013; median income of men with income and of men working full-time, year-round; percent working full-time, year-round; men in thousands as of 2014)

	total	aged 35 to 44 total	35 to 39	40 to 44	45 to 49
ASIAN MEN	**7,135**	**1,349**	**678**	**671**	**649**
Without income	**973**	**61**	**32**	**29**	**35**
With income	**6,162**	**1,287**	**645**	**642**	**614**
Under $5,000	433	24	18	7	26
$5,000 to $9,999	450	21	7	14	5
$10,000 to $14,999	451	46	25	21	37
$15,000 to $19,999	463	61	9	52	33
$20,000 to $24,999	384	71	35	35	21
$25,000 to $29,999	357	60	21	40	44
$30,000 to $34,999	307	56	19	37	34
$35,000 to $39,999	261	71	53	17	32
$40,000 to $44,999	316	41	12	29	42
$45,000 to $49,999	209	70	34	35	9
$50,000 to $54,999	259	56	35	21	20
$55,000 to $59,999	186	37	21	16	14
$60,000 to $64,999	207	51	23	28	22
$65,000 to $69,999	176	29	21	8	33
$70,000 to $74,999	196	44	21	22	26
$75,000 to $79,999	131	54	31	23	13
$80,000 to $84,999	137	40	16	24	26
$85,000 to $89,999	75	27	9	18	12
$90,000 to $94,999	133	49	25	24	21
$95,000 to $99,999	63	5	0	5	16
$100,000 or more	966	374	207	167	130
MEDIAN INCOME					
Men with income	$39,204	$62,109	$66,283	$59,475	$56,018
Working full-time	60,191	72,102	75,843	70,212	65,611
Percent full-time	52.6%	82.2%	81.5%	83.0%	75.7%
PERCENT DISTRIBUTION					
ASIAN MEN	**100.0%**	**100.0%**	**100.0%**	**100.0%**	**100.0%**
Without income	**13.6**	**4.5**	**4.8**	**4.3**	**5.4**
With income	**86.4**	**95.5**	**95.2**	**95.7**	**94.6**
Under $15,000	18.7	6.8	7.3	6.2	10.4
$15,000 to $24,999	11.9	9.7	6.5	12.9	8.3
$25,000 to $34,999	9.3	8.6	5.9	11.4	11.9
$35,000 to $49,999	11.0	13.5	14.8	12.1	12.8
$50,000 to $74,999	14.4	16.1	17.8	14.3	17.6
$75,000 to $99,999	7.6	13.0	12.2	13.9	13.5
$100,000 or more	13.5	27.7	30.6	24.8	20.0

Note: Asians are those who identify themselves as being of the race alone and those who identify themselves as being of the race in combination with other races.
Source: Bureau of the Census, 2014 Current Population Survey, Internet site http://www.census.gov/hhes/www/income/data/index .html; calculations by New Strategist

Table 5.16 Income of Men Aged 35 to 49, 2013: Black Men

(number and percent distribution of Black men aged 15 or older and aged 35 to 49 by income and age, 2013; median income of men with income and of men working full-time, year-round; percent working full-time, year-round; men in thousands as of 2014)

| | total | aged 35 to 44 | | | 45 to 49 |
		total	35 to 39	40 to 44	
BLACK MEN	**15,188**	**2,448**	**1,211**	**1,237**	**1,251**
Without income	**2,876**	**275**	**163**	**113**	**100**
With income	**12,311**	**2,172**	**1,048**	**1,124**	**1,151**
Under $5,000	1,059	69	29	40	43
$5,000 to $9,999	1,533	218	142	76	104
$10,000 to $14,999	1,224	135	66	69	53
$15,000 to $19,999	1,269	152	57	95	98
$20,000 to $24,999	1,130	221	113	108	71
$25,000 to $29,999	888	144	75	69	93
$30,000 to $34,999	736	133	70	63	82
$35,000 to $39,999	596	121	77	43	45
$40,000 to $44,999	574	110	41	69	105
$45,000 to $49,999	508	98	39	59	70
$50,000 to $54,999	468	106	61	45	62
$55,000 to $59,999	269	88	43	45	42
$60,000 to $64,999	344	100	39	60	44
$65,000 to $69,999	213	59	25	34	43
$70,000 to $74,999	221	69	26	43	28
$75,000 to $79,999	211	63	34	29	20
$80,000 to $84,999	190	89	31	58	19
$85,000 to $89,999	92	9	4	5	22
$90,000 to $94,999	97	18	6	13	19
$95,000 to $99,999	73	26	5	21	5
$100,000 or more	617	146	65	81	84
MEDIAN INCOME					
Men with income	$24,643	$35,488	$32,339	$39,816	$37,263
Working full-time	41,555	47,264	42,333	50,485	45,390
Percent full-time	40.2%	62.6%	60.0%	65.1%	64.1%
PERCENT DISTRIBUTION					
BLACK MEN	**100.0%**	**100.0%**	**100.0%**	**100.0%**	**100.0%**
Without income	**18.9**	**11.2**	**13.4**	**9.1**	**8.0**
With income	**81.1**	**88.8**	**86.6**	**90.9**	**92.0**
Under $15,000	25.1	17.2	19.6	14.9	16.0
$15,000 to $24,999	15.8	15.3	14.1	16.4	13.5
$25,000 to $34,999	10.7	11.3	12.0	10.6	14.0
$35,000 to $49,999	11.0	13.4	13.0	13.9	17.6
$50,000 to $74,999	10.0	17.2	16.0	18.3	17.5
$75,000 to $99,999	4.4	8.4	6.6	10.2	6.7
$100,000 or more	4.1	6.0	5.4	6.6	6.7

Note: Blacks are those who identify themselves as being of the race alone and those who identify themselves as being of the race in combination with other races.
Source: Bureau of the Census, 2014 Current Population Survey, Internet site http://www.census.gov/hhes/www/income/data/index .html; calculations by New Strategist

Table 5.17 Income of Men Aged 35 to 49, 2013: Hispanic Men

(number and percent distribution of Hispanic men aged 15 or older and aged 35 to 49 by income and age, 2013; median income of men with income and of men working full-time, year-round; percent working full-time, year-round; men in thousands as of 2014)

| | total | aged 35 to 44 | | | 45 to 49 |
		total	35 to 39	40 to 44	
HISPANIC MEN	**19,683**	**3,927**	**2,017**	**1,911**	**1,664**
Without income	**3,199**	**254**	**141**	**112**	**88**
With income	**16,484**	**3,674**	**1,875**	**1,798**	**1,576**
Under $5,000	1,077	107	53	54	35
$5,000 to $9,999	1,524	190	116	75	91
$10,000 to $14,999	1,598	260	146	114	80
$15,000 to $19,999	1,877	366	212	154	132
$20,000 to $24,999	2,005	488	247	240	207
$25,000 to $29,999	1,431	350	173	177	159
$30,000 to $34,999	1,299	324	169	155	122
$35,000 to $39,999	928	265	137	129	125
$40,000 to $44,999	962	267	122	145	117
$45,000 to $49,999	555	125	73	53	78
$50,000 to $54,999	579	135	59	76	86
$55,000 to $59,999	317	82	35	46	30
$60,000 to $64,999	425	129	70	59	51
$65,000 to $69,999	244	46	17	29	30
$70,000 to $74,999	224	84	31	52	26
$75,000 to $79,999	210	66	34	32	31
$80,000 to $84,999	213	73	33	40	27
$85,000 to $89,999	119	35	14	21	19
$90,000 to $94,999	131	41	15	26	15
$95,000 to $99,999	96	37	15	22	9
$100,000 or more	671	203	103	100	106
MEDIAN INCOME					
Men with income	$25,411	$30,765	$29,621	$31,820	$32,005
Working full-time	32,949	35,949	35,027	37,350	37,304
Percent full-time	50.9%	68.5%	67.7%	69.4%	72.8%
PERCENT DISTRIBUTION					
HISPANIC MEN	**100.0%**	**100.0%**	**100.0%**	**100.0%**	**100.0%**
Without income	**16.3**	**6.5**	**7.0**	**5.9**	**5.3**
With income	**83.7**	**93.5**	**93.0**	**94.1**	**94.7**
Under $15,000	21.3	14.2	15.6	12.7	12.4
$15,000 to $24,999	19.7	21.7	22.8	20.7	20.4
$25,000 to $34,999	13.9	17.1	16.9	17.4	16.9
$35,000 to $49,999	12.4	16.8	16.4	17.1	19.2
$50,000 to $74,999	9.1	12.1	10.6	13.8	13.5
$75,000 to $99,999	3.9	6.4	5.6	7.3	6.0
$100,000 or more	3.4	5.2	5.1	5.2	6.4

Source: Bureau of the Census, 2014 Current Population Survey, Internet site http://www.census.gov/hhes/www/income/data/index .html; calculations by New Strategist

Table 5.18 Income of Men Aged 35 to 49, 2013: Non-Hispanic White Men

(number and percent distribution of non-Hispanic White men aged 15 or older and aged 35 to 49 by income and age, 2013; median income of men with income and of men working full-time, year-round; percent working full-time, year-round; men in thousands as of 2014)

	total	aged 35 to 44 total	35 to 39	40 to 44	45 to 49
NON-HISPANIC WHITE MEN	**80,003**	**11,801**	**5,642**	**6,158**	**6,554**
Without income	**6,669**	**503**	**203**	**301**	**272**
With income	**73,333**	**11,297**	**5,440**	**5,858**	**6,282**
Under $5,000	**4,477**	**253**	**112**	**141**	**196**
$5,000 to $9,999	3,724	388	146	243	169
$10,000 to $14,999	4,412	398	190	208	186
$15,000 to $19,999	5,227	559	299	260	266
$20,000 to $24,999	5,383	529	323	206	258
$25,000 to $29,999	4,416	526	236	290	295
$30,000 to $34,999	4,688	573	289	285	325
$35,000 to $39,999	4,199	673	349	323	295
$40,000 to $44,999	4,146	700	394	306	344
$45,000 to $49,999	3,338	660	330	330	330
$50,000 to $54,999	3,930	645	343	301	401
$55,000 to $59,999	2,204	440	187	253	194
$60,000 to $64,999	2,872	552	239	313	275
$65,000 to $69,999	2,017	427	230	196	236
$70,000 to $74,999	1,987	406	197	209	242
$75,000 to $79,999	1,747	391	180	211	220
$80,000 to $84,999	1,673	408	207	201	217
$85,000 to $89,999	1,145	228	108	120	183
$90,000 to $94,999	1,227	237	121	117	151
$95,000 to $99,999	851	214	102	112	102
$100,000 or more	9,669	2,089	857	1,232	1,398
MEDIAN INCOME					
Men with income	$40,122	$51,839	$50,451	$55,473	$56,437
Working full-time	56,456	60,754	57,060	62,118	66,306
Percent full-time	50.9%	76.1%	77.4%	74.9%	76.4%
PERCENT DISTRIBUTION					
NON-HISPANIC WHITE MEN	**100.0%**	**100.0%**	**100.0%**	**100.0%**	**100.0%**
Without income	**8.3**	**4.3**	**3.6**	**4.9**	**4.2**
With income	**91.7**	**95.7**	**96.4**	**95.1**	**95.8**
Under $15,000	15.8	8.8	7.9	9.6	8.4
$15,000 to $24,999	13.3	9.2	11.0	7.6	8.0
$25,000 to $34,999	11.4	9.3	9.3	9.3	9.5
$35,000 to $49,999	14.6	17.2	19.0	15.6	14.8
$50,000 to $74,999	16.3	20.9	21.2	20.7	20.6
$75,000 to $99,999	8.3	12.5	12.7	12.4	13.3
$100,000 or more	12.1	17.7	15.2	20.0	21.3

Note: Non-Hispanic Whites are those who identify themselves as being White alone and not Hispanic.
Source: Bureau of the Census, 2014 Current Population Survey, Internet site http://www.census.gov/hhes/www/income/data/index .html; calculations by New Strategist

Half of Gen X Women Work Full-Time

Asian and Non-Hispanic White women have the highest incomes.

The incomes of women aged 35 to 49 are well above average (Gen Xers were aged 37 to 48 in 2013). In 2013, women aged 35 to 44 had a median income of $30,571. Among the 50 percent with a full-time job, median income was a higher $42,441. For the 53 percent of women aged 45 to 49 who work full-time, median income was about the same at $41,877.

By race and Hispanic origin, women's incomes do not vary as much as men's. Among women aged 35 to 44 who work full-time, Asians have the highest median income—$48,100 in 2013. Non-Hispanic Whites are not far behind, with a median of $46,658. Black women in the age group who work full-time had a median income of $39,099. Among Hispanics, median income was just $32,939. In the 45-to-49 age group, the median income of non-Hispanic White women who work full-time is slightly greater than the Asian median ($46,108 versus $44,475), while the Hispanic median is the lowest ($31,857).

■ Hispanic women have the lowest incomes because they are the least educated.

Among women aged 35 to 44, Hispanics have the lowest incomes

*(median income of women aged 35 to 44 who work full-time,
by race and Hispanic origin, 2013)*

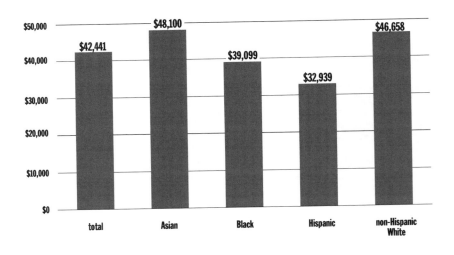

Table 5.19 Income of Women Aged 35 to 49, 2013: Total Women

(number and percent distribution of women aged 15 or older and aged 35 to 49 by income and age, 2013; median income of women with income and of women working full-time, year-round; percent working full-time, year-round; women in thousands as of 2014)

| | total | aged 35 to 44 | | | |
		total	35 to 39	40 to 44	45 to 49
TOTAL WOMEN	**129,930**	**20,196**	**9,848**	**10,348**	**10,520**
Without income	**19,975**	**2,841**	**1,487**	**1,354**	**1,154**
With income	**109,956**	**17,356**	**8,361**	**8,995**	**9,366**
Under $5,000	11,888	1,681	822	859	857
$5,000 to $9,999	13,431	1,241	589	652	726
$10,000 to $14,999	13,771	1,536	759	777	803
$15,000 to $19,999	11,145	1,406	685	721	769
$20,000 to $24,999	9,350	1,400	691	709	796
$25,000 to $29,999	7,492	1,220	564	656	584
$30,000 to $34,999	6,989	1,181	590	591	692
$35,000 to $39,999	5,478	1,017	548	469	613
$40,000 to $44,999	5,150	1,011	485	525	546
$45,000 to $49,999	3,947	819	382	437	433
$50,000 to $54,999	3,800	853	446	407	465
$55,000 to $59,999	2,267	483	237	247	215
$60,000 to $64,999	2,643	646	316	330	260
$65,000 to $69,999	1,737	344	137	208	164
$70,000 to $74,999	1,810	477	207	269	251
$75,000 to $79,999	1,441	344	167	177	176
$80,000 to $84,999	1,301	262	88	174	245
$85,000 to $89,999	740	175	77	99	80
$90,000 to $94,999	664	134	64	69	99
$95,000 to $99,999	468	99	42	57	51
$100,000 or more	4,442	1,027	464	564	543
MEDIAN INCOME					
Women with income	$22,063	$30,571	$30,411	$30,729	$30,749
Working full-time	40,597	42,441	41,931	43,732	41,877
Percent full-time	34.7%	50.1%	49.0%	51.1%	52.9%
PERCENT DISTRIBUTION					
TOTAL WOMEN	**100.0%**	**100.0%**	**100.0%**	**100.0%**	**100.0%**
Without income	**15.4**	**14.1**	**15.1**	**13.1**	**11.0**
With income	**84.6**	**85.9**	**84.9**	**86.9**	**89.0**
Under $15,000	30.1	22.1	22.0	22.1	22.7
$15,000 to $24,999	15.8	13.9	14.0	13.8	14.9
$25,000 to $34,999	11.1	11.9	11.7	12.0	12.1
$35,000 to $49,999	11.2	14.1	14.4	13.8	15.1
$50,000 to $74,999	9.4	13.9	13.6	14.1	12.9
$75,000 to $99,999	3.6	5.0	4.4	5.6	6.2
$100,000 or more	3.4	5.1	4.7	5.4	5.2

Source: Bureau of the Census, 2014 Current Population Survey, Internet site http://www.census.gov/hhes/www/income/data/index .html; calculations by New Strategist

Table 5.20 Income of Women Aged 35 to 49, 2013: Asian Women

(number and percent distribution of Asian women aged 15 or older and aged 35 to 49 by income and age, 2013; median income of women with income and of women working full-time, year-round; percent working full-time, year-round; women in thousands as of 2014)

| | | aged 35 to 44 | | | |
	total	total	35 to 39	40 to 44	45 to 49
ASIAN WOMEN	**7,877**	**1,571**	**796**	**774**	**656**
Without income	**1,834**	**318**	**202**	**116**	**105**
With income	**6,043**	**1,253**	**595**	**658**	**551**
Under $5,000	827	166	68	98	56
$5,000 to $9,999	745	71	37	34	32
$10,000 to $14,999	586	70	27	43	63
$15,000 to $19,999	447	82	41	41	40
$20,000 to $24,999	433	98	52	46	50
$25,000 to $29,999	379	75	26	49	31
$30,000 to $34,999	364	65	42	23	34
$35,000 to $39,999	253	56	24	32	29
$40,000 to $44,999	282	64	19	45	27
$45,000 to $49,999	239	64	35	29	28
$50,000 to $54,999	185	48	28	20	24
$55,000 to $59,999	111	33	7	26	7
$60,000 to $64,999	209	62	32	30	23
$65,000 to $69,999	81	20	7	12	14
$70,000 to $74,999	121	48	24	23	11
$75,000 to $79,999	100	29	17	12	8
$80,000 to $84,999	95	40	23	17	9
$85,000 to $89,999	45	14	5	9	4
$90,000 to $94,999	56	10	7	3	6
$95,000 to $99,999	27	7	3	5	2
$100,000 or more	459	131	68	62	55

MEDIAN INCOME

Women with income	$24,734	$34,802	$35,909	$32,917	$30,653
Working full-time	45,335	48,100	51,453	45,832	44,475
Percent full-time	35.5%	48.7%	45.1%	52.4%	49.4%

PERCENT DISTRIBUTION

ASIAN WOMEN	**100.0%**	**100.0%**	**100.0%**	**100.0%**	**100.0%**
Without income	**23.3**	**20.2**	**25.3**	**15.0**	**15.9**
With income	**76.7**	**79.8**	**74.7**	**85.0**	**84.1**
Under $15,000	27.4	19.5	16.7	22.5	23.0
$15,000 to $24,999	11.2	11.5	11.7	11.3	13.7
$25,000 to $34,999	9.4	8.9	8.5	9.3	9.8
$35,000 to $49,999	9.8	11.7	9.8	13.6	12.7
$50,000 to $74,999	9.0	13.4	12.5	14.4	12.1
$75,000 to $99,999	4.1	6.4	6.9	5.8	4.3
$100,000 or more	5.8	8.3	8.6	8.0	8.3

Note: Asians are those who identify themselves as being of the race alone and those who identify themselves as being of the race in combination with other races.
Source: Bureau of the Census, 2014 Current Population Survey, Internet site http://www.census.gov/hhes/www/income/data/index .html; calculations by New Strategist

Table 5.21 Income of Women Aged 35 to 49, 2013: Black Women

(number and percent distribution of Black women aged 15 or older and aged 35 to 49 by income and age, 2013; median income of women with income and of women working full-time, year-round; percent working full-time, year-round; women in thousands as of 2014)

	total	aged 35 to 44			45 to 49
		total	35 to 39	40 to 44	
BLACK WOMEN	18,038	3,005	1,486	1,518	1,494
Without income	2,999	349	189	160	146
With income	15,038	2,656	1,298	1,358	1,348
Under $5,000	1,590	212	95	117	70
$5,000 to $9,999	2,234	219	105	114	119
$10,000 to $14,999	2,063	252	117	135	174
$15,000 to $19,999	1,643	243	121	122	134
$20,000 to $24,999	1,336	219	118	101	123
$25,000 to $29,999	1,037	208	105	103	123
$30,000 to $34,999	1,009	183	92	90	104
$35,000 to $39,999	792	225	126	99	91
$40,000 to $44,999	610	159	74	84	61
$45,000 to $49,999	544	154	65	89	66
$50,000 to $54,999	450	102	49	53	67
$55,000 to $59,999	259	75	42	34	32
$60,000 to $64,999	294	81	34	46	45
$65,000 to $69,999	186	36	15	21	19
$70,000 to $74,999	218	81	31	51	24
$75,000 to $79,999	163	27	18	10	20
$80,000 to $84,999	108	28	7	21	32
$85,000 to $89,999	80	20	9	12	3
$90,000 to $94,999	60	12	11	1	5
$95,000 to $99,999	52	16	9	7	0
$100,000 or more	309	104	55	49	36
MEDIAN INCOME					
Women with income	$19,955	$29,065	$29,023	$29,098	$26,811
Working full-time	35,460	39,099	37,516	40,676	36,085
Percent full-time	37.0%	56.0%	56.6%	55.4%	58.0%
PERCENT DISTRIBUTION					
BLACK WOMEN	100.0%	100.0%	100.0%	100.0%	100.0%
Without income	16.6	11.6	12.7	10.5	9.8
With income	83.4	88.4	87.3	89.5	90.2
Under $15,000	32.6	22.7	21.3	24.1	24.3
$15,000 to $24,999	16.5	15.4	16.1	14.7	17.2
$25,000 to $34,999	11.3	13.0	13.2	12.8	15.2
$35,000 to $49,999	10.8	17.9	17.9	17.9	14.6
$50,000 to $74,999	7.8	12.5	11.5	13.5	12.6
$75,000 to $99,999	2.6	3.5	3.6	3.3	4.0
$100,000 or more	1.7	3.4	3.7	3.2	2.4

Note: Blacks are those who identify themselves as being of the race alone and those who identify themselves as being of the race in combination with other races.
Source: Bureau of the Census, 2014 Current Population Survey, Internet site http://www.census.gov/hhes/www/income/data/index .html; calculations by New Strategist

Table 5.22 Income of Women Aged 35 to 49, 2013: Hispanic Women

(number and percent distribution of Hispanic women aged 15 or older and aged 35 to 49 by income and age, 2013; median income of women with income and of women working full-time, year-round; percent working full-time, year-round; women in thousands as of 2014)

		aged 35 to 44			
	total	total	35 to 39	40 to 44	45 to 49
HISPANIC WOMEN	**19,476**	**3,825**	**1,967**	**1,858**	**1,625**
Without income	**5,442**	**938**	**477**	**461**	**352**
With income	**14,034**	**2,886**	**1,490**	**1,396**	**1,273**
Under $5,000	1,766	256	134	122	88
$5,000 to $9,999	2,211	276	135	141	123
$10,000 to $14,999	2,015	395	192	203	147
$15,000 to $19,999	1,643	325	156	169	170
$20,000 to $24,999	1,408	288	143	145	163
$25,000 to $29,999	1,050	258	148	110	89
$30,000 to $34,999	862	211	113	98	97
$35,000 to $39,999	655	195	127	68	77
$40,000 to $44,999	526	135	70	65	63
$45,000 to $49,999	367	80	41	39	44
$50,000 to $54,999	351	107	47	59	45
$55,000 to $59,999	177	51	31	20	11
$60,000 to $64,999	225	73	51	22	34
$65,000 to $69,999	117	33	15	18	19
$70,000 to $74,999	143	43	16	28	25
$75,000 to $79,999	105	33	10	22	14
$80,000 to $84,999	72	17	5	13	15
$85,000 to $89,999	46	10	6	4	9
$90,000 to $94,999	31	6	6	0	7
$95,000 to $99,999	25	12	6	6	1
$100,000 or more	239	81	37	44	32
MEDIAN INCOME					
Women with income	$17,762	$22,627	$24,237	$21,702	$22,220
Working full-time	30,799	32,939	34,031	32,156	31,857
Percent full-time	31.7%	43.5%	43.8%	43.1%	49.3%
PERCENT DISTRIBUTION					
HISPANIC WOMEN	**100.0%**	**100.0%**	**100.0%**	**100.0%**	**100.0%**
Without income	**27.9**	**24.5**	**24.2**	**24.8**	**21.6**
With income	**72.1**	**75.5**	**75.8**	**75.2**	**78.4**
Under $15,000	30.8	24.2	23.4	25.0	22.1
$15,000 to $24,999	15.7	16.0	15.2	16.9	20.5
$25,000 to $34,999	9.8	12.3	13.3	11.2	11.4
$35,000 to $49,999	8.0	10.7	12.1	9.3	11.4
$50,000 to $74,999	5.2	8.0	8.2	7.9	8.2
$75,000 to $99,999	1.4	2.1	1.7	2.5	2.8
$100,000 or more	1.2	2.1	1.9	2.4	2.0

Source: Bureau of the Census, 2014 Current Population Survey, Internet site http://www.census.gov/hhes/www/income/data/index .html; calculations by New Strategist

Table 5.23 Income of Women Aged 35 to 49, 2013: Non-Hispanic White Women

(number and percent distribution of non-Hispanic White women aged 15 or older and aged 35 to 49 by income and age, 2013; median income of women with income and of women working full-time, year-round; percent working full-time, year-round; women in thousands as of 2014)

	total	aged 35 to 44 total	35 to 39	40 to 44	45 to 49
NON-HISPANIC WHITE WOMEN	**84,038**	**11,777**	**5,606**	**6,170**	**6,697**
Without income	**9,656**	**1,243**	**626**	**617**	**548**
With income	**74,382**	**10,534**	**4,980**	**5,553**	**6,149**
Under $5,000	7,662	1,047	515	532	638
$5,000 to $9,999	8,189	658	308	351	449
$10,000 to $14,999	9,052	824	423	401	426
$15,000 to $19,999	7,370	751	360	392	415
$20,000 to $24,999	6,114	784	374	409	469
$25,000 to $29,999	4,972	678	279	398	345
$30,000 to $34,999	4,746	727	344	383	442
$35,000 to $39,999	3,767	553	298	256	411
$40,000 to $44,999	3,690	651	326	325	377
$45,000 to $49,999	2,761	516	238	278	293
$50,000 to $54,999	2,805	589	315	274	322
$55,000 to $59,999	1,719	321	156	166	165
$60,000 to $64,999	1,912	443	209	234	158
$65,000 to $69,999	1,354	257	101	156	115
$70,000 to $74,999	1,328	301	136	165	189
$75,000 to $79,999	1,065	251	122	129	134
$80,000 to $84,999	1,007	175	54	121	187
$85,000 to $89,999	561	126	54	72	64
$90,000 to $94,999	517	105	40	66	81
$95,000 to $99,999	365	66	22	44	48
$100,000 or more	3,426	712	309	403	418

MEDIAN INCOME

Women with income	$23,780	$32,719	$32,540	$32,909	$32,584
Working full-time	42,784	46,658	45,809	47,476	46,108
Percent full-time	34.9%	51.1%	49.9%	52.2%	53.3%

PERCENT DISTRIBUTION

NON-HISPANIC WHITE WOMEN	**100.0%**	**100.0%**	**100.0%**	**100.0%**	**100.0%**
Without income	**11.5**	**10.6**	**11.2**	**10.0**	**8.2**
With income	**88.5**	**89.4**	**88.8**	**90.0**	**91.8**
Under $15,000	29.6	21.5	22.2	20.8	22.6
$15,000 to $24,999	16.0	13.0	13.1	13.0	13.2
$25,000 to $34,999	11.6	11.9	11.1	12.7	11.8
$35,000 to $49,999	12.2	14.6	15.4	13.9	16.1
$50,000 to $74,999	10.9	16.2	16.3	16.1	14.2
$75,000 to $99,999	4.2	6.1	5.2	7.0	7.7
$100,000 or more	4.1	6.0	5.5	6.5	6.2

Note: Non-Hispanic Whites are those who identify themselves as being White alone and not Hispanic.
Source: Bureau of the Census, 2014 Current Population Survey, Internet site http://www.census.gov/hhes/www/income/data/index.html; calculations by New Strategist

Earnings Rise with Education

The highest earners are men with professional degrees.

A college degree has been well worth the cost for Gen Xers. The higher their educational level, the greater are their earnings. Among men aged 35 to 44 with a full-time job, those with a professional degree (such as physicians and lawyers) had median earnings of $120,534 in 2013. Among women as well, median earnings are highest for those with a professional degree, at $82,413 in 2013. The pattern is the same in the 45-to-54 age group: men and women with professional degrees earn the most.

Men aged 35 to 44 with no more than a high school diploma had median earnings of $40,802 in 2013. Those with at least a bachelor's degree had median earnings that were nearly twice as high, at $80,591. Among men aged 45 to 54, those with at least a bachelor's degree earn more than twice what high school graduates make ($86,327 versus $41,379). The pattern is the same for women, although earnings are lower. Among women aged 35 to 44 who work full-time, those with at least a bachelor's degree earned $60,080 in 2013—more than double the $29,021 earned by those who went no further than high school.

■ The steeply rising cost of a college degree may reduce the financial return of a college education in the years ahead.

College bonus is big for Gen Xers

(median earnings of people aged 35 to 44 who work full-time by educational attainment, 2013)

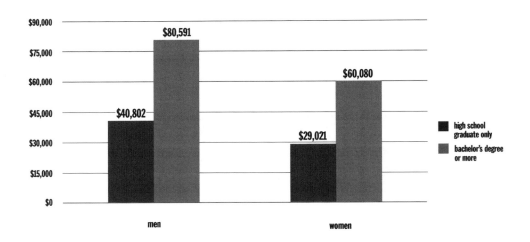

Table 5.24 Earnings of Men by Education, 2013: Aged 35 to 44

(number and percent distribution of men aged 35 to 44 who work full-time, year-round, by earnings and educational attainment, 2013; median earnings of men with earnings; men in thousands as of 2014)

	total	less than 9th grade	9th to 12th grade, no degree	high school graduate	some college	associate's degree	bachelor's degree or more				
							total	bachelor's degree	master's degree	professional degree	doctoral degree
Men aged 35 to 44 who work full-time	**14,332**	**610**	**744**	**3,833**	**2,239**	**1,486**	**5,420**	**3,354**	**1,412**	**301**	**352**
Under $5,000	42	0	1	22	6	1	12	9	1	0	3
$5,000 to $9,999	90	15	7	57	3	0	8	6	2	0	0
$10,000 to $14,999	236	44	35	95	26	8	28	28	0	0	0
$15,000 to $19,999	634	105	85	241	92	62	48	41	5	2	0
$20,000 to $24,999	895	149	151	360	99	64	71	68	3	0	0
$25,000 to $29,999	841	57	101	295	172	68	149	131	16	0	2
$30,000 to $34,999	935	81	63	376	163	114	138	111	14	10	4
$35,000 to $39,999	946	38	61	371	203	95	179	139	34	0	6
$40,000 to $44,999	977	19	73	362	165	136	223	173	43	5	2
$45,000 to $49,999	923	17	29	285	214	119	258	182	51	11	13
$50,000 to $54,999	898	17	18	288	184	95	297	211	68	6	12
$55,000 to $59,999	596	19	18	172	124	101	162	113	43	2	4
$60,000 to $64,999	775	19	26	197	118	112	303	211	63	11	18
$65,000 to $69,999	507	5	10	125	100	76	191	120	54	10	6
$70,000 to $74,999	555	5	24	64	91	70	302	198	85	13	6
$75,000 to $79,999	543	6	4	96	115	38	283	173	81	6	23
$80,000 to $84,999	587	8	15	98	63	99	304	185	89	18	12
$85,000 to $89,999	279	0	4	38	40	29	168	97	45	16	9
$90,000 to $94,999	327	2	4	28	47	14	232	140	63	4	26
$95,000 to $99,999	226	0	5	34	30	27	128	81	38	5	5
$100,000 or more	2,520	4	9	228	184	158	1,936	937	616	183	201
Median earnings	**$52,054**	**$24,365**	**$29,097**	**$40,802**	**$49,369**	**$52,090**	**$80,591**	**$71,864**	**$90,422**	**$120,534**	**$107,575**

PERCENT DISTRIBUTION

	total	less than 9th grade	9th to 12th grade, no degree	high school graduate	some college	associate's degree	bachelor's degree or more				
							total	bachelor's degree	master's degree	professional degree	doctoral degree
Men aged 35 to 44 who work full-time	100.0%	100.0%	100.0%	100.0%	100.0%	100.0%	100.0%	100.0%	100.0%	100.0%	100.0%
Under $15,000	2.6	9.7	5.9	4.5	1.6	0.6	0.9	1.3	0.2	0.0	0.7
$15,000 to $24,999	10.7	41.7	31.7	15.7	8.5	8.5	2.2	3.2	0.6	0.7	0.0
$25,000 to $34,999	12.4	22.5	22.1	17.5	15.0	12.2	5.3	7.2	2.1	3.2	1.5
$35,000 to $49,999	19.9	12.2	22.0	26.5	26.0	23.6	12.2	14.8	9.1	5.1	6.1
$50,000 to $74,999	23.2	10.6	12.9	22.1	27.5	30.5	23.2	25.4	22.2	14.0	13.1
$75,000 to $99,999	13.7	2.7	4.3	7.7	13.2	14.0	20.6	20.1	22.3	16.2	21.4
$100,000 or more	17.6	0.7	1.2	6.0	8.2	10.6	35.7	27.9	43.6	60.7	57.2

Note: Earnings include wages and salary only.
Source: Bureau of the Census, 2014 Current Population Survey, Internet site http://www.census.gov/hhes/www/income/data/index.html; calculations by New Strategist

Table 5.25 Earnings of Men by Education, 2013: Aged 45 to 54

(number and percent distribution of men aged 45 to 54 who work full-time, year-round, by earnings and educational attainment, 2013; median earnings of men with earnings; men in thousands as of 2014)

	total	less than 9th grade	9th to 12th grade, no degree	high school graduate	some college	associate's degree	bachelor's degree or more total	bachelor's degree	master's degree	professional degree	doctoral degree
Men aged 45 to 54 who work full-time	**15,019**	**505**	**806**	**4,365**	**2,225**	**1,540**	**5,578**	**3,498**	**1,417**	**295**	**369**
Under $5,000	47	0	2	21	12	6	6	1	3	2	0
$5,000 to $9,999	125	5	29	39	16	10	26	25	0	0	0
$10,000 to $14,999	222	29	30	106	24	13	21	21	0	0	0
$15,000 to $19,999	468	60	55	188	74	28	64	48	17	0	0
$20,000 to $24,999	758	114	105	324	78	76	62	49	9	2	3
$25,000 to $29,999	845	58	102	350	134	70	132	96	30	2	5
$30,000 to $34,999	951	56	78	465	125	88	139	111	16	8	4
$35,000 to $39,999	962	31	47	500	156	78	150	103	38	6	3
$40,000 to $44,999	1,056	53	75	414	161	132	220	154	47	7	12
$45,000 to $49,999	821	20	50	225	195	104	227	179	33	5	11
$50,000 to $54,999	1,137	28	72	390	237	118	294	204	64	21	5
$55,000 to $59,999	500	11	25	139	94	82	150	109	31	7	3
$60,000 to $64,999	798	11	38	230	168	111	240	185	40	8	8
$65,000 to $69,999	643	1	14	169	97	73	288	210	55	0	23
$70,000 to $74,999	607	1	7	175	109	69	246	187	41	2	16
$75,000 to $79,999	499	6	12	140	78	79	186	130	41	5	10
$80,000 to $84,999	559	0	19	90	103	74	274	188	67	8	12
$85,000 to $89,999	363	1	6	85	59	42	170	118	42	3	7
$90,000 to $94,999	415	10	11	80	47	40	228	135	68	13	12
$95,000 to $99,999	181	2	2	24	27	31	94	50	28	7	9
$100,000 or more	3,062	9	29	212	234	218	2,360	1,196	748	191	226
Median earnings	**$55,723**	**$27,251**	**$35,209**	**$41,379**	**$51,775**	**$56,767**	**$86,327**	**$76,608**	**$100,967**	**$140,401**	**$125,696**

PERCENT DISTRIBUTION

	total	less than 9th grade	9th to 12th grade, no degree	high school graduate	some college	associate's degree	bachelor's degree or more total	bachelor's degree	master's degree	professional degree	doctoral degree
Men aged 45 to 54 who work full-time	**100.0%**	**100.0%**	**100.0%**	**100.0%**	**100.0%**	**100.0%**	**100.0%**	**100.0%**	**100.0%**	**100.0%**	**100.0%**
Under $15,000	2.6	6.7	7.5	3.8	2.3	1.9	0.9	1.3	0.2	0.7	0.1
$15,000 to $24,999	8.2	34.5	19.8	11.7	6.8	6.7	2.3	2.8	1.8	0.6	0.8
$25,000 to $34,999	12.0	22.5	22.3	18.7	11.7	10.3	4.9	5.9	3.3	3.1	2.4
$35,000 to $49,999	18.9	20.6	21.4	26.1	23.0	20.3	10.7	12.5	8.3	6.0	6.9
$50,000 to $74,999	24.5	10.2	19.3	25.3	31.7	29.4	21.9	25.6	16.3	12.8	15.0
$75,000 to $99,999	13.4	3.7	6.2	9.6	14.1	17.3	17.1	17.7	17.3	12.1	13.7
$100,000 or more	20.4	1.8	3.5	4.9	10.5	14.2	42.3	34.2	52.8	64.7	61.2

Note: Earnings include wages and salary only.
Source: Bureau of the Census, 2014 Current Population Survey, Internet site http://www.census.gov/hhes/www/income/data/index.html; calculations by New Strategist

Table 5.26 Earnings of Women by Education, 2013: Aged 35 to 44

(number and percent distribution of women aged 35 to 44 who work full-time, year-round, by earnings and educational attainment, 2013; median earnings of women with earnings; women in thousands as of 2014)

	total	less than 9th grade	9th to 12th grade, no degree	high school graduate	some college	associate's degree	bachelor's degree or more				
							total	bachelor's degree	master's degree	professional degree	doctoral degree
Women aged 35 to 44 who work full-time	10,111	186	339	2,111	1,601	1,353	4,522	2,691	1,412	209	210
Under $5,000	46	2	7	13	3	2	19	19	0	0	0
$5,000 to $9,999	85	4	9	23	11	16	23	20	3	0	0
$10,000 to $14,999	305	42	61	86	50	27	40	26	12	2	0
$15,000 to $19,999	690	55	74	259	133	95	75	67	5	3	0
$20,000 to $24,999	953	33	42	435	173	142	128	99	21	2	6
$25,000 to $29,999	869	27	37	276	231	147	152	118	30	0	4
$30,000 to $34,999	881	12	58	244	197	120	250	218	31	0	1
$35,000 to $39,999	787	5	9	172	166	167	267	195	65	1	6
$40,000 to $44,999	901	2	14	186	108	143	448	284	140	21	2
$45,000 to $49,999	603	0	1	112	131	105	254	148	96	2	8
$50,000 to $54,999	726	2	1	116	147	97	364	205	142	12	5
$55,000 to $59,999	391	0	2	39	61	56	234	144	79	0	10
$60,000 to $64,999	532	0	6	70	64	66	327	169	122	10	27
$65,000 to $69,999	278	0	0	10	18	30	220	115	77	12	15
$70,000 to $74,999	398	3	13	11	23	40	307	167	100	21	20
$75,000 to $79,999	286	0	0	17	18	38	213	103	93	10	7
$80,000 to $84,999	222	0	0	7	13	15	186	96	75	10	5
$85,000 to $89,999	124	0	0	6	9	13	96	57	32	0	7
$90,000 to $94,999	100	0	1	4	3	3	90	45	38	0	6
$95,000 to $99,999	100	0	0	2	5	4	89	32	34	8	14
$100,000 or more	836	0	6	22	39	27	741	363	217	94	68
Median earnings	$41,535	$19,260	$21,706	$29,021	$35,065	$38,022	$60,080	$52,325	$62,245	$82,413	$75,949

PERCENT DISTRIBUTION

	total	less than 9th grade	9th to 12th grade, no degree	high school graduate	some college	associate's degree	bachelor's degree or more				
							total	bachelor's degree	master's degree	professional degree	doctoral degree
Women aged 35 to 44 who work full-time	100.0%	100.0%	100.0%	100.0%	100.0%	100.0%	100.0%	100.0%	100.0%	100.0%	100.0%
Under $15,000	4.3	25.8	22.6	5.7	4.0	3.3	1.8	2.4	1.1	0.8	0.0
$15,000 to $24,999	16.2	47.1	34.1	32.9	19.1	17.5	4.5	6.2	1.8	2.5	2.7
$25,000 to $34,999	17.3	21.1	27.9	24.6	26.7	19.7	8.9	12.5	4.3	0.0	2.5
$35,000 to $49,999	22.7	3.6	6.9	22.3	25.3	30.7	21.4	23.3	21.4	11.5	7.4
$50,000 to $74,999	23.0	2.5	6.4	11.7	19.5	21.3	32.1	29.7	36.9	26.2	36.5
$75,000 to $99,999	8.2	0.0	0.3	1.7	2.9	5.4	14.9	12.4	19.3	14.0	18.4
$100,000 or more	8.3	0.0	1.7	1.0	2.5	2.0	16.4	13.5	15.3	44.9	32.5

Note: Earnings include wages and salary only.
Source: Bureau of the Census, 2014 Current Population Survey, Internet site http://www.census.gov/hhes/www/income/data/index .html; calculations by New Strategist

Table 5.27 Earnings of Women by Education, 2013: Aged 45 to 54

(number and percent distribution of women aged 45 to 54 who work full-time, year-round, by earnings and educational attainment, 2013; median earnings of women with earnings; women in thousands as of 2014)

	total	less than 9th grade	9th to 12th grade, no degree	high school graduate	some college	associate's degree	bachelor's degree or more total	bachelor's degree	master's degree	professional degree	doctoral degree
Women aged 45 to 54 who work full-time	**11,644**	**244**	**381**	**3,126**	**2,047**	**1,442**	**4,404**	**2,840**	**1,193**	**187**	**184**
Under $5,000	41	1	6	8	5	9	11	8	3	0	0
$5,000 to $9,999	136	9	20	64	21	4	18	12	4	2	0
$10,000 to $14,999	290	35	32	72	59	27	66	47	14	2	3
$15,000 to $19,999	768	83	100	268	165	85	67	57	5	0	4
$20,000 to $24,999	1,085	34	75	563	150	99	164	138	27	0	0
$25,000 to $29,999	855	30	42	397	163	105	119	97	19	3	0
$30,000 to $34,999	1,256	23	37	475	282	168	270	225	37	5	3
$35,000 to $39,999	1,067	11	18	317	281	188	252	177	57	8	11
$40,000 to $44,999	936	9	18	190	195	154	369	261	85	10	12
$45,000 to $49,999	786	1	2	168	218	136	262	173	70	10	9
$50,000 to $54,999	742	6	16	157	108	100	353	241	90	11	11
$55,000 to $59,999	449	0	2	78	61	71	237	164	71	1	2
$60,000 to $64,999	456	0	1	98	50	58	248	148	80	8	12
$65,000 to $69,999	310	1	4	52	45	41	167	95	55	5	12
$70,000 to $74,999	364	0	7	38	58	41	220	148	63	3	7
$75,000 to $79,999	345	0	3	44	40	33	225	134	72	7	12
$80,000 to $84,999	348	1	0	34	28	26	260	142	102	2	14
$85,000 to $89,999	159	0	0	26	12	21	101	68	23	0	10
$90,000 to $94,999	179	0	0	11	26	11	132	74	49	4	4
$95,000 to $99,999	98	0	0	4	19	8	68	36	27	5	0
$100,000 or more	974	0	0	61	61	57	795	395	241	102	58
Median earnings	**$41,110**	**$19,727**	**$21,491**	**$31,242**	**$37,263**	**$40,801**	**$60,198**	**$54,090**	**$67,191**	**$106,649**	**$76,253**

PERCENT DISTRIBUTION

	total	less than 9th grade	9th to 12th grade, no degree	high school graduate	some college	associate's degree	bachelor's degree or more total	bachelor's degree	master's degree	professional degree	doctoral degree
Women aged 45 to 54 who work full-time	**100.0%**	**100.0%**	**100.0%**	**100.0%**	**100.0%**	**100.0%**	**100.0%**	**100.0%**	**100.0%**	**100.0%**	**100.0%**
Under $15,000	4.0	18.4	15.0	4.6	4.2	2.8	2.2	2.4	1.8	2.1	1.4
$15,000 to $24,999	15.9	47.9	45.8	26.6	15.4	12.8	5.2	6.9	2.7	0.0	2.4
$25,000 to $34,999	18.1	21.6	20.8	27.9	21.8	18.9	8.8	11.3	4.7	4.2	1.5
$35,000 to $49,999	23.9	8.6	9.7	21.6	33.9	33.2	20.1	21.5	17.8	15.0	17.5
$50,000 to $74,999	19.9	3.0	7.9	13.6	15.7	21.6	27.8	28.0	30.1	14.3	24.0
$75,000 to $99,999	9.7	0.5	0.7	3.8	6.1	6.8	17.8	16.0	22.8	9.9	21.9
$100,000 or more	8.4	0.0	0.0	1.9	3.0	3.9	18.1	13.9	20.2	54.6	31.4

Note: Earnings include wages and salary only.
Source: Bureau of the Census, 2014 Current Population Survey, Internet site http://www.census.gov/hhes/www/income/data/index .html; calculations by New Strategist

The Poverty Rate Is below Average for Gen Xers

But more than 10 percent of Gen Xers are poor.

Generation Xers (aged 37 to 48 in 2013) are less likely to be poor than the average American. Overall, 14.5 percent of Americans lived in poverty in 2013. Among people aged 35 to 44, the figure was 12.2 percent, and it was 10.6 percent among people aged 45 to 54. Children under age 18 are most likely to be poor, with a poverty rate of 19.9 percent.

Black and Hispanic Generation Xers are more than twice as likely as Asian and non-Hispanic White Gen Xers to be poor. One in five Blacks and Hispanics aged 35 to 44 is poor versus fewer than 10 percent of Asians and non-Hispanic Whites.

■ Blacks are more likely to be poor than Asians or non-Hispanic Whites because they are less likely to live in a married-couple family, the most affluent household type.

The poverty rate falls with age

(percent of people in poverty, by age, 2013)

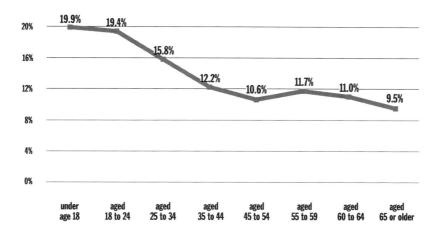

Table 5.28 People below Poverty Level by Age, Race, and Hispanic Origin, 2013

(number, percent, and percent distribution of people below poverty level by age, race, and Hispanic origin, 2013; people in thousands as of 2014)

NUMBER IN POVERTY	total	Asian	Black	Hispanic	non-Hispanic White
Total people	**45,318**	**1,974**	**11,959**	**12,744**	**18,796**
Under age 18	14,659	457	4,838	5,415	4,094
Aged 18 to 24	5,819	309	1,585	1,358	2,595
Aged 25 to 34	6,694	379	1,601	1,918	2,857
Aged 35 to 44	4,871	231	1,170	1,548	1,926
Aged 45 to 54	4,533	169	1,021	1,076	2,242
Aged 55 to 59	2,476	74	611	427	1,346
Aged 60 to 64	2,036	96	422	327	1,168
Aged 65 or older	4,231	259	712	676	2,569
PERCENT IN POVERTY					
Total people	**14.5%**	**10.4%**	**27.1%**	**23.5%**	**9.6%**
Under age 18	19.9	9.6	36.9	30.4	10.7
Aged 18 to 24	19.4	16.4	31.3	21.3	15.6
Aged 25 to 34	15.8	12.1	25.8	22.0	11.7
Aged 35 to 44	12.2	7.9	21.5	20.0	8.2
Aged 45 to 54	10.6	6.8	18.7	17.5	7.8
Aged 55 to 59	11.7	7.3	23.7	19.6	8.8
Aged 60 to 64	11.0	10.5	19.4	18.8	8.6
Aged 65 or older	9.5	13.6	17.4	19.8	7.4
PERCENT DISTRIBUTION OF POOR BY AGE					
Total in poverty	**100.0**	**100.0**	**100.0**	**100.0**	**100.0**
Under age 18	32.3	23.2	40.5	42.5	21.8
Aged 18 to 24	12.8	15.7	13.3	10.7	13.8
Aged 25 to 34	14.8	19.2	13.4	15.1	15.2
Aged 35 to 44	10.7	11.7	9.8	12.1	10.2
Aged 45 to 54	10.0	8.6	8.5	8.4	11.9
Aged 55 to 59	5.5	3.7	5.1	3.4	7.2
Aged 60 to 64	4.5	4.9	3.5	2.6	6.2
Aged 65 or older	9.3	13.1	6.0	5.3	13.7
PERCENT DISTRIBUTION OF POOR BY RACE AND HISPANIC ORIGIN					
Total in poverty	**100.0**	**4.4**	**26.4**	**28.1**	**41.5**
Under age 18	100.0	3.1	33.0	36.9	27.9
Aged 18 to 24	100.0	5.3	27.2	23.3	44.6
Aged 25 to 34	100.0	5.7	23.9	28.7	42.7
Aged 35 to 44	100.0	4.7	24.0	31.8	39.5
Aged 45 to 54	100.0	3.7	22.5	23.7	49.5
Aged 55 to 59	100.0	3.0	24.7	17.2	54.4
Aged 60 to 64	100.0	4.7	20.7	16.1	57.4
Aged 65 or older	100.0	6.1	16.8	16.0	60.7

Note: Numbers do not add to total because Asians and Blacks are those who identify themselves as being of the race alone and those who identify themselves as being of the race in combination with other races. Non-Hispanic Whites are those who identify themselves as being White alone and not Hispanic. Hispanics may be of any race.
Source: Bureau of the Census, Poverty, Internet site http://www.census.gov/hhes/www/cpstables/032014/pov/toc.htm; calculations by New Strategist

6

Labor Force

■ Generation Xers are in their prime working years. Ninety percent of Gen X men and 74 percent of Gen X women are in the labor force.

■ In 2013, Generation X (aged 37 to 48) accounted for 26 percent of the nation's workers. Larger shares of the labor force are accounted for by the Millennial generation (37 percent) and the Baby-Boom generation (31 percent).

■ Workers in the age groups that encompass Generation X account for 54 percent of CEOs, 56 percent of police, and 63 percent of computer and information system managers.

■ Between 2000 and 2012, long-term employment fell by 3 to 4 percentage points among men in the 35-to-49 age groups.

■ Between 2012 and 2022, Generation X will fill the 45-to-54 age group (Gen Xers will be aged 46 to 57 in 2022). Consequently, the number of workers in the age group will decline by more than 3 million.

Gen Xers Are in Their Prime Working Years

But the labor force participation rate is down for both men and women.

Generation Xers are in the career-building stage of their lives. But their labor force participation rate is down because of the Great Recession and lingering weakness in the economy.

Typically, labor force participation peaks among men in their thirties and forties, and that is still true today. Among men aged 35 to 44 in 2013 (Gen Xers were aged 37 to 48 in that year), nearly 91 percent were in the labor force. But this was about 2 percentage points less than for men of the same age in 2000. Among women aged 35 to 44, labor force participation was 74 percent. This was 1.9 to 4.5 percentage points lower than for their counterparts in 2000.

■ Although the labor force participation rate is down for Generation Xers, the great majority of both men and women either have a job or are looking for work.

The labor force participation rate of men aged 35 to 44 has declined

(percentage of men aged 35 to 44 in the labor force, 2000 and 2013)

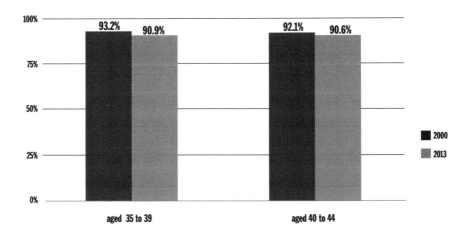

Table 6.1 Labor Force Participation Rate by Sex and Age, 2000 to 2013

(civilian labor force participation rate of people aged 16 or older, by sex and age, 2000 to 2013; percentage point change, 2010–13 and 2000–13)

	2013	2010	2000	percentage point change	
				2010–13	2000–13
Men aged 16 or older	**69.7%**	**71.2%**	**74.8%**	**–1.5**	**–5.1**
Aged 16 to 17	21.8	21.8	40.9	0.0	–19.1
Aged 18 to 19	48.3	49.6	65.0	–1.3	–16.7
Aged 20 to 24	73.9	74.5	82.6	–0.6	–8.7
Aged 25 to 29	87.6	88.4	92.5	–0.8	–4.9
Aged 30 to 34	90.7	91.1	94.2	–0.4	–3.5
Aged 35 to 39	90.9	92.2	93.2	–1.3	–2.3
Aged 40 to 44	90.6	90.7	92.1	–0.1	–1.5
Aged 45 to 49	87.3	88.5	90.2	–1.2	–2.9
Aged 50 to 54	83.9	85.1	86.8	–1.2	–2.9
Aged 55 to 59	78.0	78.5	77.0	–0.5	1.0
Aged 60 to 64	60.5	60.0	54.9	0.5	5.6
Aged 65 or older	23.5	22.1	17.7	1.4	5.8
Women aged 16 or older	**57.2**	**58.6**	**59.9**	**–1.4**	**–2.7**
Aged 16 to 17	23.5	23.0	40.8	0.5	–17.3
Aged 18 to 19	47.6	48.6	61.3	–1.0	–13.7
Aged 20 to 24	67.5	68.3	73.1	–0.8	–5.6
Aged 25 to 29	73.7	75.6	76.7	–1.9	–3.0
Aged 30 to 34	73.3	73.8	75.5	–0.5	–2.2
Aged 35 to 39	73.8	74.1	75.7	–0.3	–1.9
Aged 40 to 44	74.2	76.2	78.7	–2.0	–4.5
Aged 45 to 49	75.3	76.8	79.1	–1.5	–3.8
Aged 50 to 54	73.0	74.6	74.1	–1.6	–1.1
Aged 55 to 59	67.2	68.4	61.4	–1.2	5.8
Aged 60 to 64	50.0	50.7	40.2	–0.7	9.8
Aged 65 or older	14.9	13.8	9.4	1.1	5.5

Source: Bureau of Labor Statistics, Labor Force Statistics from the Current Population Survey, Internet site http://www.bls.gov/cps/ tables.htm#empstat; calculations by New Strategist

More than 80 Percent of Gen Xers Are in the Labor Force

Among Gen X men, labor force participation is 90 percent.

Eighty-two percent of Gen Xers (aged 37 to 48) were in the labor force in 2013. Among Gen X men, 90 percent are in the labor force. Among Gen X women, the figure is 74 percent. The labor force participation rate for men and women varies little within the age groups encompassing Generation X.

Unemployment is less common for the men and women of Gen X than for the average male or female worker. Among Gen Xers, 5.7 percent of men and 5.8 percent of women were unemployed in 2013 versus an unemployment rate of more than 7 percent for all male and female workers.

■ Gen Xers account for 26 percent of the labor force and 20 percent of the unemployed.

Most men and women of Generation X are in the labor force

(percentage of people aged 37 to 48 in the labor force, by sex, 2013)

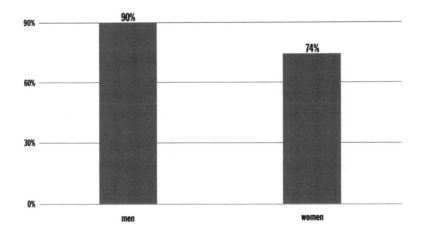

Table 6.2 Employment Status by Sex and Generation, 2013

(number and percent of people aged 16 or older in the civilian labor force by sex and generation, 2013; numbers in thousands)

| | civilian noninstitutional population | civilian labor force | | | unemployed | | not in labor force | |
		total	percent of population	employed	number	percent of labor force	number	percent of population
Total aged 16 or older	**245,679**	**155,389**	**63.2%**	**143,929**	**11,460**	**7.4%**	**90,290**	**36.8%**
iGeneration (aged 16 to 18)	12,590	4,339	34.5	3,344	995	22.9	8,252	65.5
Millennials (aged 19 to 36)	75,456	57,080	75.6	51,857	5,224	9.2	18,375	24.4
Generation Xers (aged 37 to 48)	48,677	39,842	81.9	37,552	2,290	5.7	8,834	18.1
Baby Boomers (aged 49 to 67)	74,209	48,798	65.8	46,124	2,676	5.5	25,410	34.2
Older Americans (aged 68 or older)	34,748	5,330	15.3	5,054	277	5.2	29,417	84.7
Men aged 16 or older	**118,555**	**82,667**	**69.7**	**76,353**	**6,314**	**7.6**	**35,889**	**30.3**
iGeneration (aged 16 to 18)	6,404	2,192	34.2	1,633	560	25.5	4,211	65.8
Millennials (aged 19 to 36)	37,437	30,585	81.7	27,669	2,915	9.5	6,852	18.3
Generation Xers (aged 37 to 48)	23,837	21,338	89.5	20,121	1,217	5.7	2,499	10.5
Baby Boomers (aged 49 to 67)	35,780	25,568	71.5	24,105	1,463	5.7	10,212	28.5
Older Americans (aged 68 or older)	15,098	2,983	19.8	2,824	159.4	5.3	12,114	80.2
Women aged 16 or older	**127,124**	**72,722**	**57.2**	**67,577**	**5,146**	**7.1**	**54,401**	**42.8**
iGeneration (aged 16 to 18)	6,187	2,147	34.7	1,711	436	20.3	4,040	65.3
Millennials (aged 19 to 36)	38,020	26,497	69.7	24,186	2,309	8.7	11,523	30.3
Generation Xers (aged 37 to 48)	24,839	18,502	74.5	17,429	1,074	5.8	6,335	25.5
Baby Boomers (aged 49 to 67)	38,427	23,230	60.5	22,018	1,211	5.2	15,198	39.6
Older Americans (aged 68 or older)	19,651	2,347	11.9	2,231	116	5.0	17,304	88.1

Source: Bureau of Labor Statistics, Labor Force Statistics from the Current Population Survey, Internet site http://www.bls.gov/cps/tables.htm#empstat; calculations by New Strategist

Table 6.3 Employment Status of Generation X by Sex, 2013

(number and percent of people aged 16 or older, aged 37 to 48, and in age groups that include Generation X, by sex and employment status, 2013; numbers in thousands)

| | civilian noninstitutional population | civilian labor force | | | | | | |
| | | | | | unemployed | | not in labor force | |
		total	percent of population	employed	number	percent of labor force	number	percent of population
Total, aged 16 or older	**245,679**	**155,389**	**63.2%**	**143,929**	**11,460**	**7.4%**	**90,290**	**36.8%**
Gen Xers (aged 37 to 48)	**48,677**	**39,842**	**81.9**	**37,552**	**2,290**	**5.7**	**8,834**	**18.1**
Aged 35 to 39	19,149	15,730	82.1	14,752	977	6.2	3,419	17.9
Aged 40 to 44	20,464	16,833	82.3	15,898	935	5.6	3,631	17.7
Aged 45 to 49	20,904	16,964	81.2	16,003	961	5.7	3,940	18.8
Men aged 16 or older	**118,555**	**82,667**	**69.7**	**76,353**	**6,314**	**7.6**	**35,889**	**30.3**
Gen Xers (aged 37 to 48)	**23,837**	**21,338**	**89.5**	**20,121**	**1,217**	**5.7**	**2,499**	**10.5**
Aged 35 to 39	9,383	8,525	90.9	8,014	511	6.0	858	9.1
Aged 40 to 44	10,021	9,080	90.6	8,576	504	5.6	941	9.4
Aged 45 to 49	10,233	8,929	87.3	8,421	508	5.7	1,304	12.7
Women aged 16 or older	**127,124**	**72,722**	**57.2**	**67,577**	**5,146**	**7.1**	**54,401**	**42.8**
Gen Xers (aged 37 to 48)	**24,839**	**18,502**	**74.5**	**17,429**	**1,074**	**5.8**	**6,335**	**25.5**
Aged 35 to 39	9,766	7,205	73.8	6,738	467	6.5	2,561	26.2
Aged 40 to 44	10,443	7,752	74.2	7,321	431	5.6	2,690	25.8
Aged 45 to 49	10,671	8,034	75.3	7,582	453	5.6	2,636	24.7

Source: Bureau of Labor Statistics, Labor Force Statistics from the Current Population Survey, Internet site http://www.bls.gov/cps/tables.htm#empstat; calculations by New Strategist

Table 6.4 Labor Force Status by Generation, 2013

(number and percent distribution of people aged 16 or older by labor force status and by generation, 2013; numbers in thousands)

	in labor force	employed	unemployed	not in labor force
Total aged 16 or older	**155,389**	**143,929**	**11,460**	**90,290**
iGeneration (aged 16 to 18)	4,339	3,344	995	8,252
Millennials (aged 19 to 36)	57,080	51,857	5,224	18,375
Generation Xers (aged 37 to 48)	39,842	37,552	2,290	8,834
Baby Boomers (aged 49 to 67)	48,798	46,124	2,676	25,410
Older Americans (aged 68 or older)	5,330	5,054	277	29,417
PERCENT DISTRIBUTION BY GENERATION				
Total aged 16 or older	**100.0%**	**100.0%**	**100.0%**	**100.0%**
iGeneration (aged 16 to 18)	2.8	2.3	8.7	9.1
Millennials (aged 19 to 36)	36.7	36.0	45.6	20.4
Generation Xers (aged 37 to 48)	25.6	26.1	20.0	9.8
Baby Boomers (aged 49 to 67)	31.4	32.0	23.3	28.1
Older Americans (aged 68 or older)	3.4	3.5	2.4	32.6

Source: Bureau of Labor Statistics, Labor Force Statistics from the Current Population Survey, Internet site http://www.bls.gov/cps/ tables.htm#empstat; calculations by New Strategist

Among Gen X Men, Asians Have Highest Labor Force Participation Rate

Blacks have the highest unemployment rate.

Among men aged 37 to 48 in 2013 (Generation X), a substantial 90 percent were in the labor force. The labor force includes both the employed and the unemployed. Among Gen X men, the labor force participation rate varies little by age group.

The unemployment rate is significantly higher for Black and Hispanic men than for Asians or non-Hispanic Whites. Asian Gen X men had the lowest unemployment rate, at 4.3 percent in 2013. Non-Hispanic White Gen Xers had an unemployment rate of 4.9 percent, while the figure was a higher 6.3 percent among Hispanic Gen Xers and reached 9.8 percent among Black Gen Xers.

■ Among Gen X men in the labor force, only 61 percent are non-Hispanic White.

More than 80 percent of Gen X men are in the labor force

(percentage of men aged 37 to 48 in the labor force by race and Hispanic origin, 2013)

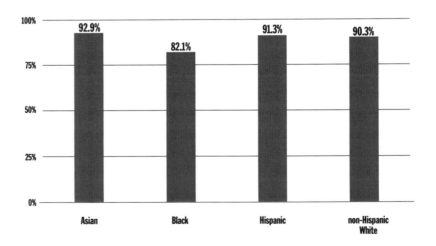

Table 6.5 Employment Status of Generation X Men by Race and Hispanic Origin, 2013

(number and percent of men aged 16 or older, aged 37 to 48, and in age groups that include Generation X, by race, Hispanic origin, and employment status, 2013; numbers in thousands)

	civilian noninstitutional population	civilian labor force					not in labor force	
					unemployed			
		total	percent of population	employed	number	percent of labor force	number	percent of population
Asian men aged 16 or older	6,225	4,547	73.0%	4,294	253	5.6%	1,678	27.0%
Asian Gen Xers (aged 37 to 48)	1,451	1,348	92.9	1,290	58	4.3	104	7.2
Aged 35 to 39	632	601	95.0	581	20	3.3	32	5.1
Aged 40 to 44	632	587	92.9	561	26	4.5	45	7.1
Aged 45 to 49	550	500	90.9	475	25	5.0	50	9.1
Black men aged 16 or older	13,747	8,733	63.5	7,497	1,236	14.2	5,014	36.5
Black Gen Xers (aged 37 to 48)	2,825	2,320	82.1	2,094	226	9.8	504	17.8
Aged 35 to 39	1,117	941	84.2	836	104	11.1	176	15.8
Aged 40 to 44	1,183	993	84.0	902	92	9.2	189	16.0
Aged 45 to 49	1,215	953	78.4	863	90	9.4	262	21.6
Hispanic men aged 16 or older	18,798	14,341	76.3	13,078	1,263	8.8	4,457	23.7
Hispanic Gen Xers (aged 37 to 48)	4,381	3,999	91.3	3,748	250	6.3	382	8.7
Aged 35 to 39	2,019	1,858	92.0	1,736	122	6.6	161	8.0
Aged 40 to 44	1,861	1,706	91.7	1,597	109	6.4	155	8.3
Aged 45 to 49	1,636	1,473	90.0	1,387	85	5.8	163	10.0
Non-Hispanic White men aged 16 or older	76,067	52,501	69.0	49,244	3,257	6.2	23,567	31.0
Non-Hispanic White Gen Xers (aged 37 to 48)	14,436	13,029	90.3	12,397	634	4.9	1,407	9.7
Aged 35 to 39	5,274	4,822	91.4	4,581	242	5.0	451	8.6
Aged 40 to 44	6,031	5,522	91.6	5,268	254	4.6	509	8.4
Aged 45 to 49	6,551	5,767	88.0	5,475	293	5.1	784	12.0

Note: Race is shown only for those who identify themselves as being of the race alone. People who selected more than one race are not included. Hispanics may be of any race. Non-Hispanic Whites are estimated by subtracting Hispanics from Whites.
Source: Bureau of Labor Statistics, Labor Force Statistics from the Current Population Survey, Internet site http://www.bls.gov/cps/ tables.htm#empstat; calculations by New Strategist

Among Gen X Women, Blacks Have Highest Labor Force Participation Rate

Hispanic women have the lowest labor force participation rate.

Among women aged 37 to 48 in 2013 (Generation X), a substantial 74 percent were in the labor force. The labor force includes both the employed and the unemployed. Among Gen X women, the labor force participation rate varies little by age group.

The unemployment rate is significantly higher for Black and Hispanic women than for Asians or non-Hispanic Whites. Asian Gen X women had the lowest unemployment rate, at 3.8 percent in 2013. Non-Hispanic White Gen Xers had an unemployment rate of 4.5 percent, while the figure was a higher 8.2 percent among Hispanic Gen Xers and reached 9.2 percent among Black Gen Xers.

■ Among Gen X women in the labor force, only 61 percent are non-Hispanic White.

The labor force participation rate of Gen X women varies by race and Hispanic origin

*(percentage of women aged 37 to 48 in the labor force
by race and Hispanic origin, 2013)*

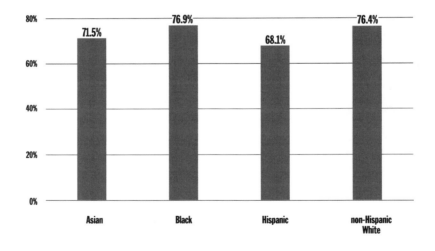

Table 6.6 Employment Status of Generation X Women by Race and Hispanic Origin, 2013

(number and percent of women aged 16 or older, aged 37 to 48, and in age groups that include Generation X, by race, Hispanic origin, and employment status, 2013; numbers in thousands)

| | civilian noninstitutional population | civilian labor force | | | | | | |
| | | total | percent of population | employed | unemployed | | not in labor force | |
					number	percent of labor force	number	percent of population
Asian women aged 16 or older	7,071	4,037	57.1%	3,842	195	4.8%	3,034	42.9%
Asian Gen Xers (aged 37 to 48)	1,652	1,182	71.5	1,136	45	3.8	469	28.4
Aged 35 to 39	739	517	70.0	495	22	4.3	222	30.0
Aged 40 to 44	708	503	71.0	486	16	3.3	205	29.0
Aged 45 to 49	626	461	73.7	441	20	4.4	164	26.2
Black women aged 16 or older	16,629	9,846	59.2	8,654	1,192	12.1	6,783	40.8
Black Gen Xers (aged 37 to 48)	3,448	2,653	76.9	2,409	245	9.2	793	23.0
Aged 35 to 39	1,386	1,089	78.6	976	113	10.4	296	21.4
Aged 40 to 44	1,447	1,120	77.5	1,016	104	9.3	326	22.5
Aged 45 to 49	1,462	1,099	75.2	1,009	91	8.2	362	24.8
Hispanic women aged 16 or older	18,719	10,430	55.7	9,437	994	9.5	8,289	44.3
Hispanic Gen Xers (aged 37 to 48)	4,286	2,920	68.1	2,681	239	8.2	1,366	31.9
Aged 35 to 39	1,952	1,302	66.7	1,184	118	9.0	650	33.3
Aged 40 to 44	1,831	1,228	67.1	1,135	93	7.5	603	32.9
Aged 45 to 49	1,605	1,138	70.9	1,044	94	8.2	466	29.0
Non-Hispanic White women aged 16 or older	80,748	46,141	57.1	43,620	2,519	5.5	34,608	42.9
Non-Hispanic White Gen Xers (aged 37 to 48)	14,665	11,204	76.4	10,703	500	4.5	3,461	23.6
Aged 35 to 39	5,349	4,070	76.1	3,876	193	4.7	1,279	23.9
Aged 40 to 44	6,111	4,659	76.2	4,456	203	4.4	1,452	23.8
Aged 45 to 49	6,681	5,129	76.8	4,902	227	4.4	1,552	23.2

Note: Race is shown only for those who identify themselves as being of the race alone. People who selected more than one race are not included. Hispanics may be of any race. Non-Hispanic Whites are estimated by subtracting Hispanics from Whites.
Source: Bureau of Labor Statistics, Labor Force Statistics from the Current Population Survey, Internet site http://www.bls.gov/cps/tables.htm#empstat; calculations by New Strategist

Most Generation X Couples Are Dual Earners

The husband is the sole support for only about one in four couples.

Dual incomes are by far the norm among married couples. Both husband and wife are in the labor force in 52 percent of the nation's couples. In another 23 percent, the husband is the only worker. Not far behind are the 18 percent of couples in which neither spouse is in the labor force. The wife is the sole worker in 8 percent of couples.

Sixty-eight percent of couples aged 37 to 48 (Gen Xers) are dual earners, while the husband is the only one in the labor force in another 25 percent. The dual-earner share varies little in the age groups that encompass Gen X.

■ Gen X couples are more likely than couples in any other generation to be dual-earner.

Few Generation X couples are supported solely by the husband

*(percent distribution of married couples aged 37 to 48 by
labor force status of husband and wife, 2013)*

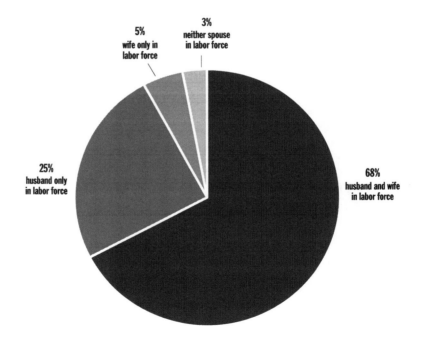

5%
wife only in
labor force

3%
neither spouse
in labor force

25%
husband only
in labor force

68%
husband and wife
in labor force

Table 6.7 Labor Force Status of Married-Couple Family Groups by Generation, 2013

(number and percent distribution of married-couple family groups by generation of reference person and labor force status of husband and wife, 2013; numbers in thousands)

	total	husband and wife in labor force	husband only in labor force	wife only in labor force	neither husband nor wife in labor force
Total married-couple family groups	**61,295**	**31,673**	**13,901**	**4,656**	**11,065**
Millennials (under age 37)	13,604	8,693	4,083	468	340
Generation Xers (aged 37 to 48)	14,367	9,699	3,558	680	428
Baby Boomers (aged 49 to 67)	23,112	12,161	4,929	2,458	3,562
Older Americans (aged 68 or older)	10,213	1,099	1,330	1,049	6,736
PERCENT DISTRIBUTION BY LABOR FORCE STATUS					
Total married-couple family groups	**100.0%**	**51.7%**	**22.7%**	**7.6%**	**18.1%**
Millennials (under age 37)	100.0	63.9	30.0	3.4	2.5
Generation Xers (aged 37 to 48)	100.0	67.5	24.8	4.7	3.0
Baby Boomers (aged 49 to 67)	100.0	52.6	21.3	10.6	15.4
Older Americans (aged 68 or older)	100.0	10.8	13.0	10.3	66.0

Source: Bureau of the Census, America's Families and Living Arrangements: 2013, Internet site http://www.census.gov/hhes/ families/data/cps2013.html; calculations by New Strategist

Table 6.8 Labor Force Status of Married-Couple Family Groups in Generation X, 2013

(number and percent distribution of total married-couple family groups, married-couple family groups headed by people aged 37 to 48, and married-couple family groups in age groups that include Generation X, by labor force status of husband and wife, 2013; numbers in thousands)

	total	husband and wife in labor force	husband only in labor force	wife only in labor force	neither husband nor wife in labor force
Total married-couple family groups	**61,295**	**31,673**	**13,901**	**4,656**	**11,065**
Generation Xers (aged 37 to 48)	**14,367**	**9,699**	**3,558**	**680**	**428**
Aged 35 to 39	5,749	3,734	1,656	232	126
Aged 40 to 44	6,585	4,494	1,687	259	145
Aged 45 to 54	13,705	9,279	3,022	821	582
PERCENT DISTRIBUTION BY LABOR FORCE STATUS					
Total married-couple family groups	**100.0%**	**51.7%**	**22.7%**	**7.6%**	**18.1%**
Generation Xers (aged 37 to 48)	**100.0**	**67.5**	**24.8**	**4.7**	**3.0**
Aged 35 to 39	100.0	65.0	28.8	4.0	2.2
Aged 40 to 44	100.0	68.2	25.6	3.9	2.2
Aged 45 to 54	100.0	67.7	22.1	6.0	4.2

Source: Bureau of the Census, America's Families and Living Arrangements: 2013, Internet site http://www.census.gov/hhes/ families/data/cps2013.html; calculations by New Strategist

Middle-Aged Workers Are the Majority of Managers

Nearly two out of three computer and information systems managers are aged 35 to 54.

Only 44 percent of all workers were aged 35 to 54 in 2013 (Generation X was aged 37 to 48 in that year), but the share varies by occupation. Workers in the broad 35-to-54 age group tend to be overrepresented in leadership positions and underrepresented in service jobs. The 35-to-54 age group accounts for 54 percent of chief executives, 56 percent of police, and 63 percent of computer and information systems managers.

The age groups that encompass Generation X account for a smaller share of workers in jobs requiring physical stamina. Only 36 percent of laborers are aged 35 to 54, for example, and an even smaller 26 percent of food prep workers and 21 percent of waiters and waitresses are in the age group.

■ Generation X was raised on computers, explaining their disproportionate presence in high-tech jobs.

People aged 35 to 54 account for a relatively large share of some occupations

(percent of workers in the 35-to-54 age group, by occupation, 2013)

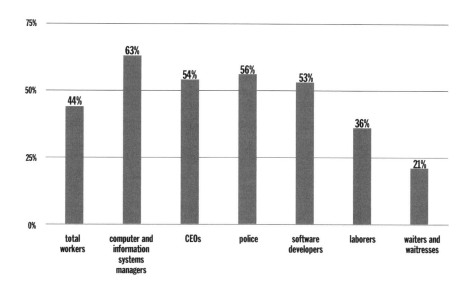

Table 6.9 Occupations of Workers Aged 35 to 54, 2013

(number of employed workers aged 16 or older, median age of workers, and number of workers aged 35 to 54, by occupation, 2013; numbers in thousands)

	total	median age	aged 35 to 54 total	35 to 44	45 to 54
TOTAL WORKERS	**143,929**	**42.4 yrs.**	**63,173**	**30,650**	**32,523**
Management and professional occupations	**54,712**	**44.4**	**26,199**	**12,993**	**13,206**
Management, business and financial operations	22,794	46.4	11,459	5,342	6,117
Management	16,037	47.5	8,263	3,762	4,501
Business and financial operations	6,757	43.6	3,196	1,580	1,616
Professional and related occupations	31,917	43.1	14,740	7,651	7,089
Computer and mathematical	3,980	41.1	2,089	1,143	946
Architecture and engineering	2,806	44.3	1,317	605	712
Life, physical, and social sciences	1,307	42.8	583	325	258
Community and social services	2,332	43.9	1,028	546	482
Legal	1,809	46.0	865	419	446
Education, training, and library	8,623	43.3	3,887	2,008	1,879
Arts, design, entertainment, sports, and media	2,879	40.5	1,131	594	537
Health care practitioner and technician	8,182	43.7	3,838	2,010	1,828
Service occupations	**25,929**	**37.9**	**9,886**	**4,956**	**4,930**
Health care support	3,537	39.1	1,434	726	708
Protective service	3,130	40.8	1,513	807	706
Food preparation and serving	8,209	29.4	2,245	1,188	1,057
Building and grounds cleaning and maintenance	5,661	44.1	2,600	1,220	1,380
Personal care and service	5,392	40.0	2,095	1,015	1,080
Sales and office occupations	**33,246**	**41.7**	**13,219**	**6,136**	**7,083**
Sales and related occupations	15,444	39.9	5,745	2,738	3,007
Office and administrative support	17,802	43.1	7,474	3,398	4,076
Natural resources, construction, and maintenance occupations	**13,058**	**41.9**	**6,199**	**3,014**	**3,185**
Farming, fishing, and forestry	964	37.2	354	189	165
Construction and extraction	7,130	41.6	3,445	1,716	1,729
Installation, maintenance, and repair	4,964	43.0	2,400	1,109	1,291
Production, transportation and material moving occupations	**16,984**	**43.1**	**7,670**	**3,551**	**4,119**
Production	8,275	43.0	3,842	1,783	2,059
Transportation and material moving	8,709	43.1	3,828	1,768	2,060

Source: Bureau of Labor Statistics, unpublished data from the 2013 Current Population Survey; calculations by New Strategist

Table 6.10 Share of Workers Aged 35 to 54, 2013

(percent of employed people aged 35 to 54 by occupation, 2013)

	total	aged 35 to 54		
		total	35 to 44	45 to 54
TOTAL WORKERS	**100.0%**	**43.9%**	**21.3%**	**22.6%**
Management and professional occupations	**100.0**	**47.9**	**23.7**	**24.1**
Management, business and financial operations	100.0	50.3	23.4	26.8
Management	100.0	51.5	23.5	28.1
Business and financial operations	100.0	47.3	23.4	23.9
Professional and related occupations	100.0	46.2	24.0	22.2
Computer and mathematical	100.0	52.5	28.7	23.8
Architecture and engineering	100.0	46.9	21.6	25.4
Life, physical, and social sciences	100.0	44.6	24.9	19.7
Community and social services	100.0	44.1	23.4	20.7
Legal	100.0	47.8	23.2	24.7
Education, training, and library	100.0	45.1	23.3	21.8
Arts, design, entertainment, sports, and media	100.0	39.3	20.6	18.7
Health care practitioner and technician	100.0	47.0	24.7	22.3
Service occupations	**100.0**	**38.1**	**19.1**	**19.0**
Health care support	100.0	40.5	20.5	20.0
Protective service	100.0	48.3	25.8	22.6
Food preparation and serving	100.0	27.3	14.5	12.9
Building and grounds cleaning and maintenance	100.0	45.9	21.6	24.4
Personal care and service	100.0	38.9	18.8	20.0
Sales and office occupations	**100.0**	**39.8**	**18.5**	**21.3**
Sales and related occupations	100.0	37.2	17.7	19.5
Office and administrative support	100.0	42.0	19.1	22.9
Natural resources, construction, and maintenance occupations	**100.0**	**47.5**	**23.1**	**24.4**
Farming, fishing, and forestry	100.0	36.7	19.6	17.1
Construction and extraction	100.0	48.3	24.1	24.2
Installation, maintenance, and repair	100.0	48.3	22.3	26.0
Production, transportation and material moving occupations	**100.0**	**45.2**	**20.9**	**24.3**
Production	100.0	46.4	21.5	24.9
Transportation and material moving	100.0	44.0	20.3	23.7

Source: Bureau of Labor Statistics, unpublished data from the 2013 Current Population Survey; calculations by New Strategist

Table 6.11 Distribution of Workers Aged 35 to 54 by Occupation, 2013

(percent distribution of total employed and employed aged 35 to 54, by occupation, 2013)

	total	aged 35 to 54 total	35 to 44	45 to 54
TOTAL WORKERS	**100.0%**	**100.0%**	**100.0%**	**100.0%**
Management and professional occupations	**38.0**	**41.5**	**42.4**	**40.6**
Management, business and financial operations	15.8	18.1	17.4	18.8
Management	11.1	13.1	12.3	13.8
Business and financial operations	4.7	5.1	5.2	5.0
Professional and related occupations	22.2	23.3	25.0	21.8
Computer and mathematical	2.8	3.3	3.7	2.9
Architecture and engineering	1.9	2.1	2.0	2.2
Life, physical, and social sciences	0.9	0.9	1.1	0.8
Community and social services	1.6	1.6	1.8	1.5
Legal	1.3	1.4	1.4	1.4
Education, training, and library	6.0	6.2	6.6	5.8
Arts, design, entertainment, sports, and media	2.0	1.8	1.9	1.7
Health care practitioner and technician	5.7	6.1	6.6	5.6
Service occupations	**18.0**	**15.6**	**16.2**	**15.2**
Health care support	2.5	2.3	2.4	2.2
Protective service	2.2	2.4	2.6	2.2
Food preparation and serving	5.7	3.6	3.9	3.3
Building and grounds cleaning and maintenance	3.9	4.1	4.0	4.2
Personal care and service	3.7	3.3	3.3	3.3
Sales and office occupations	**23.1**	**20.9**	**20.0**	**21.8**
Sales and related occupations	10.7	9.1	8.9	9.2
Office and administrative support	12.4	11.8	11.1	12.5
Natural resources, construction, and maintenance occupations	**9.1**	**9.8**	**9.8**	**9.8**
Farming, fishing, and forestry	0.7	0.6	0.6	0.5
Construction and extraction	5.0	5.5	5.6	5.3
Installation, maintenance, and repair	3.4	3.8	3.6	4.0
Production, transportation and material moving occupations	**11.8**	**12.1**	**11.6**	**12.7**
Production	5.7	6.1	5.8	6.3
Transportation and material moving	6.1	6.1	5.8	6.3

Source: Bureau of Labor Statistics, unpublished data from the 2013 Current Population Survey; calculations by New Strategist

Table 6.12 Workers Aged 35 to 54 by Detailed Occupation, 2013

(number of employed workers aged 16 or older, median age, and number aged 35 to 54 for detailed occupations with at least 500,000 workers, 2013; numbers in thousands)

	total workers	median age	aged 35 to 54 total	35 to 44	45 to 54
TOTAL WORKERS	**143,929**	**42.4 yrs.**	**63,173**	**30,650**	**32,523**
Chief executives	1,520	52.5	817	312	505
General and operations managers	1,075	45.6	620	283	337
Marketing and sales managers	907	42.8	490	249	241
Computer and information systems managers	602	44.3	381	199	182
Financial managers	1,218	43.8	624	296	328
Farmers, ranchers, and other agricultural managers	929	56.1	288	111	177
Construction managers	821	46.9	415	191	224
Education administrators	804	48.1	430	197	233
Food service managers	1,077	40.0	473	249	224
Medical and health services managers	585	48.3	309	147	162
Property, real estate, and community association managers	654	50.8	300	128	172
Human resources workers	584	42.2	291	158	133
Management analysts	811	47.2	371	168	203
Accountants and auditors	1,814	43.2	885	442	443
Computer systems analysts	534	41.6	277	152	125
Software developers, applications and systems software	1,103	40.6	580	320	260
Computer support specialists	517	40.1	232	125	107
Counselors	727	43.2	323	171	152
Social workers	727	41.4	345	195	150
Lawyers	1,092	47.1	537	279	258
Postsecondary teachers	1,313	45.7	503	255	248
Preschool and kindergarten teachers	695	39.6	303	160	143
Elementary and middle school teachers	3,038	43.0	1,521	838	683
Secondary school teachers	1,063	42.5	487	258	229
Teacher assistants	918	44.8	433	178	255
Designers	784	41.0	349	179	170
Physicians and surgeons	934	46.8	456	243	213
Registered nurses	2,892	44.2	1,377	710	667
Health practitioner support technologists and technicians	554	36.1	208	110	98
Licensed practical and licensed vocational nurses	558	43.8	284	143	141
Nursing, psychiatric, and home health aides	2,134	40.4	891	433	458
Police and sheriff's patrol officers	697	40.0	392	235	157
Security guards and gaming surveillance officers	858	41.0	313	142	171
First-line supervisors of food preparation and serving workers	581	33.8	204	106	98
Cooks	1,988	33.4	660	355	305
Food preparation workers	885	27.8	227	114	113
Waiters and waitresses	2,124	26.2	446	250	196
Janitors and building cleaners	2,275	46.8	971	410	561
Maids and housekeeping cleaners	1,401	44.3	706	342	364

	total workers	median age	aged 35 to 54		
			total	35 to 44	45 to 54
Grounds maintenance workers	1,327	38.5 yrs.	558	304	254
Hairdressers, hairstylists, and cosmetologists	786	40.3	324	175	149
Childcare workers	1,230	37.7	438	200	238
Personal care aides	1,242	44.2	498	212	286
First-line supervisors of retail sales workers	3,223	43.0	1,459	713	746
First-line supervisors of non-retail sales workers	1,188	46.4	633	286	347
Cashiers	3,254	26.7	698	355	343
Retail salespersons	3,230	34.7	922	446	476
Insurance sales agents	602	45.6	248	108	140
Sales representatives, wholesale and manufacturing	1,319	44.9	683	332	351
Real estate brokers and sales agents	769	50.7	335	140	195
First-line supervisors of office and administrative support workers	1,363	45.7	699	338	361
Bookkeeping, accounting, and auditing clerks	1,241	50.0	555	236	319
Customer service representatives	2,069	36.7	768	388	380
Receptionists and information clerks	1,326	37.6	440	206	234
Shipping, receiving, and traffic clerks	563	41.1	248	107	141
Stock clerks and order fillers	1,508	35.2	467	226	241
Secretaries and administrative assistants	2,922	48.5	1,364	543	821
Office clerks, general	1,184	42.7	484	227	257
Miscellaneous agricultural workers	679	33.7	220	122	98
First-line supervisors of construction trades and extraction workers	631	46.2	346	155	191
Carpenters	1,164	42.2	568	274	294
Construction laborers	1,536	38.8	668	346	322
Electricians	730	42.8	385	191	194
Painters, construction and maintenance	517	41.5	246	125	121
Pipelayers, plumbers, pipefitters, and steamfitters	553	41.6	267	130	137
Automotive service technicians and mechanics	863	39.4	409	194	215
First-line supervisors of production and operating workers	731	47.2	406	171	235
Miscellaneous assemblers and fabricators	1,013	41.6	465	235	230
Welding, soldering, and brazing workers	575	39.2	254	132	122
Inspectors, testers, sorters, samplers, and weighers	686	43.8	296	144	152
Bus drivers	582	52.7	260	99	161
Driver/sales workers and truck drivers	3,252	46.0	1,644	741	903
Industrial truck and tractor operators	557	40.0	246	118	128
Laborers and freight, stock, and material movers, hand	1,752	35.8	638	335	303

Source: Bureau of Labor Statistics, unpublished tables from the 2013 Current Population Survey; calculations by New Strategist

Table 6.13 Share of Workers Aged 35 to 54 by Detailed Occupation, 2013

(share of employed aged 35 to 54 by detailed occupations with at least 500,000 workers, 2013)

	total workers	aged 34 to 54		
		total	35 to 44	45 to 54
TOTAL WORKERS	**100.0%**	**43.9%**	**21.3%**	**22.6%**
Chief executives	100.0	53.8	20.5	33.2
General and operations managers	100.0	57.7	26.3	31.3
Marketing and sales managers	100.0	54.0	27.5	26.6
Computer and information systems managers	100.0	63.3	33.1	30.2
Financial managers	100.0	51.2	24.3	26.9
Farmers, ranchers, and other agricultural managers	100.0	31.0	11.9	19.1
Construction managers	100.0	50.5	23.3	27.3
Education administrators	100.0	53.5	24.5	29.0
Food service managers	100.0	43.9	23.1	20.8
Medical and health services managers	100.0	52.8	25.1	27.7
Property, real estate, and community association managers	100.0	45.9	19.6	26.3
Human resources workers	100.0	49.8	27.1	22.8
Management analysts	100.0	45.7	20.7	25.0
Accountants and auditors	100.0	48.8	24.4	24.4
Computer systems analysts	100.0	51.9	28.5	23.4
Software developers, applications and systems software	100.0	52.6	29.0	23.6
Computer support specialists	100.0	44.9	24.2	20.7
Counselors	100.0	44.4	23.5	20.9
Social workers	100.0	47.5	26.8	20.6
Lawyers	100.0	49.2	25.5	23.6
Postsecondary teachers	100.0	38.3	19.4	18.9
Preschool and kindergarten teachers	100.0	43.6	23.0	20.6
Elementary and middle school teachers	100.0	50.1	27.6	22.5
Secondary school teachers	100.0	45.8	24.3	21.5
Teacher assistants	100.0	47.2	19.4	27.8
Designers	100.0	44.5	22.8	21.7
Physicians and surgeons	100.0	48.8	26.0	22.8
Registered nurses	100.0	47.6	24.6	23.1
Health practitioner support technologists and technicians	100.0	37.5	19.9	17.7
Licensed practical and licensed vocational nurses	100.0	50.9	25.6	25.3
Nursing, psychiatric, and home health aides	100.0	41.8	20.3	21.5
Police and sheriff's patrol officers	100.0	56.2	33.7	22.5
Security guards and gaming surveillance officers	100.0	36.5	16.6	19.9
First-line supervisors of food preparation and serving workers	100.0	35.1	18.2	16.9
Cooks	100.0	33.2	17.9	15.3
Food preparation workers	100.0	25.6	12.9	12.8
Waiters and waitresses	100.0	21.0	11.8	9.2
Janitors and building cleaners	100.0	42.7	18.0	24.7
Maids and housekeeping cleaners	100.0	50.4	24.4	26.0

	total workers	aged 34 to 54		
		total	35 to 44	45 to 54
Grounds maintenance workers	100.0%	42.0%	22.9%	19.1%
Hairdressers, hairstylists, and cosmetologists	100.0	41.2	22.3	19.0
Childcare workers	100.0	35.6	16.3	19.3
Personal care aides	100.0	40.1	17.1	23.0
First-line supervisors of retail sales workers	100.0	45.3	22.1	23.1
First-line supervisors of non-retail sales workers	100.0	53.3	24.1	29.2
Cashiers	100.0	21.5	10.9	10.5
Retail salespersons	100.0	28.5	13.8	14.7
Insurance sales agents	100.0	41.2	17.9	23.3
Sales representatives, wholesale and manufacturing	100.0	51.8	25.2	26.6
Real estate brokers and sales agents	100.0	43.6	18.2	25.4
First-line supervisors of office and administrative support workers	100.0	51.3	24.8	26.5
Bookkeeping, accounting, and auditing clerks	100.0	44.7	19.0	25.7
Customer service representatives	100.0	37.1	18.8	18.4
Receptionists and information clerks	100.0	33.2	15.5	17.6
Shipping, receiving, and traffic clerks	100.0	44.0	19.0	25.0
Stock clerks and order fillers	100.0	31.0	15.0	16.0
Secretaries and administrative assistants	100.0	46.7	18.6	28.1
Office clerks, general	100.0	40.9	19.2	21.7
Miscellaneous agricultural workers	100.0	32.4	18.0	14.4
First-line supervisors of construction trades and extraction workers	100.0	54.8	24.6	30.3
Carpenters	100.0	48.8	23.5	25.3
Construction laborers	100.0	43.5	22.5	21.0
Electricians	100.0	52.7	26.2	26.6
Painters, construction and maintenance	100.0	47.6	24.2	23.4
Pipelayers, plumbers, pipefitters, and steamfitters	100.0	48.3	23.5	24.8
Automotive service technicians and mechanics	100.0	47.4	22.5	24.9
First-line supervisors of production and operating workers	100.0	55.5	23.4	32.1
Miscellaneous assemblers and fabricators	100.0	45.9	23.2	22.7
Welding, soldering, and brazing workers	100.0	44.2	23.0	21.2
Inspectors, testers, sorters, samplers, and weighers	100.0	43.1	21.0	22.2
Bus drivers	100.0	44.7	17.0	27.7
Driver/sales workers and truck drivers	100.0	50.6	22.8	27.8
Industrial truck and tractor operators	100.0	44.2	21.2	23.0
Laborers and freight, stock, and material movers, hand	100.0	36.4	19.1	17.3

Source: Bureau of Labor Statistics, unpublished tables from the 2013 Current Population Survey; calculations by New Strategist

Many Workers Have Part-Time Jobs

Nearly one in five workers aged 25 to 54 is a part-timer.

Among workers ranging in age from 25 to 54, a substantial 18 percent had a part-time job in 2013. Among those with a part-time job, many would prefer full-time employment. Among working men in the age group, 13 percent work part-time. Of those who do, more than one in three (37 percent) work part-time for economic reasons—meaning they want a full-time job. Among working women in the age group, 25 percent work part-time and 22 percent of the part-timers want a full-time position.

Among workers aged 55 or older, part-time work becomes more common—and more desired—for both men and women. Twenty-two percent of employed men and 34 percent of employed women aged 55 or older have a part-time job. Only 18 percent of the men and 14 percent of the women work part-time because they cannot find full-time work.

■ The percentage of workers who had a part-time job because they could not find full-time employment grew during the Great Recession.

Many part-time workers want full-time jobs

(percentage of employed men who work part-time but would prefer a full-time job, by age, 2013)

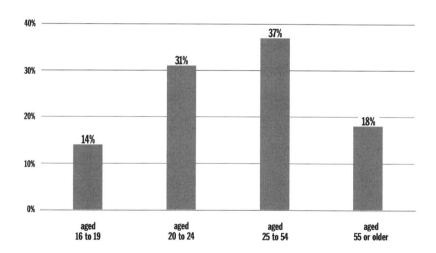

Table 6.14 Full-Time and Part-Time Workers by Age and Sex, 2013

(number and percent distribution of people aged 16 or older at work in nonagricultural industries by age, employment status, and sex, 2013; numbers in thousands)

	total			men			women		
	total	full-time	part-time	total	full-time	part-time	total	full-time	part-time
Total at work	**136,891**	**103,607**	**33,284**	**72,604**	**59,338**	**13,266**	**64,287**	**44,269**	**20,017**
Aged 16 to 19	4,209	1,048	3,161	2,028	602	1,426	2,181	446	1,735
Aged 20 to 24	13,103	7,751	5,352	6,746	4,363	2,383	6,357	3,388	2,969
Aged 25 to 54	90,260	73,589	16,672	48,422	42,348	6,075	41,838	31,241	10,597
Aged 55 or older	29,318	21,220	8,099	15,408	12,025	3,382	13,911	9,194	4,716
PERCENT DISTRIBUTION BY EMPLOYMENT STATUS									
Total at work	**100.0%**	**75.7%**	**24.3%**	**100.0%**	**81.7%**	**18.3%**	**100.0%**	**68.9%**	**31.1%**
Aged 16 to 19	100.0	24.9	75.1	100.0	29.7	70.3	100.0	20.4	79.6
Aged 20 to 24	100.0	59.2	40.8	100.0	64.7	35.3	100.0	53.3	46.7
Aged 25 to 54	100.0	81.5	18.5	100.0	87.5	12.5	100.0	74.7	25.3
Aged 55 or older	100.0	72.4	27.6	100.0	78.0	21.9	100.0	66.1	33.9
PERCENT DISTRIBUTION BY AGE									
Total at work	**100.0**	**100.0**	**100.0**	**100.0**	**100.0**	**100.0**	**100.0**	**100.0**	**100.0**
Aged 16 to 19	3.1	1.0	9.5	2.8	1.0	10.7	3.4	1.0	8.7
Aged 20 to 24	9.6	7.5	16.1	9.3	7.4	18.0	9.9	7.7	14.8
Aged 25 to 54	65.9	71.0	50.1	66.7	71.4	45.8	65.1	70.6	52.9
Aged 55 or older	21.4	20.5	24.3	21.2	20.3	25.5	21.6	20.8	23.6

Note: Part-time work is less than 35 hours per week. Part-time workers exclude those who worked less than 35 hours in the previous week because of vacation, holidays, child care problems, weather issues, and other temporary, noneconomic reasons. "Economic reasons" means a worker's hours have been reduced or worker cannot find full-time employment.
Source: Bureau of Labor Statistics, Labor Force Statistics from the Current Population Survey, Internet site http://www.bls.gov/cps/tables.htm#empstat; calculations by New Strategist

Table 6.15 Part-Time Workers by Sex, Age, and Reason, 2013

(total number of people aged 16 or older who work in nonagricultural industries part-time, and number and percent working part-time for economic reasons, by sex and age, 2013; numbers in thousands)

	total	working part-time for economic reasons	
		number	share of total
Men working part-time	**13,266**	**3,825**	**28.8%**
Aged 16 to 19	1,426	203	14.2
Aged 20 to 24	2,383	745	31.3
Aged 25 to 54	6,075	2,251	37.1
Aged 55 or older	3,382	625	18.5
Women working part-time	**20,017**	**3,998**	**20.0%**
Aged 16 to 19	1,735	204	11.8
Aged 20 to 24	2,969	748	25.2
Aged 25 to 54	10,597	2,378	22.4
Aged 55 or older	4,716	667	14.1

Note: Part-time work is less than 35 hours per week. Part-time workers exclude those who worked less than 35 hours in the previous week because of vacation, holidays, child care problems, weather issues, and other temporary, noneconomic reasons. "Economic reasons" means a worker's hours have been reduced or worker cannot find full-time employment.
Source: Bureau of Labor Statistics, Labor Force Statistics from the Current Population Survey, Internet site http://www.bls.gov/cps/tables.htm#empstat; calculations by New Strategist

Few Gen Xers Are Self-Employed

The oldest workers are most likely to be self-employed.

Despite plenty of media hype about America's entrepreneurial spirit, few Americans are self-employed. Only 6.5 percent of the nation's workers were self-employed in 2013. Men are more likely than women to be self-employed, 7.4 versus 5.5 percent. For both men and women, self-employment rises with age.

The oldest workers are most likely to be self-employed. Nineteen percent of working men and 14 percent of working women aged 65 or older work for themselves. One reason for the higher rate of self-employment among workers aged 65 or older is that they do not need to depend on an employer for health insurance. The 65-plus population has universal health insurance coverage through Medicare.

■ With the Affordable Care Act now guaranteeing access to health insurance for Americans under age 65, self-employment may rise among younger workers.

Self-employment rises with age

(percentage of workers aged 25 or older who are self-employed, by age, 2013)

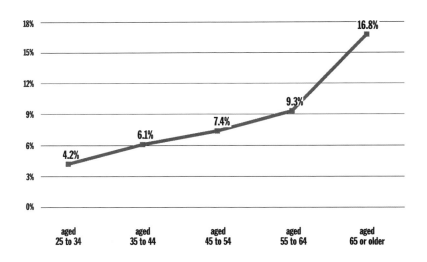

Table 6.16 Self-Employed Workers by Sex and Age, 2013

(number of employed workers aged 16 or older, number and percent who are self-employed, and percent distribution of self-employed, by age, 2013; numbers in thousands)

	total	self-employed		percent distribution of self-employed by age
		number	percent	
Total aged 16 or older	**143,929**	**9,408**	**6.5%**	**100.0%**
Aged 16 to 19	4,458	78	1.7	0.8
Aged 20 to 24	13,599	242	1.8	2.6
Aged 25 to 34	31,242	1,318	4.2	14.0
Aged 35 to 44	30,650	1,861	6.1	19.8
Aged 45 to 54	32,522	2,412	7.4	25.6
Aged 55 to 64	23,777	2,205	9.3	23.4
Aged 65 or older	7,681	1,292	16.8	13.7
Total men	**76,353**	**5,682**	**7.4**	**100.0**
Aged 16 to 19	2,177	53	2.4	0.9
Aged 20 to 24	7,013	157	2.2	2.8
Aged 25 to 34	16,907	776	4.6	13.7
Aged 35 to 44	16,590	1,092	6.6	19.2
Aged 45 to 54	17,033	1,445	8.5	25.4
Aged 55 to 64	12,376	1,346	10.9	23.7
Aged 65 or older	4,257	814	19.1	14.3
Total women	**67,577**	**3,726**	**5.5**	**100.0**
Aged 16 to 19	2,281	26	1.1	0.7
Aged 20 to 24	6,585	84	1.3	2.3
Aged 25 to 34	14,336	542	3.8	14.5
Aged 35 to 44	14,060	769	5.5	20.6
Aged 45 to 54	15,490	968	6.2	26.0
Aged 55 to 64	11,400	859	7.5	23.1
Aged 65 or older	3,424	477	13.9	12.8

Source: Bureau of Labor Statistics, Labor Force Statistics from the Current Population Survey, Internet site http://www.bls.gov/cps/ tables.htm#empstat; calculations by New Strategist

Job Tenure Has Been Stable for Men Aged 35 to 44

Long-term employment has fallen.

Job tenure (the median number of years a worker has been with his current employer) has been stable among men aged 35 to 44 over the past 12 years. In 2012, the average male worker aged 35 to 44 (Gen Xers were aged 36 to 47 in that year) had been with his current employer for 5.4 years, about the same as the 5.3 years of 2000. Among women in the age group, job tenure grew during the time period from 4.3 to 5.2 years.

Long-term employment has fallen among men ranging in age from 35 to 49 but has increased among women aged 35 to 44. Among men in the 35-to-49 age groups, the share that has been with their current employer for 10 or more years fell 3 to 4 percentage points between 2000 and 2012. Among women aged 35 to 44, the share with long-term jobs grew 2 percentage points during those years, while women aged 45 to 49 experienced a 3 percentage point decline in long-term employment.

■ The decline in long-term employment among men is due to job cuts in many sectors.

Fewer men aged 35 to 49 have long-term jobs

(percent of men aged 35 to 49 who have worked for their current employer for 10 or more years, by age, 2000 and 2012)

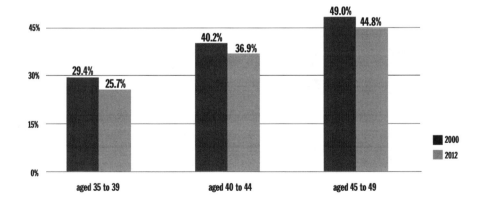

Table 6.17 Job Tenure by Sex and Age, 2000 to 2012

(median number of years workers aged 16 or older have been with their current employer by sex and age, 2000 to 2012; change in years, 2000–12)

	2012	2010	2000	change in years 2000–12
Total employed men	**4.7 yrs.**	**4.6 yrs.**	**3.8 yrs.**	**0.9 yrs.**
Aged 16 to 17	0.6	0.7	0.6	0.0
Aged 18 to 19	0.8	1.0	0.7	0.1
Aged 20 to 24	1.4	1.6	1.2	0.2
Aged 25 to 34	3.2	3.2	2.7	0.5
Aged 35 to 44	5.4	5.3	5.3	0.1
Aged 45 to 54	8.5	8.5	9.5	–1.0
Aged 55 to 64	10.7	10.4	10.2	0.5
Aged 65 or older	10.2	9.7	9.0	1.2
Total employed women	**4.6**	**4.2**	**3.3**	**1.3**
Aged 16 to 17	0.7	0.7	0.6	0.1
Aged 18 to 19	0.8	1.0	0.7	0.1
Aged 20 to 24	1.3	1.5	1.0	0.3
Aged 25 to 34	3.1	3.0	2.5	0.6
Aged 35 to 44	5.2	4.9	4.3	0.9
Aged 45 to 54	7.3	7.1	7.3	0.0
Aged 55 to 64	10.0	9.7	9.9	0.1
Aged 65 or older	10.5	10.1	9.7	0.8

Source: Bureau of Labor Statistics, Employee Tenure, Internet site http://www.bls.gov/news.release/tenure.toc.htm; calculations by New Strategist

Table 6.18 Long-Term Employment by Sex and Age, 2000 to 2012

(percent of employed wage and salary workers aged 25 or older who have been with their current employer for 10 or more years, by sex and age, 2000 to 2012; percentage point change in share, 2000–12)

	2012	2010	2000	percentage point change 2000–12
Total employed men	**34.6%**	**34.3%**	**33.4%**	**1.2**
Aged 25 to 29	2.6	3.1	3.0	−0.4
Aged 30 to 34	13.2	14.3	15.1	−1.9
Aged 35 to 39	25.7	27.2	29.4	−3.7
Aged 40 to 44	36.9	37.5	40.2	−3.3
Aged 45 to 49	44.8	43.7	49.0	−4.2
Aged 50 to 54	51.4	51.3	51.6	−0.2
Aged 55 to 59	55.7	53.6	53.7	2.0
Aged 60 to 64	56.2	56.8	52.4	3.8
Aged 65 or older	55.5	51.9	48.6	6.9
Total employed women	**32.8**	**31.9**	**29.5**	**3.3**
Aged 25 to 29	2.3	1.6	1.9	0.4
Aged 30 to 34	11.8	11.1	12.5	−0.7
Aged 35 to 39	24.7	24.0	22.3	2.4
Aged 40 to 44	33.2	32.9	31.2	2.0
Aged 45 to 49	38.3	38.0	41.4	−3.1
Aged 50 to 54	45.5	46.5	45.8	−0.3
Aged 55 to 59	52.6	51.2	52.5	0.1
Aged 60 to 64	54.0	52.2	53.6	0.4
Aged 65 or older	55.6	54.3	51.0	4.6

Source: Bureau of Labor Statistics, Employee Tenure, Internet site http://www.bls.gov/news.release/tenure.toc.htm; calculations by New Strategist

Most Minimum-Wage Workers Are Young Adults

Only 11 percent are aged 35 to 44.

Among the nation's 76 million workers who are paid hourly rates, 3.3 million (4 percent) made minimum wage or less in 2013, according to the Bureau of Labor Statistics. Nearly three out of four minimum-wage workers are under age 35, and half are under age 25. Only 11 percent are aged 35 to 44 (Gen Xers were aged 37 to 48 in 2013).

Among workers under age 25, a substantial 11 percent are paid minimum wage or less. The percentage is 4 percent among workers aged 25 to 34 and an even smaller 2.5 percent among those aged 35 to 44. The figure bottoms out at 1 percent among workers aged 55 to 64.

■ Younger workers are most likely to earn minimum wage or less because many are in entry-level jobs or are part-time workers.

Gen Xers account for few minimum-wage workers

(percent distribution of workers making minimum wage or less by age, 2013)

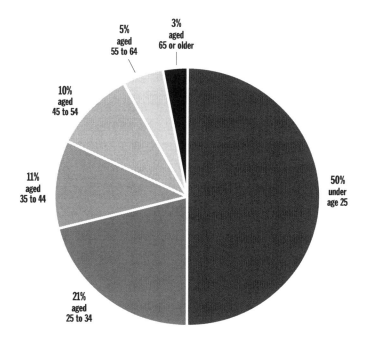

Table 6.19 Minimum-Wage Workers, 2013

(number and percent distribution of total workers paid hourly rates and those paid at or below the prevailing federal minimum wage, by age, 2013; numbers in thousands)

	total paid hourly rates	at or below minimum wage
Total aged 16 or older	**75,948**	**3,300**
Aged 16 to 24	15,110	1,663
Aged 25 to 34	17,607	703
Aged 35 to 44	14,195	354
Aged 45 to 54	15,097	314
Aged 55 to 64	10,713	154
Aged 65 or older	3,227	111
PERCENT DISTRIBUTION BY WAGE STATUS		
Total aged 16 or older	**100.0%**	**4.3%**
Aged 16 to 24	100.0	11.0
Aged 25 to 34	100.0	4.0
Aged 35 to 44	100.0	2.5
Aged 45 to 54	100.0	2.1
Aged 55 to 64	100.0	1.4
Aged 65 or older	100.0	3.4
PERCENT DISTRIBUTION BY AGE		
Total aged 16 or older	**100.0**	**100.0**
Aged 16 to 24	19.9	50.4
Aged 25 to 34	23.2	21.3
Aged 35 to 44	18.7	10.7
Aged 45 to 54	19.9	9.5
Aged 55 to 64	14.1	4.7
Aged 65 or older	4.2	3.4

Source: Bureau of Labor Statistics, Characteristics of Minimum Wage Workers: 2013, Internet site http://www.bls.gov/cps/minwage2013tbls.htm; calculations by New Strategist

Few of Today's Workers Are Represented by a Union

Only about one in seven Gen Xers is represented by a union.

Union representation has fallen sharply over the past few decades. In 2013, unions represented only 12 percent of wage and salary workers.

The percentage of workers who are represented by a union peaks in the 55-to-64 age group at 16 percent. Among 35-to-44-year-olds, unions represented a smaller 14 percent (Gen Xers were aged 37 to 48 in 2013). One reason for the decline in labor union representation is the shift from manufacturing to service jobs, with fewer service workers being unionized.

■ Union representation could rise among service workers as they demand better pay and benefits.

Few workers are represented by a union

(percentage of employed wage and salary workers who are represented by a union, by age, 2013)

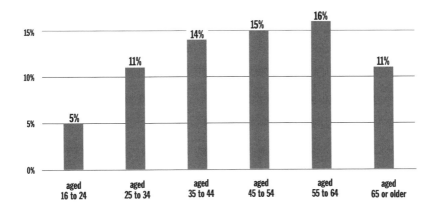

Table 6.20 Union Representation by Age, 2013

(number and percent of employed wage and salary workers aged 16 or older by age and union representation status, 2013; numbers in thousands)

	total employed	represented by a union	
		number	percent
Total aged 16 or older	**129,110**	**16,028**	**12.4%**
Aged 16 to 24	17,647	854	4.8
Aged 25 to 34	29,404	3,228	11.0
Aged 35 to 44	27,631	3,790	13.7
Aged 45 to 54	28,498	4,377	15.4
Aged 55 to 64	20,207	3,176	15.7
Aged 65 or older	5,723	603	10.5

Note: Workers represented by unions are either members of a labor union or similar employee association or workers who report no union affiliation but whose jobs are covered by a union or an employee association contract.
Source: Bureau of Labor Statistics, Labor Force Statistics from the Current Population Survey, Internet site http://www.bls.gov/cps/tables.htm#empstat; calculations by New Strategist

Number of Workers Aged 45 to 54 Will Decline

The number aged 55 or older will grow.

Between 2012 and 2022, the small Generation X will fill the 45-to-54 age group (Gen Xers will be aged 46 to 57 in 2022). Consequently, the number of workers in the age group will decline by more than 3 million. The 35-to-44 age group, in contrast, will fill with the larger Millennial generation. The number of workers aged 35 to 44 will expand by more than 2 million during the decade.

The number of older workers is projected to soar between 2012 and 2022 as Boomers enter the 65-plus age group and many postpone retirement. The Bureau of Labor Statistics projects a 66 percent increase in the number of male workers aged 65 or older during those years. The number of older female workers is projected to increase by an even larger 86 percent.

■ Generation X may find it difficult to advance on the job as Boomers, working well into their sixties, clog the ranks of upper management.

Number of workers aged 45 to 54 will decline

(percent change in number of workers aged 25 to 54, by sex and age, 2012–22)

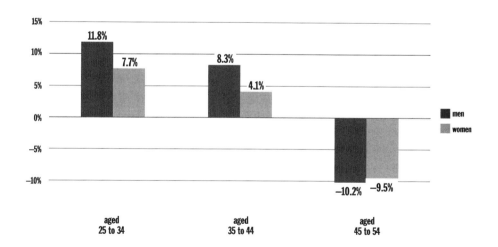

Table 6.21 Projections of the Labor Force by Sex and Age, 2012 and 2022

(number of people aged 16 or older in the civilian labor force by sex and age, 2012 and 2022; percent change, 2012–22; numbers in thousands)

	2012	2022	percent change
Total labor force	**154,975**	**163,450**	**5.5%**
Aged 16 to 19	5,823	4,473	−23.2
Aged 20 to 24	15,462	13,989	−9.5
Aged 25 to 34	33,465	36,786	9.9
Aged 35 to 44	32,734	34,810	6.3
Aged 45 to 54	35,054	31,600	−9.9
Aged 55 to 64	24,710	28,317	14.6
Aged 65 or older	7,727	13,476	74.4
Total men in labor force	**82,327**	**86,913**	**5.6**
Aged 16 to 19	2,940	2,316	−21.2
Aged 20 to 24	8,110	7,266	−10.4
Aged 25 to 34	18,083	20,212	11.8
Aged 35 to 44	17,607	19,061	8.3
Aged 45 to 54	18,363	16,495	−10.2
Aged 55 to 64	12,879	14,370	11.6
Aged 65 or older	4,345	7,193	65.5
Total women in labor force	**72,648**	**76,537**	**5.4**
Aged 16 to 19	2,883	2,156	−25.2
Aged 20 to 24	7,352	6,724	−8.5
Aged 25 to 34	15,382	16,574	7.7
Aged 35 to 44	15,127	15,749	4.1
Aged 45 to 54	16,692	15,104	−9.5
Aged 55 to 64	11,830	13,947	17.9
Aged 65 or older	3,382	6,284	85.8

Source: Bureau of Labor Statistics, Labor Force Projections to 2022: The Labor Force Participation Rate Continues to Fall, Monthly Labor Review, December 2013, Internet site http://www.bls.gov/opub/mlr/2013/article/labor-force-projections-to-2022-the-labor-force-participation-rate-continues-to-fall.htm; calculations by New Strategist

Table 6.22 Projections of Labor Force Participation by Sex and Age, 2012 and 2022

(percent of people aged 16 or older in the civilian labor force by sex and age, 2012 and 2022; percentage point change, 2012–22)

	2012	2022	percentage point change
Total labor force participation rate	**63.7%**	**61.6%**	**−2.1**
Men in labor force	**70.2**	**67.6**	**−2.6**
Aged 16 to 19	34.0	27.8	−6.2
Aged 20 to 24	74.5	69.9	−4.6
Aged 25 to 34	89.5	88.8	−0.7
Aged 35 to 44	90.7	90.4	−0.3
Aged 45 to 54	86.1	85.1	−1.0
Aged 55 to 59	78.0	77.8	−0.2
Aged 60 to 64	60.5	64.3	3.8
Aged 65 or older	23.6	27.2	3.6
Women in labor force	**57.7**	**56.0**	**−1.7**
Aged 16 to 19	34.6	26.7	−7.9
Aged 20 to 24	67.4	64.7	−2.7
Aged 25 to 34	74.1	73.4	−0.7
Aged 35 to 44	74.8	73.3	−1.5
Aged 45 to 54	74.7	74.9	0.2
Aged 55 to 59	67.3	73.3	6.0
Aged 60 to 64	50.4	55.6	5.2
Aged 65 or older	14.4	19.5	5.1

Source: Bureau of Labor Statistics, Labor Force Projections to 2022: The Labor Force Participation Rate Continues to Fall, Monthly Labor Review, December 2013, Internet site http://www.bls.gov/opub/mlr/2013/article/labor-force-projections-to-2022-the-labor-force-participation-rate-continues-to-fall.htm; calculations by New Strategist

7

Living Arrangements

■ Married couples head the 56 percent majority of Gen X households. (Gen Xers were aged 37 to 48 in 2013.)

■ Among Gen X households, non-Hispanic Whites head the 63 percent majority. But the figure varies by household type.

■ Gen Xers are in the crowded-nest lifestage. Households headed by people aged 35 to 49 average more than three people.

■ The 57 percent majority of Gen X households include children under age 18. The figure varies from a low of 51 percent among households headed by Blacks to a high of 67 percent among households headed by Asians.

■ Overall, 65 percent of Gen Xers are currently married. About half are in their first marriage and the rest are in their second or higher marriage.

Married Couples Head the Majority of Gen X Households

In middle age, Gen Xers are in the most stable lifestage.

As people age through their thirties and forties, life becomes more routine. Gen Xers (aged 37 to 48 in 2013) are now at the stage of life when work, marriage, children, and home are the central focus.

Overall, 56 percent of households headed by Gen Xers were married couples in 2013. Another 16 percent were families headed by women and 6 percent were families headed by men.

This is a lifestage when few women live by themselves. Among Gen X households, only 7 percent are women who live alone. More than 10 percent are men who live alone.

■ Gen X is in the lifestage when people look for stability as they raise their children.

Married couples dominate Gen X households

(percent distribution of households headed by people aged 37 to 48, by type, 2013)

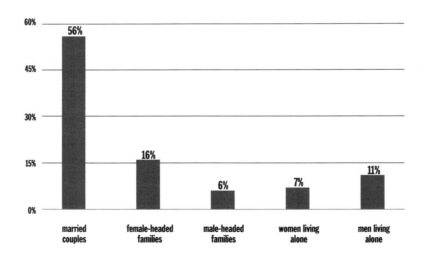

Table 7.1 Households by Generation and Household Type, 2013

(number and percent distribution of households by generation and household type, 2013; numbers in thousands)

	total	family households			female householder		male householder	
		married couple	female-headed	male-headed	total	living alone	total	living alone
Total households	**122,459**	**59,204**	**15,469**	**6,229**	**21,810**	**18,568**	**19,747**	**15,002**
Millennials (under age 37)	30,378	11,755	5,485	2,588	4,480	2,844	6,072	3,586
Generation Xers (aged 37 to 48)	26,514	14,879	4,179	1,506	2,307	1,862	3,641	2,814
Baby Boomers (aged 49 to 67)	43,003	23,036	4,152	1,626	7,452	6,552	6,738	5,606
Older Americans (aged 68 or older)	22,565	9,533	1,653	510	7,572	7,309	3,297	2,996
PERCENT DISTRIBUTION BY HOUSEHOLD TYPE								
Total households	**100.0%**	**48.3%**	**12.6%**	**5.1%**	**17.8%**	**15.2%**	**16.1%**	**12.3%**
Millennials (under age 37)	100.0	38.7	18.1	8.5	14.7	9.4	20.0	11.8
Generation Xers (aged 37 to 48)	100.0	56.1	15.8	5.7	8.7	7.0	13.7	10.6
Baby Boomers (aged 49 to 67)	100.0	53.6	9.7	3.8	17.3	15.2	15.7	13.0
Older Americans (aged 68 or older)	100.0	42.2	7.3	2.3	33.6	32.4	14.6	13.3
PERCENT DISTRIBUTION BY GENERATION OF HOUSEHOLDER								
Total households	**100.0**	**100.0**	**100.0**	**100.0**	**100.0**	**100.0**	**100.0**	**100.0**
Millennials (under age 37)	24.8	19.9	35.5	41.5	20.5	15.3	30.7	23.9
Generation Xers (aged 37 to 48)	21.7	25.1	27.0	24.2	10.6	10.0	18.4	18.8
Baby Boomers (aged 49 to 67)	35.1	38.9	26.8	26.1	34.2	35.3	34.1	37.4
Older Americans (aged 68 or older)	18.4	16.1	10.7	8.2	34.7	39.4	16.7	20.0

Source: Bureau of the Census, 2013 Current Population Survey, Internet site http://www.census.gov/hhes/www/cpstables/032013/ hhinc/toc.html; calculations by New Strategist

Table 7.2 Generation X Households by Age and Household Type, 2013

(number and percent distribution of total households, households headed by people aged 37 to 48, and in age groups that include Gen Xers, by household type, 2013; numbers in thousands)

	total	family households			female householder		male householder	
		married couple	female-headed	male-headed	total	living alone	total	living alone
Total households	122,459	59,204	15,469	6,229	21,810	18,568	19,747	15,002
Gen Xers (aged 37 to 48)	26,514	14,879	4,179	1,506	2,307	1,862	3,641	2,814
Aged 35 to 39	10,116	5,588	1,795	627	752	600	1,354	986
Aged 40 to 44	11,218	6,397	1,809	631	875	696	1,505	1,175
Aged 45 to 49	11,533	6,412	1,616	623	1,226	1,007	1,655	1,309
PERCENT DISTRIBUTION BY HOUSEHOLD TYPE								
Total households	100.0%	48.3%	12.6%	5.1%	17.8%	15.2%	16.1%	12.3%
Gen Xers (aged 37 to 48)	100.0	56.1	15.8	5.7	8.7	7.0	13.7	10.6
Aged 35 to 39	100.0	55.2	17.7	6.2	7.4	5.9	13.4	9.8
Aged 40 to 44	100.0	57.0	16.1	5.6	7.8	6.2	13.4	10.5
Aged 45 to 49	100.0	55.6	14.0	5.4	10.6	8.7	14.4	11.4

Source: Bureau of the Census, 2013 Current Population Survey, Internet site http://www.census.gov/hhes/www/cpstables/032013/hhinc/toc.html; calculations by New Strategist

Hispanics and Blacks Head Many Gen X Households

Non-Hispanic Whites head fewer than half of female-headed families.

Among all households headed by Gen Xers (aged 37 to 48 in 2013), non-Hispanic Whites head the 63 percent majority. But the figure varies greatly by type of household. Non-Hispanic Whites account for only 47 percent of Gen X female-headed families, for example, but they account for 67 percent of married couples.

Married couples dominate households headed by Asian Gen Xers, accounting for nearly 70 percent of the total. The figure is 60 percent among non-Hispanic Whites and 55 percent among Hispanics. Among households headed by Black Gen Xers, however, only 35 percent are married couples. A substantial 31 percent are female-headed families.

■ The non-Hispanic White share of households will continue to shrink as more diverse younger generation replace older people in the population.

One in three Gen X couples is Asian, Black, Hispanic, or another minority

(percent distribution of married couples aged 37 to 48 by race and Hispanic origin, 2013)

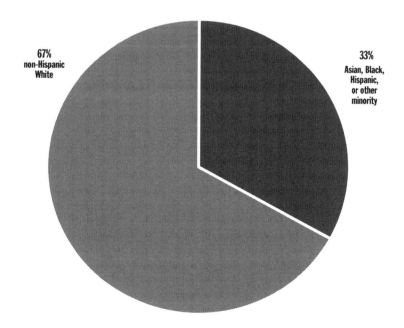

67%
non-Hispanic
White

33%
Asian, Black,
Hispanic,
or other
minority

Table 7.3 Generation X Households by Race, Hispanic Origin, and Household Type, 2013

(number and percent distribution of households headed by people aged 37 to 48, by household type, race, and Hispanic origin, 2013; numbers in thousands)

	total	family households			female householder		male householder	
		married couple	female-headed	male-headed	total	living alone	total	living alone
Total Generation X households (aged 37 to 48)	26,514	14,879	4,179	1,506	2,307	1,862	3,641	2,814
Asian	1,620	1,127	172	78	109	99	136	93
Black	3,949	1,390	1,214	275	516	454	554	458
Hispanic	4,253	2,346	888	310	209	176	499	354
Non-Hispanic White	16,680	9,968	1,945	847	1,464	1,140	2,455	1,911
PERCENT DISTRIBUTION BY HOUSEHOLD TYPE								
Total Generation X households (aged 37 to 48)	100.0%	56.1%	15.8%	5.7%	8.7%	7.0%	13.7%	10.6%
Asian	100.0	69.6	10.6	4.8	6.7	6.1	8.4	5.8
Black	100.0	35.2	30.7	7.0	13.1	11.5	14.0	11.6
Hispanic	100.0	55.2	20.9	7.3	4.9	4.1	11.7	8.3
Non-Hispanic White	100.0	59.8	11.7	5.1	8.8	6.8	14.7	11.5
PERCENT DISTRIBUTION BY RACE AND HISPANIC ORIGIN								
Total Generation X households (aged 37 to 48)	100.0	100.0	100.0	100.0	100.0	100.0	100.0	100.0
Asian	6.1	7.6	4.1	5.2	4.7	5.3	3.7	3.3
Black	14.9	9.3	29.1	18.2	22.4	24.4	15.2	16.3
Hispanic	16.0	15.8	21.3	20.6	9.1	9.4	13.7	12.6
Non-Hispanic White	62.9	67.0	46.6	56.2	63.5	61.2	67.4	67.9

Note: Numbers do not add to total because Asians and Blacks are those who identify themselves as being of the race alone and those who identify themselves as being of the race in combination with other races. Hispanics may be of any race. Non-Hispanic Whites are those who identify themselves as being White alone and not Hispanic.
Source: Bureau of the Census, 2013 Current Population Survey, Internet site http://www.census.gov/hhes/www/cpstables/032013/hhinc/toc.html; calculations by New Strategist

Table 7.4 Asian Households by Generation and Age Group, 2013

(number and percent distribution of total Asian households, households headed by Asians aged 37 to 48, and in age groups that include Gen Xers, by household type, 2013; numbers in thousands)

	total	family households			female householder		male householder	
		married couple	female-headed	male-headed	total	living alone	total	living alone
Total Asian households	**5,872**	**3,409**	**565**	**346**	**758**	**610**	**794**	**539**
Gen Xers (aged 37 to 48)	**1,620**	**1,127**	**172**	**78**	**109**	**99**	**136**	**93**
Aged 35 to 39	731	496	61	33	58	50	83	51
Aged 40 to 44	708	505	80	27	34	33	63	43
Aged 45 to 49	592	406	69	39	50	45	29	25
PERCENT DISTRIBUTION BY HOUSEHOLD TYPE								
Total Asian households	**100.0%**	**58.1%**	**9.6%**	**5.9%**	**12.9%**	**10.4%**	**13.5%**	**9.2%**
Gen Xers (aged 37 to 48)	**100.0**	**69.6**	**10.6**	**4.8**	**6.7**	**6.1**	**8.4**	**5.8**
Aged 35 to 39	100.0	67.8	8.4	4.5	8.0	6.8	11.3	7.0
Aged 40 to 44	100.0	71.3	11.3	3.8	4.8	4.7	8.9	6.1
Aged 45 to 49	100.0	68.6	11.6	6.6	8.4	7.6	4.8	4.2

Note: Asians are those who identify themselves as being of the race alone and those who identify themselves as being of the race in combination with other races.
Source: Bureau of the Census, 2013 Current Population Survey, Internet site http://www.census.gov/hhes/www/cpstables/032013/hhinc/toc.html; calculations by New Strategist

Table 7.5 Black Households by Generation and Age Group, 2013

(number and percent distribution of total Black households, households headed by Blacks aged 37 to 48, and in age groups that include Gen Xers, by household type, 2013; numbers in thousands)

	total	family households			female householder		male householder	
		married couple	female-headed	male-headed	total	living alone	total	living alone
Total Black households	**16,559**	**4,700**	**4,473**	**1,105**	**3,424**	**3,042**	**2,856**	**2,370**
Gen Xers (aged 37 to 48)	**3,949**	**1,390**	**1,214**	**275**	**516**	**454**	**554**	**458**
Aged 35 to 39	1,559	458	611	121	162	142	207	172
Aged 40 to 44	1,654	624	497	116	191	165	225	186
Aged 45 to 49	1,701	615	439	107	284	255	256	212
PERCENT DISTRIBUTION BY HOUSEHOLD TYPE								
Total Black households	**100.0%**	**28.4%**	**27.0%**	**6.7%**	**20.7%**	**18.4%**	**17.2%**	**14.3%**
Gen Xers (aged 37 to 48)	**100.0**	**35.2**	**30.7**	**7.0**	**13.1**	**11.5**	**14.0**	**11.6**
Aged 35 to 39	100.0	29.4	39.2	7.7	10.4	9.1	13.3	11.0
Aged 40 to 44	100.0	37.7	30.1	7.0	11.6	9.9	13.6	11.2
Aged 45 to 49	100.0	36.2	25.8	6.3	16.7	15.0	15.0	12.5

Note: Blacks are those who identify themselves as being of the race alone and those who identify themselves as being of the race in combination with other races.
Source: Bureau of the Census, 2013 Current Population Survey, Internet site http://www.census.gov/hhes/www/cpstables/032013/hhinc/toc.html; calculations by New Strategist

Table 7.6 Hispanic Households by Generation and Age Group, 2013

(number and percent distribution of total Hispanic households, households headed by Hispanics aged 37 to 48, and in age groups that include Gen Xers, by household type, 2013; numbers in thousands)

	total	family households			female householder		male householder	
		married couple	female-headed	male-headed	total	living alone	total	living alone
Total Hispanic households	**15,589**	**7,455**	**3,106**	**1,391**	**1,683**	**1,367**	**1,954**	**1,345**
Gen Xers (aged 37 to 48)	**4,253**	**2,346**	**888**	**310**	**209**	**176**	**499**	**354**
Aged 35 to 39	1,925	1,017	452	147	87	72	221	124
Aged 40 to 44	1,836	1,036	388	130	70	57	213	166
Aged 45 to 49	1,578	876	286	115	109	94	192	142
PERCENT DISTRIBUTION BY HOUSEHOLD TYPE								
Total Hispanic households	**100.0%**	**47.8%**	**19.9%**	**8.9%**	**10.8%**	**8.8%**	**12.5%**	**8.6%**
Gen Xers (aged 37 to 48)	**100.0**	**55.2**	**20.9**	**7.3**	**4.9**	**4.1**	**11.7**	**8.3**
Aged 35 to 39	100.0	52.8	23.5	7.6	4.5	3.7	11.5	6.4
Aged 40 to 44	100.0	56.4	21.1	7.1	3.8	3.1	11.6	9.0
Aged 45 to 49	100.0	55.5	18.1	7.3	6.9	6.0	12.2	9.0

Source: Bureau of the Census, 2013 Current Population Survey, Internet site http://www.census.gov/hhes/www/cpstables/032013/hhinc/toc.html; calculations by New Strategist

Table 7.7 Non-Hispanic White Households by Generation and Age Group, 2013

(number and percent distribution of total non-Hispanic White households, households headed by non-Hispanic Whites aged 37 to 48, and in age groups that include Gen Xers, by household type, 2013; numbers in thousands)

	total	family households			female householder		male householder	
		married couple	female-headed	male-headed	total	living alone	total	living alone
Total non-Hispanic White households	**83,792**	**43,299**	**7,317**	**3,388**	**15,833**	**13,476**	**13,955**	**10,609**
Gen Xers (aged 37 to 48)	**16,680**	**9,968**	**1,945**	**847**	**1,464**	**1,140**	**2,455**	**1,911**
Aged 35 to 39	5,928	3,610	700	333	447	345	837	627
Aged 40 to 44	7,015	4,218	862	362	571	440	1,002	779
Aged 45 to 49	7,635	4,480	829	356	781	617	1,189	945
PERCENT DISTRIBUTION BY HOUSEHOLD TYPE								
Total non-Hispanic White households	**100.0%**	**51.7%**	**8.7%**	**4.0%**	**18.9%**	**16.1%**	**16.7%**	**12.7%**
Gen Xers (aged 37 to 48)	**100.0**	**59.8**	**11.7**	**5.1**	**8.8**	**6.8**	**14.7**	**11.5**
Aged 35 to 39	100.0	60.9	11.8	5.6	7.5	5.8	14.1	10.6
Aged 40 to 44	100.0	60.1	12.3	5.2	8.1	6.3	14.3	11.1
Aged 45 to 49	100.0	58.7	10.9	4.7	10.2	8.1	15.6	12.4

Note: Non-Hispanic Whites are those who identify themselves as being White alone and not Hispanic.
Source: Bureau of the Census, 2013 Current Population Survey, Internet site http://www.census.gov/hhes/www/cpstables/032013/hhinc/toc.html; calculations by New Strategist

Gen X Households Are Crowded

Household size peaks in the 35-to-39 age group.

The average American household was home to 2.54 people in 2013. Household size peaks among householders aged 35 to 39, at 3.39 people. As householders age into their forties and fifties, the nest empties. Average household size falls below two in the 65-to-74 age group.

Householders ranging in age from 30 to 44 average more than one child per household, the figure peaking at 1.50 children in households headed by 35-to-39-year-olds. As people enter their late forties, the nest empties, and the average number of children per household falls below one.

■ The nest is emptying more slowly for Gen Xers because of the Great Recession.

The nest is fullest for householders aged 35 to 39

(average number of children under age 18 per household by selected age of householder, 2013)

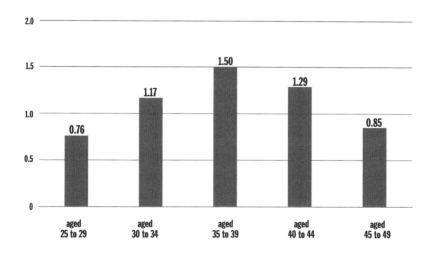

Table 7.8 Average Size of Household by Age of Householder, 2013

(number of households, average number of people per household, and average number of people under age 18 per household, by age of householder, 2013; number of households in thousands)

	number	average number of people	average number of people under age 18
Total households	**122,459**	**2.54**	**0.61**
Under age 20	740	3.05	0.90
Aged 20 to 24	5,574	2.41	0.48
Aged 25 to 29	9,251	2.59	0.76
Aged 30 to 34	10,767	2.98	1.17
Aged 35 to 39	10,116	3.39	1.50
Aged 40 to 44	11,218	3.32	1.29
Aged 45 to 49	11,533	3.01	0.85
Aged 50 to 54	12,535	2.66	0.45
Aged 55 to 59	12,217	2.30	0.23
Aged 60 to 64	10,585	2.06	0.14
Aged 65 to 74	15,349	1.91	0.09
Aged 75 or older	12,575	1.61	0.04

Source: Bureau of the Census, America's Families and Living Arrangements: 2013, Internet site http://www.census.gov/hhes/families/data/cps2013.html; calculations by New Strategist

Most Gen X Households Include Children under Age 18

Gen Xers are more likely than any other generation to have children at home.

The 57 percent majority of households headed by Generation Xers include children under age 18. (Gen Xers were aged 37 to 48 in 2013.) The figure rises to nearly two-thirds when children of any age are counted.

The majority of Gen X households, regardless of race or Hispanic origin, include children under age 18. The figure ranges from a low of 51 percent among Black Gen X households to a high of 67 percent among Asian Gen Xers.

■ The spending of Gen X households is determined by children's wants and needs.

Most Gen X households include children

(percent of households headed by people aged 37 to 48 with children under age 18 at home, by race and Hispanic origin, 2013)

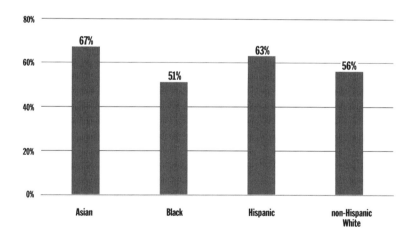

Table 7.9 Households by Generation, Age of Householder, and Presence of Children, 2013

(total number of households and number and percent with own children under age 18 or children of any age at home, by generation and age of householder, 2013; numbers in thousands)

	total	with own children under age 18		with own children, any age	
		number	percent	number	percent
Total households	**122,459**	**35,058**	**28.6%**	**48,105**	**39.3%**
Millennials (under age 37)	30,378	14,013	46.1	14,190	46.7
Generation Xers (aged 37 to 48)	26,514	15,158	57.2	17,312	65.3
Baby Boomers (aged 49 to 67)	42,249	5,645	13.4	13,691	32.4
Older Americans (aged 68 or older)	23,319	242	1.0	2,912	12.5
Total households	**122,459**	**35,058**	**28.6**	**48,105**	**39.3**
Under age 25	6,314	1,629	25.8	1,642	26.0
Aged 25 to 29	9,251	3,734	40.4	3,776	40.8
Aged 30 to 34	10,767	5,953	55.3	6,012	55.8
Aged 35 to 39	10,116	6,743	66.7	6,900	68.2
Aged 40 to 44	11,218	6,911	61.6	7,624	68.0
Aged 45 to 49	11,533	5,252	45.5	6,935	60.1
Aged 50 to 54	12,535	2,955	23.6	5,645	45.0
Aged 55 to 64	22,802	1,576	6.9	6,035	26.5
Aged 65 to 74	15,349	211	1.4	2,079	13.5
Aged 75 or older	12,575	94	0.7	1,457	11.6

Source: Bureau of the Census, America's Families and Living Arrangements: 2013, Internet site http://www.census.gov/hhes/families/data/cps2013.html; calculations by New Strategist

---

Table 7.10 Generation X Households with Children under Age 18 by Race and Hispanic Origin of Householder, 2013

(total number of households headed by people aged 37 to 48 and number and percent with own children under age 18, by race and Hispanic origin of householder, 2013; numbers in thousands)

	total	with own children under age 18	
		number	percent
Generation X households	**26,514**	**15,158**	**57.2%**
Asians	1,620	1,079	66.6
Blacks	3,949	2,009	50.9
Hispanics	4,253	2,699	63.4
Non-Hispanic Whites	16,680	9,380	56.2

Note: Numbers do not add to total because Asians and Blacks are those who identify themselves as being of the race alone and those who identify themselves as being of the race in combination with other races. Hispanics may be of any race. Non-Hispanic Whites are those who identify themselves as being White alone and not Hispanic.
Source: Bureau of the Census, America's Families and Living Arrangements: 2013, Internet site http://www.census.gov/hhes/families/data/cps2013.html; calculations by New Strategist

Table 7.11 Asian Households by Generation, Age of Householder, and Presence of Children, 2013

(total number of Asian households and number and percent with own children under age 18 or children of any age at home, by generation and age of householder, 2013; numbers in thousands)

	total	with own children under age 18		with own children, any age	
		number	percent	number	percent
Total Asian households	**5,872**	**2,076**	**35.4%**	**2,808**	**47.8%**
Millennials (under age 37)	1,943	595	30.6	604	31.1
Generation Xers (aged 37 to 48)	1,620	1,079	66.6	1,164	71.9
Baby Boomers (aged 49 to 67)	1,645	392	23.8	889	54.0
Older Americans (aged 68 or older)	662	11	1.7	152	23.0
Total Asian households	**5,872**	**2,076**	**35.4**	**2,808**	**47.8**
Under age 25	363	20	5.5	20	5.5
Aged 25 to 29	594	110	18.5	112	18.9
Aged 30 to 34	694	277	39.9	281	40.5
Aged 35 to 39	731	471	64.4	477	65.3
Aged 40 to 44	708	509	71.9	530	74.9
Aged 45 to 49	592	359	60.6	435	73.5
Aged 50 to 54	541	227	42.0	358	66.2
Aged 55 to 64	839	92	11.0	404	48.2
Aged 65 to 74	488	3	0.6	133	27.3
Aged 75 or older	320	9	2.8	59	18.4

Note: Asians are those who identify themselves as being of the race alone and those who identify themselves as being of the race in combination with other races.
Source: Bureau of the Census, America's Families and Living Arrangements: 2013, Internet site http://www.census.gov/hhes/ families/data/cps2013.html; calculations by New Strategist

Table 7.12 Black Households by Generation, Age of Householder, and Presence of Children, 2013

(total number of Black households and number and percent with own children under age 18 or children of any age at home, by generation and age of householder, 2013; numbers in thousands)

	total	with own children under age 18		with own children, any age	
		number	percent	number	percent
Total Black households	**16,559**	**5,256**	**31.7%**	**7,269**	**43.9%**
Millennials (under age 37)	5,003	2,523	50.4	2,561	51.2
Generation Xers (aged 37 to 48)	3,949	2,009	50.9	2,441	61.8
Baby Boomers (aged 49 to 67)	5,365	680	12.7	1,814	33.8
Older Americans (aged 68 or older)	2,242	46	2.0	453	20.2
Total Black households	**16,559**	**5,256**	**31.7**	**7,269**	**43.9**
Under age 25	1,217	398	32.7	400	32.9
Aged 25 to 29	1,500	729	48.6	738	49.2
Aged 30 to 34	1,663	982	59.1	997	60.0
Aged 35 to 39	1,559	1,036	66.5	1,065	68.3
Aged 40 to 44	1,654	906	54.8	1,080	65.3
Aged 45 to 49	1,701	602	35.4	902	53.0
Aged 50 to 54	1,705	349	20.5	718	42.1
Aged 55 to 64	2,825	199	7.0	810	28.7
Aged 65 to 74	1,650	38	2.3	352	21.3
Aged 75 or older	1,087	19	1.7	207	19.0

Note: Blacks are those who identify themselves as being of the race alone and those who identify themselves as being of the race in combination with other races.
Source: Bureau of the Census, America's Families and Living Arrangements: 2013, Internet site http://www.census.gov/hhes/families/data/cps2013.html; calculations by New Strategist

Table 7.13 Hispanic Households by Generation, Age of Householder, and Presence of Children, 2013

(total number of Hispanic households and number and percent with own children under age 18 or children of any age at home, by generation and age of householder, 2013; numbers in thousands)

	total	with own children under age 18		with own children, any age	
		number	percent	number	percent
Total Hispanic households	**15,589**	**6,953**	**44.6%**	**8,760**	**56.2%**
Millennials (under age 37)	5,775	3,386	58.6	3,421	59.2
Generation Xers (aged 37 to 48)	4,253	2,699	63.4	3,083	72.5
Baby Boomers (aged 49 to 67)	4,096	833	20.3	1,942	47.4
Older Americans (aged 68 or older)	1,465	34	2.3	314	21.4
Total Hispanic households	**15,589**	**6,953**	**44.6**	**8,760**	**56.2**
Under age 25	1,363	542	39.8	545	40.0
Aged 25 to 29	1,657	912	55.1	925	55.8
Aged 30 to 34	1,985	1,376	69.3	1,383	69.7
Aged 35 to 39	1,925	1,391	72.3	1,419	73.7
Aged 40 to 44	1,836	1,228	66.9	1,375	74.9
Aged 45 to 49	1,578	795	50.4	1,071	67.9
Aged 50 to 54	1,401	428	30.6	841	60.0
Aged 55 to 64	2,057	236	11.5	811	39.4
Aged 65 to 74	1,075	32	3.0	254	23.6
Aged 75 or older	712	12	1.7	136	19.1

Source: Bureau of the Census, America's Families and Living Arrangements: 2013, Internet site http://www.census.gov/hhes/ families/data/cps2013.html; calculations by New Strategist

Table 7.14 Non-Hispanic White Households by Generation, Age of Householder, and Presence of Children, 2013

(total number of non-Hispanic White households and number and percent with own children under age 18 or children of any age at home, by generation and age of householder, 2013; numbers in thousands)

	total	with own children under age 18		with own children, any age	
		number	percent	number	percent
Total non-Hispanic White households	**83,792**	**20,730**	**24.7%**	**29,107**	**34.7%**
Millennials (under age 37)	17,606	7,512	42.7	7,606	43.2
Generation Xers (aged 37 to 48)	16,680	9,380	56.2	10,622	63.7
Baby Boomers (aged 49 to 67)	30,712	3,687	12.0	8,915	29.0
Older Americans (aged 68 or older)	18,794	150	0.8	1,964	10.4
Total non-Hispanic White households	**83,792**	**20,730**	**24.7**	**29,107**	**34.7**
Under age 25	3,346	670	20.0	677	20.2
Aged 25 to 29	5,488	1,960	35.7	1,979	36.1
Aged 30 to 34	6,400	3,332	52.1	3,364	52.6
Aged 35 to 39	5,928	3,876	65.4	3,966	66.9
Aged 40 to 44	7,015	4,261	60.7	4,637	66.1
Aged 45 to 49	7,635	3,492	45.7	4,507	59.0
Aged 50 to 54	8,702	1,909	21.9	3,662	42.1
Aged 55 to 64	16,882	1,038	6.1	3,954	23.4
Aged 65 to 74	12,001	139	1.2	1,324	11.0
Aged 75 or older	10,393	53	0.5	1,037	10.0

Note: Non-Hispanic Whites are those who identify themselves as being White alone and not Hispanic.
Source: Bureau of the Census, America's Families and Living Arrangements: 2013, Internet site http://www.census.gov/hhes/ families/data/cps2013.html; calculations by New Strategist

Many Households Headed by Gen Xers Include Teenagers

Gen Xers head the majority of households with children aged 12 to 17.

Many Gen Xers (aged 37 to 48 in 2013) are the parents of teenagers. In fact, Gen X households account for the 54 percent majority of all households with 12-to-17-year-olds. Only 17 percent of Gen X households include preschoolers.

Twenty-one percent of Gen X households have one child at home and 23 percent have two children. Only 12 percent of Gen X households are home to three or more children.

■ As men and women have children, their priorities shift from pursuing their own wants and needs to meeting the needs of their children.

Children are the norm for Gen X households

(percent distribution of households headed by people aged 37 to 48 by presence of children under age 18, 2013)

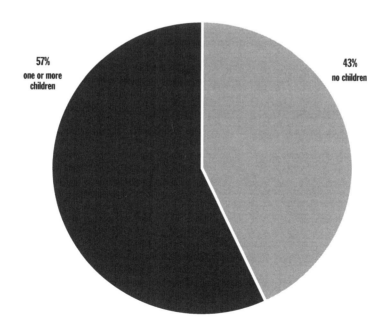

57%
one or more
children

43%
no children

Table 7.15 Generation X Households by Presence and Age of Children, 2013

(number and percent distribution of total households, households headed by people aged 37 to 48, and in age groups that include Generation Xers, by presence and age of own children at home, by age of children, 2013; numbers in thousands)

	total	Gen Xers (37 to 48)	35 to 39	40 to 44	45 to 49
Total households	**122,459**	**26,514**	**10,116**	**11,218**	**11,533**
With children of any age	**48,105**	**17,312**	**6,900**	**7,624**	**6,935**
Under age 25	41,660	17,030	6,890	7,559	6,671
Under age 18	35,058	15,158	6,743	6,911	5,252
Under age 12	25,623	10,266	5,628	4,830	2,574
Under age 6	15,046	4,412	3,334	1,892	649
Under age 1	2,743	498	460	177	56
Aged 12 to 17	16,708	9,070	3,058	4,142	3,866
PERCENT DISTRIBUTION BY AGE OF CHILD					
Total households	**100.0%**	**100.0%**	**100.0%**	**100.0%**	**100.0%**
With children of any age	**39.3**	**65.3**	**68.2**	**68.0**	**60.1**
Under age 25	34.0	64.2	68.1	67.4	57.8
Under age 18	28.6	57.2	66.7	61.6	45.5
Under age 12	20.9	38.7	55.6	43.1	22.3
Under age 6	12.3	16.6	33.0	16.9	5.6
Under age 1	2.2	1.9	4.5	1.6	0.5
Aged 12 to 17	13.6	34.2	30.2	36.9	33.5
PERCENT DISTRIBUTION BY AGE OF HOUSEHOLDER					
Total households	**100.0**	**21.7**	**8.3**	**9.2**	**9.4**
With children of any age	**100.0**	**36.0**	**14.3**	**15.8**	**14.4**
Under age 25	100.0	40.9	16.5	18.1	16.0
Under age 18	100.0	43.2	19.2	19.7	15.0
Under age 12	100.0	40.1	22.0	18.9	10.0
Under age 6	100.0	29.3	22.2	12.6	4.3
Under age 1	100.0	18.1	16.8	6.5	2.0
Aged 12 to 17	100.0	54.3	18.3	24.8	23.1

Source: Bureau of the Census, America's Families and Living Arrangements: 2013, Internet site http://www.census.gov/hhes/families/data/cps2013.html; calculations by New Strategist

Table 7.16 Generation X Households by Number of Children under Age 18, 2013

(number and percent distribution of total households, households headed by people aged 37 to 48, and in age groups that include Generation Xers, by number of own children under age 18 at home, by age of children, 2013; numbers in thousands)

	total	Gen Xers (37 to 48)	35 to 39	40 to 44	45 to 49
Total households	**122,459**	**26,514**	**10,116**	**11,218**	**11,533**
With children under age 18	**35,058**	**15,158**	**6,743**	**6,911**	**5,252**
One child	14,784	5,672	1,959	2,442	2,568
Two children	13,187	6,228	2,893	2,936	1,945
Three children	5,086	2,404	1,348	1,146	561
Four or more children	2,001	854	542	387	177
PERCENT DISTRIBUTION BY NUMBER OF CHILDREN					
Total households	**100.0%**	**100.0%**	**100.0%**	**100.0%**	**100.0%**
With children under age 18	**28.6**	**57.2**	**66.7**	**61.6**	**45.5**
One child	12.1	21.4	19.4	21.8	22.3
Two children	10.8	23.5	28.6	26.2	16.9
Three children	4.2	9.1	13.3	10.2	4.9
Four or more children	1.6	3.2	5.4	3.4	1.5
PERCENT DISTRIBUTION BY AGE OF HOUSEHOLDER					
Total households	**100.0**	**21.7**	**8.3**	**9.2**	**9.4**
With children under age 18	**100.0**	**43.2**	**19.2**	**19.7**	**15.0**
One child	100.0	38.4	13.3	16.5	17.4
Two children	100.0	47.2	21.9	22.3	14.7
Three children	100.0	47.3	26.5	22.5	11.0
Four or more children	100.0	42.7	27.1	19.3	8.8

Source: Bureau of the Census, America's Families and Living Arrangements: 2013, Internet site http://www.census.gov/hhes/ families/data/cps2013.html; calculations by New Strategist

Gen Xers Account for Few People Who Live Alone

Fewer than one in 10 Gen Xers lives alone.

Among the 34 million Americans who live alone, Gen Xers (aged 37 to 48 in 2013) account for only 14 percent. Millennials are a larger 19 percent of people who live alone, Boomers 36 percent, and Older Americans 31 percent.

The percentage of people who live alone is lowest among the nation's youngest adults (under age 25) at just 4 percent. The figure rises to about 10 percent among 25-to-34-year-olds, then falls to 8 percent in the 35-to-39 age group as people who have postponed marriage finally tie the knot. Living alone reaches a high of 36 percent among Americans aged 75 or older.

■ With advancing age, women are more likely than men to live alone.

Gen Xers are less likely than Boomers to live alone

(percent of people who live alone, by generation, 2013)

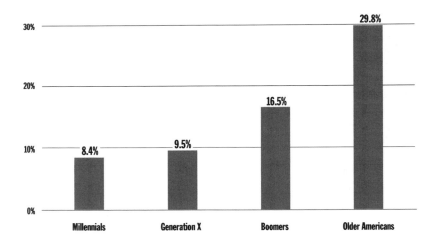

Table 7.17 People Who Live Alone by Generation and Age, 2013

(number of people aged 15 or older and number, percent, and percent distribution of people who live alone by generation and age, 2013; numbers in thousands)

		living alone		
	total	number	percent	percent distribution
Total people	250,023	33,570	13.4%	100.0%
Millennials (aged 19 to 36)	75,520	6,375	8.4	19.0
Generation Xers (aged 37 to 48)	49,037	4,676	9.5	13.9
Baby Boomers (aged 49 to 67)	73,752	12,158	16.5	36.2
Older Americans (aged 68 or older)	34,625	10,304	29.8	30.7
Total people	250,023	33,570	13.4	100.0
Aged 15 to 24	43,124	1,548	3.6	4.6
Aged 25 to 29	21,138	2,098	9.9	6.3
Aged 30 to 34	20,659	2,152	10.4	6.4
Aged 35 to 39	19,221	1,587	8.3	4.7
Aged 40 to 44	20,657	1,871	9.1	5.6
Aged 45 to 49	21,060	2,317	11.0	6.9
Aged 50 to 54	22,386	2,995	13.4	8.9
Aged 55 to 59	20,880	3,424	16.4	10.2
Aged 60 to 64	17,611	3,491	19.8	10.4
Aged 65 to 69	14,437	2,972	20.6	8.9
Aged 70 to 74	10,264	2,450	23.9	7.3
Aged 75 or older	18,585	6,665	35.9	19.9

Source: Bureau of the Census, 2013 Current Population Survey, Internet site http://www.census.gov/hhes/www/cpstables/032013/ hhinc/toc.html; calculations by New Strategist

Living Arrangements Differ by Generation

Most Gen Xers are a married-couple householder or spouse.

The living arrangements of generations differ depending on their lifestage. Many Millennials still live with their parents (29 percent of Millennial men and 23 percent of Millennial women). Among Generation Xers and Boomers, most men and women are married-couple householders or spouses. Among Older Americans, a substantial 37 percent of women live alone and only 42 percent are a married-couple householder or spouse.

Women marry at a younger age than men, and they are more likely than men to be widowed and live alone in old age. Among Gen Xers, women and men are equally likely to be a married-couple householder or spouse (61 percent). The proportion of Gen X men who are married and living with their spouse is likely to rise with age. For Gen X women, however, the proportion is likely to shrink. Only 42 percent of women aged 68 or older are married and living with their spouse.

■ The wants and needs of men and women diverge as lifestyle differences grow with age.

Women are less likely than men to live with a spouse in old age

(percent of Americans who are married and living with their spouse, by generation and sex, 2013)

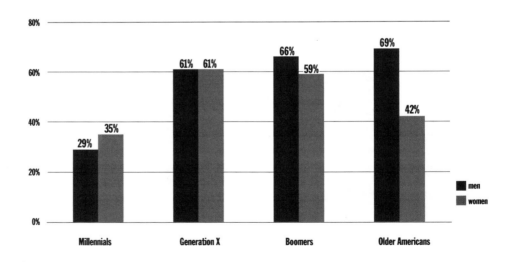

Table 7.18 Men by Living Arrangement and Generation, 2013

(number and percent distribution of men aged 15 or older by living arrangement and generation, 2013; numbers in thousands)

	total	iGeneration (under age 19)	Millennials (aged 19 to 36)	Generation X (aged 37 to 48)	Baby Boom (aged 49 to 67)	Older Americans (68 or older)
Total men	**121,067**	**8,668**	**37,719**	**24,087**	**34,781**	**15,812**
Householder	85,180	221	19,248	19,881	31,030	14,801
Married-couple householder or spouse	59,203	19	10,793	14,733	22,815	10,843
Other family householder	6,231	145	2,442	1,506	1,609	530
Living alone	15,001	25	3,561	2,814	5,509	3,092
Living with nonrelatives	4,745	33	2,451	828	1,096	337
Not a householder	35,885	8,448	18,472	4,204	3,750	1,011
Child of householder	20,834	7,535	11,061	1,452	755	31
Other relative of householder	6,667	696	2,698	1,036	1,522	715
In nonfamily household	8,384	217	4,713	1,716	1,473	265
PERCENT DISTRIBUTION BY LIVING ARRANGEMENT						
Total men	**100.0%**	**100.0%**	**100.0%**	**100.0%**	**100.0%**	**100.0%**
Householder	70.4	2.5	51.0	82.5	89.2	93.6
Married-couple householder or spouse	48.9	0.2	28.6	61.2	65.6	68.6
Other family householder	5.1	1.7	6.5	6.3	4.6	3.4
Living alone	12.4	0.3	9.4	11.7	15.8	19.6
Living with nonrelatives	3.9	0.4	6.5	3.4	3.2	2.1
Not a householder	29.6	97.5	49.0	17.5	10.8	6.4
Child of householder	17.2	86.9	29.3	6.0	2.2	0.2
Other relative of householder	5.5	8.0	7.2	4.3	4.4	4.5
In nonfamily household	6.9	2.5	12.5	7.1	4.2	1.7

Source: Bureau of the Census, America's Families and Living Arrangements: 2013, Internet site http://www.census.gov/hhes/ families/data/cps2013.html; calculations by New Strategist

Table 7.19 Women by Living Arrangement and Age, 2013

(number and percent distribution of women aged 15 or older by living arrangement and generation, 2013; numbers in thousands)

	total	iGeneration (under age 19)	Millennials (aged 19 to 36)	Generation X (aged 37 to 48)	Baby Boom (aged 49 to 67)	Older Americans (68 or older)
Total women	**128,827**	**8,351**	**37,803**	**24,932**	**37,695**	**20,047**
Householder	96,479	269	22,945	21,819	33,732	17,714
Married-couple householder or spouse	59,203	38	13,214	15,333	22,259	8,359
Other family householder	15,469	164	5,320	4,179	4,101	1,704
Living alone	18,566	33	2,812	1,862	6,492	7,369
Living with nonrelatives	3,241	34	1,599	445	880	283
Not a householder	32,339	8,081	14,854	3,111	3,962	2,331
Child of householder	17,394	7,095	8,777	936	554	33
Other relative of householder	7,891	737	1,886	988	2,238	2,043
In nonfamily household	7,054	250	4,191	1,188	1,170	255
PERCENT DISTRIBUTION BY LIVING ARRANGEMENT						
Total women	**100.0%**	**100.0%**	**100.0%**	**100.0%**	**100.0%**	**100.0%**
Householder	74.9	3.2	60.7	87.5	89.5	88.4
Married-couple householder or spouse	46.0	0.5	35.0	61.5	59.1	41.7
Other family householder	12.0	2.0	14.1	16.8	10.9	8.5
Living alone	14.4	0.4	7.4	7.5	17.2	36.8
Living with nonrelatives	2.5	0.4	4.2	1.8	2.3	1.4
Not a householder	25.1	96.8	39.3	12.5	10.5	11.6
Child of householder	13.5	85.0	23.2	3.8	1.5	0.2
Other relative of householder	6.1	8.8	5.0	4.0	5.9	10.2
In nonfamily household	5.5	3.0	11.1	4.8	3.1	1.3

Source: Bureau of the Census, America's Families and Living Arrangements: 2013, Internet site http://www.census.gov/hhes/ families/data/cps2013.html; calculations by New Strategist

Most Gen Xers Are Married

Some are in their second marriage, however.

Overall, 65 percent of Gen Xers (aged 37 to 48 in 2013) are married. A substantial 18 percent of Gen Xers have not yet married, and 13 percent are currently divorced.

Although nearly two-thirds of Gen Xers are currently married, many have married more than once. Among men aged 40 to 44, half are in their first marriage and 15 percent are in a second or higher marriage. Among women aged 40 to 44, the figures are nearly identical.

■ Cohabitation is a common living arrangement for Millennials and Gen Xers.

Most Gen Xers are married, but relationships are complex

(percent distribution of people aged 40 to 44 by current marital/union status, by sex, 2006–2010)

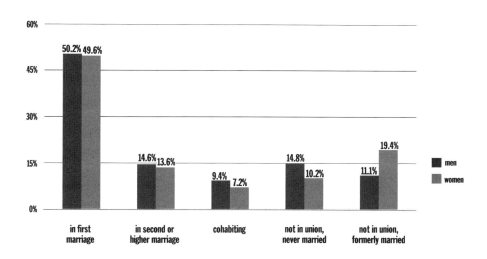

Table 7.20 Marital Status by Generation and Age, 2013

(number and percent distribution of people aged 15 or older by current marital status, by generation and age groups that include Gen Xers, 2013; numbers in thousands)

	total	never married	married	separated	divorced	widowed
Total people	**249,893**	**78,499**	**126,055**	**5,600**	**25,388**	**14,349**
Millennials (aged 19 to 36)	75,520	44,172	26,275	1,633	3,214	227
Generation Xers (aged 37 to 48)	49,018	8,657	31,856	1,634	6,365	507
Baby Boomers (aged 49 to 67)	72,476	7,411	47,599	1,851	12,011	3,603
Older Americans (aged 68 or older)	35,859	1,540	20,189	368	3,762	10,002
PERCENT DISTRIBUTION BY MARITAL STATUS AND GENERATION						
Total people	**100.0%**	**31.4%**	**50.4%**	**2.2%**	**10.2%**	**5.7%**
Millennials (under age 37)	100.0	58.5	34.8	2.2	4.3	0.3
Generation Xers (aged 37 to 48)	100.0	17.7	65.0	3.3	13.0	1.0
Baby Boomers (aged 49 to 67)	100.0	10.2	65.7	2.6	16.6	5.0
Older Americans (aged 68 or older)	100.0	4.3	56.3	1.0	10.5	27.9
PERCENT DISTRIBUTION BY MARITAL STATUS AND AGE						
Total people	**100.0**	**31.4**	**50.5**	**2.2**	**10.2**	**5.7**
Generation Xers (aged 37 to 48)	**100.0**	**17.7**	**65.0**	**3.3**	**13.0**	**1.0**
Aged 35 to 39	100.0	23.4	62.8	3.3	9.8	0.6
Aged 40 to 44	100.0	17.5	65.5	3.3	12.7	1.0
Aged 45 to 49	100.0	14.0	65.8	3.4	15.5	1.4

Source: Bureau of the Census, America's Families and Living Arrangements: 2013, Internet site http://www.census.gov/hhes/families/data/cps2013.html; calculations by New Strategist

Table 7.21 Marital Status of Men by Generation and Age, 2013

(number and percent distribution of men aged 15 or older by current marital status, by generation and age groups that include Gen Xers, 2013; numbers in thousands)

	total	never married	married	separated	divorced	widowed
Total men	**121,067**	**41,620**	**62,934**	**2,435**	**10,954**	**3,124**
Millennials (aged 19 to 36)	37,719	23,766	11,846	677	1,371	60
Generation Xers (aged 37 to 48)	24,087	4,742	15,619	707	2,881	136
Baby Boomers (aged 49 to 67)	34,781	3,881	24,034	830	5,228	807
Older Americans (aged 68 or older)	15,812	701	11,387	159	1,454	2,111
PERCENT DISTRIBUTION BY MARITAL STATUS AND GENERATION						
Total men	**100.0%**	**34.4%**	**52.0%**	**2.0%**	**9.0%**	**2.6%**
Millennials (aged 19 to 36)	100.0	63.0	31.4	1.8	3.6	0.2
Generation Xers (aged 37 to 48)	100.0	19.7	64.8	2.9	12.0	0.6
Baby Boomers (aged 49 to 67)	100.0	11.2	69.1	2.4	15.0	2.3
Older Americans (aged 68 or older)	100.0	4.4	72.0	1.0	9.2	13.4
PERCENT DISTRIBUTION BY MARITAL STATUS AND AGE						
Total men	**100.0**	**34.4**	**52.0**	**2.0**	**9.0**	**2.6**
Generation Xers (aged 37 to 48)	**100.0**	**19.7**	**64.8**	**2.9**	**12.0**	**0.6**
Aged 35 to 39	100.0	25.9	62.4	2.7	8.7	0.3
Aged 40 to 44	100.0	19.6	65.3	3.0	11.5	0.5
Aged 45 to 49	100.0	15.5	65.9	3.0	14.7	0.8

Source: Bureau of the Census, America's Families and Living Arrangements: 2013, Internet site http://www.census.gov/hhes/families/data/cps2013.html; calculations by New Strategist

Table 7.22 Marital Status of Women by Generation and Age, 2013

(number and percent distribution of women aged 15 or older by current marital status, by generation and age groups that include Gen Xers, 2013; numbers in thousands)

	total	never married	married	separated	divorced	widowed
Total women	**128,826**	**36,879**	**63,122**	**3,165**	**14,434**	**11,225**
Millennials (aged 19 to 36)	37,803	20,407	14,430	957	1,842	167
Generation Xers (aged 37 to 48)	24,932	3,916	16,238	927	3,482	369
Baby Boomers (aged 49 to 67)	37,695	3,532	23,565	1,021	6,783	2,795
Older Americans (aged 68 or older)	20,047	838	8,802	209	2,307	7,891

PERCENT DISTRIBUTION BY MARITAL STATUS AND GENERATION

	total	never married	married	separated	divorced	widowed
Total women	**100.0%**	**28.6%**	**49.0%**	**2.5%**	**11.2%**	**8.7%**
Millennials (aged 19 to 36)	100.0	54.0	38.2	2.5	4.9	0.4
Generation Xers (aged 37 to 48)	100.0	15.7	65.1	3.7	14.0	1.5
Baby Boomers (aged 49 to 67)	100.0	9.4	62.5	2.7	18.0	7.4
Older Americans (aged 68 or older)	100.0	4.2	43.9	1.0	11.5	39.4

PERCENT DISTRIBUTION BY MARITAL STATUS AND AGE

	total	never married	married	separated	divorced	widowed
Total women	**100.0**	**28.6**	**49.0**	**2.5**	**11.2**	**8.7**
Generation Xers (aged 37 to 48)	**100.0**	**15.7**	**65.1**	**3.7**	**14.0**	**1.5**
Aged 35 to 39	100.0	21.1	63.2	3.8	10.9	0.9
Aged 40 to 44	100.0	15.4	65.7	3.7	13.8	1.4
Aged 45 to 49	100.0	12.4	65.7	3.7	16.2	1.9

Source: Bureau of the Census, America's Families and Living Arrangements: 2013, Internet site http://www.census.gov/hhes/ families/data/cps2013.html; calculations by New Strategist

Table 7.23 Current Marital Status of Men, 2006–2010

(total number of men aged 15 to 44, and percent distribution by current marital status, by selected characteristics, 2006–2010; numbers in thousands)

| | total | | in a union | | | | not in a union | |
	number	percent	total	first marriage	second or higher marriage	cohabiting	never married	formerly married
Total men aged 15 to 44	**62,128**	**100.0%**	**49.8%**	**32.8%**	**4.8%**	**12.2%**	**45.0%**	**5.2%**
Aged 15 to 19	10,816	100.0	2.6	0.3	0.0	2.3	97.3	–
Aged 20 to 24	10,394	100.0	26.3	11.3	–	15.0	72.6	0.8
Aged 25 to 29	10,758	100.0	53.7	32.8	1.4	19.5	43.1	3.1
Aged 30 to 34	9,228	100.0	71.1	50.9	5.2	15.0	22.0	7.0
Aged 35 to 39	10,405	100.0	74.3	54.1	7.9	12.3	16.0	9.7
Aged 40 to 44	10,526	100.0	74.2	50.2	14.6	9.4	14.8	11.1
Number of biologial children								
None	34,307	100.0	23.5	13.3	0.8	9.4	74.1	2.4
One or more children	27,821	100.0	82.1	56.7	9.8	15.6	9.1	8.7
Race and Hispanic origin								
Asian	2,406	100.0	50.0	44.7	1.9	3.4	49.4	0.7
Black	7,341	100.0	39.7	24.2	2.7	12.8	55.1	5.2
Hispanic	11,847	100.0	52.5	31.7	3.2	17.6	42.0	5.4
Non-Hispanic White	37,283	100.0	50.5	34.3	5.9	10.3	44.0	5.6
Education								
Not a high school graduate	9,004	100.0	70.1	37.7	5.8	26.6	23.3	6.7
High school graduate or GED	12,068	100.0	61.5	40.6	8.3	12.6	28.6	9.9
Some college, no degree	13,206	100.0	59.1	37.8	7.2	14.1	34.7	6.3
Bachelor's degree	8,924	100.0	62.3	48.6	4.1	9.6	32.9	4.7
Master's degree or more	3,857	100.0	74.9	65.7	4.2	5.0	20.7	4.3

Note: Asians and Blacks are those who identify themselves as being of the race alone. Education categories include only people aged 22 to 44. "–" means sample is too small to make a reliable estimate.
Source: National Center for Health Statistics, First Marriages in the United States: Data from the 2006–2010 National Survey of Family Growth, National Health Statistics Reports, No. 49, 2012; Internet site http://www.cdc.gov/nchs/nsfg.htm

Table 7.24 Current Marital Status of Women, 2006–2010

(total number of women aged 15 to 44, and percent distribution by current marital status, by selected characteristics, 2006–2010; numbers in thousands)

| | total | | in a union | | | | not in a union | |
	number	percent	total	first marriage	second or higher marriage	cohabiting	never married	formerly married
Total women aged 15 to 44	**61,755**	**100.0 %**	**52.7%**	**36.4%**	**5.1%**	**11.2%**	**38.2%**	**9.2%**
Aged 15 to 19	10,478	100.0	5.9	1.1	0.0	4.8	94.1	0.0
Aged 20 to 24	10,365	100.0	36.0	17.3	–	18.7	60.8	2.9
Aged 25 to 29	10,535	100.0	61.3	42.3	2.2	16.8	31.3	7.4
Aged 30 to 34	9,188	100.0	71.4	53.7	5.6	12.1	18.1	10.5
Aged 35 to 39	10,538	100.0	72.4	55.9	8.7	7.8	13.0	14.6
Aged 40 to 44	10,652	100.0	70.4	49.6	13.6	7.2	10.2	19.4
Number of biologial children								
None	27,401	100.0	27.6	17.0	1.3	9.3	69.1	3.2
One or more births	34,353	100.0	72.6	51.8	8.1	12.7	13.5	13.9
Race and Hispanic origin								
Asian	2,456	100.0	56.2	48.5	4.2	3.5	38.7	5.2
Black	8,451	100.0	33.3	21.3	2.7	9.3	55.1	11.6
Hispanic	10,474	100.0	55.2	35.9	4.2	15.1	35.5	9.3
Non-Hispanic White	37,384	100.0	56.8	40.2	5.9	10.7	34.3	8.9
Education								
Not a high school graduate	6,844	100.0	64.5	36.6	7.7	20.2	19.1	16.5
High school graduate or GED	11,578	100.0	64.2	39.5	9.2	15.5	20.3	15.6
Some college, no degree	13,702	100.0	61.1	42.1	7.4	11.6	26.4	12.6
Bachelor's degree	11,024	100.0	68.4	58.3	3.3	6.8	25.5	6.1
Master's degree or more	4,059	100.0	72.9	63.0	4.4	5.5	20.1	7.0

Note: Asians and Blacks are those who identify themselves as being of the race alone. Education categories include only people aged 22 to 44. "–" means sample is too small to make a reliable estimate.
Source: National Center for Health Statistics, First Marriages in the United States: Data from the 2006–2010 National Survey of Family Growth, National Health Statistics Reports, No. 49, 2012; Internet site http://www.cdc.gov/nchs/nsfg.htm

8

Population

■ Generation X numbers 49 million, a figure that includes all those born between 1965 and 1976 (aged 37 to 48 in 2013). Generation Xers account for 16 percent of the population.

■ Sixty-one percent of Generation Xers are non-Hispanic White. Eighteen percent of Gen Xers are Hispanic, 14 percent are Black, and 7 percent are Asian.

■ Twenty-two percent of 35-to-44-year-olds were born in another country—much greater than the 13 percent of all U.S. residents who are foreign-born.

■ The Gen X share of state populations ranges from a high of 16.7 percent in New Jersey and Georgia to a low of 13.4 percent in North Dakota.

■ With Gen Xers in middle age, most go to the polls in presidential elections. The 57 percent majority of American citizens aged 25 to 44 voted in 2012.

Generation X Is Sandwiched between Larger Generations

Age groups shrink when Generation X moves in.

Generation X numbers 49 million, a figure that includes all those born between 1965 and 1976 (aged 37 to 48 in 2013). Generation Xers account for 16 percent of the total population. They are surrounded by the two largest generations: Boomers (24 percent of the population) and Millennials (25 percent).

As Generation X moves through the age structure, age groups shrink. Between 2010 and 2013, the number of 45-to-49-year-olds fell by 6 percent as Generation Xers replaced Boomers in the age group. The number of 35-to-44-year-olds also fell during those years.

■ Generation X may be relatively small, but the cohort accounts for a large share of the nation's parents and workers.

Generation X is smaller than most other generations

(number of people by generation, 2013)

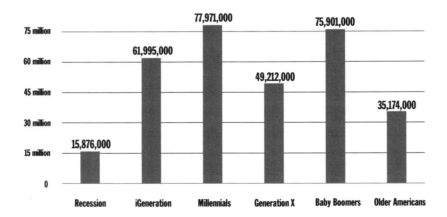

Table 8.1 Population by Age and Generation, 2013

(number and percent distribution of people by age and generation, 2013; numbers in thousands)

	number	percent distribution
Total people	**316,129**	**100.0%**
Under age 5	19,868	6.3
Aged 5 to 9	20,571	6.5
Aged 10 to 14	20,650	6.5
Aged 15 to 19	21,159	6.7
Aged 20 to 24	22,795	7.2
Aged 25 to 29	21,580	6.8
Aged 30 to 34	21,264	6.7
Aged 35 to 39	19,604	6.2
Aged 40 to 44	20,849	6.6
Aged 45 to 49	21,208	6.7
Aged 50 to 54	22,559	7.1
Aged 55 to 59	21,194	6.7
Aged 60 to 64	18,122	5.7
Aged 65 to 69	14,609	4.6
Aged 70 to 74	10,608	3.4
Aged 75 to 79	7,678	2.4
Aged 80 to 84	5,769	1.8
Aged 85 or older	6,041	1.9
Total people	**316,129**	**100.0**
Recession (aged 0 to 3)	15,876	5.0
iGeneration (aged 4 to 18)	61,995	19.6
Millennial (aged 19 to 36)	77,971	24.7
Generation X (aged 37 to 48)	49,212	15.6
Baby Boom (aged 49 to 67)	75,901	24.0
Older Americans (aged 68 or older)	35,174	11.1

Source: Bureau of the Census, Population Estimates, Internet site http://www.census.gov/popest/; calculations by New Strategist

Table 8.2 Population by Age, Generation, and Sex, 2013

(number of people by age, generation, and sex, and sex ratio by age and generation, 2013; numbers in thousands)

	total	female	male	sex ratio
Total people	316,129	160,477	155,652	97
Under age 5	19,868	9,716	10,152	104
Aged 5 to 9	20,571	10,062	10,509	104
Aged 10 to 14	20,650	10,098	10,553	105
Aged 15 to 19	21,159	10,313	10,846	105
Aged 20 to 24	22,795	11,116	11,679	105
Aged 25 to 29	21,580	10,620	10,960	103
Aged 30 to 34	21,264	10,583	10,682	101
Aged 35 to 39	19,604	9,819	9,785	100
Aged 40 to 44	20,849	10,489	10,360	99
Aged 45 to 49	21,208	10,710	10,498	98
Aged 50 to 54	22,559	11,488	11,071	96
Aged 55 to 59	21,194	10,912	10,282	94
Aged 60 to 64	18,122	9,448	8,674	92
Aged 65 to 69	14,609	7,696	6,913	90
Aged 70 to 74	10,608	5,724	4,884	85
Aged 75 to 79	7,678	4,288	3,390	79
Aged 80 to 84	5,769	3,398	2,370	70
Aged 85 or older	6,041	3,999	2,042	51
Total people	316,129	160,477	155,652	97
Recession (aged 0 to 3)	15,876	7,761	8,116	105
iGeneration (aged 4 to 18)	61,995	30,300	31,695	105
Millennial (aged 19 to 36)	77,971	38,427	39,544	103
Generation X (aged 37 to 48)	49,212	24,758	24,453	99
Baby Boom (aged 49 to 67)	75,901	39,127	36,774	94
Older Americans (aged 68 or older)	35,174	20,105	15,069	75

Note: The sex ratio is the number of males per 100 females.
Source: Bureau of the Census, Population Estimates, Internet site http://www.census.gov/popest/; calculations by New Strategist

Table 8.3 Generation X by Single Year of Age, 2013

(number of people aged 37 to 48 by single year of age and sex, and sex ratio by age, 2013; numbers in thousands)

	total	female	male	sex ratio
Total Gen Xers	**49,212**	**24,758**	**24,453**	**99**
Aged 37	3,843	1,925	1,918	100
Aged 38	3,964	1,983	1,981	100
Aged 39	3,842	1,930	1,912	99
Aged 40	3,905	1,968	1,937	98
Aged 41	4,085	2,056	2,029	99
Aged 42	4,324	2,178	2,146	99
Aged 43	4,381	2,198	2,183	99
Aged 44	4,155	2,089	2,066	99
Aged 45	4,070	2,048	2,022	99
Aged 46	4,077	2,058	2,019	98
Aged 47	4,156	2,097	2,059	98
Aged 48	4,410	2,227	2,183	98

Note: The sex ratio is the number of males per 100 females.
Source: Bureau of the Census, Population Estimates, Internet site http://www.census.gov/popest/; calculations by New Strategist

Table 8.4 Population by Age, 2010 and 2013

(number of people by age, 2010 and 2013; percent change, 2010–13; numbers in thousands)

	2013	2010	percent change 2010–13
Total people	**316,129**	**309,326**	**2.2%**
Under age 5	19,868	20,189	−1.6
Aged 5 to 9	20,571	20,332	1.2
Aged 10 to 14	20,650	20,680	−0.1
Aged 15 to 19	21,159	21,979	−3.7
Aged 20 to 24	22,795	21,702	5.0
Aged 25 to 29	21,580	21,144	2.1
Aged 30 to 34	21,264	20,068	6.0
Aged 35 to 39	19,604	20,078	−2.4
Aged 40 to 44	20,849	20,904	−0.3
Aged 45 to 49	21,208	22,636	−6.3
Aged 50 to 54	22,559	22,353	0.9
Aged 55 to 59	21,194	19,795	7.1
Aged 60 to 64	18,122	16,990	6.7
Aged 65 to 69	14,609	12,521	16.7
Aged 70 to 74	10,608	9,336	13.6
Aged 75 to 79	7,678	7,319	4.9
Aged 80 to 84	5,769	5,759	0.2
Aged 85 or older	6,041	5,543	9.0
Aged 18 to 24	31,458	30,762	2.3
Aged 18 or older	242,543	235,206	3.1
Aged 65 or older	44,704	40,477	10.4

Source: Bureau of the Census, Population Estimates, Internet site http://www.census.gov/popest/; calculations by New Strategist

Generation X Is Slightly More Diverse than Average

It is less diverse than children and young adults, however.

Sixty-one percent of Generation Xers are non-Hispanic White, according to the Census Bureau's 2013 population estimates. This figure is slightly smaller than the 63 percent for the population as a whole, but larger than the share among the youngest Americans—only 50 percent of children under age 5 are non-Hispanic White. Older generations are much less diverse than Generation X. Among Boomers, 72 percent are non-Hispanic White. Among Older Americans (aged 68 or older), the share is 79 percent.

Within Generation X, Hispanics outnumber Blacks. Eighteen percent of Gen Xers are Hispanic, 14 percent are Black, and 7 percent are Asian. Among the Asian and Hispanic populations, Gen Xers outnumber Boomers.

■ The differing racial and ethnic makeup of older versus younger generations of Americans may give rise to political tension in the years ahead.

Just over 60 percent of Generation Xers are non-Hispanic White

(non-Hispanic White share of population by generation, 2013)

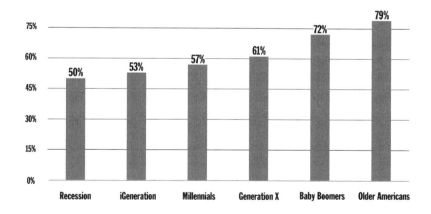

Table 8.5 Population by Generation, Race, and Hispanic Origin, 2013

(number and percent distribution of people by generation, race, and Hispanic origin, 2013; numbers in thousands)

	total	Asian	Black	Hispanic	non-Hispanic White
Total people	**316,129**	**19,437**	**45,004**	**54,071**	**197,836**
Recession (aged 0 to 3)	15,876	1,139	2,928	4,101	7,926
iGeneration (aged 4 to 18)	61,995	4,048	10,825	14,575	32,987
Millennial (aged 19 to 36)	77,971	5,564	12,258	16,020	44,314
Generation X (aged 37 to 48)	49,212	3,446	6,806	8,798	30,117
Baby Boom (aged 49 to 67)	75,901	3,811	9,074	8,011	54,592
Older Americans (aged 68 or older)	35,174	1,429	3,112	2,567	27,900
PERCENT DISTRIBUTION BY RACE AND HISPANIC ORIGIN					
Total people	**100.0%**	**6.1%**	**14.2%**	**17.1%**	**62.6%**
Recession (aged 0 to 3)	100.0	7.2	18.4	25.8	49.9
iGeneration (aged 4 to 18)	100.0	6.5	17.5	23.5	53.2
Millennial (aged 19 to 36)	100.0	7.1	15.7	20.5	56.8
Generation X (aged 37 to 48)	100.0	7.0	13.8	17.9	61.2
Baby Boom (aged 49 to 67)	100.0	5.0	12.0	10.6	71.9
Older Americans (aged 68 or older)	100.0	4.1	8.8	7.3	79.3
PERCENT DISTRIBUTION BY GENERATION					
Total people	**100.0**	**100.0**	**100.0**	**100.0**	**100.0**
Recession (aged 0 to 3)	5.0	5.9	6.5	7.6	4.0
iGeneration (aged 4 to 18)	19.6	20.8	24.1	27.0	16.7
Millennial (aged 19 to 36)	24.7	28.6	27.2	29.6	22.4
Generation X (aged 37 to 48)	15.6	17.7	15.1	16.3	15.2
Baby Boom (aged 49 to 67)	24.0	19.6	20.2	14.8	27.6
Older Americans (aged 68 or older)	11.1	7.4	6.9	4.7	14.1

Note: Asians and Blacks are those who identify themselves as being of the race alone and those who identify themselves as being of the race in combination with other races. Non-Hispanic Whites are those who identify themselves as being White alone and not Hispanic. Numbers do not add to total because not all races are shown and Hispanics may be of any race.
Source: Bureau of the Census, Population Estimates, Internet site http://www.census.gov/popest/; calculations by New Strategist

Table 8.6 Population by Age, Race, and Hispanic Origin, 2013

(number of people by age, race, and Hispanic origin, 2013; numbers in thousands)

	total	Asian	Black	Hispanic	non-Hispanic White
Total people	**316,129**	**19,437**	**45,004**	**54,071**	**197,836**
Under age 5	19,868	1,420	3,659	5,119	9,937
Aged 5 to 9	20,571	1,419	3,635	5,126	10,594
Aged 10 to 14	20,650	1,324	3,566	4,767	11,118
Aged 15 to 19	21,159	1,287	3,668	4,599	11,678
Aged 20 to 24	22,795	1,489	3,948	4,676	12,736
Aged 25 to 29	21,580	1,592	3,275	4,396	12,369
Aged 30 to 34	21,264	1,616	3,112	4,366	12,223
Aged 35 to 39	19,604	1,524	2,792	4,044	11,276
Aged 40 to 44	20,849	1,500	2,877	3,746	12,708
Aged 45 to 49	21,208	1,285	2,880	3,285	13,699
Aged 50 to 54	22,559	1,186	2,914	2,797	15,552
Aged 55 to 59	21,194	1,061	2,591	2,196	15,226
Aged 60 to 64	18,122	882	2,035	1,623	13,474
Aged 65 to 69	14,609	654	1,436	1,177	11,254
Aged 70 to 74	10,608	458	996	810	8,285
Aged 75 to 79	7,678	324	701	583	6,033
Aged 80 to 84	5,769	218	467	403	4,659
Aged 85 or older	6,041	200	450	357	5,015

PERCENT DISTRIBUTION BY RACE AND HISPANIC ORIGIN

Total people	**100.0%**	**6.1%**	**14.2%**	**17.1%**	**62.6%**
Under age 5	100.0	7.1	18.4	25.8	50.0
Aged 5 to 9	100.0	6.9	17.7	24.9	51.5
Aged 10 to 14	100.0	6.4	17.3	23.1	53.8
Aged 15 to 19	100.0	6.1	17.3	21.7	55.2
Aged 20 to 24	100.0	6.5	17.3	20.5	55.9
Aged 25 to 29	100.0	7.4	15.2	20.4	57.3
Aged 30 to 34	100.0	7.6	14.6	20.5	57.5
Aged 35 to 39	100.0	7.8	14.2	20.6	57.5
Aged 40 to 44	100.0	7.2	13.8	18.0	61.0
Aged 45 to 49	100.0	6.1	13.6	15.5	64.6
Aged 50 to 54	100.0	5.3	12.9	12.4	68.9
Aged 55 to 59	100.0	5.0	12.2	10.4	71.8
Aged 60 to 64	100.0	4.9	11.2	9.0	74.4
Aged 65 to 69	100.0	4.5	9.8	8.1	77.0
Aged 70 to 74	100.0	4.3	9.4	7.6	78.1
Aged 75 to 79	100.0	4.2	9.1	7.6	78.6
Aged 80 to 84	100.0	3.8	8.1	7.0	80.8
Aged 85 or older	100.0	3.3	7.5	5.9	83.0

Note: Asians and Blacks are those who identify themselves as being of the race alone and those who identify themselves as being of the race in combination with other races. Non-Hispanic Whites are those who identify themselves as being White alone and not Hispanic. Numbers do not add to total because not all races are shown and Hispanics may be of any race.
Source: Bureau of the Census, Population Estimates, Internet site http://www.census.gov/popest/; calculations by New Strategist

Table 8.7 Generation X by Single Year of Age, Race, and Hispanic Origin, 2013

(number and percent distribution of people aged 37 to 48 by single year of age, race, and Hispanic origin, 2013; numbers in thousands)

	total	Asian	Black	Hispanic	non-Hispanic White
Total Gen Xers	**49,212**	**3,446**	**6,806**	**8,798**	**30,117**
Aged 37	3,843	303	546	805	2,196
Aged 38	3,964	312	559	813	2,285
Aged 39	3,842	305	539	779	2,221
Aged 40	3,905	308	555	769	2,275
Aged 41	4,085	307	573	762	2,441
Aged 42	4,324	301	598	758	2,663
Aged 43	4,381	302	598	755	2,722
Aged 44	4,155	283	554	704	2,607
Aged 45	4,070	269	556	686	2,552
Aged 46	4,077	249	554	659	2,606
Aged 47	4,156	252	573	652	2,668
Aged 48	4,410	257	601	657	2,880

PERCENT DISTRIBUTION BY RACE AND HISPANIC ORIGIN

	total	Asian	Black	Hispanic	non-Hispanic White
Total Gen Xers	**100.0%**	**7.0%**	**13.8%**	**17.9%**	**61.2%**
Aged 37	100.0	7.9	14.2	21.0	57.2
Aged 38	100.0	7.9	14.1	20.5	57.7
Aged 39	100.0	7.9	14.0	20.3	57.8
Aged 40	100.0	7.9	14.2	19.7	58.3
Aged 41	100.0	7.5	14.0	18.6	59.8
Aged 42	100.0	7.0	13.8	17.5	61.6
Aged 43	100.0	6.9	13.6	17.2	62.1
Aged 44	100.0	6.8	13.3	16.9	62.8
Aged 45	100.0	6.6	13.7	16.9	62.7
Aged 46	100.0	6.1	13.6	16.2	63.9
Aged 47	100.0	6.1	13.8	15.7	64.2
Aged 48	100.0	5.8	13.6	14.9	65.3

Note: Asians and Blacks are those who identify themselves as being of the race alone and those who identify themselves as being of the race in combination with other races. Non-Hispanic Whites are those who identify themselves as being White alone and not Hispanic. Numbers do not add to total because not all races are shown and Hispanics may be of any race.
Source: Bureau of the Census, Population Estimates, Internet site http://www.census.gov/popest/; calculations by New Strategist

Rapid Growth Is Projected for the Older Population

Some age groups will shrink during the coming decades.

As large and small generations grow older, age groups expand and contract. Between 2012 and 2050, the largest expansion will be among people aged 65 or older, according to Census Bureau population projections. The number of people aged 65 or older will climb from 43 million in 2012 to 84 million in 2050. In 2050, Generation X will count among the nation's elderly, spanning the ages from 74 to 85.

Several age groups will shrink during the decades as Generation X passes through. The number of 45-to-54-year-olds is projected to decline between 2012 and 2020, and the number of 55-to-64-year-olds will decline between 2020 and 2030.

■ Not evident in these projections is the baby bust emerging from the Great Recession, which occurred too recently to be included in the Census Bureau's fertility assumptions.

Number of Americans aged 65 or older will nearly double in the next few decades

(number of people aged 65 or older, 2012 and 2050)

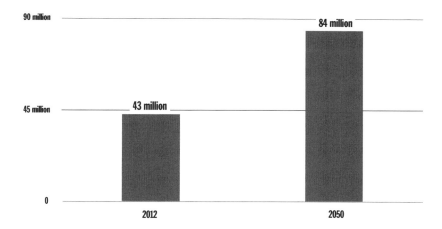

Table 8.8 Population Projections by Age, 2012 to 2050

(projected number of people by age, 2012 to 2050; percent change for selected years; numbers in thousands)

	2012	2020	2030	2040	2050
Total people	**314,004**	**333,896**	**358,471**	**380,016**	**399,803**
Under age 5	20,274	21,808	22,252	23,004	24,115
Aged 5 to 9	20,457	21,307	22,451	22,886	23,983
Aged 10 to 14	20,639	20,616	22,365	22,893	23,682
Aged 15 to 19	21,326	20,806	21,946	23,174	23,642
Aged 20 to 24	22,554	21,651	21,940	23,863	24,463
Aged 25 to 29	21,375	23,366	22,712	24,151	25,493
Aged 30 to 34	20,901	22,906	23,340	23,924	25,949
Aged 35 to 39	19,479	21,869	24,423	24,002	25,513
Aged 40 to 44	21,017	20,361	23,403	24,000	24,655
Aged 45 to 49	21,678	20,008	21,935	24,595	24,262
Aged 50 to 54	22,572	20,467	20,083	23,176	23,866
Aged 55 to 59	20,769	21,747	19,393	21,384	24,094
Aged 60 to 64	17,808	21,017	19,454	19,242	22,348
Aged 65 or older	43,155	55,969	72,774	79,719	83,739

PERCENT CHANGE	2012–20	2020–30	2030–40	2040–50	2012–2050
Total people	**6.3%**	**7.4%**	**6.0%**	**5.2%**	**27.3%**
Under age 5	7.6	2.0	3.4	4.8	18.9
Aged 5 to 9	4.2	5.4	1.9	4.8	17.2
Aged 10 to 14	–0.1	8.5	2.4	3.4	14.7
Aged 15 to 19	–2.4	5.5	5.6	2.0	10.9
Aged 20 to 24	–4.0	1.3	8.8	2.5	8.5
Aged 25 to 29	9.3	–2.8	6.3	5.6	19.3
Aged 30 to 34	9.6	1.9	2.5	8.5	24.1
Aged 35 to 39	12.3	11.7	–1.7	6.3	31.0
Aged 40 to 44	–3.1	14.9	2.6	2.7	17.3
Aged 45 to 49	–7.7	9.6	12.1	–1.4	11.9
Aged 50 to 54	–9.3	–1.9	15.4	3.0	5.7
Aged 55 to 59	4.7	–10.8	10.3	12.7	16.0
Aged 60 to 64	18.0	–7.4	–1.1	16.1	25.5
Aged 65 or older	29.7	30.0	9.5	5.0	94.0

Note: Numbers are for July 1 of each year.
Source: Bureau of the Census, Population Projections, Internet site http://www.census.gov/population/projections/; calculations by New Strategist

Minorities Are Close to Becoming the Majority

Minorities may account for well over half of children under age 5 by 2020.

Children are far more diverse than older Americans, and this diversity will intensify over the next decade. In 2020, fewer than half of children under age 5 will be non-Hispanic White, according to Census Bureau projections. More than one in four will be Hispanic. In contrast, 76 percent of people aged 65 or older will be non-Hispanic White and only 9 percent will be Hispanic.

The number of Hispanics will more than double between 2012 and 2050. Asians are also projected to more than double during those years, and Blacks will grow 56 percent. Meanwhile, the number of non-Hispanic Whites will shrink by 6 percent. Between 2040 and 2050, non-Hispanic Whites will fall below 50 percent of the population and the nation's minorities will become the majority.

■ By 2030, minorities will account for the majority of Americans under age 30.

The generation gap will be a racial and ethnic divide

(minority share of selected age groups, 2030)

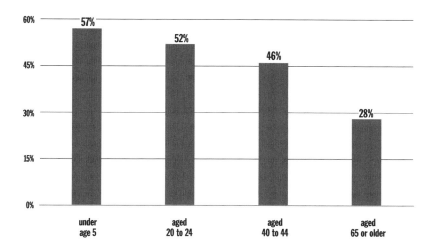

Table 8.9 Minority Population, 2012 to 2050

(projected number of minorities by age, and minority share of total population, 2012 to 2050, percent and percentage point change for selected years; numbers in thousands)

	2012	2020	2030	2040	2050	percent change 2012–50
Total minorities	**116,242**	**134,583**	**159,654**	**186,129**	**213,469**	**83.6%**
Under age 5	10,160	11,517	12,725	14,253	15,805	55.6
Aged 5 to 9	9,781	10,993	12,391	13,742	15,386	57.3
Aged 10 to 14	9,424	10,292	11,986	13,261	14,819	57.3
Aged 15 to 19	9,486	9,904	11,550	13,019	14,397	51.8
Aged 20 to 24	9,825	10,111	11,444	13,286	14,620	48.8
Aged 25 to 29	9,059	10,879	11,560	13,457	15,021	65.8
Aged 30 to 34	8,862	10,266	11,577	13,151	15,076	70.1
Aged 35 to 39	8,232	9,524	11,809	12,668	14,617	77.6
Aged 40 to 44	8,020	8,807	10,744	12,167	13,784	71.9
Aged 45 to 49	7,460	8,263	9,686	12,034	12,938	73.4
Aged 50 to 54	6,835	7,585	8,750	10,702	12,167	78.0
Aged 55 to 59	5,731	7,086	8,038	9,465	11,814	106.2
Aged 60 to 64	4,457	6,147	7,213	8,383	10,319	131.5
Aged 65 or older	8,913	13,207	20,181	26,540	32,706	267.0

MINORITY SHARE OF TOTAL POPULATION	2012	2020	2030	2040	2050	percentage point change 2012–50
Total minorities	**37.0%**	**40.3%**	**44.5%**	**49.0%**	**53.4%**	**16.4**
Under age 5	50.1	52.8	57.2	62.0	65.5	15.4
Aged 5 to 9	47.8	51.6	55.2	60.0	64.2	16.3
Aged 10 to 14	45.7	49.9	53.6	57.9	62.6	16.9
Aged 15 to 19	44.5	47.6	52.6	56.2	60.9	16.4
Aged 20 to 24	43.6	46.7	52.2	55.7	59.8	16.2
Aged 25 to 29	42.4	46.6	50.9	55.7	58.9	16.5
Aged 30 to 34	42.4	44.8	49.6	55.0	58.1	15.7
Aged 35 to 39	42.3	43.6	48.4	52.8	57.3	15.0
Aged 40 to 44	38.2	43.3	45.9	50.7	55.9	17.8
Aged 45 to 49	34.4	41.3	44.2	48.9	53.3	18.9
Aged 50 to 54	30.3	37.1	43.6	46.2	51.0	20.7
Aged 55 to 59	27.6	32.6	41.4	44.3	49.0	21.4
Aged 60 to 64	25.0	29.2	37.1	43.6	46.2	21.1
Aged 65 or older	20.7	23.6	27.7	33.3	39.1	18.4

Note: Minorities are calculated by subtracting non-Hispanic Whites from the total population.
Source: Bureau of the Census, Population Projections, Internet site http://www.census.gov/population/projections/; calculations by New Strategist

Table 8.10 Asian Population Projections, 2012 to 2050

(projected number of Asians by age, and Asian share of total population, 2012 to 2050, percent and percentage point change, 2012–50; numbers in thousands)

	2012	2020	2030	2040	2050	percent change 2012–50
Total Asians	**18,647**	**22,384**	**27,482**	**32,876**	**38,407**	**106.0%**
Under age 5	1,414	1,664	1,912	2,238	2,558	80.9
Aged 5 to 9	1,378	1,602	1,878	2,169	2,505	81.7
Aged 10 to 14	1,270	1,489	1,817	2,079	2,409	89.8
Aged 15 to 19	1,247	1,447	1,750	2,036	2,329	86.8
Aged 20 to 24	1,430	1,474	1,788	2,136	2,403	68.0
Aged 25 to 29	1,514	1,689	1,964	2,309	2,604	72.0
Aged 30 to 34	1,535	1,825	2,009	2,367	2,725	77.6
Aged 35 to 39	1,493	1,779	2,053	2,359	2,710	81.5
Aged 40 to 44	1,436	1,627	2,036	2,241	2,601	81.2
Aged 45 to 49	1,252	1,571	1,893	2,181	2,487	98.7
Aged 50 to 54	1,137	1,360	1,676	2,088	2,295	101.9
Aged 55 to 59	1,012	1,221	1,575	1,897	2,187	116.0
Aged 60 to 64	836	1,086	1,339	1,649	2,055	145.9
Aged 65 or older	1,694	2,550	3,792	5,126	6,539	286.0

ASIAN SHARE OF TOTAL POPULATION	2012	2020	2030	2040	2050	percentage point change 2012–50
Total Asians	**5.9%**	**6.7%**	**7.7%**	**8.7%**	**9.6%**	**3.7**
Under age 5	7.0	7.6	8.6	9.7	10.6	3.6
Aged 5 to 9	6.7	7.5	8.4	9.5	10.4	3.7
Aged 10 to 14	6.2	7.2	8.1	9.1	10.2	4.0
Aged 15 to 19	5.8	7.0	8.0	8.8	9.9	4.0
Aged 20 to 24	6.3	6.8	8.2	9.0	9.8	3.5
Aged 25 to 29	7.1	7.2	8.6	9.6	10.2	3.1
Aged 30 to 34	7.3	8.0	8.6	9.9	10.5	3.2
Aged 35 to 39	7.7	8.1	8.4	9.8	10.6	3.0
Aged 40 to 44	6.8	8.0	8.7	9.3	10.5	3.7
Aged 45 to 49	5.8	7.9	8.6	8.9	10.3	4.5
Aged 50 to 54	5.0	6.6	8.3	9.0	9.6	4.6
Aged 55 to 59	4.9	5.6	8.1	8.9	9.1	4.2
Aged 60 to 64	4.7	5.2	6.9	8.6	9.2	4.5
Aged 65 or older	3.9	4.6	5.2	6.4	7.8	3.9

Note: Asians are those who identify themselves as being of the race alone and those who identify themselves as being of the race in combination with other races.
Source: Bureau of the Census, Population Projections, Internet site http://www.census.gov/population/projections/; calculations by New Strategist

Table 8.11 Black Population Projections, 2012 to 2050

(projected number of Blacks by age, and Black share of total population, 2012 to 2050, percent and percentage point change, 2012–50; numbers in thousands)

	2012	2020	2030	2040	2050	percent change 2012–50
Total Blacks	**44,462**	**49,338**	**55,727**	**62,350**	**69,525**	**56.4%**
Under age 5	3,748	4,179	4,408	4,809	5,321	42.0
Aged 5 to 9	3,559	3,990	4,348	4,625	5,147	44.6
Aged 10 to 14	3,574	3,719	4,252	4,503	4,923	37.8
Aged 15 to 19	3,718	3,547	4,067	4,446	4,740	27.5
Aged 20 to 24	3,830	3,666	3,866	4,439	4,723	23.3
Aged 25 to 29	3,192	4,024	3,766	4,350	4,782	49.8
Aged 30 to 34	3,049	3,631	3,870	4,138	4,763	56.2
Aged 35 to 39	2,760	3,172	4,150	3,951	4,575	65.8
Aged 40 to 44	2,877	2,935	3,687	3,966	4,266	48.3
Aged 45 to 49	2,919	2,787	3,171	4,165	4,002	37.1
Aged 50 to 54	2,893	2,754	2,878	3,639	3,942	36.3
Aged 55 to 59	2,505	2,809	2,666	3,068	4,056	61.9
Aged 60 to 64	1,966	2,584	2,558	2,717	3,471	76.5
Aged 65 or older	3,871	5,541	8,039	9,534	10,814	179.3

BLACK SHARE OF TOTAL POPULATION	2012	2020	2030	2040	2050	percentage point change 2012–50
Total Blacks	**14.2%**	**14.8%**	**15.5%**	**16.4%**	**17.4%**	**3.2**
Under age 5	18.5	19.2	19.8	20.9	22.1	3.6
Aged 5 to 9	17.4	18.7	19.4	20.2	21.5	4.1
Aged 10 to 14	17.3	18.0	19.0	19.7	20.8	3.5
Aged 15 to 19	17.4	17.0	18.5	19.2	20.0	2.6
Aged 20 to 24	17.0	16.9	17.6	18.6	19.3	2.3
Aged 25 to 29	14.9	17.2	16.6	18.0	18.8	3.8
Aged 30 to 34	14.6	15.9	16.6	17.3	18.4	3.8
Aged 35 to 39	14.2	14.5	17.0	16.5	17.9	3.8
Aged 40 to 44	13.7	14.4	15.8	16.5	17.3	3.6
Aged 45 to 49	13.5	13.9	14.5	16.9	16.5	3.0
Aged 50 to 54	12.8	13.5	14.3	15.7	16.5	3.7
Aged 55 to 59	12.1	12.9	13.7	14.3	16.8	4.8
Aged 60 to 64	11.0	12.3	13.1	14.1	15.5	4.5
Aged 65 or older	9.0	9.9	11.0	12.0	12.9	3.9

Note: Blacks are those who identify themselves as being of the race alone and those who identify themselves as being of the race in combination with other races.
Source: Bureau of the Census, Population Projections, Internet site http://www.census.gov/population/projections/; calculations by New Strategist

Table 8.12 Hispanic Population Projections, 2012 to 2050

(projected number of Hispanics by age, and Hispanic share of total population, 2012 to 2050, percent and percentage point change, 2012–50; numbers in thousands)

	2012	2020	2030	2040	2050	percent change 2012–50
Total Hispanics	**53,274**	**63,784**	**78,655**	**94,876**	**111,732**	**109.7%**
Under age 5	5,267	6,035	6,924	7,970	8,930	69.5
Aged 5 to 9	5,026	5,715	6,597	7,591	8,628	71.7
Aged 10 to 14	4,689	5,329	6,289	7,211	8,264	76.2
Aged 15 to 19	4,579	5,069	6,063	6,987	7,988	74.4
Aged 20 to 24	4,616	5,079	6,065	7,117	8,061	74.6
Aged 25 to 29	4,401	5,239	6,027	7,173	8,130	84.7
Aged 30 to 34	4,326	4,878	5,837	6,958	8,031	85.6
Aged 35 to 39	4,001	4,633	5,701	6,579	7,731	93.2
Aged 40 to 44	3,680	4,295	5,100	6,112	7,241	96.8
Aged 45 to 49	3,215	3,910	4,687	5,788	6,675	107.6
Aged 50 to 54	2,688	3,434	4,249	5,057	6,083	126.3
Aged 55 to 59	2,093	2,968	3,805	4,566	5,673	171.0
Aged 60 to 64	1,548	2,370	3,288	4,072	4,876	214.9
Aged 65 or older	3,142	4,831	8,023	11,695	15,421	390.8

HISPANIC SHARE OF TOTAL POPULATION	2012	2020	2030	2040	2050	percentage point change 2012–50
Total Hispanics	**17.0%**	**19.1%**	**21.9%**	**25.0%**	**27.9%**	**11.0**
Under age 5	26.0	27.7	31.1	34.6	37.0	11.0
Aged 5 to 9	24.6	26.8	29.4	33.2	36.0	11.4
Aged 10 to 14	22.7	25.8	28.1	31.5	34.9	12.2
Aged 15 to 19	21.5	24.4	27.6	30.1	33.8	12.3
Aged 20 to 24	20.5	23.5	27.6	29.8	33.0	12.5
Aged 25 to 29	20.6	22.4	26.5	29.7	31.9	11.3
Aged 30 to 34	20.7	21.3	25.0	29.1	30.9	10.2
Aged 35 to 39	20.5	21.2	23.3	27.4	30.3	9.8
Aged 40 to 44	17.5	21.1	21.8	25.5	29.4	11.9
Aged 45 to 49	14.8	19.5	21.4	23.5	27.5	12.7
Aged 50 to 54	11.9	16.8	21.2	21.8	25.5	13.6
Aged 55 to 59	10.1	13.6	19.6	21.3	23.5	13.5
Aged 60 to 64	8.7	11.3	16.9	21.2	21.8	13.1
Aged 65 or older	7.3	8.6	11.0	14.7	18.4	11.1

Source: Bureau of the Census, Population Projections, Internet site http://www.census.gov/population/projections/; calculations by New Strategist

Table 8.13 Non-Hispanic White Population, 2012 to 2050

(projected number of non-Hispanic Whites by age, and non-Hispanic White share of total population, 2012 to 2050, percent and percentage point change, 2012–50; numbers in thousands)

	2012	2020	2030	2040	2050	percent change 2012–50
Total non-Hispanic Whites	**197,762**	**199,313**	**198,817**	**193,887**	**186,334**	**−5.8%**
Under age 5	10,114	10,291	9,527	8,751	8,311	−17.8
Aged 5 to 9	10,676	10,314	10,060	9,144	8,597	−19.5
Aged 10 to 14	11,215	10,324	10,379	9,631	8,863	−21.0
Aged 15 to 19	11,840	10,902	10,396	10,155	9,245	−21.9
Aged 20 to 24	12,729	11,539	10,496	10,577	9,843	−22.7
Aged 25 to 29	12,315	12,486	11,153	10,694	10,472	−15.0
Aged 30 to 34	12,040	12,639	11,763	10,773	10,873	−9.7
Aged 35 to 39	11,248	12,344	12,613	11,334	10,896	−3.1
Aged 40 to 44	12,998	11,554	12,659	11,833	10,870	−16.4
Aged 45 to 49	14,219	11,745	12,249	12,562	11,324	−20.4
Aged 50 to 54	15,737	12,882	11,333	12,474	11,700	−25.7
Aged 55 to 59	15,038	14,661	11,356	11,920	12,279	−18.3
Aged 60 to 64	13,351	14,870	12,241	10,860	12,029	−9.9
Aged 65 or older	34,243	42,761	52,594	53,180	51,033	49.0

NON-HISPANIC WHITE SHARE OF TOTAL POPULATION	2012	2020	2030	2040	2050	percentage point change 2012–50
Total non-Hispanic Whites	**63.0%**	**59.7%**	**55.5%**	**51.0%**	**46.6%**	**−16.4**
Under age 5	49.9	47.2	42.8	38.0	34.5	−15.4
Aged 5 to 9	52.2	48.4	44.8	40.0	35.8	−16.3
Aged 10 to 14	54.3	50.1	46.4	42.1	37.4	−16.9
Aged 15 to 19	55.5	52.4	47.4	43.8	39.1	−16.4
Aged 20 to 24	56.4	53.3	47.8	44.3	40.2	−16.2
Aged 25 to 29	57.6	53.4	49.1	44.3	41.1	−16.5
Aged 30 to 34	57.6	55.2	50.4	45.0	41.9	−15.7
Aged 35 to 39	57.7	56.4	51.6	47.2	42.7	−15.0
Aged 40 to 44	61.8	56.7	54.1	49.3	44.1	−17.8
Aged 45 to 49	65.6	58.7	55.8	51.1	46.7	−18.9
Aged 50 to 54	69.7	62.9	56.4	53.8	49.0	−20.7
Aged 55 to 59	72.4	67.4	58.6	55.7	51.0	−21.4
Aged 60 to 64	75.0	70.8	62.9	56.4	53.8	−21.1
Aged 65 or older	79.3	76.4	72.3	66.7	60.9	−18.4

Note: Non-Hispanic Whites are those who identify themselves as being White alone and not Hispanic.
Source: Bureau of the Census, Population Projections, Internet site http://www.census.gov/population/projections/; calculations by New Strategist

Nearly Half of Gen Xers Live in Their State of Birth

Among 35-to-44-year-olds, more than one in five is foreign-born.

According to the 2012 American Community Survey, most Americans live in the state in which they were born. In the Gen X age groups (Gen Xers were aged 36 to 47 in 2012), the share who live in their state of birth is just under 50 percent. Slightly fewer than one-third were born in the United States but live in a state other than the one in which they were born. A substantial 22 percent of 35-to-44-year-olds were born in another country.

In 2013, nearly 1 million legal immigrants were admitted to the United States. A substantial 25 percent were aged 35 to 49, adding to the Gen X population.

Sixty-two million residents of the United States speak a language other than English at home, according to the Census Bureau's 2012 American Community Survey—21 percent of the population aged 5 or older. Among working-age adults (aged 18 to 64), 22 percent do not speak English at home. Most of those who do not speak English at home speak Spanish.

■ Among people aged 18 to 64 who speak Spanish at home, most also speak English "very well."

Many Gen Xers were born in another country

(percent distribution of people aged 35 to 44 or older by place of birth, 2012)

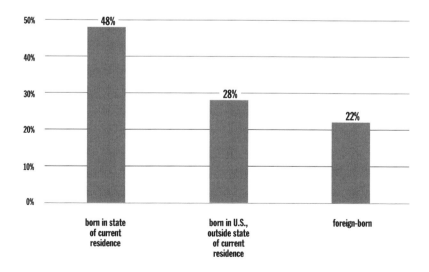

Table 8.14 Population by Age and Place of Birth, 2012

(number and percent distribution of people by age and place of birth, 2012; numbers in thousands)

| | | born in United States | | | |
	total	in state of current residence	outside state of current residence	citizen born outside United States	foreign-born
Total people	**313,914**	**184,556**	**84,147**	**4,386**	**40,825**
Under age 5	19,910	17,835	1,711	129	236
Aged 5 to 17	53,800	42,565	8,315	592	2,328
Aged 18 to 24	31,472	20,472	7,335	459	3,207
Aged 25 to 34	42,101	22,560	11,080	693	7,769
Aged 35 to 44	40,698	19,467	11,571	720	8,939
Aged 45 to 54	44,205	21,881	14,039	755	7,529
Aged 55 to 59	20,622	10,371	7,014	308	2,930
Aged 60 to 61	7,539	3,756	2,673	93	1,018
Aged 62 to 64	10,426	5,103	3,805	140	1,378
Aged 65 to 74	24,005	11,260	9,297	296	3,151
Aged 75 or older	19,136	9,287	7,308	200	2,340
PERCENT DISTRIBUTION BY PLACE OF BIRTH					
Total people	**100.0%**	**58.8%**	**26.8%**	**1.4%**	**13.0%**
Under age 5	100.0	89.6	8.6	0.6	1.2
Aged 5 to 17	100.0	79.1	15.5	1.1	4.3
Aged 18 to 24	100.0	65.0	23.3	1.5	10.2
Aged 25 to 34	100.0	53.6	26.3	1.6	18.5
Aged 35 to 44	100.0	47.8	28.4	1.8	22.0
Aged 45 to 54	100.0	49.5	31.8	1.7	17.0
Aged 55 to 59	100.0	50.3	34.0	1.5	14.2
Aged 60 to 61	100.0	49.8	35.5	1.2	13.5
Aged 62 to 64	100.0	48.9	36.5	1.3	13.2
Aged 65 to 74	100.0	46.9	38.7	1.2	13.1
Aged 75 or older	100.0	48.5	38.2	1.0	12.2

Source: Bureau of the Census, 2012 American Community Survey, Internet site http://factfinder2.census.gov/faces/nav/jsf/pages/index.xhtml; calculations by New Strategist

Table 8.15 Immigrants by Age, 2013

(number and percent distribution of immigrants by age, 2013)

	number	percent distribution
Total immigrants	**990,553**	**100.0%**
Under age 1	3,507	0.4
Aged 1 to 4	30,243	3.1
Aged 5 to 9	46,203	4.7
Aged 10 to 14	56,988	5.8
Aged 15 to 19	75,497	7.6
Aged 20 to 24	90,396	9.1
Aged 25 to 29	112,244	11.3
Aged 30 to 34	122,446	12.4
Aged 35 to 39	104,210	10.5
Aged 40 to 44	81,892	8.3
Aged 45 to 49	63,818	6.4
Aged 50 to 54	50,001	5.0
Aged 55 to 59	40,195	4.1
Aged 60 to 64	31,529	3.2
Aged 65 to 74	36,117	3.6
Aged 75 or older	12,758	1.3

Note: Immigrants are those granted legal permanent residence in the United States. They either arrive in the United States with immigrant visas issued abroad or adjust their status in the United States from temporary to permanent residence. Numbers may not sum to total because "age not stated" is not shown.
Source: Department of Homeland Security, 2013 Yearbook of Immigration Statistics, Internet site http://www.dhs.gov/yearbook-immigration-statistics-2013-lawful-permanent-residents

Table 8.16 Language Spoken at Home by People Aged 18 to 64, 2012

(number and percent distribution of people aged 5 or older and aged 18 to 64 who speak a language other than English at home by language spoken at home and ability to speak English "very well," 2012; numbers in thousands)

	total		aged 18 to 64	
	number	percent distribution	number	percent distribution
Total, aged 5 or older	**294,004**	**100.0%**	**197,063**	**100.0%**
Speak only English at home	232,126	79.0	153,444	77.9
Speak a language other than English at home	61,877	21.0	43,619	22.1
Speak English less than "very well"	25,088	8.5	18,908	9.6
Total who speak a language other than English at home	**61,877**	**100.0**	**43,619**	**100.0**
Speak Spanish at home	38,325	61.9	26,861	61.6
Speak other Indo-European language at home	11,035	17.8	7,517	17.2
Speak Asian or Pacific Island language at home	9,752	15.8	7,224	16.6
Speak other language at home	2,765	4.5	2,017	4.6
Speak Spanish at home	38,325	100.0	26,861	100.0
Speak English less than "very well"	16,149	42.1	12,566	46.8
Speak other Indo-European language at home	11,035	100.0	7,517	100.0
Speak English less than "very well"	3,462	31.4	2,296	30.5
Speak Asian or Pacific Island language at home	9,752	100.0	7,224	100.0
Speak English less than "very well"	4,618	47.4	3,406	47.1
Speak other language at home	2,765	100.0	2,017	100.0
Speak English less than "very well"	859	31.1	640	31.7

Source: Bureau of the Census, 2012 American Community Survey, Internet site http://factfinder2.census.gov/faces/nav/jsf/pages/index.xhtml; calculations by New Strategist

Largest Share of Generation X Lives in the South

Gen X accounts for 15 to 16 percent of the population in every region.

The South is home to the largest share of the population, and consequently to the largest share of Generation X. Thirty-eight percent of Gen Xers live in the South, where the generation accounts for 16 percent of the population.

The Gen X share of state populations does not vary much. The proportion ranges from a high of 16.7 percent in New Jersey and Georgia to a low of 13.4 percent in North Dakota.

■ Gen Xers outnumber Older Americans (aged 68 or older) in every state.

The Northeast is home to just 18 percent of Gen Xers

(percent distribution of the Generation X by region, 2013)

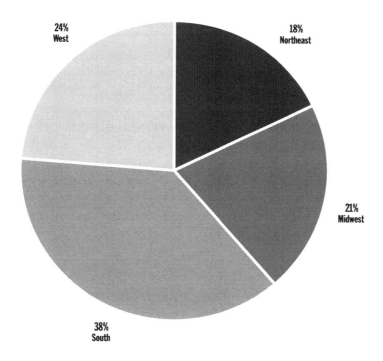

Table 8.17 Population by Generation and Region, 2013

(number and percent distribution of people by generation and region, 2013; numbers in thousands)

	total	Northeast	Midwest	South	West
Total people	**316,129**	**55,943**	**67,548**	**118,383**	**74,254**
Recession (aged 0 to 3)	15,876	2,557	3,349	6,085	3,903
iGeneration (aged 4 to 18)	61,995	10,306	13,380	23,486	14,949
Millennial (aged 19 to 36)	77,971	13,398	16,121	29,085	19,108
Generation X (aged 37 to 48)	49,212	8,897	10,300	18,689	11,692
Baby Boom (aged 49 to 67)	75,901	13,934	16,466	27,656	16,826
Older Americans (aged 68 or older)	35,174	6,850	7,931	13,382	7,776
PERCENT DISTRIBUTION BY GENERATION					
Total people	**100.0%**	**100.0%**	**100.0%**	**100.0%**	**100.0%**
Recession (aged 0 to 3)	5.0	4.6	5.0	5.1	5.3
iGeneration (aged 4 to 18)	19.6	18.4	19.8	19.8	20.1
Millennial (aged 19 to 36)	24.7	24.0	23.9	24.6	25.7
Generation X (aged 37 to 48)	15.6	15.9	15.2	15.8	15.7
Baby Boom (aged 49 to 67)	24.0	24.9	24.4	23.4	22.7
Older Americans (aged 68 or older)	11.1	12.2	11.7	11.3	10.5
PERCENT DISTRIBUTION BY REGION					
Total people	**100.0**	**17.7**	**21.4**	**37.4**	**23.5**
Recession (aged 0 to 3)	100.0	16.1	21.1	38.3	24.6
iGeneration (aged 4 to 18)	100.0	16.6	21.6	37.9	24.1
Millennial (aged 19 to 36)	100.0	17.2	20.7	37.3	24.5
Generation X (aged 37 to 48)	100.0	18.1	20.9	38.0	23.8
Baby Boom (aged 49 to 67)	100.0	18.4	21.7	36.4	22.2
Older Americans (aged 68 or older)	100.0	19.5	22.5	38.0	22.1

*Source: Bureau of the Census, State Population Estimates, Internet site http://www.census.gov/popest/data/state/asrh/2013/index
.html; calculations by New Strategist*

Table 8.18 Population by Age and Region, 2013

(number and percent distribution of people by age and region, 2013; numbers in thousands)

	total	Northeast	Midwest	South	West
Total people	**316,129**	**55,943**	**67,548**	**118,383**	**74,254**
Under age 5	19,868	3,196	4,186	7,607	4,879
Aged 5 to 9	20,571	3,287	4,405	7,855	5,023
Aged 10 to 14	20,650	3,410	4,468	7,840	4,932
Aged 15 to 19	21,159	3,713	4,588	7,837	5,022
Aged 20 to 24	22,795	3,900	4,810	8,551	5,534
Aged 25 to 29	21,580	3,796	4,377	8,044	5,363
Aged 30 to 34	21,264	3,621	4,407	7,956	5,280
Aged 35 to 39	19,604	3,345	4,024	7,417	4,818
Aged 40 to 44	20,849	3,696	4,304	7,905	4,944
Aged 45 to 49	21,208	3,993	4,477	7,917	4,822
Aged 50 to 54	22,559	4,237	4,959	8,308	5,055
Aged 55 to 59	21,194	3,968	4,737	7,736	4,754
Aged 60 to 64	18,122	3,335	4,014	6,683	4,090
Aged 65 to 69	14,609	2,660	3,101	5,575	3,273
Aged 70 to 74	10,608	1,924	2,284	4,082	2,317
Aged 75 to 79	7,678	1,425	1,683	2,922	1,649
Aged 80 to 84	5,769	1,145	1,303	2,101	1,219
Aged 85 or older	6,041	1,292	1,420	2,047	1,282
PERCENT DISTRIBUTION BY REGION					
Total people	**100.0%**	**17.7%**	**21.4%**	**37.4%**	**23.5%**
Under age 5	100.0	16.1	21.1	38.3	24.6
Aged 5 to 9	100.0	16.0	21.4	38.2	24.4
Aged 10 to 14	100.0	16.5	21.6	38.0	23.9
Aged 15 to 19	100.0	17.5	21.7	37.0	23.7
Aged 20 to 24	100.0	17.1	21.1	37.5	24.3
Aged 25 to 29	100.0	17.6	20.3	37.3	24.9
Aged 30 to 34	100.0	17.0	20.7	37.4	24.8
Aged 35 to 39	100.0	17.1	20.5	37.8	24.6
Aged 40 to 44	100.0	17.7	20.6	37.9	23.7
Aged 45 to 49	100.0	18.8	21.1	37.3	22.7
Aged 50 to 54	100.0	18.8	22.0	36.8	22.4
Aged 55 to 59	100.0	18.7	22.3	36.5	22.4
Aged 60 to 64	100.0	18.4	22.2	36.9	22.6
Aged 65 to 69	100.0	18.2	21.2	38.2	22.4
Aged 70 to 74	100.0	18.1	21.5	38.5	21.8
Aged 75 to 79	100.0	18.6	21.9	38.1	21.5
Aged 80 to 84	100.0	19.8	22.6	36.4	21.1
Aged 85 or older	100.0	21.4	23.5	33.9	21.2

Source: Bureau of the Census, State Population Estimates, Internet site http://www.census.gov/popest/data/state/asrh/2013/index .html; calculations by New Strategist

Table 8.19 Population by State and Generation, 2013

(number of people by state and generation, 2013; numbers in thousands)

	total population	Recession (0 to 3)	iGeneration (4 to 18)	Millennial (19 to 36)	Generation X (37 to 48)	Baby Boom (49 to 67)	Older Americans (68 or older)
United States	**316,129**	**15,876**	**61,995**	**77,971**	**49,212**	**75,901**	**35,174**
Alabama	4,834	238	940	1,157	745	1,177	577
Alaska	735	44	153	206	110	172	50
Arizona	6,627	345	1,363	1,620	992	1,488	819
Arkansas	2,959	154	593	706	443	697	365
California	38,333	2,006	7,719	10,061	6,204	8,496	3,847
Colorado	5,268	268	1,042	1,363	849	1,237	509
Connecticut	3,596	154	689	809	581	921	442
Delaware	926	45	173	219	140	231	118
District of Columbia	646	33	93	231	101	129	59
Florida	19,553	863	3,398	4,460	3,006	4,841	2,985
Georgia	9,992	535	2,099	2,501	1,668	2,251	938
Hawaii	1,404	73	251	361	210	333	176
Idaho	1,612	91	358	387	233	366	178
Illinois	12,882	639	2,562	3,196	2,050	3,025	1,409
Indiana	6,571	337	1,344	1,575	1,013	1,565	737
Iowa	3,090	156	616	731	445	747	395
Kansas	2,894	160	606	714	416	668	330
Kentucky	4,395	220	851	1,043	695	1,080	506
Louisiana	4,625	247	926	1,187	689	1,087	490
Maine	1,328	52	227	275	206	380	188
Maryland	5,929	294	1,133	1,446	970	1,452	634
Massachusetts	6,693	292	1,217	1,647	1,073	1,664	799
Michigan	9,896	458	1,929	2,274	1,520	2,517	1,198
Minnesota	5,420	278	1,075	1,306	828	1,320	613
Mississippi	2,991	159	623	732	449	695	333
Missouri	6,044	301	1,178	1,453	902	1,475	735
Montana	1,015	49	189	237	140	269	132
Nebraska	1,869	104	388	458	269	433	216
Nevada	2,790	143	550	695	457	647	298
New Hampshire	1,323	53	239	287	215	369	161
New Jersey	8,899	427	1,705	2,047	1,488	2,193	1,040
New Mexico	2,085	111	426	508	297	500	244
New York	19,651	939	3,587	4,989	3,133	4,707	2,296
North Carolina	9,848	490	1,939	2,366	1,599	2,337	1,118
North Dakota	723	39	137	199	97	166	85
Ohio	11,571	553	2,257	2,670	1,768	2,904	1,420
Oklahoma	3,851	212	788	960	561	888	442
Oregon	3,930	184	723	955	606	979	483
Pennsylvania	12,774	573	2,339	2,947	1,946	3,260	1,709
Rhode Island	1,052	44	191	256	163	265	132
South Carolina	4,775	234	916	1,146	734	1,172	574
South Dakota	845	48	173	203	116	202	104

	total population	Recession (0 to 3)	iGeneration (4 to 18)	Millennial (19 to 36)	Generation X (37 to 48)	Baby Boom (49 to 67)	Older Americans (68 or older)
Tennessee	6,496	320	1,256	1,553	1,032	1,579	757
Texas	26,448	1,553	5,857	6,886	4,227	5,573	2,353
Utah	2,901	203	735	812	412	512	227
Vermont	627	24	111	140	94	176	81
Virginia	8,260	410	1,575	2,080	1,344	1,974	878
Washington	6,971	356	1,325	1,757	1,100	1,683	752
West Virginia	1,854	82	324	412	285	495	257
Wisconsin	5,743	275	1,115	1,343	875	1,445	690
Wyoming	583	31	115	146	83	145	63

Source: Bureau of the Census, State Population Estimates, Internet site http://www.census.gov/popest/data/state/asrh/2013/index .html; calculations by New Strategist

Table 8.20 Distribution of State Population by Generation, 2013

(percent distribution of people by state and generation, 2013)

	total population	Recession (0 to 3)	iGeneration (4 to 18)	Millennial (19 to 36)	Generation X (37 to 48)	Baby Boom (49 to 67)	Older Americans (68 or older)
United States	**100.0%**	**5.0%**	**19.6%**	**24.7%**	**15.6%**	**24.0%**	**11.1%**
Alabama	100.0	4.9	19.4	23.9	15.4	24.3	11.9
Alaska	100.0	6.0	20.8	28.0	14.9	23.4	6.8
Arizona	100.0	5.2	20.6	24.4	15.0	22.5	12.4
Arkansas	100.0	5.2	20.1	23.9	15.0	23.6	12.3
California	100.0	5.2	20.1	26.2	16.2	22.2	10.0
Colorado	100.0	5.1	19.8	25.9	16.1	23.5	9.7
Connecticut	100.0	4.3	19.2	22.5	16.2	25.6	12.3
Delaware	100.0	4.9	18.7	23.6	15.2	25.0	12.7
District of Columbia	100.0	5.1	14.4	35.8	15.6	19.9	9.1
Florida	100.0	4.4	17.4	22.8	15.4	24.8	15.3
Georgia	100.0	5.4	21.0	25.0	16.7	22.5	9.4
Hawaii	100.0	5.2	17.9	25.7	15.0	23.7	12.6
Idaho	100.0	5.6	22.2	24.0	14.5	22.7	11.0
Illinois	100.0	5.0	19.9	24.8	15.9	23.5	10.9
Indiana	100.0	5.1	20.5	24.0	15.4	23.8	11.2
Iowa	100.0	5.0	19.9	23.7	14.4	24.2	12.8
Kansas	100.0	5.5	20.9	24.7	14.4	23.1	11.4
Kentucky	100.0	5.0	19.4	23.7	15.8	24.6	11.5
Louisiana	100.0	5.3	20.0	25.7	14.9	23.5	10.6
Maine	100.0	3.9	17.1	20.7	15.5	28.6	14.2
Maryland	100.0	5.0	19.1	24.4	16.4	24.5	10.7
Massachusetts	100.0	4.4	18.2	24.6	16.0	24.9	11.9
Michigan	100.0	4.6	19.5	23.0	15.4	25.4	12.1
Minnesota	100.0	5.1	19.8	24.1	15.3	24.4	11.3
Mississippi	100.0	5.3	20.8	24.5	15.0	23.2	11.1
Missouri	100.0	5.0	19.5	24.0	14.9	24.4	12.2
Montana	100.0	4.8	18.6	23.3	13.8	26.5	13.0
Nebraska	100.0	5.6	20.8	24.5	14.4	23.1	11.6
Nevada	100.0	5.1	19.7	24.9	16.4	23.2	10.7
New Hampshire	100.0	4.0	18.1	21.7	16.2	27.9	12.2
New Jersey	100.0	4.8	19.2	23.0	16.7	24.6	11.7
New Mexico	100.0	5.3	20.4	24.4	14.2	24.0	11.7
New York	100.0	4.8	18.3	25.4	15.9	24.0	11.7
North Carolina	100.0	5.0	19.7	24.0	16.2	23.7	11.3
North Dakota	100.0	5.4	19.0	27.6	13.4	23.0	11.7
Ohio	100.0	4.8	19.5	23.1	15.3	25.1	12.3
Oklahoma	100.0	5.5	20.5	24.9	14.6	23.1	11.5
Oregon	100.0	4.7	18.4	24.3	15.4	24.9	12.3
Pennsylvania	100.0	4.5	18.3	23.1	15.2	25.5	13.4
Rhode Island	100.0	4.2	18.2	24.4	15.5	25.2	12.6
South Carolina	100.0	4.9	19.2	24.0	15.4	24.5	12.0
South Dakota	100.0	5.7	20.4	24.0	13.7	23.9	12.3

	total population	Recession (0 to 3)	iGeneration (4 to 18)	Millennial (19 to 36)	Generation X (37 to 48)	Baby Boom (49 to 67)	Older Americans (68 or older)
Tennessee	100.0%	4.9%	19.3%	23.9%	15.9%	24.3%	11.7%
Texas	100.0	5.9	22.1	26.0	16.0	21.1	8.9
Utah	100.0	7.0	25.3	28.0	14.2	17.7	7.8
Vermont	100.0	3.9	17.7	22.3	15.1	28.0	13.0
Virginia	100.0	5.0	19.1	25.2	16.3	23.9	10.6
Washington	100.0	5.1	19.0	25.2	15.8	24.1	10.8
West Virginia	100.0	4.4	17.5	22.2	15.4	26.7	13.8
Wisconsin	100.0	4.8	19.4	23.4	15.2	25.2	12.0
Wyoming	100.0	5.3	19.7	25.1	14.2	24.9	10.7

Source: Bureau of the Census, State Population Estimates, Internet site http://www.census.gov/popest/data/state/asrh/2013/index .html; calculations by New Strategist

Table 8.21 Generation X by State, 2013

(number of total people, people aged 37 to 48, and in age groups that include Gen Xers, by state, 2013; numbers in thousands)

	total population	Gen Xers (37 to 48)	35 to 39	40 to 44	45 to 49
Total population	**316,129**	**49,212**	**19,604**	**20,849**	**21,208**
Alabama	4,834	745	292	315	319
Alaska	735	110	45	45	47
Arizona	6,627	992	409	421	407
Arkansas	2,959	443	179	186	187
California	38,333	6,204	2,526	2,623	2,581
Colorado	5,268	849	352	363	344
Connecticut	3,596	581	207	241	270
Delaware	926	140	52	58	63
District of Columbia	646	101	48	42	38
Florida	19,553	3,006	1,140	1,261	1,326
Georgia	9,992	1,668	657	715	698
Hawaii	1,404	210	87	88	87
Idaho	1,612	233	99	98	95
Illinois	12,882	2,050	825	861	868
Indiana	6,571	1,013	400	427	434
Iowa	3,090	445	178	184	193
Kansas	2,894	416	171	173	176
Kentucky	4,395	695	273	292	299
Louisiana	4,625	689	279	284	297
Maine	1,328	206	72	86	96
Maryland	5,929	970	367	403	433
Massachusetts	6,693	1,073	398	444	487
Michigan	9,896	1,520	563	640	678
Minnesota	5,420	828	327	341	363
Mississippi	2,991	449	181	189	190
Missouri	6,044	902	355	376	392
Montana	1,015	140	57	58	60
Nebraska	1,869	269	112	112	113
Nevada	2,790	457	184	195	189
New Hampshire	1,323	215	72	90	102
New Jersey	8,899	1,488	562	619	664
New Mexico	2,085	297	121	123	126
New York	19,651	3,133	1,223	1,297	1,377
North Carolina	9,848	1,599	623	686	674
North Dakota	723	97	41	39	41
Ohio	11,571	1,768	671	746	775
Oklahoma	3,851	561	232	236	233
Oregon	3,930	606	254	258	245
Pennsylvania	12,774	1,946	717	812	879
Rhode Island	1,052	163	59	67	75
South Carolina	4,775	734	284	310	316
South Dakota	845	116	47	47	50

	total population	Gen Xers (37 to 48)	35 to 39	40 to 44	45 to 49
Tennessee	6,496	1,032	402	439	439
Texas	26,448	4,227	1,771	1,804	1,700
Utah	2,901	412	201	171	149
Vermont	627	94	34	39	44
Virginia	8,260	1,344	525	564	581
Washington	6,971	1,100	448	466	457
West Virginia	1,854	285	111	121	123
Wisconsin	5,743	875	335	359	394
Wyoming	583	83	35	34	34

Source: Bureau of the Census, State Population Estimates, Internet site http://www.census.gov/popest/data/state/asrh/2013/index .html; calculations by New Strategist

Table 8.22 Generation X Share of State Populations, 2013

(percent of population aged 37 to 48 and in age groups that include Gen Xers, by state, 2013)

	total population	Gen Xers (37 to 48)	35 to 39	40 to 44	45 to 49
United States	**100.0%**	**15.6%**	**6.2%**	**6.6%**	**6.7%**
Alabama	100.0	15.4	6.0	6.5	6.6
Alaska	100.0	14.9	6.1	6.2	6.4
Arizona	100.0	15.0	6.2	6.4	6.1
Arkansas	100.0	15.0	6.0	6.3	6.3
California	100.0	16.2	6.6	6.8	6.7
Colorado	100.0	16.1	6.7	6.9	6.5
Connecticut	100.0	16.2	5.8	6.7	7.5
Delaware	100.0	15.2	5.7	6.3	6.8
District of Columbia	100.0	15.6	7.4	6.5	5.9
Florida	100.0	15.4	5.8	6.5	6.8
Georgia	100.0	16.7	6.6	7.2	7.0
Hawaii	100.0	15.0	6.2	6.3	6.2
Idaho	100.0	14.5	6.1	6.1	5.9
Illinois	100.0	15.9	6.4	6.7	6.7
Indiana	100.0	15.4	6.1	6.5	6.6
Iowa	100.0	14.4	5.8	6.0	6.3
Kansas	100.0	14.4	5.9	6.0	6.1
Kentucky	100.0	15.8	6.2	6.6	6.8
Louisiana	100.0	14.9	6.0	6.1	6.4
Maine	100.0	15.5	5.4	6.5	7.2
Maryland	100.0	16.4	6.2	6.8	7.3
Massachusetts	100.0	16.0	6.0	6.6	7.3
Michigan	100.0	15.4	5.7	6.5	6.8
Minnesota	100.0	15.3	6.0	6.3	6.7
Mississippi	100.0	15.0	6.0	6.3	6.3
Missouri	100.0	14.9	5.9	6.2	6.5
Montana	100.0	13.8	5.6	5.7	6.0
Nebraska	100.0	14.4	6.0	6.0	6.1
Nevada	100.0	16.4	6.6	7.0	6.8
New Hampshire	100.0	16.2	5.5	6.8	7.7
New Jersey	100.0	16.7	6.3	7.0	7.5
New Mexico	100.0	14.2	5.8	5.9	6.0
New York	100.0	15.9	6.2	6.6	7.0
North Carolina	100.0	16.2	6.3	7.0	6.8
North Dakota	100.0	13.4	5.6	5.4	5.7
Ohio	100.0	15.3	5.8	6.4	6.7
Oklahoma	100.0	14.6	6.0	6.1	6.1
Oregon	100.0	15.4	6.5	6.6	6.2
Pennsylvania	100.0	15.2	5.6	6.4	6.9
Rhode Island	100.0	15.5	5.6	6.4	7.1
South Carolina	100.0	15.4	6.0	6.5	6.6
South Dakota	100.0	13.7	5.6	5.6	5.9

	total population	Gen Xers (37 to 48)	35 to 39	40 to 44	45 to 49
Tennessee	100.0%	15.9%	6.2%	6.8%	6.8%
Texas	100.0	16.0	6.7	6.8	6.4
Utah	100.0	14.2	6.9	5.9	5.1
Vermont	100.0	15.1	5.4	6.2	7.0
Virginia	100.0	16.3	6.4	6.8	7.0
Washington	100.0	15.8	6.4	6.7	6.6
West Virginia	100.0	15.4	6.0	6.5	6.6
Wisconsin	100.0	15.2	5.8	6.3	6.9
Wyoming	100.0	14.2	6.0	5.9	5.9

Source: Bureau of the Census, State Population Estimates, Internet site http://www.census.gov/popest/data/state/asrh/2013/index .html; calculations by New Strategist

Young Adults Are Least Likely to Vote

People aged 65 or older are most likely to vote.

The older people are, the more likely they are to vote. This has long been true, but the gap between young and old has widened over the years. In the 1972 presidential election (the first in which 18-to-20-year-olds could vote), 63.5 percent of people aged 65 or older reported voting compared with 49.6 percent of those aged 18 to 24 (a 13.9 percentage point difference). In the 2012 election, 72.0 percent of citizens aged 65 or older voted versus only 41.2 percent of citizens aged 18 to 24 (a 30.8 percentage point difference). (The voting rates of citizens by age are not available before 2004.)

Despite the excitement generated by Barack Obama during the 2008 presidential campaign, the overall voting rate fell slightly between 2004 and 2008. Young adults were the only ones who boosted their voting rate, the percentage of 18-to-24-year-olds who voted rising from 46.7 to 48.5 percent. In the 2012 presidential election, however, the voting rate of young adults fell by more than 7 percentage points to 41.2 percent. Voting rates also fell among citizens ranging in age from 25 to 64, but the rate increased among citizens aged 65 or older.

■ Non-Hispanic Whites aged 45 or older accounted for only 48 percent of voters in the 2012 presidential election.

Less than half of young adults vote

(percent of citizens aged 18 or older voting in the 2012 presidential election, by age)

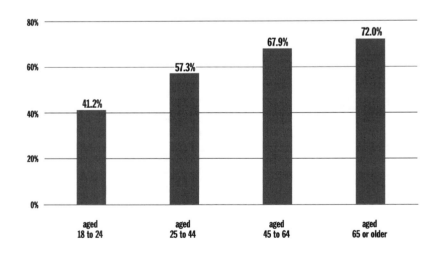

Table 8.23 Voting Rate in Presidential Elections by Age, 1972 to 2012

(percent of people aged 18 or older who reported voting in presidential elections by age, and index of age group to total, 1972 to 2012)

	total people of voting age	18 to 24	25 to 44	45 to 64	65 or older
Citizen population					
2012	61.8%	41.2%	57.3%	67.9%	72.0%
2008	63.6	48.5	60.0	69.2	70.3
2004	63.8	46.7	60.1	70.4	71.0
Total population					
2000	54.7	32.3	49.8	64.1	67.6
1996	54.2	32.4	49.2	64.4	67.0
1992	61.3	42.8	58.3	70.0	70.1
1988	57.4	36.2	54.0	67.9	68.8
1984	59.9	40.8	58.4	69.8	67.7
1980	59.3	39.9	58.7	69.3	65.1
1976	59.2	42.2	58.7	68.7	62.2
1972	63.0	49.6	62.7	70.8	63.5
INDEX OF AGE GROUP TO TOTAL					
Citizen population					
2012	100	67	93	110	117
2008	100	76	94	109	111
2004	100	73	94	110	111
Total population					
2000	100	59	91	117	124
1996	100	60	91	119	124
1992	100	70	95	114	114
1988	100	63	94	118	120
1984	100	68	97	117	113
1980	100	67	99	117	110
1976	100	71	99	116	105
1972	100	79	100	112	101

Note: Voting rates of citizens by age are not available before 2004. The index is calculated by dividing the voting rate of each age group by the total voting rate and multiplying by 100.
Source: Bureau of the Census, Voting and Registration, Internet site http://www.census.gov/hhes/www/socdemo/voting/index.html; calculations by New Strategist

Table 8.24 Voters by Age, Race, and Hispanic Origin, 2012

(number, percent distribution, and share of people who reported voting in the presidential election by age, race, and Hispanic origin, 2012; numbers in thousands)

	total	Asian	Black	Hispanic	non-Hispanic White
Total voters	**132,948**	**4,331**	**18,558**	**11,188**	**98,041**
Aged 18 to 24	11,353	408	2,306	1,677	6,933
Aged 25 to 44	39,942	1,652	6,595	4,365	27,216
Aged 45 to 64	52,013	1,522	6,890	3,609	39,507
Aged 65 or older	29,641	748	2,767	1,537	24,385
PERCENT DISTRIBUTION OF VOTERS BY RACE AND HISPANIC ORIGIN					
Total voters	**100.0%**	**3.3%**	**14.0%**	**8.4%**	**73.7%**
Aged 18 to 24	100.0	3.6	20.3	14.8	61.1
Aged 25 to 44	100.0	4.1	16.5	10.9	68.1
Aged 45 to 64	100.0	2.9	13.2	6.9	76.0
Aged 65 or older	100.0	2.5	9.3	5.2	82.3
SHARE OF VOTERS BY AGE GROUP, RACE, AND HISPANIC ORIGIN					
Under age 45	38.6	1.5	6.7	4.5	25.7
Aged 45 or older	61.4	1.7	7.3	3.9	48.1

Note: Asians and Blacks are those who identify themselves as being of the race alone and those who identify themselves as being of the race in combination with other races. Non-Hispanic Whites are those who identify themselves as being White alone and not Hispanic.
Source: Bureau of the Census, Voting and Registration, Internet site http://www.census.gov/hhes/www/socdemo/voting/index.html; calculations by New Strategist

9

Spending

■ The average household reduced its spending by 8.6 percent between 2006 (the year overall household spending peaked) and 2013, after adjusting for inflation. The spending of households headed by people aged 35 to 44 (Gen Xers were aged 37 to 48 in 2013) fell by a larger 11.5 percent during those years, and the spending of householders aged 45 to 54 fell 9.0 percent.

■ One reason for the decline in spending among households headed by people ranging in age from 35 to 54 is less spending on mortgage interest. Householders aged 35 to 44 reduced their spending on mortgage interest by 26 percent between 2006 and 2013, after adjusting for inflation, as some lost their home and others decided to rent rather than buy. Householders aged 45 to 54 cut their mortgage interest spending by 29 percent during those years.

■ Households headed by people aged 35 to 54 are in their peak earning years and they spend 15 to 18 percent more than average. Those aged 35 to 44 spent $58,784 in 2013, disproportionately spending on items commonly purchased by parents with children under age 18. Those aged 45 to 54 spent an even larger $60,524 in 2013, including above-average spending on education.

Spending of Householders Aged 35 to 54 Has Fallen

Gen Xers spent less in 2013 than their counterparts did in 2000.

Gen Xers are perhaps the generation hardest hit by the Great Recession. Between 2006 and 2013, the average household headed by a 35-to-44-year old (Generation X was aged 37 to 48 in 2013) slashed its spending by a substantial 11 percent, after adjusting for inflation. Householders aged 45 to 54 cut their spending by 9 percent. Households in both age groups spent less in 2013 than their counterparts did in 2000.

Households headed by people aged 35 to 44 spent an average of $58,784 in 2013, down from $66,416 in 2006, after adjusting for inflation. One factor behind the decline is the drop in spending on mortgage interest. Many Gen Xers bought homes during the housing bubble. The average annual spending on mortgage interest of householders aged 35 to 44 was as high as $6,834 in 2006, fully 17 percent more than in 2000. Between 2006 and 2013, however, mortgage interest payments by households in the age group fell 26 percent, to $5,078, as some lost their home and others decided not to buy.

Householders aged 45 to 54 spent $60,524 in 2013, well below the $66,516 of 2006, after adjusting for inflation. This age group also cut its spending on mortgage interest dramatically, with the figure falling 29 percent from $5,567 in 2006 to just $3,950 in 2013. The spending of households in the 35-to-44 and 45-to-54 age groups continued to decline faster than average in the more recent 2010-to-2013 time period, but some categories made gains. Most notably, householders aged 35 to 44 spent 24 percent more on new cars and trucks in 2013 than in 2010, and householders aged 45 to 54 spent 31 percent more.

■ The Great Recession was a setback for Gen Xers, and it will take years for them to recover.

The average Gen X household spends close to $60,000 a year

(average annual household spending by age of householder, 2013)

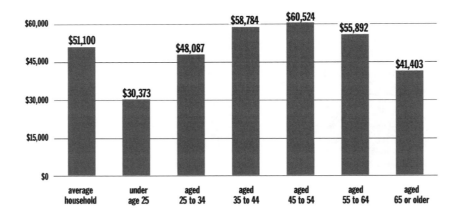

Table 9.1 Average Household Spending, 2000 to 2013

(average annual spending of consumer units on products and services, 2000 to 2013; percent change for selected years; in 2013 dollars)

	average spending				percent change		
	2013	2010	2006	2000	2010–13	2006–13	2000–06
Number of consumer units (in 000s)	125,670	121,107	118,843	109,367	3.8%	5.7%	8.7%
Average annual spending of consumer units	$51,100	$51,397	$55,926	$51,468	–0.6	–8.6	8.7
FOOD	6,602	6,548	7,062	6,978	0.8	–6.5	1.2
Food at home	3,977	3,872	3,948	4,087	2.7	0.7	–3.4
Cereals and bakery products	544	536	515	613	1.4	5.6	–15.9
Cereals and cereal products	185	176	165	211	4.9	12.0	–21.7
Bakery products	359	360	351	402	–0.3	2.2	–12.6
Meats, poultry, fish, and eggs	856	838	921	1,075	2.2	–7.1	–14.4
Beef	219	232	273	322	–5.5	–19.7	–15.3
Pork	170	159	181	226	6.8	–6.3	–19.7
Other meats	119	125	121	137	–4.8	–1.9	–11.2
Poultry	170	147	163	196	15.3	4.3	–16.9
Fish and seafood	122	125	141	149	–2.4	–13.5	–5.3
Eggs	56	49	43	46	14.0	31.0	–7.0
Dairy products	414	406	425	440	2.0	–2.6	–3.3
Fresh milk and cream	152	151	162	177	0.9	–6.0	–8.7
Other dairy products	262	256	263	261	2.2	–0.6	0.9
Fruits and vegetables	751	725	684	705	3.5	9.8	–2.9
Fresh fruits	270	248	225	221	8.9	19.8	2.2
Fresh vegetables	236	224	223	215	5.2	5.8	3.7
Processed fruits	115	121	126	156	–4.7	–8.7	–19.0
Processed vegetables	130	132	110	114	–1.9	18.4	–3.4
Other food at home	1,412	1,365	1,401	1,254	3.4	0.8	11.7
Sugar and other sweets	143	141	144	158	1.4	–1.0	–8.7
Fats and oils	117	110	99	112	6.3	17.7	–11.5
Miscellaneous foods	728	713	725	591	2.2	0.5	22.6
Nonalcoholic beverages	384	356	384	338	7.9	0.1	13.4
Food prepared by consumer unit on trips	42	46	50	54	–8.6	–15.5	–8.2
Food away from home	2,625	2,676	3,113	2,891	–1.9	–15.7	7.7
ALCOHOLIC BEVERAGES	445	440	574	503	1.1	–22.5	14.1
HOUSING	17,148	17,688	18,912	16,665	–3.1	–9.3	13.5
Shelter	10,080	10,483	11,178	9,624	–3.8	–9.8	16.1
Owned dwellings	6,108	6,706	7,530	6,226	–8.9	–18.9	20.9
Mortgage interest and charges	3,078	3,580	4,337	3,570	–14.0	–29.0	21.5
Property taxes	1,848	1,938	1,905	1,541	–4.6	–3.0	23.7
Maintenance, repair, insurance, other expenses	1,182	1,188	1,288	1,116	–0.5	–8.3	15.4
Rented dwellings	3,324	3,098	2,993	2,752	7.3	11.1	8.8
Other lodging	649	678	655	647	–4.3	–0.9	1.3

	average spending				percent change		
	2013	**2010**	**2006**	**2000**	**2010–13**	**2006–13**	**2000–06**
Utilities, fuels, and public services	**$3,737**	**$3,910**	**$3,925**	**$3,367**	**–4.4%**	**–4.8%**	**16.6%**
Natural gas	393	470	588	415	–16.4	–33.2	41.6
Electricity	1,422	1,510	1,463	1,232	–5.8	–2.8	18.7
Fuel oil and other fuels	142	150	159	131	–5.1	–11.0	21.5
Telephone services	1,271	1,258	1,256	1,186	1.0	1.2	5.9
Residential telephone, VOIP, and phone cards	358	447	651	1,025	–19.8	–45.0	–36.6
Cellular phone service	913	812	606	161	12.5	50.8	276.1
Water and other public services	509	522	459	400	–2.6	11.0	14.6
Household services	**1,144**	**1,076**	**1,095**	**925**	**6.3**	**4.4**	**18.4**
Personal services	368	363	454	441	1.3	–19.0	3.0
Other household services	776	713	641	484	8.9	21.0	32.4
Housekeeping supplies	**645**	**654**	**740**	**652**	**–1.3**	**–12.8**	**13.4**
Laundry and cleaning supplies	154	160	174	177	–3.9	–11.7	–1.5
Other household products	350	351	381	306	–0.4	–8.2	24.7
Postage and stationery	140	141	184	170	–0.7	–23.8	7.8
Household furnishings and equipment	**1,542**	**1,567**	**1,974**	**2,096**	**–1.6**	**–21.9**	**–5.8**
Household textiles	97	109	178	143	–11.0	–45.5	24.1
Furniture	382	379	535	529	0.7	–28.6	1.1
Floor coverings	20	38	55	60	–48.0	–63.9	–6.8
Major appliances	214	223	278	256	–4.2	–23.2	8.9
Small appliances and miscellaneous housewares	100	114	126	118	–12.5	–20.6	7.0
Miscellaneous household equipment	727	702	801	989	3.6	–9.2	–19.0
APPAREL AND RELATED SERVICES	**1,604**	**1,816**	**2,165**	**2,511**	**–11.7**	**–25.9**	**–13.8**
Men and boys	**374**	**408**	**513**	**595**	**–8.4**	**–27.1**	**–13.8**
Men, aged 16 or older	304	325	408	465	–6.4	–25.5	–12.3
Boys, aged 2 to 15	70	83	105	130	–16.0	–33.4	–19.0
Women and girls	**636**	**708**	**868**	**981**	**–10.2**	**–26.7**	**–11.5**
Women, aged 16 or older	527	600	727	821	–12.2	–27.5	–11.5
Girls, aged 2 to 15	109	108	141	160	1.0	–22.7	–11.7
Children under age 2	**75**	**97**	**111**	**111**	**–22.9**	**–32.4**	**0.0**
Footwear	**307**	**324**	**351**	**464**	**–5.2**	**–12.6**	**–24.3**
Other apparel products and services	**211**	**279**	**324**	**360**	**–24.3**	**–34.8**	**–10.1**
TRANSPORTATION	**9,004**	**8,202**	**9,831**	**10,034**	**9.8**	**–8.4**	**–2.0**
Vehicle purchases	**3,271**	**2,765**	**3,953**	**4,624**	**18.3**	**–17.3**	**–14.5**
Cars and trucks, new	1,563	1,302	2,078	2,171	20.0	–24.8	–4.3
Cars and trucks, used	1,669	1,408	1,812	2,395	18.5	–7.9	–24.3
Gasoline and motor oil	**2,611**	**2,278**	**2,573**	**1,747**	**14.6**	**1.5**	**47.3**
Other vehicle expenses	**2,584**	**2,632**	**2,721**	**3,086**	**–1.8**	**–5.0**	**–11.8**
Vehicle finance charges	204	260	344	444	–21.4	–40.8	–22.4
Maintenance and repairs	835	841	795	844	–0.7	5.0	–5.8
Vehicle insurance	1,013	1,079	1,024	1,053	–6.1	–1.1	–2.7
Vehicle rentals, leases, licenses, other charges	533	452	557	745	17.9	–4.3	–25.3
Public transportation	**537**	**527**	**584**	**578**	**2.0**	**–8.0**	**1.0**

	average spending				percent change		
	2013	2010	2006	2000	2010–13	2006–13	2000–06
HEALTH CARE	$3,631	$3,373	$3,196	$2,795	7.7%	13.6%	14.4%
Health insurance	2,229	1,956	1,693	1,330	13.9	31.7	27.3
Medical services	796	771	774	768	3.2	2.8	0.8
Drugs	470	518	594	563	–9.3	–20.9	5.5
Medical supplies	135	127	135	134	6.2	–0.1	0.9
ENTERTAINMENT	2,482	2,675	2,746	2,520	–7.2	–9.6	8.9
Fees and admissions	569	621	700	697	–8.3	–18.7	0.5
Audio and visual equipment and services	964	1,019	1,047	841	–5.4	–7.9	24.4
Pets, toys, and playground equipment	596	647	476	452	–7.9	25.2	5.4
Pets	460	513	365	283	–10.3	26.0	29.1
Toys, hobbies, and playground equipment	136	134	111	169	1.8	22.6	–34.4
Other entertainment products and services	353	389	521	532	–9.2	–32.3	–2.0
PERSONAL CARE PRODUCTS AND SERVICES	608	622	676	763	–2.2	–10.1	–11.4
READING	102	107	135	198	–4.5	–24.6	–31.5
EDUCATION	1,138	1,147	1,026	855	–0.8	10.9	20.0
TOBACCO PRODUCTS AND SMOKING SUPPLIES	330	387	378	432	–14.7	–12.7	–12.4
MISCELLANEOUS	645	907	978	1,050	–28.9	–34.0	–6.9
CASH CONTRIBUTIONS	1,834	1,745	2,160	1,613	5.1	–15.1	33.9
PERSONAL INSURANCE AND PENSIONS	5,528	5,740	6,090	4,552	–3.7	–9.2	33.8
Life and other personal insurance	319	340	372	540	–6.1	–14.3	–31.1
Pensions and Social Security*	5,209	5,399	5,718	4,012	–3.5	–8.9	*
GIFTS FOR PEOPLE IN OTHER HOUSEHOLDS	1,078	1,099	1,333	1,465	–1.9	–19.2	–9.0

*Recent spending on pensions and Social Security is not comparable with 2000 because of changes in methodology.
Note: The Bureau of Labor Statistics uses consumer unit rather than household as the sampling unit in the Consumer Expenditure Survey. For the definition of consumer unit, see the glossary. Spending on gifts is also included in the preceding product and service categories.
Source: Bureau of Labor Statistics, 2000, 2006, 2010, and 2013 Consumer Expenditure Surveys, Internet site http://www.bls.gov/cex/; calculations by New Strategist

Table 9.2 Average Spending of Householders Aged 35 to 44, 2000 to 2013

(average annual spending of consumer units headed by people aged 35 to 44, 2000 to 2013; percent change for selected years; in 2013 dollars)

	average spending				percent change		
	2013	2010	2006	2000	2010–13	2006–13	2000–06
Number of consumer units aged 35 to 44 (in 000s)	21,257	21,912	23,950	23,983	–3.0%	–11.2%	–0.1%
Average annual spending of consumer units	$58,784	$59,769	$66,416	$61,079	–1.6	–11.5	8.7
FOOD	**7,920**	**7,994**	**8,471**	**8,241**	**–0.9**	**–6.5**	**2.8**
Food at home	**4,641**	**4,546**	**4,770**	**4,713**	**2.1**	**–2.7**	**1.2**
Cereals and bakery products	646	648	639	718	–0.4	1.1	–11.0
Cereals and cereal products	233	226	214	257	2.9	9.0	–16.8
Bakery products	412	422	426	461	–2.4	–3.4	–7.6
Meats, poultry, fish, and eggs	993	957	1,112	1,242	3.7	–10.7	–10.5
Beef	276	246	314	365	12.3	–12.2	–14.0
Pork	184	184	215	252	0.1	–14.4	–14.6
Other meats	138	150	151	162	–7.7	–8.8	–6.8
Poultry	215	179	214	241	19.8	0.6	–11.2
Fish and seafood	119	141	165	170	–15.6	–28.0	–3.1
Eggs	61	58	52	50	5.7	17.3	3.9
Dairy products	495	489	522	518	1.2	–5.2	0.8
Fresh milk and cream	196	189	207	212	3.7	–5.2	–2.6
Other dairy products	299	300	315	306	–0.4	–5.2	3.2
Fruits and vegetables	866	841	775	747	3.0	11.7	3.8
Fresh fruits	312	292	253	229	7.0	23.3	10.7
Fresh vegetables	259	249	239	222	4.0	8.3	7.8
Processed fruits	136	143	151	169	–5.0	–10.2	–10.5
Processed vegetables	158	156	132	124	1.3	19.9	5.8
Other food at home	1,641	1,611	1,722	1,489	1.9	–4.7	15.6
Sugar and other sweets	157	165	168	199	–4.6	–6.3	–15.7
Fats and oils	128	127	112	122	0.7	14.2	–7.9
Miscellaneous foods	881	853	916	701	3.3	–3.9	30.8
Nonalcoholic beverages	435	410	473	406	6.0	–8.0	16.5
Food prepared by consumer unit on trips	41	57	52	62	–27.6	–21.2	–16.4
Food away from home	**3,280**	**3,448**	**3,701**	**3,527**	**–4.9**	**–11.4**	**4.9**
ALCOHOLIC BEVERAGES	**443**	**531**	**573**	**568**	**–16.6**	**–22.7**	**0.9**
HOUSING	**20,619**	**21,411**	**23,461**	**20,443**	**–3.7**	**–12.1**	**14.8**
Shelter	**12,271**	**12,969**	**14,381**	**12,081**	**–5.4**	**–14.7**	**19.0**
Owned dwellings	7,981	8,706	10,359	8,703	–8.3	–23.0	19.0
Mortgage interest and charges	5,078	5,551	6,834	5,820	–8.5	–25.7	17.4
Property taxes	1,964	2,110	2,238	1,686	–6.9	–12.3	32.8
Maintenance, repair, insurance, other expenses	939	1,045	1,287	1,196	–10.1	–27.1	7.6
Rented dwellings	3,834	3,712	3,395	2,796	3.3	12.9	21.4
Other lodging	455	550	625	582	–17.3	–27.2	7.5

	average spending				percent change		
	2013	**2010**	**2006**	**2000**	**2010–13**	**2006–13**	**2000–06**
Utilities, fuels, and public services	**$4,299**	**$4,356**	**$4,453**	**$3,801**	**–1.3%**	**–3.5%**	**17.2%**
Natural gas	445	531	646	473	–16.2	–31.1	36.4
Electricity	1,635	1,674	1,640	1,365	–2.3	–0.3	20.1
Fuel oil and other fuels	121	112	181	131	7.9	–33.3	38.3
Telephone services	1,508	1,457	1,469	1,377	3.5	2.7	6.6
Residential telephone, VOIP, and phone cards	298	431	718	1,164	–30.9	–58.5	–38.3
Cellular phone service	1,209	1,026	750	213	17.9	61.2	251.4
Water and other public services	590	581	519	455	1.5	13.7	14.1
Household services	**1,612**	**1,511**	**1,595**	**1,212**	**6.7**	**1.1**	**31.6**
Personal services	825	785	937	733	5.1	–12.0	27.8
Other household services	787	725	658	479	8.5	19.7	37.3
Housekeeping supplies	**674**	**708**	**879**	**771**	**–4.8**	**–23.4**	**14.0**
Laundry and cleaning supplies	170	197	218	212	–13.5	–22.2	2.8
Other household products	368	355	477	379	3.8	–22.9	26.0
Postage and stationery	136	158	184	180	–14.0	–26.0	2.1
Household furnishings and equipment	**1,763**	**1,867**	**2,154**	**2,578**	**–5.6**	**–18.1**	**–16.5**
Household textiles	108	119	162	168	–8.9	–33.2	–3.6
Furniture	449	478	619	675	–6.0	–27.5	–8.2
Floor coverings	17	45	46	72	–62.1	–63.2	–35.5
Major appliances	268	280	314	287	–4.3	–14.7	9.6
Small appliances and miscellaneous housewares	102	112	131	126	–9.1	–21.9	3.8
Miscellaneous household equipment	819	833	881	1,253	–1.7	–7.0	–29.7
APPAREL AND RELATED SERVICES	**1,960**	**2,179**	**2,736**	**3,143**	**–10.1**	**–28.4**	**–12.9**
Men and boys	**533**	**520**	**664**	**745**	**2.4**	**–19.8**	**–10.9**
Men, aged 16 or older	378	342	466	496	10.6	–18.8	–6.2
Boys, aged 2 to 15	154	177	199	249	–13.2	–22.5	–20.2
Women and girls	**718**	**817**	**1,065**	**1,265**	**–12.1**	**–32.6**	**–15.8**
Women, aged 16 or older	513	593	775	936	–13.5	–33.8	–17.2
Girls, aged 2 to 15	205	224	290	327	–8.6	–29.3	–11.4
Children under age 2	**109**	**125**	**148**	**142**	**–12.8**	**–26.3**	**4.1**
Footwear	**398**	**442**	**467**	**542**	**–10.0**	**–14.7**	**–13.9**
Other apparel products and services	**202**	**276**	**391**	**448**	**–26.7**	**–48.3**	**–12.8**
TRANSPORTATION	**10,519**	**9,362**	**11,529**	**11,772**	**12.4**	**–8.8**	**–2.1**
Vehicle purchases	**4,010**	**3,104**	**4,688**	**5,406**	**29.2**	**–14.5**	**–13.3**
Cars and trucks, new	1,774	1,433	2,310	2,332	23.8	–23.2	–1.0
Cars and trucks, used	2,218	1,579	2,280	2,974	40.5	–2.7	–23.3
Gasoline and motor oil	**3,218**	**2,710**	**3,046**	**2,133**	**18.7**	**5.6**	**42.8**
Other vehicle expenses	**2,740**	**2,966**	**3,149**	**3,622**	**–7.6**	**–13.0**	**–13.1**
Vehicle finance charges	288	331	432	549	–13.0	–33.4	–21.3
Maintenance and repairs	841	950	860	958	–11.5	–2.2	–10.2
Vehicle insurance	1,019	1,147	1,128	1,196	–11.2	–9.6	–5.7
Vehicle rentals, leases, licenses, other charges	592	537	729	920	10.2	–18.8	–20.7
Public transportation	**552**	**582**	**646**	**610**	**–5.2**	**–14.5**	**5.9**

	average spending				percent change		
	2013	**2010**	**2006**	**2000**	**2010–13**	**2006–13**	**2000–06**
HEALTH CARE	**$3,188**	**$2,760**	**$2,639**	**$2,400**	**15.5%**	**20.8%**	**10.0%**
Health insurance	1,944	1,552	1,403	1,150	25.2	38.6	22.0
Medical services	786	728	733	751	8.0	7.3	–2.4
Drugs	343	363	399	384	–5.6	–14.0	3.8
Medical supplies	116	116	104	115	–0.4	11.5	–9.6
ENTERTAINMENT	**2,958**	**3,267**	**3,427**	**3,333**	**–9.5**	**–13.7**	**2.8**
Fees and admissions	736	907	969	967	–18.9	–24.1	0.2
Audio and visual equipment and services	1,139	1,152	1,216	1,067	–1.1	–6.3	13.9
Pets, toys, and playground equipment	638	765	574	610	–16.6	11.1	–5.9
Pets	473	570	423	357	–17.1	11.8	18.4
Toys, hobbies, and playground equipment	165	195	151	253	–15.3	9.0	–40.1
Other entertainment products and services	446	442	668	689	0.8	–33.2	–3.0
PERSONAL CARE PRODUCTS AND SERVICES	**672**	**729**	**795**	**871**	**–7.8**	**–15.5**	**–8.7**
READING	**105**	**85**	**129**	**204**	**22.9**	**–18.9**	**–36.6**
EDUCATION	**903**	**1,029**	**990**	**832**	**–12.2**	**–8.8**	**19.0**
TOBACCO PRODUCTS AND SMOKING SUPPLIES	**331**	**382**	**409**	**578**	**–13.5**	**–19.1**	**–29.2**
MISCELLANEOUS	**643**	**985**	**1,090**	**1,153**	**–34.7**	**–41.0**	**–5.5**
CASH CONTRIBUTIONS	**1,440**	**1,637**	**1,973**	**1,357**	**–12.0**	**–27.0**	**45.4**
PERSONAL INSURANCE AND PENSIONS	**7,081**	**7,419**	**8,193**	**6,182**	**–4.5**	**–13.6**	**32.5**
Life and other personal insurance	290	299	421	557	–3.1	–31.1	–24.5
Pensions and Social Security	6,791	7,119	7,772	5,625	–4.6	–12.6	38.2
GIFTS FOR PEOPLE IN OTHER HOUSEHOLDS	**604**	**782**	**896**	**1,354**	**–22.8**	**–32.6**	**–33.9**

Note: The Bureau of Labor Statistics uses consumer unit rather than household as the sampling unit in the Consumer Expenditure Survey. For the definition of consumer unit, see the glossary. Spending on gifts is also included in the preceding product and service categories.
Source: Bureau of Labor Statistics, 2000, 2006, 2010, and 2013 Consumer Expenditure Surveys, Internet site http://www.bls.gov/cex/; calculations by New Strategist

Table 9.3 Average Spending of Householders Aged 45 to 54, 2000 to 2013

(average annual spending of consumer units headed by people aged 45 to 54, 2000 to 2013; percent change for selected years; in 2013 dollars)

	average spending				percent change		
	2013	2010	2006	2000	2010–13	2006–13	2000–06
Number of consumer units aged 45 to 54 (in 000s)	24,501	25,054	24,696	21,874	–2.2%	–0.8%	12.9%
Average annual spending of consumer units	$60,524	$61,737	$66,516	$62,447	–2.0	–9.0	6.5
FOOD	7,907	7,724	8,468	8,516	2.4	–6.6	–0.6
Food at home	4,701	4,668	4,664	4,947	0.7	0.8	–5.7
Cereals and bakery products	650	641	589	758	1.4	10.3	–22.2
Cereals and cereal products	222	213	187	244	4.4	18.6	–23.1
Bakery products	428	428	402	514	–0.1	6.4	–21.8
Meats, poultry, fish, and eggs	1,048	1,032	1,123	1,312	1.5	–6.7	–14.4
Beef	249	281	356	400	–11.4	–30.0	–11.1
Pork	211	194	223	268	8.5	–5.4	–16.7
Other meats	154	157	153	164	–1.9	1.0	–6.8
Poultry	213	186	184	229	14.6	15.9	–19.6
Fish and seafood	159	154	164	198	3.4	–3.1	–16.9
Eggs	63	59	45	54	7.2	39.8	–16.7
Dairy products	475	484	485	510	–1.9	–2.1	–4.8
Fresh milk and cream	171	175	174	198	–2.4	–2.0	–11.7
Other dairy products	304	309	310	314	–1.5	–1.8	–1.3
Fruits and vegetables	857	875	789	847	–2.1	8.6	–6.8
Fresh fruits	302	293	260	253	3.2	16.2	2.8
Fresh vegetables	275	268	270	272	2.6	1.7	–0.6
Processed fruits	127	143	136	180	–11.3	–6.9	–24.2
Processed vegetables	152	170	122	142	–10.5	24.1	–13.8
Other food at home	1,672	1,637	1,677	1,521	2.2	–0.3	10.3
Sugar and other sweets	171	173	180	193	–1.2	–5.1	–6.8
Fats and oils	133	132	112	138	0.4	18.7	–18.8
Miscellaneous foods	854	833	845	714	2.5	1.1	18.3
Nonalcoholic beverages	465	448	477	406	3.9	–2.6	17.6
Food prepared by consumer unit on trips	49	51	61	70	–4.4	–20.0	–12.9
Food away from home	3,206	3,057	3,804	3,569	4.9	–15.7	6.6
ALCOHOLIC BEVERAGES	545	442	707	564	23.2	–22.9	25.4
HOUSING	19,001	20,192	21,235	19,182	–5.9	–10.5	10.7
Shelter	11,208	12,304	12,591	11,224	–8.9	–11.0	12.2
Owned dwellings	7,378	8,721	9,272	8,068	–15.4	–20.4	14.9
Mortgage interest and charges	3,950	4,986	5,567	4,813	–20.8	–29.1	15.7
Property taxes	2,180	2,452	2,348	1,990	–11.1	–7.2	18.0
Maintenance, repair, insurance, other expenses	1,248	1,282	1,358	1,265	–2.7	–8.1	7.3
Rented dwellings	2,938	2,663	2,385	2,183	10.3	23.2	9.2
Other lodging	892	920	933	973	–3.0	–4.3	–4.1

	average spending				percent change		
	2013	2010	2006	2000	2010–13	2006–13	2000–06
Utilities, fuels, and public services	**$4,277**	**$4,501**	**$4,520**	**$3,865**	**–5.0%**	**–5.4%**	**17.0%**
Natural gas	442	541	691	465	–18.2	–36.0	48.5
Electricity	1,575	1,686	1,670	1,414	–6.6	–5.7	18.1
Fuel oil and other fuels	156	160	173	147	–2.7	–10.0	17.5
Telephone services	1,534	1,526	1,466	1,362	0.6	4.6	7.6
Residential telephone, VOIP, and phone cards	403	502	742	1,165	–19.7	–45.7	–36.3
Cellular phone service	1,131	1,023	725	198	10.5	56.1	266.8
Water and other public services	571	589	519	476	–3.0	10.1	9.0
Household services	**1,020**	**999**	**916**	**789**	**2.1**	**11.3**	**16.2**
Personal services	162	205	222	199	–21.0	–27.0	11.6
Other household services	859	794	694	588	8.2	23.7	18.0
Housekeeping supplies	**751**	**694**	**840**	**720**	**8.1**	**–10.6**	**16.7**
Laundry and cleaning supplies	176	176	185	185	–0.2	–4.8	–0.2
Other household products	424	368	426	334	15.4	–0.6	27.6
Postage and stationery	151	150	229	199	1.0	–34.0	15.1
Household furnishings and equipment	**1,745**	**1,693**	**2,369**	**2,585**	**3.1**	**–26.3**	**–8.4**
Household textiles	117	116	202	169	0.5	–42.1	19.6
Furniture	398	347	658	637	14.6	–39.5	3.2
Floor coverings	18	40	55	69	–54.5	–67.5	–19.6
Major appliances	252	235	329	302	7.2	–23.5	9.2
Small appliances and miscellaneous housewares	117	120	172	170	–2.2	–32.0	1.0
Miscellaneous household equipment	844	837	952	1,238	0.9	–11.4	–23.1
APPAREL AND RELATED SERVICES	**1,826**	**2,100**	**2,514**	**3,208**	**–13.1**	**–27.4**	**–21.6**
Men and boys	**453**	**501**	**622**	**781**	**–9.6**	**–27.1**	**–20.4**
Men, aged 16 or older	372	417	507	652	–10.7	–26.7	–22.2
Boys, aged 2 to 15	81	84	116	129	–4.0	–29.9	–10.1
Women and girls	**690**	**895**	**1,055**	**1,322**	**–22.9**	**–34.6**	**–20.2**
Women, aged 16 or older	546	771	904	1,150	–29.2	–39.6	–21.4
Girls, aged 2 to 15	144	124	151	170	16.2	–4.9	–11.2
Children under age 2	**39**	**63**	**83**	**73**	**–38.1**	**–53.1**	**13.9**
Footwear	**404**	**385**	**396**	**593**	**5.0**	**1.9**	**–33.1**
Other apparel products and services	**240**	**257**	**359**	**440**	**–6.8**	**–33.2**	**–18.3**
TRANSPORTATION	**10,782**	**9,887**	**11,684**	**11,941**	**9.0**	**–7.7**	**–2.2**
Vehicle purchases	**3,958**	**3,249**	**4,603**	**5,226**	**21.8**	**–14.0**	**–11.9**
Cars and trucks, new	2,077	1,581	2,412	2,286	31.4	–13.9	5.5
Cars and trucks, used	1,817	1,626	2,093	2,879	11.7	–13.2	–27.3
Gasoline and motor oil	**3,093**	**2,751**	**3,112**	**2,154**	**12.4**	**–0.6**	**44.5**
Other vehicle expenses	**3,074**	**3,230**	**3,257**	**3,880**	**–4.8**	**–5.6**	**–16.0**
Vehicle finance charges	245	318	386	529	–23.0	–36.5	–27.0
Maintenance and repairs	1,071	1,012	1,001	1,084	5.9	7.0	–7.7
Vehicle insurance	1,153	1,348	1,277	1,356	–14.5	–9.7	–5.8
Vehicle rentals, leases, licenses, other charges	605	551	594	912	9.7	1.9	–34.9
Public transportation	**657**	**658**	**712**	**683**	**–0.2**	**–7.7**	**4.2**

	average spending				percent change		
	2013	**2010**	**2006**	**2000**	**2010–13**	**2006–13**	**2000–06**
HEALTH CARE	**$3,801**	**$3,484**	**$3,186**	**$2,976**	**9.1%**	**19.3%**	**7.0%**
Health insurance	2,242	1,866	1,514	1,320	20.1	48.1	14.6
Medical services	918	939	922	946	−2.2	−0.4	−2.5
Drugs	489	531	577	551	−7.9	−15.2	4.7
Medical supplies	151	146	174	160	3.2	−13.5	9.3
ENTERTAINMENT	**3,070**	**3,299**	**3,201**	**3,018**	**−6.9**	**−4.1**	**6.1**
Fees and admissions	747	833	875	862	−10.4	−14.6	1.5
Audio and visual equipment and services	1,064	1,095	1,179	942	−2.8	−9.7	25.2
Pets, toys, and playground equipment	728	786	574	519	−7.4	26.8	10.6
Pets	586	641	478	380	−8.6	22.6	25.8
Toys, hobbies, and playground equipment	141	145	96	139	−3.0	47.0	−31.2
Other entertainment products and services	531	585	572	695	−9.3	−7.2	−17.7
PERSONAL CARE PRODUCTS AND SERVICES	**723**	**719**	**804**	**923**	**0.6**	**−10.1**	**−12.8**
READING	**88**	**111**	**154**	**241**	**−20.8**	**−42.7**	**−36.2**
EDUCATION	**1,970**	**2,237**	**2,006**	**1,550**	**−11.9**	**−1.8**	**29.4**
TOBACCO PRODUCTS AND SMOKING SUPPLIES	**447**	**480**	**500**	**509**	**−6.8**	**−10.7**	**−1.6**
MISCELLANEOUS	**686**	**1,002**	**1,122**	**1,254**	**−31.5**	**−38.9**	**−10.5**
CASH CONTRIBUTIONS	**2,007**	**1,866**	**2,447**	**2,079**	**7.5**	**−18.0**	**17.7**
PERSONAL INSURANCE AND PENSIONS	**7,672**	**8,192**	**8,489**	**6,487**	**−6.3**	**−9.6**	**30.9**
Life and other personal insurance	367	471	477	743	−22.1	−23.1	−35.7
Pensions and Social Security	7,305	7,721	8,011	5,744	−5.4	−8.8	39.5
GIFTS FOR PEOPLE IN OTHER HOUSEHOLDS	**1,724**	**1,734**	**2,096**	**2,332**	**−0.6**	**−17.8**	**−10.1**

Note: The Bureau of Labor Statistics uses consumer unit rather than household as the sampling unit in the Consumer Expenditure Survey. For the definition of consumer unit, see the glossary. Spending on gifts is also included in the preceding product and service categories.
Source: Bureau of Labor Statistics, 2000, 2006, 2010, and 2013 Consumer Expenditure Surveys, Internet site http://www.bls.gov/cex/; calculations by New Strategist

Householders Aged 35 to 44 Spend More than Average

Most households in the age group include children, which accounts for their above-average spending.

Households headed by people aged 35 to 44 and 45 to 54 spend more than other age groups—15 to 18 percent more than the average household. Gen Xers were aged 37 to 48 in 2013 and straddle these two age groups. With average annual spending at $60,524 in 2013, householders aged 45 to 54 spend more than any other. Those aged 35 to 44 are not far behind, spending $58,784 in 2013. Behind the higher spending of these households is their higher income because they are in their peak earning years. Another factor in their higher spending is their larger household size because many are raising children.

Householders aged 35 to 44 spend significantly more than average on items commonly purchased by parents with children under age 18. They spend 29 percent more than the average household on milk and about twice the average on children's clothing. Many in this age group bought homes during the housing bubble, which explains why their mortgage interest payments are 65 percent above average.

Householders aged 45 to 54 spend more than average on items enjoyed by empty nesters—such as travel. Their spending on "other lodging," a category that includes hotels and motels as well as college dorms, is 37 percent above average. They spend 22 percent more on public transportation—a category that includes airline fares. Not surprisingly, this age group spends 73 percent more than average on education since many have children in college.

■ The spending of householders aged 35 to 44 is determined by children, which reduces their spending on other items.

Householders aged 35 to 44 spend more than average on items for children

(indexed spending of householders aged 35 to 44 on selected items, 2013; 100 is the index for the average household)

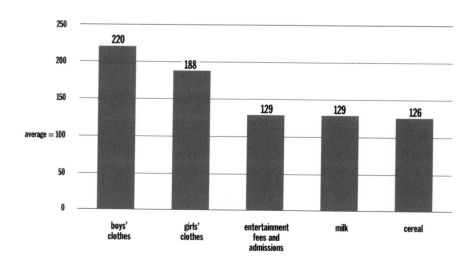

Table 9.4 Average, Indexed, and Market Share of Spending by Householders Aged 35 to 44, 2013

(average annual spending of total consumer units and average annual, indexed, and market share of spending by consumer units headed by people aged 35 to 44, 2013)

	total consumer units	consumer units headed by 35-to-44-year-olds		
		average spending	indexed spending	market share
Number of consumer units (in 000s)	125,670	21,257	–	16.9%
Average annual spending	$51,100	$58,784	115	19.5
FOOD	**6,602**	**7,920**	**120**	**20.3**
Food at home	**3,977**	**4,641**	**117**	**19.7**
Cereals and bakery products	544	646	119	20.1
Cereals and cereal products	185	233	126	21.3
Bakery products	359	412	115	19.4
Meats, poultry, fish, and eggs	856	993	116	19.6
Beef	219	276	126	21.3
Pork	170	184	108	18.3
Other meats	119	138	116	19.6
Poultry	170	215	126	21.4
Fish and seafood	122	119	98	16.5
Eggs	56	61	109	18.4
Dairy products	414	495	120	20.2
Fresh milk and cream	152	196	129	21.8
Other dairy products	262	299	114	19.3
Fruits and vegetables	751	866	115	19.5
Fresh fruits	270	312	116	19.5
Fresh vegetables	236	259	110	18.6
Processed fruits	115	136	118	20.0
Processed vegetables	130	158	122	20.6
Other food at home	1,412	1,641	116	19.7
Sugar and other sweets	143	157	110	18.6
Fats and oils	117	128	109	18.5
Miscellaneous foods	728	881	121	20.5
Nonalcoholic beverages	384	435	113	19.2
Food prepared by consumer unit on trips	42	41	98	16.5
Food away from home	**2,625**	**3,280**	**125**	**21.1**
ALCOHOLIC BEVERAGES	**445**	**443**	**100**	**16.8**
HOUSING	**17,148**	**20,619**	**120**	**20.3**
Shelter	**10,080**	**12,271**	**122**	**20.6**
Owned dwellings	6,108	7,981	131	22.1
Mortgage interest and charges	3,078	5,078	165	27.9
Property taxes	1,848	1,964	106	18.0
Maintenance, repair, insurance, other expenses	1,182	939	79	13.4
Rented dwellings	3,324	3,834	115	19.5
Other lodging	649	455	70	11.9

	total consumer units	consumer units headed by 35-to-44-year-olds		
		average spending	indexed spending	market share
Utilities, fuels, and public services	**$3,737**	**$4,299**	**115**	**19.5%**
Natural gas	393	445	113	19.2
Electricity	1,422	1,635	115	19.4
Fuel oil and other fuels	142	121	85	14.4
Telephone services	1,271	1,508	119	20.1
Residential telephone, VOIP, and phone cards	358	298	83	14.1
Cellular phone service	913	1,209	132	22.4
Water and other public services	509	590	116	19.6
Household services	**1,144**	**1,612**	**141**	**23.8**
Personal services	368	825	224	37.9
Other household services	776	787	101	17.2
Housekeeping supplies	**645**	**674**	**104**	**17.7**
Laundry and cleaning supplies	154	170	110	18.7
Other household products	350	368	105	17.8
Postage and stationery	140	136	97	16.4
Household furnishings and equipment	**1,542**	**1,763**	**114**	**19.3**
Household textiles	97	108	111	18.8
Furniture	382	449	118	19.9
Floor coverings	20	17	85	14.4
Major appliances	214	268	125	21.2
Small appliances and miscellaneous housewares	100	102	102	17.3
Miscellaneous household equipment	727	819	113	19.1
APPAREL AND RELATED SERVICES	**1,604**	**1,960**	**122**	**20.7**
Men and boys	**374**	**533**	**143**	**24.1**
Men, aged 16 or older	304	378	124	21.0
Boys, aged 2 to 15	70	154	220	37.2
Women and girls	**636**	**718**	**113**	**19.1**
Women, aged 16 or older	527	513	97	16.5
Girls, aged 2 to 15	109	205	188	31.8
Children under age 2	**75**	**109**	**145**	**24.6**
Footwear	**307**	**398**	**130**	**21.9**
Other apparel products and services	**211**	**202**	**96**	**16.2**
TRANSPORTATION	**9,004**	**10,519**	**117**	**19.8**
Vehicle purchases	**3,271**	**4,010**	**123**	**20.7**
Cars and trucks, new	1,563	1,774	113	19.2
Cars and trucks, used	1,669	2,218	133	22.5
Gasoline and motor oil	**2,611**	**3,218**	**123**	**20.8**
Other vehicle expenses	**2,584**	**2,740**	**106**	**17.9**
Vehicle finance charges	204	288	141	23.9
Maintenance and repairs	835	841	101	17.0
Vehicle insurance	1,013	1,019	101	17.0
Vehicle rentals, leases, licenses, other charges	533	592	111	18.8
Public transportation	**537**	**552**	**103**	**17.4**

	total consumer units	consumer units headed by 35-to-44-year-olds		
		average spending	indexed spending	market share
HEALTH CARE	**$3,631**	**$3,188**	**88**	**14.9%**
Health insurance	2,229	1,944	87	14.8
Medical services	796	786	99	16.7
Drugs	470	343	73	12.3
Medical supplies	135	116	86	14.5
ENTERTAINMENT	**2,482**	**2,958**	**119**	**20.2**
Fees and admissions	569	736	129	21.9
Audio and visual equipment and services	964	1,139	118	20.0
Pets, toys, and playground equipment	596	638	107	18.1
Pets	460	473	103	17.4
Toys, hobbies, and playground equipment	136	165	121	20.5
Other entertainment products and services	353	446	126	21.4
PERSONAL CARE PRODUCTS AND SERVICES	**608**	**672**	**111**	**18.7**
READING	**102**	**105**	**103**	**17.4**
EDUCATION	**1,138**	**903**	**79**	**13.4**
TOBACCO PRODUCTS AND SMOKING SUPPLIES	**330**	**331**	**100**	**17.0**
MISCELLANEOUS	**645**	**643**	**100**	**16.9**
CASH CONTRIBUTIONS	**1,834**	**1,440**	**79**	**13.3**
PERSONAL INSURANCE AND PENSIONS	**5,528**	**7,081**	**128**	**21.7**
Life and other personal insurance	319	290	91	15.4
Pensions and Social Security	5,209	6,791	130	22.1
GIFTS FOR PEOPLE IN OTHER HOUSEHOLDS	**1,078**	**604**	**56**	**9.5**

Note: The Bureau of Labor Statistics uses consumer unit rather than household as the sampling unit in the Consumer Expenditure Survey. For the definition of consumer unit, see the glossary. Spending on gifts is also included in the preceding product and service categories. "–" means not applicable.
Source: Bureau of Labor Statistics, 2013 Consumer Expenditure Survey, Internet site http://www.bls.gov/cex/; calculations by New Strategist

Table 9.5 Average, Indexed, and Market Share of Spending by Householders Aged 45 to 54, 2013

(average annual spending of total consumer units and average annual, indexed, and market share of spending by consumer units headed by people aged 45 to 54, 2013)

	total consumer units	consumer units headed by 45-to-54-year-olds		
		average spending	indexed spending	market share
Number of consumer units (in 000s)	125,670	24,501	–	19.5%
Average annual spending	$51,100	$60,524	118	23.1
FOOD	6,602	7,907	120	23.4
Food at home	3,977	4,701	118	23.0
Cereals and bakery products	544	650	119	23.3
Cereals and cereal products	185	222	120	23.4
Bakery products	359	428	119	23.2
Meats, poultry, fish, and eggs	856	1,048	122	23.9
Beef	219	249	114	22.2
Pork	170	211	124	24.2
Other meats	119	154	129	25.2
Poultry	170	213	125	24.4
Fish and seafood	122	159	130	25.4
Eggs	56	63	113	21.9
Dairy products	414	475	115	22.4
Fresh milk and cream	152	171	113	21.9
Other dairy products	262	304	116	22.6
Fruits and vegetables	751	857	114	22.2
Fresh fruits	270	302	112	21.8
Fresh vegetables	236	275	117	22.7
Processed fruits	115	127	110	21.5
Processed vegetables	130	152	117	22.8
Other food at home	1,412	1,672	118	23.1
Sugar and other sweets	143	171	120	23.3
Fats and oils	117	133	114	22.2
Miscellaneous foods	728	854	117	22.9
Nonalcoholic beverages	384	465	121	23.6
Food prepared by consumer unit on trips	42	49	117	22.7
Food away from home	2,625	3,206	122	23.8
ALCOHOLIC BEVERAGES	445	545	122	23.9
HOUSING	17,148	19,001	111	21.6
Shelter	10,080	11,208	111	21.7
Owned dwellings	6,108	7,378	121	23.6
Mortgage interest and charges	3,078	3,950	128	25.0
Property taxes	1,848	2,180	118	23.0
Maintenance, repair, insurance, other expenses	1,182	1,248	106	20.6
Rented dwellings	3,324	2,938	88	17.2
Other lodging	649	892	137	26.8

	total consumer units	consumer units headed by 45-to-54-year-olds		
		average spending	indexed spending	market share
Utilities, fuels, and public services	**$3,737**	**$4,277**	**114**	**22.3%**
Natural gas	393	442	112	21.9
Electricity	1,422	1,575	111	21.6
Fuel oil and other fuels	142	156	110	21.4
Telephone services	1,271	1,534	121	23.5
Residential telephone, VOIP, and phone cards	358	403	113	21.9
Cellular phone service	913	1,131	124	24.2
Water and other public services	509	571	112	21.9
Household services	**1,144**	**1,020**	**89**	**17.4**
Personal services	368	162	44	8.6
Other household services	776	859	111	21.6
Housekeeping supplies	**645**	**751**	**116**	**22.7**
Laundry and cleaning supplies	154	176	114	22.3
Other household products	350	424	121	23.6
Postage and stationery	140	151	108	21.0
Household furnishings and equipment	**1,542**	**1,745**	**113**	**22.1**
Household textiles	97	117	121	23.5
Furniture	382	398	104	20.3
Floor coverings	20	18	90	17.5
Major appliances	214	252	118	23.0
Small appliances and miscellaneous housewares	100	117	117	22.8
Miscellaneous household equipment	727	844	116	22.6
APPAREL AND RELATED SERVICES	**1,604**	**1,826**	**114**	**22.2**
Men and boys	**374**	**453**	**121**	**23.6**
Men, aged 16 or older	304	372	122	23.9
Boys, aged 2 to 15	70	81	116	22.6
Women and girls	**636**	**690**	**108**	**21.2**
Women, aged 16 or older	527	546	104	20.2
Girls, aged 2 to 15	109	144	132	25.8
Children under age 2	**75**	**39**	**52**	**10.1**
Footwear	**307**	**404**	**132**	**25.7**
Other apparel products and services	**211**	**240**	**114**	**22.2**
TRANSPORTATION	**9,004**	**10,782**	**120**	**23.3**
Vehicle purchases	**3,271**	**3,958**	**121**	**23.6**
Cars and trucks, new	1,563	2,077	133	25.9
Cars and trucks, used	1,669	1,817	109	21.2
Gasoline and motor oil	**2,611**	**3,093**	**118**	**23.1**
Other vehicle expenses	**2,584**	**3,074**	**119**	**23.2**
Vehicle finance charges	204	245	120	23.4
Maintenance and repairs	835	1,071	128	25.0
Vehicle insurance	1,013	1,153	114	22.2
Vehicle rentals, leases, licenses, other charges	533	605	114	22.1
Public transportation	**537**	**657**	**122**	**23.9**

	total consumer units	consumer units headed by 45-to-54-year-olds		
		average spending	indexed spending	market share
HEALTH CARE	$3,631	$3,801	105	20.4%
Health insurance	2,229	2,242	101	19.6
Medical services	796	918	115	22.5
Drugs	470	489	104	20.3
Medical supplies	135	151	112	21.8
ENTERTAINMENT	2,482	3,070	124	24.1
Fees and admissions	569	747	131	25.6
Audio and visual equipment and services	964	1,064	110	21.5
Pets, toys, and playground equipment	596	728	122	23.8
Pets	460	586	127	24.8
Toys, hobbies, and playground equipment	136	141	104	20.2
Other entertainment products and services	353	531	150	29.3
PERSONAL CARE PRODUCTS AND SERVICES	608	723	119	23.2
READING	102	88	86	16.8
EDUCATION	1,138	1,970	173	33.8
TOBACCO PRODUCTS AND SMOKING SUPPLIES	330	447	135	26.4
MISCELLANEOUS	645	686	106	20.7
CASH CONTRIBUTIONS	1,834	2,007	109	21.3
PERSONAL INSURANCE AND PENSIONS	5,528	7,672	139	27.1
Life and other personal insurance	319	367	115	22.4
Pensions and Social Security	5,209	7,305	140	27.3
GIFTS FOR PEOPLE IN OTHER HOUSEHOLDS	1,078	1,724	160	31.2

Note: The Bureau of Labor Statistics uses consumer unit rather than household as the sampling unit in the Consumer Expenditure Survey. For the definition of consumer unit, see the glossary. Spending on gifts is also included in the preceding product and service categories. "–" means not applicable.
Source: Bureau of Labor Statistics, 2013 Consumer Expenditure Survey, Internet site http://www.bls.gov/cex/; calculations by New Strategist

10

Time Use

■ People aged 35 to 44 have the least amount of leisure time because most are juggling work and family responsibilities.

■ The middle aged spend the most time at work. On an average day (including weekdays and weekends), men aged 35 to 44 spend 5.43 hours per day at work versus the 3.88 hours spent at work or in work-related activities by the average man.

■ Women aged 35 to 44 spend twice as much time as the average woman caring for household children. They spend 37 percent more time at work than the average woman.

■ Women aged 35 to 44 have 21 percent less leisure time than the average woman. Men aged 35 to 44 have 22 percent less leisure time than the average man.

Gen X Spends More Time at Work than at Play

People aged 35 to 44 spend 40 percent more time at work than the average person.

Time use varies sharply by age. The middle aged are the ones who spend the most time at work and the least time at play, according to the Bureau of Labor Statistics' American Time Use Survey. On an average day (including weekdays and weekends), men aged 35 to 44 spend 5.43 hours at work versus the 3.88 hours spent at work or in work-related activities by the average man. Women aged 35 to 44 spend 37 percent more time at work than the average woman. They spend twice as much time as the average woman caring for household children.

People aged 35 to 44 have the least amount of leisure time because most are juggling both work and family responsibilities. Women aged 35 to 44 have 21 percent less leisure time than the average woman. Men in the age group have 22 percent less leisure time than the average man.

■ As their children grow up, Gen Xers will have more leisure time.

Time at work peaks in middle age

(average number of hours per day men spend working or in work-related activities, by age, 2013)

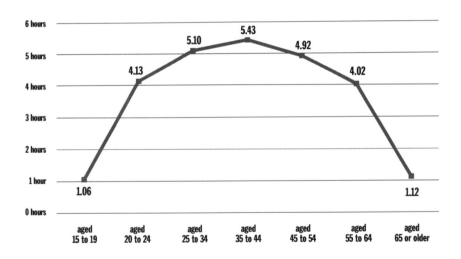

Table 10.1 Detailed Time Use of People Aged 35 to 44, 2013

(hours per day spent in primary activities by total people aged 15 or older and people aged 35 to 44, index of age group to total, and number and percent of people aged 35 to 44 participating in activity on an average day, 2013)

	average hours per day for total people	average hours per day for people aged 35 to 44	index, 35 to 44 to total	people aged 35 to 44 participating in activity	
				number (in 000s)	percent
Total, all activities	**24.00 hrs.**	**24.00 hrs.**	**100**	**39,613**	**100.0%**
Personal care activities	9.53	9.26	97	39,613	100.0
Sleeping	8.74	8.52	97	39,613	100.0
Grooming	0.70	0.68	97	32,904	83.1
Health-related self-care	0.09	0.06	67	1,545	3.9
Household activities	1.78	1.85	104	30,985	78.2
Housework	0.57	0.67	118	15,266	38.5
Food preparation and cleanup	0.57	0.69	121	24,893	62.8
Lawn, garden, and houseplants	0.18	0.12	67	2,672	6.7
Animals and pets	0.10	0.07	70	5,481	13.8
Vehicles	0.04	0.04	100	757	1.9
Household management	0.18	0.14	78	9,569	24.2
Financial management	0.03	0.02	67	1,131	2.9
Household and personal organization and planning	0.10	0.08	80	5,658	14.3
Household and personal mail and messages (except email)	0.01	0.01	100	1,396	3.5
Household and personal email and messages	0.03	0.03	100	2,639	6.7
Caring for and helping household members	0.44	0.97	220	20,290	51.2
Caring for and helping household children	0.36	0.82	228	18,724	47.3
Caring for household adults	0.02	0.01	50	640	1.6
Helping household adults	0.01	0.01	100	1,539	3.9
Caring for and helping people in other households	0.14	0.08	57	3,877	9.8
Caring for and helping children in other households	0.07	0.02	29	1,321	3.3
Caring for adults in other households	0.01	–	–	128	0.3
Helping adults in other households	0.05	0.05	100	2,582	6.5
Working and work-related activities	3.20	4.45	139	23,073	58.2
Working	3.14	4.39	140	22,415	56.6
Job search and interviewing	0.04	0.05	125	654	1.7
Educational activities	0.45	0.09	20	886	2.2
Taking class	0.26	0.03	12	364	0.9
Homework and research	0.18	0.06	33	579	1.5
Consumer purchases	0.37	0.39	105	16,515	41.7
Grocery shopping	0.11	0.13	118	6,393	16.1
Shopping (except groceries, food, and gas)	0.24	0.23	96	8,498	21.5
Professional and personal care services	0.08	0.07	88	2,659	6.7
Medical and care services	0.05	0.04	80	1,196	3.0

	average hours per day for total people	average hours per day for people aged 35 to 44	index, 35 to 44 to total	people aged 35 to 44 participating in activity	
				number (in 000s)	percent
Eating and drinking	1.11 hrs.	1.06 hrs.	95	38,108	96.2%
Socializing, relaxing, and leisure	4.71	3.69	78	36,523	92.2
Socializing and communicating	0.65	0.60	92	13,208	33.3
Attending or hosting social events	0.07	0.07	100	777	2.0
Relaxing and leisure	3.91	2.94	75	34,581	87.3
Television and movies	2.77	2.24	81	30,376	76.7
Playing games	0.22	0.12	55	2,512	6.3
Computer use for leisure (except games)	0.21	0.16	76	5,479	13.8
Reading for personal interest	0.32	0.16	50	5,170	13.1
Arts and entertainment (other than sports)	0.08	0.08	100	1,134	2.9
Attending movies	0.03	0.03	100	463	1.2
Sports, exercise, and recreation	0.32	0.25	78	6,292	15.9
Participating in sports, exercise, and recreation	0.30	0.23	77	6,049	15.3
Attending sporting or recreational events	0.03	0.02	67	292	0.7
Religious and spiritual activities	0.14	0.12	86	3,201	8.1
Volunteer activities	0.14	0.11	79	2,400	6.1
Telephone calls	0.10	0.06	60	4,164	10.5
Traveling	1.18	1.31	111	36,197	91.4

Note: Primary activities are those respondents identified as their main activity. Other activities done simultaneously are not included. Travel related to activities is reported separately. Numbers do not sum to total because not all activities are shown. The index is calculated by dividing time spent by age group by time spent by the average person and multiplying by 100. "−" means sample is too small to make a reliable estimate.
Source: Bureau of Labor Statistics, unpublished tables from the 2013 American Time Use Survey, Internet site http://www.bls .gov/tus/home.htm; calculations by New Strategist

Table 10.2 Detailed Time Use of Men Aged 35 to 44, 2013

(hours per day spent in primary activities by total men aged 15 or older and men aged 35 to 44, index of age group to total, and number and percent of men aged 35 to 44 participating in activity on an average day, 2013)

	average hours per day for total men	average hours per day for men aged 35 to 44	index, 35 to 44 to total	men aged 35 to 44 participating in activity	
				number (in 000s)	percent
Total, all activities	**24.00 hrs.**	**24.00 hrs.**	**100**	**19,432**	**100.0%**
Personal care activities	9.29	8.95	96	19,432	100.0
Sleeping	8.65	8.37	97	19,432	100.0
Grooming	0.57	0.55	96	15,504	79.8
Health-related self-care	0.60	0.02	3	517	2.7
Household activities	1.34	1.31	98	13,142	67.6
Housework	0.25	0.30	120	4,282	22.0
Food preparation and cleanup	0.33	0.44	133	9,598	49.4
Lawn, garden, and houseplants	0.25	0.17	68	1,497	7.7
Animals and pets	0.09	0.07	78	2,239	11.5
Vehicles	0.08	0.07	88	633	3.3
Household management	0.14	0.10	71	3,689	19.0
Financial management	0.02	0.02	100	412	2.1
Household and personal organization and planning	0.08	0.06	75	2,161	11.1
Household and personal mail and messages (except email)	0.01	0.01	100	383	2.0
Household and personal email and messages	0.03	0.02	67	980	5.0
Caring for and helping household members	0.30	0.75	250	8,448	43.5
Caring for and helping household children	0.24	0.63	263	7,567	38.9
Caring for household adults	0.01	–	–	178	0.9
Helping household adults	0.01	0.01	100	830	4.3
Caring for and helping people in other households	0.12	0.11	92	2,079	10.7
Caring for and helping children in other households	0.05	0.04	80	706	3.6
Caring for adults in other households	0.01	–	–	37	0.2
Helping adults in other households	0.06	0.06	100	1,399	7.2
Working and work-related activities	3.88	5.43	140	12,816	66.0
Working	3.80	5.36	141	12,453	64.1
Job search and interviewing	0.05	0.06	120	328	1.7
Educational activities	0.45	0.05	11	239	1.2
Taking class	0.27	–	–	48	0.2
Homework and research	0.17	0.03	18	171	0.9
Consumer purchases	0.29	0.30	103	7,033	36.2
Grocery shopping	0.07	0.08	114	2,205	11.3
Shopping (except groceries, food, and gas)	0.19	0.18	95	3,681	18.9
Professional and personal care services	0.06	0.05	83	1,004	5.2
Medical and care services	0.04	0.04	100	531	2.7

	average hours per day for total men	average hours per day for men aged 35 to 44	index, 35 to 44 to total	men aged 35 to 44 participating in activity	
				number (in 000s)	percent
Eating and drinking	1.14 hrs.	1.12 hrs.	98	18,839	96.9%
Socializing, relaxing, and leisure	4.94	3.83	78	17,935	92.3
Socializing and communicating	0.60	0.52	87	5,670	29.2
Attending or hosting social events	0.06	0.08	133	459	2.4
Relaxing and leisure	4.20	3.16	75	17,161	88.3
Television and movies	2.98	2.40	81	15,146	77.9
Playing games	0.32	0.15	47	1,463	7.5
Computer use for leisure (except games)	0.22	0.17	77	2,426	12.5
Reading for personal interest	0.26	0.11	42	1,967	10.1
Arts and entertainment (other than sports)	0.08	0.07	88	523	2.7
Attending movies	0.03	0.03	100	239	1.2
Sports, exercise, and recreation	0.42	0.31	74	3,435	17.7
Participating in sports, exercise, and recreation	0.40	0.29	73	3,329	17.1
Attending sporting or recreational events	0.02	–	–	113	0.6
Religious and spiritual activities	0.12	0.13	108	1,525	7.8
Volunteer activities	0.13	0.08	62	857	4.4
Telephone calls	0.06	0.03	50	1,367	7.0
Traveling	1.21	1.35	112	18,122	93.3

Note: Primary activities are those respondents identified as their main activity. Other activities done simultaneously are not included. Travel related to activities is reported separately. Numbers do not sum to total because not all activities are shown. The index is calculated by dividing time spent by age group by time spent by the average man and multiplying by 100. "–" means sample is too small to make a reliable estimate.
Source: Bureau of Labor Statistics, unpublished tables from the 2013 American Time Use Survey, Internet site http://www.bls .gov/tus/home.htm; calculations by New Strategist

Table 10.3 Detailed Time Use of Women Aged 35 to 44, 2013

(hours per day spent in primary activities by total women aged 15 or older and women aged 35 to 44, index of age group to total, and number and percent of women aged 35 to 44 participating in activity on an average day, 2013)

	average hours per day for total women	average hours per day for women aged 35 to 44	index, 35 to 44 to total	women aged 35 to 44 participating in activity	
				number (in 000s)	percent
Total, all activities	**24.00 hrs.**	**24.00 hrs.**	**100**	**20,181**	**100.0%**
Personal care activities	9.75	9.56	98	20,181	100.0
Sleeping	8.82	8.67	98	20,181	100.0
Grooming	0.82	0.79	96	17,400	86.2
Health-related self-care	0.11	0.10	91	1,028	5.1
Household activities	2.20	2.36	107	17,842	88.4
Housework	0.87	1.02	117	10,984	54.4
Food preparation and cleanup	0.80	0.93	116	15,295	75.8
Lawn, garden, and houseplants	0.12	0.07	58	1,174	5.8
Animals and pets	0.11	0.08	73	3,242	16.1
Vehicles	0.01	–	–	124	0.6
Household management	0.21	0.19	90	5,880	29.1
Financial management	0.04	0.02	50	719	3.6
Household and personal organization and planning	0.12	0.11	92	3,497	17.3
Household and personal mail and messages (except email)	0.02	0.01	50	1,012	5.0
Household and personal email and messages	0.04	0.04	100	1,659	8.2
Caring for and helping household members	0.58	1.18	203	11,842	58.7
Caring for and helping household children	0.47	0.99	211	11,157	55.3
Caring for household adults	0.03	0.01	33	462	2.3
Helping household adults	0.01	0.01	100	708	3.5
Caring for and helping people in other households	0.16	0.05	31	1,797	8.9
Caring for and helping children in other households	0.10	0.01	10	614	3.0
Caring for adults in other households	0.01	–	–	91	0.5
Helping adults in other households	0.05	0.04	80	1,184	5.9
Working and work-related activities	2.57	3.51	137	10,257	50.8
Working	2.52	3.46	137	9,962	49.4
Job search and interviewing	0.03	0.04	133	325	1.6
Educational activities	0.45	0.13	29	647	3.2
Taking class	0.25	0.05	20	316	1.6
Homework and research	0.19	0.08	42	408	2.0
Consumer purchases	0.45	0.47	104	9,483	47.0
Grocery shopping	0.14	0.17	121	4,187	20.7
Shopping (except groceries, food, and gas)	0.28	0.27	96	4,817	23.9
Professional and personal care services	0.10	0.08	80	1,655	8.2
Medical and care services	0.07	0.04	57	665	3.3

	average hours per day for total women	average hours per day for women aged 35 to 44	index, 35 to 44 to total	women aged 35 to 44 participating in activity	
				number (in 000s)	percent
Eating and drinking	1.09 hrs.	1.00 hrs.	92	19,269	95.5%
Socializing, relaxing, and leisure	4.50	3.55	79	18,587	92.1
Socializing and communicating	0.70	0.68	97	7,538	37.4
Attending or hosting social events	0.08	0.05	63	318	1.6
Relaxing and leisure	3.63	2.72	75	17,420	86.3
Television and movies	2.56	2.09	82	15,230	75.5
Playing games	0.13	0.08	62	1,049	5.2
Computer use for leisure (except games)	0.20	0.16	80	3,054	15.1
Reading for personal interest	0.38	0.20	53	3,202	15.9
Arts and entertainment (other than sports)	0.09	0.10	111	611	3.0
Attending movies	0.03	0.03	100	224	1.1
Sports, exercise, and recreation	0.23	0.20	87	2,858	14.2
Participating in sports, exercise, and recreation	0.20	0.17	85	2,721	13.5
Attending sporting or recreational events	0.03	0.03	100	179	0.9
Religious and spiritual activities	0.17	0.12	71	1,675	8.3
Volunteer activities	0.15	0.14	93	1,543	7.6
Telephone calls	0.14	0.09	64	2,797	13.9
Traveling	1.15	1.28	111	18,074	89.6

Note: Primary activities are those respondents identified as their main activity. Other activities done simultaneously are not included. Travel related to activities is reported separately. Numbers do not sum to total because not all activities are shown. The index is calculated by dividing time spent by age group by time spent by the average woman and multiplying by 100. "−" means sample is too small to make a reliable estimate.
Source: Bureau of Labor Statistics, unpublished tables from the 2013 American Time Use Survey, Internet site http://www.bls .gov/tus/home.htm; calculations by New Strategist

11

Wealth

■ Households headed by 35-to-44-year-olds (Gen Xers were aged 37 to 48 in 2013) saw their median net worth decline by a substantial 53 percent between 2007 and 2013, after adjusting for inflation—a larger decline than any other age group.

■ The median value of the financial assets owned by householders aged 35 to 44 fell 47 percent between 2007 and 2010, after adjusting for inflation. This age group recovered some ground between 2010 and 2013, with the median value of their financial assets rising 32 percent to a modest $20,400.

■ The median value of the nonfinancial assets owned by householders aged 35 to 44 fell to $135,800 in 2013—34 percent lower than in 2007, after adjusting for inflation. Two factors were behind the decline: a lower homeownership rate and a drop in housing values.

■ Households headed by 35-to-44-year-olds cut their debt by 19 percent between 2007 and 2013, after adjusting for inflation. Behind the decline was the drop in homeownership from 66 percent in 2013 to 62 percent in 2013.

■ Workers aged 35 to 44 are worried about retirement. In 2014, only 15 percent were "very confident" they would have enough money to live comfortably in retirement.

Net Worth Continues to Decline

Several age groups experienced double-digit percentage declines in net worth between 2010 and 2013.

Net worth is what remains when a household's debts are subtracted from its assets. During and after the Great Recession, the value of houses, stocks, and retirement accounts fell sharply. At the same time, debt increased. Consequently, median net worth fell 39 percent between 2007 and 2010, after adjusting for inflation. Between 2010 and 2013, median household net worth fell by another 2 percent, with double-digit percentage declines experienced by householders ranging in age from 45 to 64 and by householders aged 75 or older.

Some age groups made gains in the 2010-to-2013 time period. Householders under age 45 saw their net worth rise 3 to 4 percent, and the net worth of householders aged 65 to 74 gained 5 percent, after adjusting for inflation. But for households in every age group, 2013 net worth was far below net worth in 2007. Householders aged 65 to 74 experienced the smallest decline: their 2013 net worth was 14 percent below what it was in 2007. Householders aged 35 to 44 experienced the biggest decline—a stunning 53 percent drop during those years.

■ Net worth rises with age as people pay off their debt. In 2013, net worth peaked in the 65-to-74 age group at $232,100.

Net worth peaks among householders aged 65 to 74

(median household net worth by age of householder, 2013)

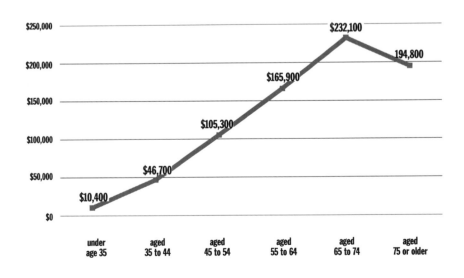

Table 11.1 Net Worth of Households, 2007 to 2013

(median net worth of households by age of householder, 2007 to 2013; percent change, 2007–13; in 2013 dollars)

	2013	2010	2007	percent change 2010–13	percent change 2007–13
Total households	**$81,200**	**$82,800**	**$135,400**	**−1.9%**	**−40.0%**
Under age 35	10,400	10,000	13,200	4.0	−21.2
Aged 35 to 44	46,700	45,200	99,100	3.3	−52.9
Aged 45 to 54	105,300	126,300	207,600	−16.6	−49.3
Aged 55 to 64	165,900	192,300	285,300	−13.7	−41.9
Aged 65 to 74	232,100	221,500	268,800	4.8	−13.7
Aged 75 or older	194,800	232,300	239,700	−16.1	−18.7

Source: Federal Reserve Board, Survey of Consumer Finances, Internet site http://www.federalreserve.gov/econresdata/scf/scfindex .html; calculations by New Strategist

Financial Asset Value Has Declined in Every Age Group

Some households made gains between 2010 and 2013, however.

Most households own financial assets, which range from transaction accounts (checking and saving) to stocks, mutual funds, retirement accounts, and life insurance. The median value of the financial assets owned by the average household stood at $21,200 in 2013. This was 35 percent below the median in 2007, after adjusting for inflation. Householders aged 35 to 44 and aged 65 to 74 were the only ones who made financial asset gains between 2010 and 2013.

Transaction accounts, the most commonly owned financial asset, are held by 93 percent of households. Their median value was just $4,100 in 2013—slightly lower than the $4,500 of 2007, after adjusting for inflation. Retirement accounts are the second most commonly owned financial asset, with 49 percent of households owning them. In 2007, a larger 53 percent of households owned retirement accounts. Most retirement accounts are modest, with an overall median value of just $59,000 in 2013.

Only 14 percent of households owned stock directly in 2013 (outside of a retirement account or mutual fund). The median value of stock owned by stockholding households was $27,000 in 2013, a substantial 41 percent greater than the value in 2007 after adjusting for inflation.

■ Financial asset value peaks in the 65-to-74 age group, at $72,000.

The value of retirement accounts peaks in the 65-to-74 age group

(median value of retirement accounts owned by households, by age of householder, 2013)

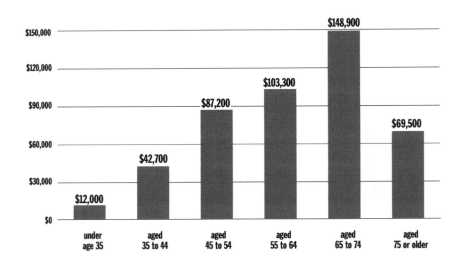

Table 11.2 Ownership and Value of Financial Assets, 2007 to 2013

(percentage of households owning any financial asset and median value for owners, by age of householder, 2007 to 2013; percentage point change in ownership and percent change in value, 2010–13 and 2007–13; in 2013 dollars)

PERCENT OWNING FINANCIAL ASSETS	2013	2010	2007	percentage point change	
				2010–13	2007–13
Total households	**94.5%**	**94.0%**	**93.9%**	**0.5**	**0.6**
Under age 35	92.5	91.3	89.2	1.2	3.3
Aged 35 to 44	93.1	92.7	93.1	0.4	0.0
Aged 45 to 54	93.3	94.2	93.3	−0.9	0.0
Aged 55 to 64	95.7	95.8	97.8	−0.1	−2.1
Aged 65 to 74	97.4	96.2	96.1	1.2	1.3
Aged 75 or older	96.9	96.4	97.4	0.5	−0.5

MEDIAN VALUE OF FINANCIAL ASSETS	2013	2010	2007	percent change	
				2010–13	2007–13
Total households	**$21,200**	**$23,000**	**$32,400**	**−7.8%**	**−34.6%**
Under age 35	5,800	5,900	7,600	−1.7	−23.7
Aged 35 to 44	20,400	15,500	29,200	31.6	−30.1
Aged 45 to 54	31,500	36,100	61,000	−12.7	−48.4
Aged 55 to 64	52,100	59,800	82,800	−12.9	−37.1
Aged 65 to 74	72,000	48,400	76,400	48.8	−5.8
Aged 75 or older	28,000	46,900	46,600	−40.3	−39.9

Source: Federal Reserve Board, Survey of Consumer Finances, Internet site http://www.federalreserve.gov/econresdata/scf/scfindex .html; calculations by New Strategist

Table 11.3 Ownership and Value of Transaction Accounts, 2007 to 2013

(percentage of households owning transactions accounts and median value for owners, by age of householder, 2007 to 2013; percentage point change in ownership and percent change in value, 2010–13 and 2007–13; in 2013 dollars)

				percentage point change	
PERCENT OWNING TRANSACTION ACCOUNTS	2013	2010	2007	2010–13	2007–13
Total households	**93.2%**	**92.5%**	**92.1%**	**0.7**	**1.1**
Under age 35	90.2	89.0	87.3	1.2	2.9
Aged 35 to 44	91.8	90.6	91.2	1.2	0.6
Aged 45 to 54	91.8	92.5	91.7	–0.7	0.1
Aged 55 to 64	94.6	94.2	96.4	0.4	–1.8
Aged 65 to 74	97.1	95.8	94.6	1.3	2.5
Aged 75 or older	96.7	96.4	95.3	0.3	1.4

				percent change	
MEDIAN VALUE OF TRANSACTION ACCOUNTS	2013	2010	2007	2010–13	2007–13
Total households	**$4,100**	**$3,800**	**$4,500**	**7.9%**	**–8.9%**
Under age 35	2,200	2,200	2,700	0.0	–18.5
Aged 35 to 44	3,800	2,700	3,900	40.7	–2.6
Aged 45 to 54	4,000	3,800	5,600	5.3	–28.6
Aged 55 to 64	5,000	5,400	5,800	–7.4	–13.8
Aged 65 to 74	7,000	6,100	8,600	14.8	–18.6
Aged 75 or older	7,000	7,700	6,800	–9.1	2.9

Source: Federal Reserve Board, Survey of Consumer Finances, Internet site http://www.federalreserve.gov/econresdata/scf/scfindex .html; calculations by New Strategist

Table 11.4 Ownership and Value of Cash Value Life Insurance, 2007 to 2013

(percentage of households owning cash value life insurance and median value for owners, by age of householder, 2007 to 2013; percentage point change in ownership and percent change in value, 2010–13 and 2007–13; in 2013 dollars)

PERCENT OWNING CASH VALUE LIFE INSURANCE	2013	2010	2007	percentage point change	
				2010–13	2007–13
Total households	**19.2%**	**19.7%**	**23.0%**	**–0.5**	**–3.8**
Under age 35	9.2	9.6	11.4	–0.4	–2.2
Aged 35 to 44	13.3	12.3	17.5	1.0	–4.2
Aged 45 to 54	17.1	19.8	22.3	–2.7	–5.2
Aged 55 to 64	24.4	25.7	35.2	–1.3	–10.8
Aged 65 to 74	29.4	28.4	34.4	1.0	–5.0
Aged 75 or older	30.4	32.4	27.6	–2.0	2.8

MEDIAN VALUE OF CASH VALUE LIFE INSURANCE	2013	2010	2007	percent change	
				2010–13	2007–13
Total households	**$8,000**	**$7,800**	**$9,000**	**2.6%**	**–11.1%**
Under age 35	2,500	2,300	3,100	8.7	–19.4
Aged 35 to 44	7,000	5,400	9,300	29.6	–24.7
Aged 45 to 54	8,000	10,700	11,200	–25.2	–28.6
Aged 55 to 64	9,800	10,000	11,200	–2.0	–12.5
Aged 65 to 74	9,800	10,700	11,200	–8.4	–12.5
Aged 75 or older	8,000	7,500	5,600	6.7	42.9

Source: Federal Reserve Board, Survey of Consumer Finances, Internet site http://www.federalreserve.gov/econresdata/scf/scfindex .html; calculations by New Strategist

Table 11.5 Ownership and Value of Certificates of Deposit, 2007 to 2013

(percentage of households owning certificates of deposit and median value for owners, by age of householder, 2007 to 2013; percentage point change in ownership and percent change in value, 2010–13 and 2007–13; in 2013 dollars)

PERCENT OWNING CERTIFICATES OF DEPOSIT	2013	2010	2007	percentage point change 2010–13	2007–13
Total households	7.8%	12.2%	16.1%	−4.4	−8.3
Under age 35	5.2	5.7	6.7	−0.5	−1.5
Aged 35 to 44	4.4	5.7	9.0	−1.3	−4.6
Aged 45 to 54	6.7	10.0	14.3	−3.3	−7.6
Aged 55 to 64	5.8	14.6	20.5	−8.8	−14.7
Aged 65 to 74	11.7	20.6	24.2	−8.9	−12.5
Aged 75 or older	18.8	27.2	37.0	−8.4	−18.2

MEDIAN VALUE OF CERTIFICATES OF DEPOSIT	2013	2010	2007	percent change 2010–13	2007–13
Total households	$16,000	$21,400	$22,500	−25.2%	−28.9%
Under age 35	4,000	5,600	5,600	−28.6	−28.6
Aged 35 to 44	6,300	7,500	5,600	−16.0	12.5
Aged 45 to 54	10,000	17,100	16,800	−41.5	−40.5
Aged 55 to 64	25,000	21,400	25,800	16.8	−3.1
Aged 65 to 74	31,000	26,800	26,100	15.7	18.8
Aged 75 or older	22,000	34,500	33,700	−36.2	−34.7

Source: Federal Reserve Board, Survey of Consumer Finances, Internet site http://www.federalreserve.gov/econresdata/scf/scfindex .html; calculations by New Strategist

Table 11.6 Ownership and Value of Stock, 2007 to 2013

(percentage of households owning stock and median value for owners, by age of householder, 2007 to 2013; percentage point change in ownership and percent change in value, 2010–13 and 2007–13; in 2013 dollars)

PERCENT OWNING STOCK	2013	2010	2007	percentage point change 2010–13	percentage point change 2007–13
Total households	**13.8%**	**15.1%**	**17.9%**	**−1.3**	**−4.1**
Under age 35	7.2	10.1	13.7	−2.9	−6.5
Aged 35 to 44	14.3	12.1	17.0	2.2	−2.7
Aged 45 to 54	14.7	16.0	18.7	−1.3	−4.0
Aged 55 to 64	15.5	19.5	21.3	−4.0	−5.8
Aged 65 to 74	18.4	16.1	19.1	2.3	−0.7
Aged 75 or older	15.3	20.1	20.2	−4.8	−4.9

MEDIAN VALUE OF STOCK	2013	2010	2007	percent change 2010–13	percent change 2007–13
Total households	**$27,000**	**$21,400**	**$19,100**	**26.2%**	**41.4%**
Under age 35	6,600	5,800	3,400	13.8	94.1
Aged 35 to 44	20,000	10,700	16,800	86.9	19.0
Aged 45 to 54	16,000	32,200	20,200	−50.3	−20.8
Aged 55 to 64	30,000	37,500	26,900	−20.0	11.5
Aged 65 to 74	50,000	51,400	42,700	−2.7	17.1
Aged 75 or older	76,400	48,200	44,900	58.5	70.2

Note: Stock ownership is defined as direct ownership outside of a retirement account or mutual fund.
*Source: Federal Reserve Board, Survey of Consumer Finances, Internet site http://www.federalreserve.gov/econresdata/scf/scfindex
.html; calculations by New Strategist*

Table 11.7 Ownership and Value of Retirement Accounts, 2007 to 2013

(percentage of households owning retirement accounts and median value for owners, by age of householder, 2007 to 2013; percentage point change in ownership and percent change in value, 2010–13 and 2007–13; in 2013 dollars)

				percentage point change	
PERCENT OWNING RETIREMENT ACCOUNTS	2013	2010	2007	2010–13	2007–13
Total households	**49.2%**	**50.4%**	**53.0%**	**–1.2**	**–3.8**
Under age 35	39.3	41.1	42.1	–1.8	–2.8
Aged 35 to 44	55.4	52.2	57.8	3.2	–2.4
Aged 45 to 54	56.5	60.0	65.4	–3.5	–8.9
Aged 55 to 64	59.3	59.8	61.2	–0.5	–1.9
Aged 65 to 74	48.0	49.0	51.7	–1.0	–3.7
Aged 75 or older	29.0	32.8	30.0	–3.8	–1.0

				percent change	
MEDIAN VALUE OF RETIREMENT ACCOUNTS	2013	2010	2007	2010–13	2007–13
Total households	**$59,000**	**$47,200**	**$50,500**	**25.0%**	**16.8%**
Under age 35	12,000	11,300	10,700	6.2	12.1
Aged 35 to 44	42,700	33,400	41,500	27.8	2.9
Aged 45 to 54	87,200	64,300	70,700	35.6	23.3
Aged 55 to 64	103,300	107,200	112,300	–3.6	–8.0
Aged 65 to 74	148,900	107,200	86,500	38.9	72.1
Aged 75 or older	69,500	57,900	39,300	20.0	76.8

Source: Federal Reserve Board, Survey of Consumer Finances, Internet site http://www.federalreserve.gov/econresdata/scf/scfindex .html; calculations by New Strategist

Table 11.8 Ownership and Value of Pooled Investment Funds, 2007 to 2013

(percentage of households owning pooled investment funds and median value for owners, by age of householder, 2007 to 2013; percentage point change in ownership and percent change in value, 2010–13 and 2007–13; in 2013 dollars)

PERCENT OWNING POOLED INVESTMENT FUNDS	2013	2010	2007	percentage point change	
				2010–13	2007–13
Total households	**8.2%**	**8.7%**	**11.4%**	**–0.5**	**–3.2**
Under age 35	4.2	3.6	5.3	0.6	–1.1
Aged 35 to 44	6.3	7.7	11.6	–1.4	–5.3
Aged 45 to 54	8.2	9.6	12.6	–1.4	–4.4
Aged 55 to 64	10.6	11.3	14.3	–0.7	–3.7
Aged 65 to 74	11.7	11.1	14.6	0.6	–2.9
Aged 75 or older	10.3	11.9	13.2	–1.6	–2.9

MEDIAN VALUE OF POOLED INVESTMENT FUNDS	2013	2010	2007	percent change	
				2010–13	2007–13
Total households	**$80,000**	**$85,700**	**$62,900**	**–6.7%**	**27.2%**
Under age 35	10,300	9,100	20,200	13.2	–49.0
Aged 35 to 44	48,000	43,900	25,300	9.3	89.7
Aged 45 to 54	53,000	117,900	56,100	–55.0	–5.5
Aged 55 to 64	143,000	117,900	125,800	21.3	13.7
Aged 65 to 74	155,000	123,200	96,600	25.8	60.5
Aged 75 or older	145,000	128,600	84,200	12.8	72.2

Note: Pooled investment funds exclude money market funds and indirectly held mutual funds. They include open-end and closed-end mutual funds, real estate investment trusts, and hedge funds.
Source: Federal Reserve Board, Survey of Consumer Finances, Internet site http://www.federalreserve.gov/econresdata/scf/scfindex .html; calculations by New Strategist

Nonfinancial Assets Are the Basis of Household Wealth

The average household saw the value of its nonfinancial assets fall steeply between 2007 and 2013.

The median value of the nonfinancial assets owned by the average American household stood at $148,400 in 2013, far surpassing the $21,200 median value of the average household's financial assets. Between 2007 and 2010, the value of the nonfinancial assets owned by the average household fell 17 percent, after adjusting for inflation. Between 2010 and 2013, the median fell by another 10 percent. Every age group saw its nonfinancial assets lose value in both time periods, primarily because of the decline in housing values.

Eighty-six percent of households own a vehicle, the most commonly held nonfinancial asset. The median value of vehicles owned by the average household fell 9 percent between 2007 and 2013, after adjusting for inflation. Behind the decline was vehicle depreciation because of Americans' reluctance to buy new vehicles during and after the Great Recession.

The second most commonly owned nonfinancial asset is a home, owned by 65 percent of households. Homes are by far the most valuable asset owned by Americans, and they account for the largest share of net worth. In 2013, the median value of the average owned home was $170,000, a hefty 24 percent below the $224,600 median of 2007 (in 2013 dollars).

■ Housing has a bigger impact on household net worth than any other asset.

Median housing value peaks in the 55-to-64 age group

(median value of the primary residence among homeowners, by age of householder, 2013)

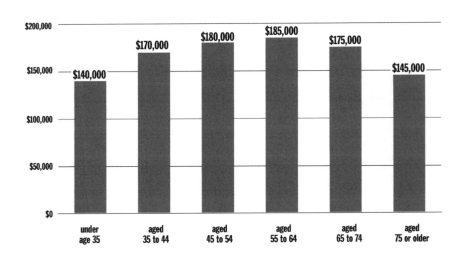

Table 11.9 Ownership and Value of Nonfinancial Assets, 2007 to 2013

(percentage of households owning any nonfinancial asset and median value for owners, by age of householder, 2007 to 2013; percentage point change in ownership and percent change in value, 2010–13 and 2007–13; in 2013 dollars)

PERCENT OWNING NONFINANCIAL ASSETS	2013	2010	2007	percentage point change 2010–13	2007–13
Total households	91.0%	91.3%	92.0%	−0.3	−1.0
Under age 35	84.9	82.8	88.2	2.1	−3.3
Aged 35 to 44	92.8	92.7	91.3	0.1	1.5
Aged 45 to 54	91.8	94.7	95.0	−2.9	−3.2
Aged 55 to 64	92.9	94.4	95.6	−1.5	−2.7
Aged 65 to 74	95.9	92.6	94.5	3.3	1.4
Aged 75 or older	89.6	93.0	87.3	−3.4	2.3

MEDIAN VALUE OF NONFINANCIAL ASSETS	2013	2010	2007	percent change 2010–13	2007–13
Total households	$148,400	$165,600	$199,200	−10.4%	−25.5%
Under age 35	22,000	36,700	34,700	−40.1	−36.6
Aged 35 to 44	135,800	153,000	205,000	−11.2	−33.8
Aged 45 to 54	174,900	205,100	252,500	−14.7	−30.7
Aged 55 to 64	189,600	221,400	261,700	−14.4	−27.6
Aged 65 to 74	206,800	214,200	238,300	−3.5	−13.2
Aged 75 or older	158,100	180,300	176,300	−12.3	−10.3

Source: Federal Reserve Board, Survey of Consumer Finances, Internet site http://www.federalreserve.gov/econresdata/scf/scfindex .html; calculations by New Strategist

Table 11.10 Ownership and Value of Primary Residence, 2007 to 2013

(percentage of households owning their primary residence and median value for owners, by age of householder, 2007 to 2013; percentage point change in ownership and percent change in value, 2010–13 and 2007–13; in 2013 dollars)

PERCENT OWNING PRIMARY RESIDENCE	2013	2010	2007	percentage point change 2010–13	2007–13
Total households	**65.2%**	**67.3%**	**68.6%**	**−2.1**	**−3.4**
Under age 35	35.6	37.5	40.6	−1.9	−5.0
Aged 35 to 44	61.7	63.8	66.1	−2.1	−4.4
Aged 45 to 54	69.1	75.2	77.3	−6.1	−8.2
Aged 55 to 64	74.2	78.1	81.0	−3.9	−6.8
Aged 65 to 74	85.8	82.6	85.5	3.2	0.3
Aged 75 or older	80.2	81.9	77.0	−1.7	3.2

MEDIAN VALUE OF PRIMARY RESIDENCE	2013	2010	2007	percent change 2010–13	2007–13
Total households	**$170,000**	**$182,200**	**$224,600**	**−6.7%**	**−24.3%**
Under age 35	140,000	150,000	196,500	−6.7	−28.8
Aged 35 to 44	170,000	182,200	230,200	−6.7	−26.2
Aged 45 to 54	180,000	214,300	258,200	−16.0	−30.3
Aged 55 to 64	185,000	198,300	235,800	−6.7	−21.5
Aged 65 to 74	175,000	176,800	224,600	−1.0	−22.1
Aged 75 or older	145,000	160,800	168,400	−9.8	−13.9

Source: Federal Reserve Board, Survey of Consumer Finances, Internet site http://www.federalreserve.gov/econresdata/scf/scfindex .html; calculations by New Strategist

Table 11.11 Ownership and Value of Other Residential Property, 2007 to 2013

(percentage of households owning other residential property and median value for owners, by age of householder, 2007 to 2013; percentage point change in ownership and percent change in value, 2010–13 and 2007–13; in 2013 dollars)

PERCENT OWNING OTHER RESIDENTIAL PROPERTY	2013	2010	2007	percentage point change	
				2010–13	2007–13
Total households	**13.2%**	**14.3%**	**13.8%**	**–1.1**	**–0.6**
Under age 35	4.7	4.5	5.6	0.2	–0.9
Aged 35 to 44	9.2	9.7	12.0	–0.5	–2.8
Aged 45 to 54	15.8	17.0	15.7	–1.2	0.1
Aged 55 to 64	18.4	22.1	20.9	–3.7	–2.5
Aged 65 to 74	21.3	22.8	18.9	–1.5	2.4
Aged 75 or older	12.8	14.6	13.4	–1.8	–0.6

MEDIAN VALUE OF OTHER RESIDENTIAL PROPERTY	2013	2010	2007	percent change	
				2010–13	2007–13
Total households	**$123,800**	**$128,600**	**$165,100**	**–3.7%**	**–25.0%**
Under age 35	102,500	77,200	95,400	32.8	7.4
Aged 35 to 44	107,000	80,400	168,400	33.1	–36.5
Aged 45 to 54	100,000	110,900	168,400	–9.8	–40.6
Aged 55 to 64	150,000	176,800	176,300	–15.2	–14.9
Aged 65 to 74	137,000	134,000	168,400	2.2	–18.6
Aged 75 or older	120,000	134,000	112,300	–10.4	6.9

Source: Federal Reserve Board, Survey of Consumer Finances, Internet site http://www.federalreserve.gov/econresdata/scf/scfindex .html; calculations by New Strategist

Table 11.12 Ownership and Value of Nonresidential Property, 2007 to 2013

(percentage of households owning nonresidential property and median value for owners, by age of householder, 2007 to 2013; percentage point change in ownership and percent change in value, 2010–13 and 2007–13; in 2013 dollars)

PERCENT OWNING NONRESIDENTIAL PROPERTY	2013	2010	2007	percentage point change 2010–13	2007–13
Total households	7.2%	7.7%	8.1%	–0.5	–0.9
Under age 35	1.8	2.3	3.2	–0.5	–1.4
Aged 35 to 44	5.7	3.9	7.5	1.8	–1.8
Aged 45 to 54	7.0	7.5	9.5	–0.5	–2.5
Aged 55 to 64	8.9	12.6	11.5	–3.7	–2.6
Aged 65 to 74	14.1	11.0	12.3	3.1	1.8
Aged 75 or older	8.9	13.4	6.8	–4.5	2.1

MEDIAN VALUE OF NONRESIDENTIAL PROPERTY	2013	2010	2007	percent change 2010–13	2007–13
Total households	$60,000	$69,700	$84,200	–13.9%	–28.7%
Under age 35	45,000	25,700	56,100	75.1	–19.8
Aged 35 to 44	54,200	53,600	56,100	1.1	–3.4
Aged 45 to 54	37,000	53,600	89,800	–31.0	–58.8
Aged 55 to 64	96,000	109,300	101,100	–12.2	–5.0
Aged 65 to 74	96,500	64,300	84,200	50.1	14.6
Aged 75 or older	55,000	69,700	123,500	–21.1	–55.5

Source: Federal Reserve Board, Survey of Consumer Finances, Internet site http://www.federalreserve.gov/econresdata/scf/scfindex .html; calculations by New Strategist

Table 11.13 Ownership and Value of Vehicles, 2007 to 2013

(percentage of households owning vehicles and median value for owners, by age of householder, 2007 to 2013; percentage point change in ownership and percent change in value, 2010–13 and 2007–13; in 2013 dollars)

PERCENT OWNING VEHICLES	2013	2010	2007	percentage point change 2010–13	2007–13
Total households	**86.3%**	**86.7%**	**87.0%**	**–0.4**	**–0.7**
Under age 35	82.7	79.4	85.4	3.3	–2.7
Aged 35 to 44	89.9	88.9	87.5	1.0	2.4
Aged 45 to 54	87.7	91.0	90.3	–3.3	–2.6
Aged 55 to 64	89.2	90.3	92.2	–1.1	–3.0
Aged 65 to 74	89.4	86.5	90.6	2.9	–1.2
Aged 75 or older	76.0	83.4	71.5	–7.4	4.5

MEDIAN VALUE OF VEHICLES	2013	2010	2007	percent change 2010–13	2007–13
Total households	**$15,800**	**$16,300**	**$17,300**	**–3.1%**	**–8.7%**
Under age 35	12,500	13,200	15,000	–5.3	–16.7
Aged 35 to 44	16,800	17,700	19,600	–5.1	–14.3
Aged 45 to 54	19,200	19,700	21,000	–2.5	–8.6
Aged 55 to 64	17,100	19,000	19,500	–10.0	–12.3
Aged 65 to 74	16,400	17,200	16,400	–4.7	0.0
Aged 75 or older	10,500	11,400	10,600	–7.9	–0.9

Source: Federal Reserve Board, Survey of Consumer Finances, Internet site http://www.federalreserve.gov/econresdata/scf/scfindex .html; calculations by New Strategist

Table 11.14 Ownership and Value of Business Equity, 2007 to 2013

(percentage of households owning business equity and median value for owners, by age of householder, 2007 to 2013; percentage point change in ownership and percent change in value, 2010–13 and 2007–13; in 2013 dollars)

PERCENT OWNING BUSINESS EQUITY	2013	2010	2007	percentage point change 2010–13	2007–13
Total households	11.7%	13.3%	13.6%	–1.6	–1.9
Under age 35	6.5	8.4	8.0	–1.9	–1.5
Aged 35 to 44	15.6	11.2	18.2	4.4	–2.6
Aged 45 to 54	14.6	16.8	17.2	–2.2	–2.6
Aged 55 to 64	15.5	19.6	18.1	–4.1	–2.6
Aged 65 to 74	11.0	15.9	11.2	–4.9	–0.2
Aged 75 or older	4.4	6.0	4.5	–1.6	–0.1

MEDIAN VALUE OF BUSINESS EQUITY	2013	2010	2007	percent change 2010–13	2007–13
Total households	$67,500	$84,400	$103,500	–20.0%	–34.8%
Under age 35	23,800	32,200	39,300	–26.1	–39.4
Aged 35 to 44	50,000	53,600	66,200	–6.7	–24.5
Aged 45 to 54	93,200	85,700	86,200	8.8	8.1
Aged 55 to 64	110,000	107,200	112,300	2.6	–2.0
Aged 65 to 74	100,000	107,200	336,800	–6.7	–70.3
Aged 75 or older	157,500	236,700	252,600	–33.5	–37.6

Source: Federal Reserve Board, Survey of Consumer Finances, Internet site http://www.federalreserve.gov/econresdata/scf/scfindex .html; calculations by New Strategist

Most Households Are in Debt

Among households with debt, the amount owed fell between 2010 and 2013.

Three out of four households are in debt, owing a median of $60,400 in 2013. The median amount of debt owed by the average debtor household fell 20 percent between 2010 and 2013, after adjusting for inflation. Householders aged 35 to 54 are most likely to be in debt, with 82 to 85 percent owing money. Debt declines with age, falling to a low of 41 percent among householders aged 75 or older. The percent of householders aged 75 or older who are in debt has climbed by a hefty 10 percentage points since 2007.

Four types of debt are relatively common—mortgage debt, which is held by 41.5 percent of households; credit card debt (38 percent); vehicle loans (31 percent); and education loans (20 percent). Mortgages account for the largest share of debt. The average homeowner with a mortgage owed $116,000 in 2013. Education loans are second in size, the average household with education loans owing a median of $16,000—more than the $11,900 owed by (the more numerous) households with vehicle loans. Credit card debt is tiny by comparison, the average household with a credit card balance owing only $2,300.

■ Americans have paid off a substantial portion of their debt, but household net worth continues to decline because asset values are falling faster than debt.

Education loans are common among young and middle-aged householders

(percentage of households with education loans, by age of householder, 2013)

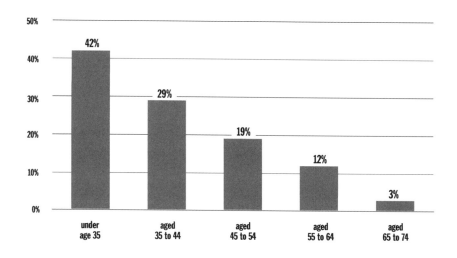

Table 11.15 Debt of Households, 2007 to 2013

(percentage of households with debt and median amount of debt for debtors, by age of householder, 2007 to 2013; percentage point change in households with debt and percent change in amount of debt, 2010–13 and 2007–13; in 2013 dollars)

PERCENT WITH DEBT	2013	2010	2007	percentage point change 2010–13	percentage point change 2007–13
Total households	74.5%	74.9%	77.0%	–0.4	–2.5
Under age 35	77.1	77.8	83.6	–0.7	–6.5
Aged 35 to 44	84.8	86.0	86.2	–1.2	–1.4
Aged 45 to 54	82.3	84.1	86.8	–1.8	–4.5
Aged 55 to 64	78.7	77.7	81.8	1.0	–3.1
Aged 65 to 74	66.4	65.2	65.5	1.2	0.9
Aged 75 or older	41.4	38.5	31.4	2.9	10.0

MEDIAN AMOUNT OWED	2013	2010	2007	percent change 2010–13	percent change 2007–13
Total households	$60,400	$75,800	$75,600	–20.3%	–20.1%
Under age 35	31,100	42,500	40,600	–26.8	–23.4
Aged 35 to 44	96,500	115,700	119,200	–16.6	–19.0
Aged 45 to 54	100,000	98,400	107,700	1.6	–7.1
Aged 55 to 64	63,400	82,500	67,700	–23.2	–6.4
Aged 65 to 74	44,000	48,300	45,100	–8.9	–2.4
Aged 75 or older	20,000	32,200	14,600	–37.9	37.0

Source: Federal Reserve Board, Survey of Consumer Finances, Internet site http://www.federalreserve.gov/econresdata/scf/scfindex .html; calculations by New Strategist

Table 11.16 Households with Mortgage Debt, 2007 to 2013

(percentage of households with mortgage debt and median amount of debt for debtors, by age of householder, 2007 to 2013; percentage point change in households with debt and percent change in amount of debt, 2010–13 and 2007–13; in 2013 dollars)

PERCENT WITH MORTGAGE DEBT	2013	2010	2007	percentage point change 2010–13	2007–13
Total households	**41.5%**	**45.2%**	**46.3%**	**−3.7**	**−4.8**
Under age 35	28.6	33.9	37.2	−5.3	−8.6
Aged 35 to 44	52.7	57.3	59.3	−4.6	−6.6
Aged 45 to 54	55.3	58.5	63.8	−3.2	−8.5
Aged 55 to 64	45.8	50.6	50.2	−4.8	−4.4
Aged 65 to 74	38.9	36.6	35.5	2.3	3.4
Aged 75 or older	18.6	21.2	11.0	−2.6	7.6

MEDIAN AMOUNT OWED	2013	2010	2007	percent change 2010–13	2007–13
Total households	**$116,000**	**$117,900**	**$123,500**	**−1.6%**	**−6.1%**
Under age 35	120,000	128,600	149,300	−6.7	−19.6
Aged 35 to 44	140,000	146,100	140,300	−4.2	−0.2
Aged 45 to 54	120,000	120,000	120,100	0.0	−0.1
Aged 55 to 64	107,000	101,800	101,100	5.1	5.8
Aged 65 to 74	87,000	84,700	95,100	2.7	−8.5
Aged 75 or older	59,000	62,200	56,100	−5.1	5.2

Source: Federal Reserve Board, Survey of Consumer Finances, Internet site http://www.federalreserve.gov/econresdata/scf/scfindex .html; calculations by New Strategist

Table 11.17 Households with Home Equity Line of Credit Debt, 2007 to 2013

(percentage of households with home equity line of credit debt and median amount of debt for debtors, by age of householder, 2007 to 2013; percentage point change in households with debt and percent change in amount of debt, 2010–13 and 2007–13; in 2013 dollars)

				percentage point change	
PERCENT WITH HELOC DEBT	2013	2010	2007	2010–13	2007–13
Total households	**5.0%**	**7.2%**	**8.5%**	**–2.2**	**–3.5**
Under age 35	–	2.3	4.0	–	–
Aged 35 to 44	5.2	5.6	8.8	–0.4	–3.6
Aged 45 to 54	5.7	10.9	11.7	–5.2	–6.0
Aged 55 to 64	8.8	10.6	12.6	–1.8	–3.8
Aged 65 to 74	6.8	8.7	9.6	–1.9	–2.8
Aged 75 or older	2.3	4.9	3.4	–2.6	–1.1

				percent change	
MEDIAN AMOUNT OWED	2013	2010	2007	2010–13	2007–13
Total households	**25,000**	**28,300**	**26,900**	**–11.7%**	**–7.1%**
Under age 35	–	16,100	26,900	–	–
Aged 35 to 44	25,000	32,200	22,500	–22.4	11.1
Aged 45 to 54	20,000	32,200	28,100	–37.9	–28.8
Aged 55 to 64	27,000	22,500	22,500	20.0	20.0
Aged 65 to 74	30,000	31,100	16,800	–3.5	78.6
Aged 75 or older	16,000	21,400	28,100	–25.2	–43.1

Note: "–" means sample is too small to make a reliable estimate.
Source: Federal Reserve Board, Survey of Consumer Finances, Internet site http://www.federalreserve.gov/econresdata/scf/scfindex .html; calculations by New Strategist

Table 11.18 Households with Credit Card Debt, 2007 to 2013

(percentage of households with credit card balances and median amount of debt for debtors, by age of householder, 2007 to 2013; percentage point change in households with debt and percent change in amount of debt, 2010–13 and 2007–13; in 2013 dollars)

PERCENT WITH CREDIT CARD BALANCES	2013	2010	2007	percentage point change 2010–13	2007–13
Total households	**38.1%**	**39.4%**	**46.1%**	**–1.3**	**–8.0**
Under age 35	36.8	38.7	48.5	–1.9	–11.7
Aged 35 to 44	41.7	45.7	51.7	–4.0	–10.0
Aged 45 to 54	44.3	46.2	53.6	–1.9	–9.3
Aged 55 to 64	43.4	41.3	49.9	2.1	–6.5
Aged 65 to 74	32.8	31.9	37.0	0.9	–4.2
Aged 75 or older	21.1	21.7	18.8	–0.6	2.3

MEDIAN AMOUNT OWED	2013	2010	2007	percent change 2010–13	2007–13
Total households	**$2,300**	**$2,800**	**$3,400**	**–17.9%**	**–32.4%**
Under age 35	1,500	1,700	2,000	–11.8	–25.0
Aged 35 to 44	2,500	3,800	3,900	–34.2	–35.9
Aged 45 to 54	2,600	3,800	4,000	–31.6	–35.0
Aged 55 to 64	3,000	3,000	4,000	0.0	–25.0
Aged 65 to 74	2,300	2,300	3,400	0.0	–32.4
Aged 75 or older	1,900	1,900	900	0.0	111.1

Source: Federal Reserve Board, Survey of Consumer Finances, Internet site http://www.federalreserve.gov/econresdata/scf/scfindex .html; calculations by New Strategist

Table 11.19 Households with Education Loans, 2007 to 2013

(percentage of households with education loans and median amount of debt for debtors, by age of householder, 2007 to 2013; percentage point change in households with debt and percent change in amount of debt, 2010–13 and 2007–13; in 2013 dollars)

PERCENT WITH EDUCATION LOANS	2013	2010	2007	percentage point change 2010–13	2007–13
Total households	**20.0%**	**19.2%**	**15.2%**	**0.8**	**4.8**
Under age 35	41.7	40.1	33.8	1.6	7.9
Aged 35 to 44	28.7	26.5	14.9	2.2	13.8
Aged 45 to 54	18.6	17.6	14.5	1.0	4.1
Aged 55 to 64	12.0	9.3	10.6	2.7	1.4
Aged 65 to 74	3.1	4.2	–	–1.1	–
Aged 75 or older	–	–	–	–	–

MEDIAN AMOUNT OWED	2013	2010	2007	percent change 2010–13	2007–13
Total households	**$16,000**	**$13,900**	**$13,500**	**15.1%**	**18.5%**
Under age 35	17,200	13,900	14,600	23.7	17.8
Aged 35 to 44	17,000	14,400	13,500	18.1	25.9
Aged 45 to 54	13,200	12,900	13,500	2.3	–2.2
Aged 55 to 64	17,200	16,100	7,900	6.8	117.7
Aged 65 to 74	17,000	12,900	–	31.8	–
Aged 75 or older	–	–	–	–	–

Note: "–" means sample is too small to make a reliable estimate.
Source: Federal Reserve Board, Survey of Consumer Finances, Internet site http://www.federalreserve.gov/econresdata/scf/scfindex .html; calculations by New Strategist

Table 11.20 Households with Vehicle Loans, 2007 to 2013

(percentage of households with vehicle loans and median amount of debt for debtors, by age of householder, 2007 to 2013; percentage point change in households with debt and percent change in amount of debt, 2010–13 and 2007–13; in 2013 dollars)

PERCENT WITH VEHICLE LOANS	2013	2010	2007	percentage point change 2010–13	2007–13
Total households	**30.9%**	**30.2%**	**34.9%**	**0.7**	**–4.0**
Under age 35	35.2	32.2	44.3	3.0	–9.1
Aged 35 to 44	37.0	40.8	42.6	–3.8	–5.6
Aged 45 to 54	36.5	35.9	39.1	0.6	–2.6
Aged 55 to 64	30.8	28.2	35.2	2.6	–4.4
Aged 65 to 74	24.4	22.8	21.6	1.6	2.8
Aged 75 or older	10.7	8.1	6.1	2.6	4.6

MEDIAN AMOUNT OWED	2013	2010	2007	percent change 2010–13	2007–13
Total households	**$11,900**	**$10,700**	**$13,000**	**11.2%**	**–8.5%**
Under age 35	11,000	10,600	13,000	3.8	–15.4
Aged 35 to 44	12,500	11,900	13,900	5.0	–10.1
Aged 45 to 54	12,100	10,500	13,000	15.2	–6.9
Aged 55 to 64	11,700	10,100	12,100	15.8	–3.3
Aged 65 to 74	10,500	10,600	13,400	–0.9	–21.6
Aged 75 or older	13,400	10,800	9,900	24.1	35.4

Source: Federal Reserve Board, Survey of Consumer Finances, Internet site http://www.federalreserve.gov/econresdata/scf/scfindex .html; calculations by New Strategist

Americans of All Ages Are Worried about Retirement

The expected age of retirement is climbing.

Only 18 percent of American workers are "very" confident in having enough money to live comfortably throughout retirement, according to the Employee Benefit Research Institute's Retirement Confidence Survey. Workers should be worried about their retirement security. More than one-third (36 percent) have less than $1,000 in savings and the 52 percent majority has less than $10,000 saved. Among workers aged 55 or older, one in four has saved less than $1,000 and one in three has saved less than $10,000. Only 42 percent of the oldest workers have saved $100,000 or more.

Among all workers, the share expecting to retire at age 65 or earlier has fallen from 65 percent in 2007—before the start of the Great Recession—to 50 percent in 2014. Among workers aged 55 or older, the percentage expecting to retire at age 66 or later climbed from 37 to 52 percent during those years.

■ Although most workers say they are saving for retirement, only about one-third contribute to a workplace retirement savings plan.

Most workers aged 55 or older expect to retire at age 66 or later

(percent of workers aged 55 or older who expect to retire at age 66 or older, including never retire, 2007 and 2014)

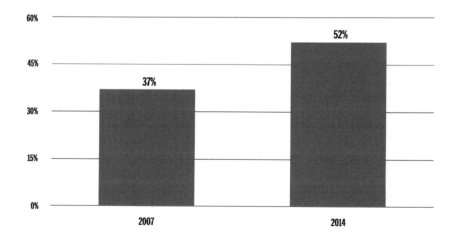

Table 11.21 Retirement Attitudes and Planning by Age, 2014

(percentage of workers aged 25 or older responding by age, 2014)

	total workers	25 to 34	35 to 44	45 to 54	55 or older
Percent very confident in having enough money to live comfortably throughout retirement	18%	21%	15%	17%	21%
Worker and/or spouse are currently saving for retirement	57	42	57	60	71
Have an IRA (includes rollover IRA)	43	27	48	42	57
Contribute to a workplace retirement savings plan	34	26	33	37	44
TOTAL SAVINGS AND INVESTMENTS (NOT INCLUDING VALUE OF PRIMARY RESIDENCE OR DEFINED BENEFIT PLANS)					
Less than $1,000	36%	43%	37%	34%	24%
$1,000 to $9,999	16	27	15	11	10
$10,000 to $24,999	8	11	7	8	7
$25,000 to $49,999	9	8	8	13	9
$50,000 to $99,999	9	8	11	7	8
$100,000 to $249,999	11	4	8	15	19
$250,000 or more	11	0	15	12	23

Source: Employee Benefit Research Institute, American Savings Education Council, and Mathew Greenwald & Associates, Inc., 2014 Retirement Confidence Survey, Internet site http://www.ebri.org/surveys/rcs/2014/

Table 11.22 Expected Age of Retirement by Age, 2007 and 2014

(percentage of workers aged 25 or older by expected age of retirement, by age, 2007 and 2014)

	2014	2007	percentage point change
Total workers			
Under age 60	9%	17%	–8
Aged 60 to 64	18	21	–3
Aged 65	23	27	–4
Aged 66 or older	33	24	9
Never retire	10	6	4
Don't know/refused	8	6	2
Workers aged 25 to 34			
Under age 60	12	26	–14
Aged 60 to 64	19	19	0
Aged 65	26	24	2
Aged 66 or older	28	19	9
Never retire	8	6	2
Don't know/refused	7	6	1
Workers aged 35 to 44			
Under age 60	13	16	–3
Aged 60 to 64	13	20	–7
Aged 65	25	30	–5
Aged 66 or older	31	22	9
Never retire	10	5	5
Don't know/refused	6	7	–1
Workers aged 45 to 54			
Under age 60	7	16	–9
Aged 60 to 64	20	20	0
Aged 65	20	28	–8
Aged 66 or older	34	26	8
Never retire	8	6	2
Don't know/refused	11	3	8
Workers aged 55 or older			
Under age 60	2	8	–6
Aged 60 to 64	21	25	–4
Aged 65	19	22	–3
Aged 66 or older	38	32	6
Never retire	14	5	9
Don't know/refused	6	7	–1

Source: Employee Benefit Research Institute, American Savings Education Council, and Mathew Greenwald & Associates, Inc., 2014 Retirement Confidence Survey, Internet site http://www.ebri.org/surveys/rcs/2014/

Glossary

adjusted for inflation A dollar value that has been adjusted for the rise in the cost of living by use of the consumer price index.

age Classification by age is based on the age of the person at his/her last birthday.

American Community Survey The ACS is an ongoing nationwide survey of 250,000 households per month, providing detailed demographic data at the community level. Designed to replace the census long-form questionnaire, the ACS includes more than 60 questions that formerly appeared on the long form, such as questions about language spoken at home, income, and education. ACS data are available for areas as small as census tracts.

American Housing Survey The AHS collects national and metropolitan-level data on the nation's housing, including apartments, single-family homes, and mobile homes. The Census Bureau conducts the nationally representative survey, with a sample of 55,000 households, for the Department of Housing and Urban Development every other year.

American Indians American Indians include Alaska Natives unless those groups are shown separately.

American Time Use Survey Under contract with the Bureau of Labor Statistics, the Census Bureau collects ATUS information, revealing how people spend their time. The ATUS sample is drawn from U.S. households completing their final month of interviews for the Current Population Survey. One individual from each selected household is chosen to participate in the ATUS. Respondents are interviewed by telephone about their time use during the previous 24 hours.

Asian The term "Asian" includes Native Hawaiians and other Pacific Islanders unless those groups are shown separately.

baby boom Americans born between 1946 and 1964.

baby bust Americans born between 1965 and 1976. Also known as Generation X.

Behavioral Risk Factor Surveillance System The BRFSS is a collaborative project of the Centers for Disease Control and Prevention and U.S. states and territories. It is an ongoing data collection program designed to measure behavioral risk factors in the adult population aged 18 or older. All 50 states, three territories, and the District of Columbia take part in the survey, making the BRFSS the primary source of information on the health-related behaviors of Americans.

Black The Black racial category includes those who identified themselves as "Black" or "African American."

Consumer Expenditure Survey The CEX is an ongoing study of the day-to-day spending of American households administered by the Bureau of Labor Statistics. The CEX includes an interview survey and a diary survey. The average spending figures shown are the integrated data from both the diary and interview components of the survey. Two separate, nationally representative samples are used for the interview and diary surveys. For the interview survey, about 7,500 consumer units are interviewed on a rotating panel basis each quarter for five consecutive quarters. For the diary survey, 7,500 consumer units keep weekly diaries of spending for two consecutive weeks.

consumer unit *(on spending tables only)* For convenience, the terms consumer unit and household are used interchangeably, although consumer units are somewhat different from the Census Bureau's households. A consumer unit includes all the related members of a household or any financially independent member of a household. A household may include more than one consumer unit.

Current Population Survey The CPS is a nationally representative survey of the civilian noninstitutional population aged 15 or older. It is taken monthly by the Census Bureau for the Bureau of Labor Statistics, collecting information from 60,000 households on employment and unemployment. In March of each year, the survey includes the Annual Social and Economic Supplement, which is the source of most national data on the characteristics of Americans, such as educational attainment, living arrangements, and incomes.

disability The National Health Interview Survey estimates the number of people aged 18 or older who have difficulty in physical functioning, probing whether respondents could perform nine activities by themselves without using special equipment. The categories are walking a quarter mile; standing for two hours; sitting for two hours; walking up 10 steps without resting; stooping, bending, kneeling; reaching over one's head; grasping or handling small objects; carrying a 10-pound object; and pushing/pulling a large object. Adults who reported that any of these activities was very difficult or they could not do it at all were defined as having physical difficulties.

dual-earner couple A married couple in which both the householder and the householder's spouse are in the labor force.

earnings A type of income, earnings is the amount of money a person receives from his or her job. *See also* Income.

employed All civilians who did any work as a paid employee or farmer/self-employed worker or who worked 15 hours or more as an unpaid farm worker or in a family-owned business during the reference period. All those who have jobs but are temporarily absent from their jobs due to illness, bad weather, vacation, labor management dispute, or personal reasons are considered employed.

expenditure The transaction cost including excise and sales taxes of goods and services acquired during the survey period. The full cost of each purchase is recorded even though full payment may not have been made at the date of purchase. Average expenditure figures may be artificially low for infrequently purchased items such as cars because figures are calculated using all consumer units within a demographic segment rather than just purchasers. Expenditure estimates include money spent on gifts for others.

family A group of two or more people (one of whom is the householder) related by birth, marriage, or adoption and living in the same household.

family household A household maintained by a householder who lives with one or more people related to him or her by blood, marriage, or adoption.

female/male householder A woman or man who maintains a household without a spouse present. May head family or nonfamily household.

foreign-born population People who are not U.S. citizens at birth.

full-time employment Full-time is 35 or more hours of work per week during the majority of weeks worked.

full-time, year-round Indicates 50 or more weeks of full-time employment during the previous calendar year.

General Social Survey The GSS is a biennial survey of the attitudes of Americans taken by the University of Chicago's National Opinion Research Center. NORC conducts the GSS through face-to-face interviews with an independently drawn, representative sample of 1,500 to 3,000 noninstitutionalized people aged 18 or older who live in the United States.

generation X Americans born between 1965 and 1976. Also known as the baby-bust generation.

Hispanic Because Hispanic is an ethnic origin rather than a race, Hispanics may be of any race. While most Hispanics are White, there are Black, Asian, American Indian, and even Native Hawaiian Hispanics.

household All the persons who occupy a housing unit. A household includes the related family members and all the unrelated persons, if any, such as lodgers, foster children, wards, or employees who share the housing unit. A person living alone is counted as a household. A group of unrelated people who share a housing unit as roommates or unmarried partners is also counted as a household. Households do not include group quarters such as college dormitories, prisons, or nursing homes.

household, race/ethnicity of Households are categorized according to the race or ethnicity of the householder only.

householder The householder is the person (or one of the persons) in whose name the housing unit is owned or rented or, if there is no such person, any adult member. With married couples, the householder may be either the husband or wife. The householder is the reference person for the household.

householder, age of The age of the householder is used to categorize households into age groups such as those used in this book. Married couples, for example, are classified according to the age of either the husband or wife, depending on which one identified him- or herself as the householder.

housing unit A housing unit is a house, an apartment, a group of rooms, or a single room occupied or intended for occupancy as separate living quarters. Separate living quarters are those in which the occupants do not live and eat with any other persons in the structure and that have direct access from the outside of the building or through a common hall that is used or intended for use by the occupants of another unit or by the general public. The occupants may be a single family, one person living alone, two or more families living together, or any other group of related or unrelated persons who share living arrangements.

Housing Vacancy Survey The HVS is a supplement to the Current Population Survey, providing quarterly and annual data on rental and homeowner vacancy rates, characteristics of units available for occupancy, and homeownership rates by age, household type, region, state, and metropolitan area. The Current Population Survey sample includes 60,000 occupied housing units and about 9,000 vacant units.

housing value The respondent's estimate of how much his or her house and lot would sell for if it were for sale.

iGeneration Americans born between 1995 and 2009.

immigrants Aliens admitted for legal permanent residence in the United States.

income Money received in the preceding calendar year by a person aged 15 or older from any of the following sources: earnings from longest job (or self-employment), earnings from jobs other than longest job, unemployment compensation, workers' compensation, Social Security, Supplemental Security income, public assistance, veterans' payments, survivor benefits, disability benefits, retirement pensions, interest, dividends, rents and royalties or estates and trusts, educational assistance, alimony, child support, financial assistance from outside the household, and other periodic income. Income is reported in several ways in this book. Household income is the combined income of all household members. Income of persons is all income accruing to a person from all sources. Earnings are the money a person receives from his or her job.

industry Refers to the industry in which a person worked longest in the preceding calendar year.

job tenure The length of time a person has been employed continuously by the same employer.

labor force The labor force tables in this book show the civilian labor force only. The labor force includes both the employed and the unemployed (people who are looking for work). People are counted as in the labor force if they were working or looking for work during the reference week in which the Census Bureau fields the Current Population Survey.

labor force participation rate The percent of the civilian noninstitutional population that is in the civilian labor force, which includes both the employed and the unemployed.

male householder *See* Female/Male Householder.

married couples with or without children under age 18 Refers to married couples with or without own children under age 18 living in the same household. Couples without children under age 18 may be parents of grown children who live elsewhere or they could be childless couples.

median The median is the amount that divides the population or households into two equal portions: one below and one above the median. Medians can be calculated for income, age, and many other characteristics.

median income The amount that divides the income distribution into two equal groups, half having incomes above the median, half having incomes below the median. The medians for households or families are based on all households or families. The median for persons are based on all persons aged 15 or older with income.

metropolitan statistical area To be defined as an MSA, an area must include a city with 50,000 or more inhabitants, or a Census Bureau–defined urbanized area of at least 50,000 inhabitants and a total metropolitan population of at least 100,000 (75,000 in New England). The county (or counties) that contains the largest city becomes the "central county" (counties), along with any adjacent counties that have at least 50 percent of their population in the urbanized area surrounding the largest city. Additional "outlying counties" are included in the MSA if they meet specified requirements of commuting to the central counties and other selected requirements of metropolitan character (such as population density and percent urban). In New England, MSAs are defined in terms of cities and towns rather than counties. For this reason, the concept of New England County Metropolitan Area is used to define metropolitan areas in the New England division.

millennial generation Americans born between 1977 and 1994.

mobility status People are classified according to their mobility status on the basis of a comparison between their place of residence at the time of the March Current Population Survey and their place of residence in March of the previous year. Nonmovers are people living in the same house at the end of the period as at the beginning of the period. Movers are people living in a different house at the end of the period from that at the beginning of the period. Movers from abroad are either citizens or aliens whose place of residence is outside the United States at the beginning of the period, that is, in an outlying area under the jurisdiction of the United States or in a foreign country. The mobility status for children is fully allocated from the mother if she is in the household; otherwise it is allocated from the householder.

National Health and Nutrition Examination Survey The NHANES is a continuous survey of a representative sample of the U.S. civilian noninstitutionalized population. Respondents are interviewed at home about their health and nutrition, and the interview is followed up by a physical examination that measures such things as height and weight in mobile examination centers.

National Health Interview Survey The NHIS is a continuing nationwide sample survey of the civilian noninstitutional population of the United States conducted by the Census Bureau for the National Center for Health Statistics. In interviews each year, data are collected from more than 100,000 people about their illnesses, injuries, impairments, chronic and acute conditions, activity limitations, and use of health services.

National Household Education Survey Sponsored by the National Center for Education Statistics, the NHES provides descriptive data on the educational activities of the U.S. population, including after-school care and adult education. The NHES is a system of telephone surveys of a representative sample of 45,000 to 60,000 households in the United States.

National Survey of Family Growth Sponsored by the National Center for Health Statistics, the NSFG is a periodic nationally representative survey of the civilian noninstitutionalized population aged 15 to 44. In-person interviews are completed with men and women, collecting data on marriage, divorce, contraception, and infertility. The 2006–10 survey updates previous NSFG surveys taken in 1973, 1976, 1988, 1995, and 2002.

National Survey on Drug Use and Health The NSDUH is an annual survey of a nationally representative sample of people aged 12 or older living in households, noninstitutional group quarters (such as college dorms), and military bases in the United States. It is the primary source of information about illegal drug use in the United States and has been conducted since 1971. Interviews are held in person and incorporate procedures (such as anonymity and computer-assisted interviewing) that will increase respondents' cooperation and willingness to report honestly about their illicit drug use behavior.

Native Hawaiian and Other Pacific Islander The 2000 census identified this group for the first time as a separate racial category from Asians. In most survey data, however, the population is included with Asians.

nonfamily household A household maintained by a householder who lives alone or who lives with people to whom he or she is not related.

nonfamily householder A householder who lives alone or with nonrelatives.

non-Hispanic People who do not identify themselves as Hispanic are classified as non-Hispanic. Non-Hispanics may be of any race.

non-Hispanic White People who identify their race as White and who do not indicate a Hispanic origin.

nonmetropolitan area Counties that are not classified as metropolitan areas.

occupation Occupational classification is based on the kind of work a person did at his or her job during the previous calendar year. If a person changed jobs during the year, the data refer to the occupation of the job held the longest during that year.

occupied housing units A housing unit is classified as occupied if a person or group of people is living in it or if the occupants are only temporarily absent— on vacation, for example. By definition, the count of occupied housing units is the same as the count of households.

outside principal city The portion of a metropolitan county or counties that falls outside of the principal city or cities; generally regarded as the suburbs.

own children Own children are sons and daughters, including stepchildren and adopted children, of the householder. The totals include never-married children living away from home in college dormitories.

owner occupied A housing unit is "owner occupied" if the owner lives in the unit, even if it is mortgaged or not fully paid for. A cooperative or condominium unit is "owner occupied" only if the owner lives in it. All other occupied units are classified as "renter occupied."

part-time employment Part-time is less than 35 hours of work per week in a majority of the weeks worked during the year.

percent change The change (either positive or negative) in a measure that is expressed as a proportion of the starting measure. When median income changes from $20,000 to $25,000, for example, this is a 25 percent increase.

percentage point change The change (either positive or negative) in a value that is already expressed as a percentage. When a labor force participation rate changes from 70 percent to 75 percent, for example, this is a 5 percentage point increase.

poverty level The official income threshold below which families and people are classified as living in poverty. The threshold rises each year with inflation and varies depending on family size and age of householder.

principal city The largest city in a metropolitan area is called the principal or central city. The balance of the metropolitan area outside the principal or central city is regarded as the "suburbs."

proportion or share The value of a part expressed as a percentage of the whole. If there are 4 million people aged 25 and 3 million of them are White, then the White proportion is 75 percent.

race Race is self-reported and can be defined in three ways. The "race alone" population comprises people who identify themselves as being of only one race. The "race in combination" population comprises people who identify themselves as being of more than one race, such as White and Black. The "race, alone or in combination" population includes both those who identify themselves as being of one race and those who identify themselves as being of more than one race.

recession generation Americans born from 2010 to the present.

regions The four major regions and nine census divisions of the United States are the state groupings as shown below:
Northeast:
—New England: Connecticut, Maine, Massachusetts, New Hampshire, Rhode Island, and Vermont
—Middle Atlantic: New Jersey, New York, and Pennsylvania
Midwest:
—East North Central: Illinois, Indiana, Michigan, Ohio, and Wisconsin
—West North Central: Iowa, Kansas, Minnesota, Missouri, Nebraska, North Dakota, and South Dakota
South:
—South Atlantic: Delaware, District of Columbia, Florida, Georgia, Maryland, North Carolina, South Carolina, Virginia, and West Virginia
—East South Central: Alabama, Kentucky, Mississippi, and Tennessee
—West South Central: Arkansas, Louisiana, Oklahoma, and Texas
West:
—Mountain: Arizona, Colorado, Idaho, Montana, Nevada, New Mexico, Utah, and Wyoming
—Pacific: Alaska, California, Hawaii, Oregon, and Washington

renter occupied *See* Owner Occupied.

Retirement Confidence Survey The RCS— sponsored by the Employee Benefit Research Institute, the American Savings Education Council, and Mathew Greenwald & Associates—is an annual survey of a nationally representative sample of 1,000 people aged 25 or older. Respondents are asked a core set of questions that have been included in the survey since 1996, measuring attitudes and behavior toward retirement, as well as additional questions about current retirement issues.

rounding Percentages are rounded to the nearest tenth of a percent; therefore, the percentages in a distribution do not always add exactly to 100.0 percent. The totals, however, are always shown as 100.0. Moreover, individual figures are rounded to the nearest thousand without being adjusted to group totals, which are independently rounded; percentages are based on the unrounded numbers.

self-employment A person is categorized as self-employed if he or she was self-employed in the job held longest during the reference period. Persons who report self-employment from a second job are excluded, but those who report wage and salary income from a second job are included. Unpaid workers in family businesses are excluded. Self-employment statistics include only nonagricultural workers and exclude people who work for themselves in incorporated business.

sex ratio The number of men per 100 women.

suburbs *See* Outside Principal City.

Survey of Consumer Finances The Survey of Consumer Finances is a triennial survey taken by the Federal Reserve Board. It collects data on the assets, debt, and net worth of approximately 6,000 nationally representative American households.

Survey of Income and Program Participation The SIPP is a continuous, monthly panel survey of up to 36,700 households conducted by the Census Bureau. It is designed to measure the effectiveness of existing federal, state, and local programs and to measure economic well-being, including wealth, asset ownership, and debt.

unemployed Unemployed people are those who, during the survey period, had no employment but were available and looking for work. Those who were laid off from their jobs and were waiting to be recalled are also classified as unemployed.

White People who identify their race as White. The "White" racial category includes many Hispanics (who may be of any race) unless the term "non-Hispanic White" is used.

Youth Risk Behavior Surveillance System The Centers for Disease Control created the YRBBS to monitor health risks being taken by young people at the national, state, and local level. The national survey is taken every two years based on a nationally representative sample of 16,000 students in 9th through 12th grade in public and private schools.

Bibliography

Agency for Healthcare Research and Quality

Internet site http://www.ahrq.gov/

—Medical Expenditure Panel Survey, Internet site http://meps.ahrq.gov/mepsweb/survey_comp/household.jsp

Bureau of Labor Statistics

Internet site http://www.bls.gov

—2013 American Time Use Survey, Internet site http://www.bls.gov/tus/home.htm

—College Enrollment and Work Activity of 2012 High School Graduates, Internet site http://www.bls.gov/news.release/hsgec.nr0.htm

—Consumer Expenditure Surveys, various years, Internet site http://www.bls.gov/cex/home.htm

—Employee Tenure, Internet site http://www.bls.gov/news.release/tenure.toc.htm

—Employment Characteristics of Families, Internet site http://www.bls.gov/news.release/famee.toc.htm

—Employment Projections, Internet site http://www.bls.gov/emp/

—Labor Force Statistics from the Current Population Survey—Annual Averages, Internet site http://www.bls.gov/cps/tables.htm#empstat

—*Monthly Labor Review*, "Labor Force Projections to 2020: A More Slowly Growing Workforce," January 2012, Internet site http://www.bls.gov/opub/mlr/

—Table 15. Employed persons by detailed occupation, sex, and age, Annual Average 2013 (Source: Current Population Survey), unpublished table received from the BLS by special request

Bureau of the Census

Internet site http://www.census.gov

—2010 Census, American Factfinder, Internet site http://factfinder2.census.gov/faces/nav/jsf/pages/index.xhtml

—American Community Survey, American Factfinder, Internet site http://factfinder2.census.gov/faces/nav/jsf/pages/index.xhtml

—America's Families and Living Arrangements, Current Population Survey Annual Social and Economic Supplement, Internet site http://www.census.gov/hhes/families/

—Current Population Survey Annual Social and Economic Supplement, Internet site http://www.census.gov/hhes/www/income/data/

—Educational Attainment, CPS Historical Time Series Tables, Internet site http://www.census .gov/hhes/socdemo/education/data/cps/historical/index.html

—Educational Attainment, Current Population Survey Annual Social and Economic Supplement, Internet site http://www.census.gov/hhes/socdemo/education/

—Families and Living Arrangements, Historical Tables—Households, Internet site http://www .census.gov/hhes/families/data/historical.html

—Fertility of American Women: 2012, Detailed Tables, Internet site http://www.census.gov/ hhes/fertility/data/cps/2012.html

—Geographic Mobility/Migration, Current Population Survey Annual Social and Economic Supplements, Internet site http://www.census.gov/hhes/migration/

—Health Insurance, Current Population Survey Annual Social and Economic Supplements, Internet site http://www.census.gov/hhes/www/hlthins/

—Historical Income Data, Current Population Survey Annual Social and Economic Supplements, Internet site http://www.census.gov/hhes/www/income/data/historical/index.html

—Housing Vacancy Survey, Internet site http://www.census.gov/housing/hvs/

—Income, Current Population Survey Annual Social and Economic Supplements, Internet site http://www.census.gov/hhes/www/income/data/index.html

—Number, Timing, and Duration of Marriages and Divorces: 2009, Detailed Tables, Internet site http://www.census.gov/hhes/socdemo/marriage/data/sipp/2009/tables.html

—Population Estimates, Internet site http://www.census.gov/popest/data/index.html

—Population Projections, Internet site http://www.census.gov/population/projections/

—Poverty, Current Population Survey Annual Social and Economic Supplements, Internet site http://www.census.gov/hhes/www/poverty/index.html

—School Enrollment, CPS Historical Time Series Tables on School Enrollment, Internet site http://www.census.gov/hhes/school/data/cps/historical/index.html

—School Enrollment, CPS October 2013, Detailed Tables, Internet site http://www.census.gov/ hhes/school/data/cps/2013/tables.html

—Voting and Registration, Internet site http://www.census.gov/hhes/www/socdemo/voting/ index.html

Centers for Disease Control and Prevention

Internet site http://www.cdc.gov

—Behavioral Risk Factor Surveillance System, Prevalence and Trends Data, Internet site http://apps.nccd.cdc.gov/brfss/

—Diagnosis of HIV Infection in the United States and Dependent Areas, 2011, Internet site http://www.cdc.gov/hiv/surveillance/resources/reports/2011report/index.htm

—Youth Risk Behavior Surveillance—United States, 2013, Internet site http://www.cdc.gov/HealthyYouth/yrbs/index.htm

Employee Benefit Research Institute

Internet site http://www.ebri.org/

—Retirement Confidence Surveys, Internet site http://www.ebri.org/surveys/rcs/

Federal Interagency Forum on Child and Family Statistics

Internet site http://childstats.gov

—America's Children: Key National Indicators of Well-Being, 2013, Internet site http://www.childstats.gov/

Federal Reserve Board

Internet site http://www.federalreserve.gov

—Survey of Consumer Finances, Internet site http://www.federalreserve.gov/econresdata/scf/scfindex.htm

Homeland Security

Internet site http://www.dhs.gov/index.shtm

—Yearbook of Immigration Statistics, Internet site http://www.dhs.gov/yearbook-immigration-statistics

National Center for Education Statistics

Internet site http://nces.ed.gov

—Digest of Education Statistics: 2013, Internet site http://nces.ed.gov/programs/digest/2013menu_tables.asp

—Parent and Family Involvement in Education, from the National Household Education Surveys Program of 2012, Internet site http://nces.ed.gov/pubsearch/pubsinfo.asp?pubid=2013028

—Projections of Education Statistics to 2021, Internet site http://nces.ed.gov/programs/projections/projections2021/

National Center for Health Statistics

Internet site http://www.cdc.gov/nchs

—*Anthropometric Reference Data for Children and Adults: United States, 2007–2010*, National Health Statistics Reports, Series 11, No. 252, 2012, Internet site http://www.cdc.gov/nchs/nhanes.htm

—Birth Data, Internet site http://www.cdc.gov/nchs/births.htm

—*Births: Preliminary Data for 2013*, National Vital Statistics Reports, Vol. 63, No. 2, 2014, Internet site http://www.cdc.gov/nchs/births.htm

—*Current Contraceptive Use in the United States, 2006–2010, and Changes in Patterns of Use since 1995*, National Health Statistics Reports, No. 60, 2012, Internet site http://www.cdc.gov/nchs/nsfg.htm

—*Deaths: Preliminary Data for 2011*, National Vital Statistics Reports, Vol. 61, No. 6, 2012, Internet site http://www.cdc.gov/nchs/deaths.htm

—*Fathers' Involvement with Their Children: United States, 2006–2010*, National Health Statistics Reports, No. 71, 2013, Internet site http://www.cdc.gov/nchs/nsfg.htm

—*First Marriages in the United States: Data from the 2006–2010 National Survey of Family Growth*, National Health Statistics Reports, No. 49, 2012, Internet site http://www.cdc.gov/nchs/nsfg.htm

—*Health, United States, 2013*, Internet site http://www.cdc.gov/nchs/hus.htm

—Mortality data, Internet site http://www.cdc.gov/nchs/deaths.htm

—*Sexual Behavior, Sexual Attraction, and Sexual Identity in the United States: Data from the 2006–2008 National Survey of Family Growth*, National Health Statistics Reports, No. 36, 2011, Internet site http://www.cdc.gov/nchs/nsfg/new_nsfg.htm

—*Summary Health Statistics for the U.S. Population: National Health Interview Survey, 2012*, Series 10, No. 259, 2013, Internet site http://www.cdc.gov/nchs/nhis.htm

—*Summary Health Statistics for U.S. Adults: National Health Interview Survey, 2012*, Series 10, No. 260, 2014, Internet site http://www.cdc.gov/nchs/products/series/series10.htm

—*Summary Health Statistics for U.S. Children: National Health Interview Survey, 2012*, Series 10, No. 258, 2013, Internet site http://www.cdc.gov/nchs/nhis.htm

Substance Abuse and Mental Health Services Administration

Internet site http://www.samhsa.gov

—National Survey on Drug Use and Health, 2012, Internet site http://www.samhsa.gov

Survey Documentation and Analysis, Computer-assisted Survey Methods Program, University of California, Berkeley

Internet site http://sda.berkeley.edu/

—General Social Surveys, 1972–2012 Cumulative Data Files, Internet site http://sda.berkeley.edu/cgi-bin/hsda?harcsda+gss12

Index

married couples. *See* Households, married-couple.
Medicaid health insurance coverage, 75
Medicare health insurance coverage, 75
men
    college enrollment, 46
    earnings, 149–150
    educational attainment, 38, 42
    employment status, 157, 159–160, 163, 178–179,
      181
    income, 134–135, 137–141
    job tenure, 183–184
    life expectancy, 93
    living arrangements, 215
    marital status, 219, 221
    physical activity, 52
    population, 226–227
    prescription drug use, 84
    projections of labor force, 190–191
    school enrollment, 45–46
    self-employed, 181
    sexual activity, 54, 56
    sexual attraction, 55
    sexual orientation, 56
    time use, 281–282
    weight status, 51
middle-class membership, 24
migraines. *See* Headaches.
military health insurance coverage, 75
minimum-wage workers, 186
minority population projections, 236
mobile homes, living in, 108–110
mobility, geographic
    by generation, 112
    rate, 112–114
    reason for, 115
moderate political leanings, 21
mortgage debt, 305. *See also* Housing, spending on.
Moslem religious preference, 10
movers. *See* Mobility, geographic.
mutual funds, as household asset, 295

net worth, household, 287
never-married. *See* Marital status.
news, sources of, 5, 7
newspapers, as source of news, 5, 7
non-Hispanic Whites. *See* White, Non-Hispanic
    Americans.

obesity. *See* Weight.
occupation, 170–176
out-of-wedlock births, 69
overweight. *See* Weight.

parents' standard of living, 28
people living alone. *See* Households, single-person.
personal care products and services, spending on,
    261–276
pet care, time spent, 279–284

physical activity, 52
physician visits. *See* Health care visits.
pill, as birth control, 58
pneumonia and influenza, as leading cause of death,
    92
political leanings, 21
political party, 21
population projections, 234–240
poverty status, 154
prescription drugs, 84–86
premarital sex, 15
projections
    of labor force, 190–191
    of population, 234–240
property
    nonresidential, as household asset, 300
    other residential, as household asset, 299
    primary residence, 298
    taxes, spending on, 261–276
Protestant, as religious preference, 10
public transportation, spending on, 261–276

race. *See* individual race and Hispanic origin groups.
radio, as source of news, 5, 7
reading
    newspapers, 5
    spending on, 261–276
    time spent, 279–284
recreational activities, time spent in, 279–284
regions
    homeownership by, 103
    moving between, 112–114
    population of, 246–247
religious
    activities, time spent in, 279–284
    attendance, 10
    beliefs, 11–12
    preferences, 10
renters. *See also* Homeowners.
    by type of structure, 110
    number of, 99–100
Republican party affiliation, 21
retirement
    accounts as household asset, 294
    age of, expected, 312
    as reason for moving, 115
    attitude toward, 311
    savings, 311

savings, 311
school enrollment, 45–46. *See also* Educational
    attainment.
science, attitude toward, 7
self-employment, 181
sex
    homosexuality, attitude toward, 15–16
    premarital, attitude toward, 15
    roles, attitude toward, 14